2017 Edition

How to Collect When You Win a Lawsuit in California

By Andres Schonviesner, Paul Young Esq. and
Joseph Chora Esq.

In Association with the California Association of Judgment Professionals

Published by Quik Know Publishing - www.QuikKnowPublishing.com

By Andres Schonviesner, Paul Young, Esq. and Joseph Chora Esq.

In Association with the California Association of Judgment Professionals

ISBN 978-0-9970677-3-6

Copyright © 2017

ALL RIGHTS RESERVED. Printed in the USA

No part of this publication may be reproduced, stored in a retrieval system or transmitted in any form or by any means, electronic, mechanical, photocopying, recording or otherwise without the prior written permission of the publisher and the authors.

Reproduction prohibitions do not apply to the forms contained in this product when reproduced for personal use.

About the Authors

Andres Schonviesner

Andres Schonviesner is the President and founder of Affirmative Judgment Services. Mr. Schonviesner has been enforcing civil judgments since 2007. Andres also holds, or has held, licenses as a Real Estate Broker, Insurance Salesperson, Tax Preparer, and Mortgage Lender. Mr. Schonviesner owns (or has owned) judgment enforcement, mortgage, real estate, and credit report reselling companies.

Mr. Schonviesner joined the California Association of Judgment Professionals in 2007, and has since served on its Board of Directors; as its President (2015), Vice President (2014), Immediate Past President (2016), and Secretary (2011-2013) and Advisor (2017).

Paul P. Young, Esq.

Paul Young is a founder and partner at Chora Young LLP, with a practice focused on the enforcement of civil judgments; the representation of creditors in collection actions, and in the U.S. Bankruptcy Courts.

Besides being a licensed California attorney, Mr. Young is also a licensed private investigator and Certified Fraud Examiner (ACFE). Mr. Young is currently (2017) serving as the Immediate Past President of the California Association of Judgment Professionals (CAJP).

Joseph Chora, Esq.

Joseph Chora is an attorney and a private investigator. His practice is exclusively focused on the Enforcement of judgments in California and throughout the United States. His firm, Chora Young LLP, is licensed to practice in all state and federal courts in California.

Mr. Chora is a member of the Los Angeles County Bar Association, and their remedies section, the Federal Bar Association and the California Judgment Professionals.

Appreciation and Acknowledgment

Paul Young, Andres Schonviesner, Joseph Chora and Quik Know Publishing appreciate and gratefully acknowledge the many valuable contributions of the following individuals to this book.

Main Editors and Contributors

Gretchen Lichtenberger

Phil Erkenbrack

Contributors

Mike Rosen

Bonnie Nicholson

Gregg Roberts

Karen Good

Richard Morrison

Robert S. Stack

Ran Bush

Bert Friedman

Brian Johnston

A Special Thank You, to two of our contributors, Mandy Powers and David Summers, who sadly, are now chasing their debtors, at the great big courthouse in Heaven. You will be missed.

Quik Know Publishing
READ a little, LEARN a lot

READ THIS FIRST

Disclaimer:

The information in this book is as up to date and accurate as we can make it. But it's important to realize that law changes frequently, as do fees, forms, and procedures. If you are handling your own legal matters, it is up to you to be sure that all the information you use, including the information in this book, is accurate.

The information contained in this book is provided for informational purposes only, and should not be construed as legal advice on any subject matter. No recipients of content from this book, client, or otherwise, should act or refrain from acting on the basis of any content included in this book without seeking the appropriate legal or other professional advice on the particular facts and circumstances at issue from an attorney licensed in the recipient's state. The content of the book contains general information and may not reflect current legal developments, verdicts, or settlements. The authors, editors, and contributors, expressly disclaim all liability in respect to actions taken or not taken based on any or all of the contents of this book.

Need more information, updates, or resource links?

Register at www.quikknowpublishing.com to be on our mailing list

Table of Contents

A. Please Read to Understand Basics

1. How to Use This Book

A. Nineteen Ways to Enforce a Court Judgment	1/3
B. Laying the Groundwork	1/3
C. Creating an Enforcement Plan	1/6
D. Special Situations	1/8
E. Miscellaneous Information About Enforcement	1/14

2. Getting Started

A. How Long Must You Wait?	2/2
B. If You Can't Locate the Debtor	2/5

3. Enforcement Practices to Avoid

A. Debt Enforcement Laws (aka Collection Laws)	3/2
B. Common Sense	3/3
C. Communicating with the Debtor	3/3
D. Communicating with Others about the Debtor	3/4
E. Giving and Getting Information About the Debtor	3/5

4. Creating Liens on the Debtor's Property

A. Real Estate Liens	4/3
B. Business Asset Liens	4/8
C. Personal Property Liens	4/10

5. Getting the Debtor to Pay Voluntarily

A. Ask for Your Money	5/2
B. Send a Final Demand Letter	5/3
C. Negotiate an Installment Plan	5/5
D. Accept Less than the Judgment as Full Payment	5/7
E. Respond to the Debtor's Claims of "No Money"	

5B. Default in Payment Agreement

A. Payment Plan Categories	5B/2
B. Debtor Defaulted	5B/2
C. Default in Small Claims	5B/3
D. Default in Civil Court	5B/4

6. Determining What the Debtor Owns

A. Debtor's Statement of Assets	6/2
B. Family Court Records	6/2
C. Schedule a Debtor's Exam	6/3
D. Obtain a Subpoena Duces Tecum	6/6
E. Have the Documents Served	6/9
F. Prepare for the Examination	6/12
G. Conduct the Examination	6/12
H. If the Debtor Doesn't Show	6/13

7. Obtaining a Writ of Execution

A. Complete the Writ of Execution Form	7/2
B. Have Court Issue Writ	7/5
C. What to Do With Your Writ	7/5

8. Enforcement from Deposit Accounts

A. Finding Deposit Accounts	8/2
B. Figuring Out if the Funds are Exempt	8/4
C. Levying on Joint and Business Accounts	8/6
D. How to Levy on Bank Accounts and Safe-Deposit Boxes	8/7

9. Collecting from Wages

A. Limits on Wage Garnishments	9/3
B. How to Garnish Wages	9/4

10. Collecting from Money/Property Owed

A. Locating Money or Property Owed Debtor	10/2
B. How to Levy on Money or Property held by Third Party	10/5

11. Collecting from a Business

A. Levying Against Cash Receipts or Business Assets	11/2
B. How to Levy Against Cash Receipts	11/4
C. How to Levy Against Business Assets	11/5

12. Seizing a Motor Vehicle

A. Limitations on Vehicle Levies	12/2
B. How to Levy on a Vehicle	12/3

13. Seizing Tangible Personal Property

A. Limitations on Personal Property Levies	13/2
B. How to Levy on Personal Property	13/5

14. Seizing Real Estate

A. Limitations on Real Estate Levies	14/2
B. Finding Debtor's Real Estate	14/3
C. Forcing a Sale of Property	14/5

15. Opposing a Claim of Exemption

A. Wage Garnishment	15/2
B. Property Seizure	15/5

16. Recovering Costs and Interest

A. Post-Judgment Costs	16/2
B. Post-Judgment Interest	16/4
C. Memorandum of Costs	16/6

17. If the Debtor Files for Bankruptcy

A. Types of Bankruptcy	17/3
B. Bankruptcy and Enforcement	17/3
C. Examine the Bankruptcy Papers You Receive	17/5
D. File Proof of Claim	17/6
E. After Filing the Proof of Claim	17/8
F. What Else Can You Do?	17/9

18. If the Debtor Passes Away

A. Recovering Your Judgment through Probate	18/2
B. Recovering Outside of Probate	18/6

19. Help from a Judge: Filing Motions to Force Enforcement

A. Seizure and Turnover Orders	19/2
B. Assignment and Restraining Orders	19/5
C. After You Prepare the Papers	19/7

20. Renewing Your Judgment and Liens

A. Renewing a Judgment	20/2
B. Renewing Liens	20/4

21. Serving Papers on a Judgment Debtor

A. Who Can Serve Papers	21/2
B. Personal Service	21/3
C. Service by Mail	21/5
D. Proof of Service Form	21/6

22. After the Judgment is Paid

A. Why File an Acknowledgment	22/2
B. Release Any Liens	22/4

Appendix

Blank Page

Chapter A

Please Read to Understand Basics

Thank you for buying our book. We have updated every part of this book as of January 2017. Laws can change at any time. You should always use the most up-to- date material you can, especially since using outdated information can cost you money and time. This is especially true when dealing with legal matters.

There are some things that you should know before reading this book. Some of these things are matters that we don't want to repeat in every chapter, while others have to do with understanding what we did, to make your experience using this book, easier and more comprehensive.

Why do we use "enforcement" and "enforce" instead of "collection" and "collect" in the book?

You were owed money for some time. Before you went to court, you were trying to "collect" or "recover" your money. Once you went to court and won the case, you are now trying to "enforce" your judgment and recover your money. It's one of those "potatoe vs potauto" things. We are just trying to help you use the correct terminology since you will be dealing with the courts and sheriff.

What is a "caption"?

A caption is the top portion of your court documents. It includes the location of the court, the parties involved, the case number, and the name of the action taken. To see a sample of a "caption", take a look at Chapter 19, page 21. The "caption" is lines 1 thru 19, from left to right. Please note that the party's names on a caption (also known as the "title") will always remain as they were on day one, it does not change. You may add other parties or correct the spelling, or names, of a party, later on in a case but the name of the case always remains the same. If your title has too many names, you can enter the first full name and then ", et al". Et Al means "and others". This change is acceptable in future filings with the court.

What is a case" title" and "short title"?

The "title" of your case is as follows:
    Plaintiff's name(s) v. Defendant's name(s).
The "short title" is using only the last name of the first party of each category. Example: Right v. Isbad. An example of both can be found in Chapter 7, pages 9 & 10. Page 9, the "title" is the Plaintiff/Defendant section, third box down from the top of the page. The "short title" is on page 10 at the very top left corner. Always make

sure you complete this part of the second page, on any court form, even when you will be leaving the rest of the page blank.

What forms should I use?
Although we have included a copy of every form that we use, in this book, we always suggest that you get your court forms from **www.courts.ca.gov/forms**. Not only will you be using the most up-to-date forms available, but you can actually type them up online and print them out, ready to go.

Always remember to keep a set of any and all documents you are sending the court, or anyone else, in your own file. The mail gets lost, clerks misfile documents, and weather happens. Be prepared for the worst always.

What is "Pro Per", and why is it below my name on many of the legal forms?
"Pro Per" is Latin for "I'm representing myself, your Honor". When you are not using the services of an attorney, it is important to let the court system and judge know it. You will sometimes see "Pro Se" instead (not in our book but within the court system). Both "Pro Per" and "Pro Se" mean the same thing, "Pro Per" is usually used in State court, while "Pro Se" is used in Federal court. But they are interchangeable.

How have we made this book easier to use?
This book has many examples and samples. In order to make things easier to understand, we have always used the same two parties in these examples and samples. Let me introduce you to our actors.

Plaintiff/Creditor/Good Gal/You - Amy Right will be our victim here. Amy will be the person who was taken advantage of and who sued to defend her rights. She won in court and is now trying to recover her money. You probably purchased this book because someone owes you money. Amy will be you. To make it easier, Amy lives at 1000 My st, in Mytown, Ca 90000. When filling out any form, just replace Amy's name and information with yours.

Defendant/Debtor/Bad Guy/Your debtor - Jeff Isbad will be our debtor here. Jeff lost the court case and now owes Amy some money. We are not saying that everyone that owes money is bad, but some are. We used "Isbad" just to make it easier for you to remember who he represents. Jeff will not cooperate with Amy and pay his debt. To make it easier, Jeff lives at 666 e. Cra P st (pronounced "cra....P" and not "crappy", thank you), Helltown, Ca 90666. When filling out any form, just replace your debtor's name and information for Jeff's.

Throughout the book you will see references to "CCP". "CCP" stands for Code of Civil Procedure. You can look up any of the codes that we mention, in the book, by searching them on the web. Make sure you are reading the California laws. Do NOT Google a code, always go to www.leginfo.legislature.ca.gov.

We have set up a link page on our website so that we can keep adding links that will help you, throughout the year. You should check it every so often to see what is new. Go to www.QuikKnowPublishing.com.

What if collecting the debt yourself is too time consuming or difficult?

If after reading this book, or attempting to collect the money owed, you find the task too time consuming, expensive, or difficult, you do have other options.

Here is a quick explanation of each.

1) Hire an attorney

One option is to hire an attorney. If the judgment is large, you believe the chances of recovering the money are good, and you can afford it, you may want to spend money upfront in order to get the biggest amount at the end. This can become expensive as you will be paying for legal fees, investigatory fees, court fees, third party fees, etc. Some attorneys may work on a contingency basis. Contingency means that they take a portion of the amount recovered instead of getting paid up front. Other attorneys may take work on an assignment basis (read option 3). Each attorney works, and gets paid, in a different way so make sure that you understand what you are agreeing to before you sign anything.

All attorneys specialize in separate parts of the law. An attorney may be a great corporate lawyer, but know nothing about car accidents. Make sure you hire someone with judgment enforcement expertise. You can find attorneys who specialize in judgment enforcement at   www.cajp.org.

2) Hire a Collection company

Another option is to work with a collection company. Collection companies may charge you a small fee up front and will usually try to collect the money by mailing letters, making phone calls, and making sure that the debt appears on the debtor's credit report. Their fees are usually low, compared to other options, but the amount of work they will do is also relatively small. Each collection company works differently so ask a lot of questions. You will probably have to assign the judgment to them (explained below).

3) Hire a Judgment Enforcement Professional

A good option is to work with a Judgment Professional. These professionals do nothing but go after judgment debtors and recover the money they owe. These individuals may agree to purchase the judgment from you for cash or for a promise to pay (Assignment of Judgment, explained below). While all professionals work differently, they usually do not ask for money up front and they only get paid if they are successful in enforcing (collecting) your judgment.

Let me say that again, **THEY ONLY GET PAID WHEN YOU DO**.

a) If you are getting paid cash for your judgment you should expect to receive 5-15% of the face value. It will vary between judgment professional and not many will be willing to pay up front, but there is always a chance. This is called selling your judgment.

b) If you assign the judgment to them you will be paid a negotiated percentage of the amount recovered, but not until the money is recovered from your debtor. The percentage will be higher than with option a.

In either case, the judgment professional will usually cover all court, investigative, third party fees, etc. so you will not be spending much money out of your pocket. As always, make sure you understand and agree with the terms before you sign any contract. The only dumb question is the one that goes unanswered, so ask all of your questions and make sure you are comfortable with the answer. We suggest you work with a professional that is local to where the court and/or your debtor lives/works. If the debtor has moved then use someone close to the debtor, whenever possible.

You can find a list of Judgment Professionals at www.cajp.org

The California Association of Judgment Professional (CAJP) is a Non-Profit Mutual Benefit Corporation whose members are professional Judgment Recovery Specialists. CAJP has members nationwide though the Association is primarily focused on California cases. Each member is an independent business person with no direct affiliation to CAJP other than as a member of a professional organization. CAJP exists to help educate its members to increase their knowledge of the laws and events unique to judgment enforcement. CAJP does not control its members' business activities nor does CAJP have any responsibility for its members' business practices. CAJP has a website where the public may search for a Judgment Recovery Specialist in his/her own area to find a person willing to take assignment of a judgment. CAJP does not endorse any particular member or any members' private business practices. CAJP will not recommend anyone to you, you must choose from the listing available on the website.

Assigning a judgment means that you give a third party ownership of the judgment. The debt is now owed to them. In exchange, the third party agrees to pay you a percentage of what they collect from the debtor.

A court judgment is considered a "right to payment" of money and is therefore a "thing in action" under the law [*Civil Code §953*]. As a "thing in action", a judgment may be transferred to someone else [*Civil Code §954*]. The Judgment Creditor owns the judgment as well as the right to payment from the Judgment Debtor for that judgment. The Judgment Creditor can sell and transfer his/her right to payment represented by the judgment to another person. A "person" includes a natural person, a corporation, a limited liability company and a partnership [*Code of Civil Procedure §680.280*].

The way a judgment is sold and transferred under the law is by assignment. The Judgment Creditor can assign the right represented by a judgment to another person who becomes the Assignee of Record for the judgment and hence the new Judgment Creditor. This transfer of the right to payment is done by the Judgment Creditor completing a notarized *Acknowledgement of Assignment of Judgment* transferring all rights, title and interest to the Assignee [*Code of Civil Procedure §673*]. The *Acknowledgement of Assignment of Judgment* is then filed with the court where the judgment was entered. The Assignee then owns the judgment and the right to receive payment on the judgment and has complete standing to enforce the judgment [*Code of Civil Procedure §681.020*]. This is similar to selling a car and transferring title to the car to the new owner or selling your house to a new owner.

Blank Page

Chapter 1

How to Use This Book

A. Nineteen Ways to Collect a Court judgment	1/3
B. Laying the Groundwork	1/3
1. Set Up a Case File	1/3
2. Establish Liens	1/5
3. Know What You Can and Can't Do	1/5
4. Attempt Voluntary Collection	1/5
5. Find Out About the Debtor's job and Assets	1/5
6. Obtain a Writ of Execution	1/5
C. Create an Enforcement Plan	1/6
1. Make a Cost-Benefit Analysis	1/6
2. Use Rating Charts	1/6
3. Select One or More Procedures	1/7
D. Special Situations	1/8
1. Judgment from Small Claims Court	1/8
2. Judgment from Federal Court	1/8
3. Judgment Stemming From Motor Vehicle Accident	1/8
4. Judgment or Order For Child or Spousal Support	1/9
5. You Have a Restitution Order	1/10
6. Debtor Is Married	1/11
7. Debtor Is Government Agency	1/11
8. Debtor Is Federal Employee or on Active Military Duty	1/12
9. Debtor Is Licensed Contractor	1/12
10. Debtor Is Licensed Real Estate Agent	1/12
11. Debtor Is Private Vocational School	1/13
12. Debtor Is Subject to Conservatorship or Guardianship	1/13
13. Judgment Does Not Reflect Debtor's Correct Name	1/13

E. Miscellaneous Information About Enforcement — 1/14
   1. Notify Court of Change of Address — 1/14
   2. Find Out About Fees and Deposits — 1/14
   3. Use the Correct Forms and Court Documents — 1/14
   4. Substitute Yourself for Your Attorney — 1/15

Congratulations! You have a court judgment ordering someone to pay you money. You won your small claims court case or your case in regular civil court, a California state court, or maybe even a federal court. You've spent some time celebrating, after all, you were wronged and deserve to be compensated, and a judge, even perhaps a jury, agreed.

But your celebration is not yet complete. While the court decided in your favor, the court did not pay you or force the defendant to write you a check on the spot. Enforcing a civil judgment is your job, not the courts. You may have no idea where or how to begin. If you've made some attempts at collecting, you may be frustrated and feel like you keep hitting a dead end.

While it may be true, that some judgments are uncollectible, those judgments are the minority. With information and perseverance, most people can collect what they are owed without having to hire an attorney and often without much additional expense.

If you don't yet have a court judgment

This book is for people who already have been to court and been awarded a court judgment. If you have not yet filed your case or your case is still pending and you don't yet have a judgment, there are other resources you may wish to use, including consulting with an
attorney, contacting a legal document Assistant or professional judgment recovery specialist, or seeking other referral sources.

A. Nineteen Ways to Collect a Court Judgment

This book covers 19 different ways to collect a court judgment. The methods are introduced in this chapter and explained in detail in other chapters. After you read this chapter please read the other chapters so you become familiar with other ways to recover your judgment. It is much better to be prepared in case your debtor knows more about evading paying your judgment than you know about recovering your judgment.

Bankruptcy or death of debtor

If the debtor has either filed for bankruptcy or died, your enforcement options may be greatly limited. Instead of reading the rest of this chapter, go directly to Chapter 17 (bankruptcy of the debtor) or Chapter 18 (death of the debtor) to find out more.

B. Laying the Groundwork

No matter what type of judgment you have (small claims or regular civil) and what kind of debtor owes you money (individual or business), you should take several steps right away to put yourself in the best possible position to enforce your judgment.

1. Set Up a Case File

You may have already organized all of your documents relating to the debtor when you prepared your case for court. Using those organizational skills, or using new ones if you didn't arrange anything before going to court, set up a system for all documents related to your enforcement efforts. One possible method is to use an accordion folder for your papers, creating separate sections for court papers (such as the judgment), letters you write and receipts for costs you incur in trying to collect. If your collection efforts are extensive, you can set up files by the type of assets the debtor owns, such as vehicles, bank accounts, real estate and wages.

Keeping complete records of your enforcement efforts is well worth the trouble and will pay off in the end. You are entitled to recover not only your judgment, but also all of your judicially allowed costs of enforcing your judgment and accrued interest from the date of the judgment. Chapter 16 includes instructions and worksheets for keeping track of payments received, costs incurred and interest due.

Nineteen Ways to Enforce a Court Judgment

Basic Enforcement Techniques
(Least Costly, Generally Most Effective)

1. Place lien (legal claim) on real estate	Chapter 4
2. Place lien on business property	Chapter 4
3. Negotiate voluntary payments	Chapter 5
4. Conduct a debtor's examination; have debtor turn over property at exam	Chapter 6
5. Seize wages	Chapter 9
6. Seize bank accounts and contents of safe-deposit boxes	Chapter 8
7. Collect from business debtor's cash register (till tap)	Chapter 11
8. Collect money from business as it comes in, for specified time (keeper)	Chapter 11
9. File proof of claim, if debtor files for bankruptcy	Chapter 17
10. File creditor's claim, if debtor has died	Chapter 18
11. Seize debts owed to debtor by third parties	Chapter 10
12. Have debtor's driver's license suspended	Chapter 1

Advanced Collection Techniques
(Often Expensive, Usually least Effective)

13. Seize and sell business assets	Chapter 11
14. Seize and sell vehicle	Chapter 12
15. Seize and sell personal assets	Chapter 13
16. Obtain court order to seize property located in private home	Chapter 19
17. Obtain court order requiring debtor to hand over specific property	Chapter 19
18. Obtain court order requiring debtor to assign (transfer) to you right to receive payments	Chapter 19
19. Force sale of real estate	Chapter 14

2. Establish Liens

A lien is a legal assertion that you have a claim of a specific value against certain property, in which the debtor has an interest, such as real property. In other words, a lien changes your general judgment against the debtor into a specific claim against whatever property is subject to the lien. Anytime a court judgment is awarded, you can use the judgment to create liens. When a debtor sells, refinances or transfers the property, all liens against the property must be paid or otherwise dealt with beforehand. In theory, you can also collect on your lien by forcing the sale of the debtor's house, but this is very costly and time consuming, and the reader is advised to seek advice of counsel if they intend on such a foreclosure.

Liens are paid in the order they were placed against the property. For example, if the debtor still owes money to their lender, such as a mortgage, the lender will be paid ahead of you and any other creditors who filed liens, because the lender's lien was established at the time of the original purchase. You and the other creditors, such as the taxing authority, will be paid out of the balance of the proceeds, if any, when the property is sold or refinanced. If there aren't any proceeds left to pay the creditors, the debtor will have to get the money elsewhere.

Chapter 4 discusses liens in detail and tells you how to create real estate liens and personal property liens, if the debtor is a business.

3. Know What You Can and Can't Do

Debtors have certain legal rights and protections, such as the right to appeal their case in most instances, before you begin enforcement efforts and protections against collection harassment. Read Chapter 2, to figure out when to start collecting, and Chapter 3, for an overview of actions you must avoid when collecting your judgment.

4. Attempt to get Voluntary Payments

A debtor who has lost in court may finally be willing to pay you. If you get the debtor to make voluntary payments, you won't need to engage in active collection measures. But you won't know if the debtor will voluntarily pay unless you ask. Chapter 5 gives suggestions for negotiating voluntary payments.

Establish liens regardless

Even if your debtor agrees to pay voluntarily, you will want to create liens. If the debtor stops paying or declares bankruptcy you want to be on record as a lienholder and because earlier liens are paid first, you should get your liens on registered as soon as possible.

5. Find Out About the Debtor's Job and Assets

If the debtor won't make voluntary payments, you'll have to force enforcement, often by garnishing the debtor's wages (where a portion of debtor's wages are diverted to you) or seizing, called levying on, certain assets owned by the debtor. If you don't know where the debtor works or what property the debtor owns, you can use routine information discovery procedures, such as debtor's examinations, subpoenas and investigation of court files. We discuss these information gathering tools in Chapter 6. You need to know where the debtor works and what kinds of assets the debtor has before you can decide on the best methods of collecting.

6. Obtain a Writ of Execution

If you will have to force the debtor to give up their money because the debtor doesn't voluntarily pay, you will need a Writ of Execution, an order from the court authorizing the Sheriff to take assets of the debtor. This may be in the county where the debtor lives or works, or anywhere the debtor owns property, for example, a debtor who lives in Los Angeles may also own a vacation house on Lake Tahoe. Chapter 7 tells you how to obtain a Writ of Execution.

C. Create an Enforcement Plan

Coming up with an enforcement strategy isn't that difficult. Nevertheless, there's no set formula that will work for every judgment and every debtor. Other than the steps described in Section B, the enforcement process you use depend almost entirely on you and the debtor. No one procedure is right for enforcing every judgment, even the order in which the various procedures might be used will vary depending on the circumstances.

For example, in some cases, the best approach will be to go after the debtor's wages. In a wage garnishment (Earnings Withholding Order) you may receive a set amount each month (up to 25% of the Judgment Debtor's net income) until the debt is paid off, unless the debtor quits their job. But some debtors are self-employed or earn income that's hard to track and garnish, such as tips earned waiting tables. In those situations, a wage garnishment is likely to come up empty either because the self-employed person will ignore your attempts to collect or because the person doesn't earn enough to have their wages garnished. In those instances, a combination of using a bank account levy, an Assignment Order and/or other tactics may be what you need.

Similarly, forcing the sale of a debtor's real estate after you have created a lien is extremely costly and complex and usually requires a lawyer's help. Most people wait until the debtor sells or refinances to be paid, rather than forcing a sale. But if you have a very large judgment and the debtor has a lot of equity in their house, forcing the sale may be the best way to collect.

1. Make a Cost-Benefit Analysis

How do you assess how much time, money and energy you'll have to spend to enforce your judgment? The answer, of course, depends on your situation and personality. It also depends on luck. Judgment enforcement can be unpredictable. You may think you can easily garnish the debtor's wages, until the debtor quits their job. Or you may believe you'll never see your money, until a single letter convinces the debtor to pay up.

Collecting From Multiple Debtors

If the court awarded you a judgment against two or more defendants, the judgment debtors are usually considered jointly and separately liable for the full amount of the judgment, unless the judgment says otherwise. Joint and separate liability means that you are entitled to collect the entire judgment from a single defendant (separate liability), or portions of it from each defendant (joint liability).

If multiple debtors are liable on your judgment, a good strategy is to seek to enforce from them simultaneously, unless you know one will be especially easy to get money from. If you collect more than "their share" from a particular debtor, that's their problem, it is up to them to get the other debtors to chip in their fair share.

Consider the following factors in evaluating the costs and benefits of using specific enforcement techniques:
- size of your judgment
- current value of the debtor's assets
- whether the debtor is likely to come into assets in the future
- whether the debtor's assets are protected against enforcement ("exempt," in legalese)
- cost of undertaking a particular enforcement method
- competition from other creditors seeking to collect
- time and energy you're willing to put into your collection efforts, and
- any special circumstances affecting your likelihood of collecting.

2. Use Rating Charts

To help you choose among the collection procedures, each chapter describing a collection method opens with the following rating chart, with "X" marks in the appropriate columns.

Collection Factor		
High	Moderate	Low
Potential cost to you		
Potential for producing		
Potential for settlement		
Potential time & trouble		
Potential for bankruptcy		

The charts will quickly tell you if the method will be costly or time consuming, and whether it has a high potential for producing cash, meaning that you'll be able to grab actual cash or an item that can easily be sold. The charts also assess how likely the method is to convince the debtor to enter into a payment schedule (a settlement).

The more coercive the enforcement method, the more likely the debtor will want to settle the matter rather than lose property.

Finally, the chart indicates if the method is likely to send the debtor to bankruptcy court. There are three kinds of bankruptcy, liquidation (Chapter 7 bankruptcy) and reorganization (Chapter 13 bankruptcy for individuals or Chapter 11 bankruptcy for corporations or individuals with extremely high debt burdens). If a debtor files for bankruptcy, you must cease all enforcement efforts immediately, unless you file a motion with the bankruptcy court and are granted an order allowing you to proceed. Most judgments are either wiped out in bankruptcy or paid off at a fraction of their worth. Even if you've created a lien against the debtor's property, there's a chance the debtor will be able to wipe it out in bankruptcy. Some judgments survive bankruptcy. We deal with bankrupt debtors in Chapter 17.

Most of the time, you don't want to pursue aggressive enforcement techniques that will push a debtor into bankruptcy. Judgments last for ten years and can be renewed for another ten years, over and over again. If the debtor is having serious financial difficulties, you may want to wait for their luck to change.

If the debtor threatens to file for bankruptcy, how can you assess whether he's really in dire financial straits or is just making threats to scare you off? There's no foolproof way to tell, but the greater their total debt burden, the more likely they are to go bankrupt. If you're the only one trying to collect on the debt, they're not likely to file. But if they owe a great deal of money to several creditors (or if the debt to you is very large), they may be a good candidate for bankruptcy.

3. Select One or More Procedures

For most creditors holding a court judgment, the best enforcement methods are those that are the most direct and simple. Consider these examples:

EXAMPLE 1: Amy Right obtained a small claims court judgment against her former friend, Jeff Isbad, for $3,000. She wrote several letters demanding payment, with no results. Amy knew that Jeff was employed and owned a late model car and his home. Amy created a lien on Jeff's home. She decided not to seize his car or force the sale of his home because the potential cost of both was likely to be greater than any money Amy would get. Amy also decided to garnish Jeff's wages, figuring he was unlikely to quit his job or file for bankruptcy. Through the garnishment, Amy's judgment, including enforcement costs, was paid in six months.

EXAMPLE 2: Amy Right, doing business as Small Press, a book publisher, obtained a $3,000 judgment against Jeff Isbad and his small bookstore, Protos. Small Press knew that Protos did a brisk business and had a relatively extensive inventory. Jeff owned a BMW automobile, a house and a 25-foot cabin cruiser, which he kept docked at a local marina. Small Press discovered that the BMW and boat were heavily financed, and that the cost of having them seized, stored and sold probably exceeded the amount of money Small Press would get. Small Press did create a lien on Jeff's house, but decided not to force a sale because of the cost involved.

Small Press decided that the best way to get the money was to impose a "keeper" on the business, where a law enforcement officer stands by the cash register and collects money as it comes in. The law enforcement officer charged a fee of about $285. When the sheriff phoned Jeff at the bookstore and told him he was sending a deputy down to stand by his cash register, Jeff quickly came to terms with Small Press, signing an agreement to pay off the judgment in installments over the next six months. Small Press knew that if Jeff didn't honor the terms of the agreement, it could send the keeper and even have the sheriff seize and sell the bookstore's inventory and assets to satisfy the judgment.

D. Special Situations

In several collection situations, you have remedies other than the 19 listed in Section A, or there are limitations on how you can collect. Keep reading if any of the following are true:
- you have a judgment from small claims court
- you have a judgment from a federal court
- you have a judgment stemming from a motor vehicle accident
- you have a judgment for child or spousal support
- you have a restitution order (Criminal case)
- the debtor is married
- the debtor is a government agency
- the debtor is on active military duty
- the debtor is a licensed contractor
- the debtor is a licensed real estate agent
- the debtor is a private vocational school
- the debtor is subject to a conservatorship or guardianship, or
- the judgment doesn't reflect the debtor's correct name.

1. Judgment from Small Claims Court

Sometimes a judgment debtor is willing to pay up, but doesn't want to deal directly with you, the judgment creditor. A small claims court judgment debtor has the option of paying a judgment directly to the court [CCP 116.860(a)]. The court can charge the debtor up to $20 for this service [CCP 116.860(h)].

If your judgment debtor opts for this, the court will notify you once it receives payment. You have three years to claim the payments. Make sure you notify the small claims court clerk if you change your address (See Section E1, below). If you fail to collect within three years, the state gets to keep your money [CCP 116.860(g) and GC 68084.1].

If you receive notice from the court that the debtor is paying off the judgment through the court, it makes sense to cease all other enforcement efforts. Otherwise, the debtor will probably get angry and stop making the payments.

Once the judgment is paid off, read Chapter 22 for information on the few additional steps you'll need to take.

2. Judgment from Federal Court

In general, federal judgments are enforced only in federal courts. But still, state law governs procedures for enforcing judgments if a specific state law applies. In California, the procedures described in this book apply if you are enforcing a judgment awarded by a federal or state court in California.

However, even though the rules apply, the forms may not. Instead, you will have to use forms for enforcing federal court judgments. One book that might help, available at a law library, is *West's Federal Forms*. Look at forms 5501 through 5671.

If the federal court that awarded the judgment is not within California, you must register the judgment with a federal district court in California by filing a certified copy of the judgment with the court (28 U.S.C. 1963). Once registered, the judgment may be enforced as if it had been initially awarded by a federal court within California.

3. Judgment Stemming from Motor Vehicle Accident

If you get a judgment against a California licensed driver and the debtor doesn't pay, the Department of Motor Vehicles (DMV) can suspend the debtor's license.

- **The accident occurred on a California road, and the judgment is for $750 or less and remains unpaid at least 90 days from the date judgment was finalized.** DMV will notify the debtor and give them 20 days to pay or prove that insurance will cover the damage. If the debtor does neither, their license will be suspended for 90 days [CCP 116.880, Vehicle Code 16370.5].

- **The judgment is for more than $750, or for personal injury or death, and resulted from an accident caused by an uninsured debtor's operation of a motor vehicle.** DMV will suspend the debtor's license until the judgment is paid or converted to a judgment under which payments are made in installments [CCP 116.870, Vehicle Code 16371].

If the debtor drives to work, license suspension may lead to job loss, leaving you with no source from which to collect. The debtor might even file for bankruptcy. Before taking the drastic step of getting the debtor's license suspended, negotiate with the debtor. You may be able to work out a payment plan.

If you decide to proceed with the suspension, gather together the following:
- a certified copy of your judgment or a docket entry showing the judgment

- the required fee, and
- Form DL-30, Certificate of Facts Re Unsatisfied Judgment.

The court may have Form DL-30 because the court must complete part of it. Otherwise you can request a copy from DMV at 800-777-0133 or go online at http://dmv.ca.gov and search for form DL-30. Currently, the fee the DMV charges is $20 (this is a separate fee from any the court may charge). Send the judgment, fee and form to the DMV at the address indicated on the form.
training, and

4. Judgment or Order for Child or Spousal Support
The California Department of Child Support Services, or sometimes another government agency charged with support enforcement, will provide free help collecting support orders or judgments. Unfortunately, these offices usually have more cases than they can handle, and the backlog means that it may take years before they get to your case. Still, if you want a support enforcement agency to take over enforcement of your support order or judgment, check with the Department of Child Support Services (DCSS) by going to their website to find a local office www.childsup.ca.gov.

Enforcement can be tricky

Child and spousal support orders (and judgments) can require a softer touch than other judgments. There may be continuing contact and relationships between the parties. If you will do it yourself or use the services of a third party, make sure that you and/or they do their homework and consider all repercussions. If you use a third party make sure that they are experienced with family court and any problems or limitations that using a third party may cause.

If you decide to enforce your own support order or judgment, we'll point out where your enforcement efforts may be slightly different from what we explain in the book. In addition, you may have enforcement methods available to you that are not available to other creditors, including the following:

- automatic deduction from the debtor's paycheck, called a wage withholding order
- suspension of the debtor's professional or business licenses
- requiring the debtor to deposit one year's worth of child support payments in a special
  security fund or post two years' worth of child support with the court
- requiring the debtor to prove they are looking for work or undergoing job

- interception of the debtor's income tax refund
  or lottery winnings.

You can use some of these collection methods if you simply have a court order for support; for others, you will have to turn that order into a court judgment. You may need a lawyer's help. If you want to try on your own, take a look at California Practice Guide: Enforcing Judgments and Debts, published by the Rutter Group and available in most law libraries.

5. You Have a Restitution Order

California law requires a judge who sentences a person, convicted of a crime, to also order the person to compensate the victims of the crime for any economic losses they suffered, called making restitution [Penal Code 1202.4(f)]. The judge must calculate the amount of the restitution at the time of the sentencing or later, at the judge's discretion.

You can convert a restitution order to a civil judgment and enforce that judgment by using the procedures outlined in this book. To do so, take the following steps:

1. Visit the clerk of the court in which the defendant was sentenced and give the clerk the defendant's name and the court docket number, this should appear on the papers sent to you by the district attorney's office.

2. Ask the clerk to provide you with a free certified copy of the sentencing order, which will include the restitution order [Penal Code 1214(b)].

3. Use this certified copy of the restitution order as your "civil judgment" to enforce and recover the money owed to you.

In addition to ordering the defendant to make restitution for your economic losses, the court usually will impose what's called a "restitution fine," which the defendant must pay to the state Restitution Fund. This Fund is responsible for paying restitution to victims for their noneconomic injuries such as emotional distress caused by the murder of a loved one. You can get information on how to apply for recovery from this fund through the victims'

Is Trying to Collect From a Person Convicted of a Crime Worth the Effort?

You have the best chance of collecting from a defendant who is not sentenced to jail, but is fined or placed on probation and required to make restitution payments as a condition of staying out of jail.

But what if the defendant is sentenced to prison? For starters, you aren't likely to collect while he's in jail. Defendants rarely have assets that can be seized to satisfy a judgment, at least at the time of their sentencing, and may well shield what assets they do have. Defendants can take advantage of the California exemption laws (see Chapters 9-14), which protect basic necessities from being grabbed to satisfy a judgment. And even if the defendant has assets, it may cost you more to try to seize them than you are willing to risk.

Once the defendant is released and on parole, however, you might be able to collect if they find a job. In addition, the parole board may order them to make restitution payments as a condition of remaining free.

As a victim due restitution, you can act as a squeaky wheel to make sure the appropriate agency (probation or parole) knows you expect to be paid and are watching to make sure that a restitution order is not ignored. If the person, on probation or parole, truly can't pay, they won't be forced to do so.

If the defendant files for bankruptcy, your restitution order cannot be discharged (wiped out). Stop your collection efforts while the bankruptcy is pending, but feel free to resume them when the case ends (See Chapter 17).

assistance division of your local district attorney's office or by calling 800-777-9229. Their website is at http://www.vcgcb.ca.gov. If you receive money from the fund for any losses covered by your restitution order, do not attempt to recover that money directly from the defendant.

If you enforce your restitution order in full, plus interest and the costs of collection, inform the court clerk for the court in which the defendant was convicted by filing a Satisfaction of Judgment.

6. Debtor Is Married

If your judgment debtor is married, you may have more assets available to you for enforcement. This is because California follows what is known as "community property" laws for married couples. Under community property laws, income earned by either spouse and most property accumulated during the marriage is considered jointly owned, which means you can go after it to satisfy your judgment against either spouse [Family Code 910(a)]. The only property considered the separate property of one spouse is property 1) they brought into the marriage or acquired after permanent separation, 2) property purchased during the marriage with separate funds, 3) received as a gift or inherited or 4) property made separate under a written agreement.

Of course, if your judgment is against both spouses, you can go after their community property and each spouse's separate property. If your judgment is against only one spouse, you can recover your judgment from that person's wages and separate property.

Furthermore, you can usually go after community property, even if the judgment is for a debt incurred before marriage. For example, if a debtor and his wife own a grand piano, you can go after the whole piano even though the wife owns half as her community property share.

Going after the wages or separate property of the non-debtor spouse is tricky, but not impossible. You can garnish the non-debtor spouse's wages if you obtain a court order [CCP 706.109]. If the debt was incurred before marriage, you cannot collect from the non-debtor spouse's wages, if they are deposited in a separate bank account to which the debtor has no access. You can recover from the non-debtor spouse's separate property, such as the property they owned before marriage, only if your judgment is for a debt incurred during marriage for food, clothing, shelter or other necessaries of life.

If the couple divorces after you created liens on community property, the liens will remain. For example, if a non-debtor spouse is awarded the family home as part of a divorce settlement, any real estate lien you have created will remain intact. Of course, if the non-debtor spouse tries to refinance the mortgage during the divorce, you're likely to get paid (See Section B2, above).

And if the non-debtor spouse has taken responsibility for a debt in the divorce decree, you have the right to recover money from that spouse, even if the other spouse incurred the debt.

7. Debtor Is Government Agency

If you have a money judgment against a California government agency, including the State; a county, city or district; a public authority or agency; or any other political subdivision, you must follow special procedures to collect [CCP 708.710, Government Code 970].

As soon as you receive notice that the judgment has been entered (finalized), do the following:

1) Prepare a written declaration under penalty of perjury specifying that you have a judgment, identifying the agency, stating that you want to be paid and indication the amount. See the sample.

2) Obtain a certified copy of the judgment or an abstract of judgment from the court clerk.

3) A fee of $ 6 will have to be paid to the public agency when filing the abstract or judgment [CCP 708.785(a)]

Your next step is to deliver these documents to the agency. Legally, you must let the agency and the court know that you've delivered the documents to the agency. So first you should take or send the documents to the agency. Then, have a friend mail the photocopies of the declaration and judgment to the agency and sign and file a proof of service with the court (see Chapter 21, Section E for information on signing and filing proofs of service). Be sure to keep copies for yourself.

The agency must notify its controller, who is required to deposit the money owed to you with the court. Make sure the court has your most current address on file (See Section E1).

Sample Declaration

I, Amy Right, declare as follows:

1. I have a judgment against the City of Los Angeles (Los Angeles Municipal Court case # 11212).

2. I desire the relief provided by Code of Civil Procedure Sections 708.710 – 708.795.

3. The exact amount required to satisfy the judgment is $ 3,566.90, plus interest at the rate allowed by law from February 16, 2015, until the judgment is paid in full.

I declare under penalty of perjury, under the laws of the State of California that the foregoing is true and correct.

02/17/2015   (sign name)
Date   Amy Right

8. Debtor Is Federal Employee or Active Military Duty

If the debtor is an employee of a federal government agency or is on active military duty, you will need to follow rules established by the federal government if you want to use a wage garnishment as part of your enforcement activities. These special rules are explained in Chapter 9. You may be restricted in trying to enforce your judgment in any way against a person on active military duty.

9. Debtor Is Licensed Contractor

If your judgment is against a California licensed contractor for a matter arising out of their contracting business, you can ask the Contractors State License Board (www.cslb.ca.gov) for help in collecting. Submit a legible copy of the judgment and the complaint you filed in the case or a statement briefly describing the reasons for the lawsuit to: Registrar of the Contractors State License Board, Judgment Unit, P.O. Box 26000, Sacramento, CA 95826, or call 800-321-2752.

The Board will send a notice to the contractor, usually within a month. The contractor has 90 days to pay the judgment in full, sign a written agreement before a notary public to pay in installments or post bond. If the contractor doesn't pay the judgment or post bond, the Board will suspend their license [Bus. & Prof. Code 7071.17].

10. Debtor Is Licensed Real Estate Agent

If your judgment is against a California licensed real estate agent or broker for activities related to their license, you can ask the California Department of Real Estate for help in enforcing your judgment, or at least in disciplining the agent or broker. The Department may suspend or revoke an agent's license for fraudulent or dishonest acts. If the court not only awarded you money but also found that the agent or broker engaged in any of these types of misconduct, you'll want to contact the Department if Real Estate Agent:

- made a substantial misrepresentation
- made a false promise
- acted for more than one party to a transaction without the consent of all
- commingled money entrusted to them with their own money
- made a secret profit
- demonstrated negligence or incompetence in performing an act that requires a real estate license,
- failed to reasonably supervise an agent

Contact the Department of Real Estate at:

877-373-4542

In addition, you can try to recover your judgment out of the California Real Estate Recovery Fund [Bus. & Prof. Code 10471]. You must complete and return a form available from the Department of Real Estate; go to www.dre.ca.gov and search for form RE 807.

11. Debtor Is Private Vocational School

If your judgment is against a private vocational school—perhaps for failing to refund your money after you dropped out—a couple of places may be able to help you get your money.

Vocational schools must post a bond before opening their doors. Contact the Bureau for Private Postsecondary and Vocational Education, at 2535 Capitol Oaks Drive, Suite 400, Sacramento, Ca 95833, or call (916) 431-6959, for more information, or visit the Bureau's website at www.bppve.ca.gov. If the bond money is all used up, you may be eligible to collect from the California Student Tuition Recovery Fund. The Bureau can give you more information.

Other Recovery Funds

Recovery funds that will pay you money you are owed by a licensed contractor, a licensed real estate broker or agent or a private vocational school have been around a while. Every so often, other recovery funds are established, sometimes for the long haul and sometimes temporarily.

If you have a judgment against any licensed professional, check to find out whether there's a recovery fund where you can submit a claim. The California Department of Consumer Affairs licenses more than 2.1 million Californians in more than 180 different professions, ranging from doctors to accountants to mechanics to security guards. Call 800-952-5210 or visit www.dca.ca.gov.

12. Debtor Is Subject to Conservatorship or Guardianship

The property of a person subject to a conservatorship or guardianship is under the jurisdiction of a probate court. This means that the property isn't accessible to creditors through traditional channels, and therefore you cannot use the enforcement methods described in this book. But the property may not be completely beyond your reach. You can file a motion in the probate court asking that your judgment be paid out of the property under the court's jurisdiction [CCP 709.030]. How to pursue enforcement in this situation is beyond the scope of this book.

13. Judgment Does Not Reflect Debtor's Correct Name

If the judgment incorrectly lists the judgment debtor's name or neglects to list all names by which the debtor is known, you will have to file a form called an Affidavit of Identity [CCP 680.135]. This form is only used when you request a writ of execution (see Chapter 7) [CCP 699.510(c)] or an abstract of judgment (see Chapter 4) [CCP 674(c) (1)].

In the Affidavit of Identity, you must list the case name and number, the name of the debtor as stated in the judgment, the additional name or names the debtor uses and the facts on which you base your assertions. Some counties have created their own forms for the Affidavit of Identity, check with the court that issued your judgment to see whether it has a form you can use. If your county does not have a local form, you can adapt the sample, below, to meet your needs. Make sure to put the affidavit on numbered pleading paper (you'll find a blank sheet in the Appendix) and sign your name.

You can only use the Affidavit of Identity to include additional names for the debtor, not to add a new debtor. For example, you can state, in the Affidavit, that Harry Smith also goes by the name Harvey Smithers. However, if Harry Smith and Harvey Smithers are two different people, you cannot use an Affidavit to add one of them to your judgment.

And the Affidavit can be used only for a writ of execution or an abstract of judgment. If you want to use one of the more complicated enforcement procedures (for example, getting an assignment order, see Chapter 19), you will have to file a motion to amend the judgment to reflect the debtor's additional names.

Sample Affidavit of Identity

I, Amy Right, declare as follows

1. I obtained a judgment against Jeff Isbad from the Los Angeles County Superior Court on January 1, 2014 (Right v. Isbad, Case # 14K5000

2. At the time of the judgment, I knew the judgment debtor only as Jeff Isbad. He used this name in our correspondence and on his business card. Therefore, I sued him and obtained a judgment against him under that name.

3. Since I obtained this judgment, I have learned that Jeff Isbad has also used the name Jeffrey Bebad and owns property under this name. I questioned Mr. Isbad during a debtor's examination on August 22, 2015. Mr. Isbad said that he owned a home at 346 Magnolia lane in Long Beach, California. Mr. Isbad also stated that he used to use the name Jeffrey Bebad, and that he might have purchased this property under that name. I checked at the Los Angeles County Recorder's Office, and found that this property is owned by Jeffrey Bebad.

4. I make this Declaration of my own personal knowledge of all facts stated in this declaration and if called as a witness, I could and would testify competently to the matters stated under oath.

I declare under penalty of perjury under the laws of the State of California that the foregoing is true and correct.

September 10, 2015   (sign your name)
Date   Amy Right

E. Miscellaneous Information About Enforcement

There are a few things you can do to make recovery of your court judgment go as smoothly as possible.

1. Notify Court of Change of Address

Promptly report any change of your address to the court, and to the judgment debtor(s). Even years after you get your judgment, the court might need to notify you, especially if the debtor wants to pay off the judgment or wants to have a lien removed after paying the judgment. Similarly, if the debtor files for bankruptcy, they'll need to notify you of the new proceeding. And if the debtor dies, the executor of the estate should notify you.

A blank court form is included in the Appendix. You can notify the court by simply sending a completed copy. Be more formal with the debtor. Have the debtor served either in person or by mail and file a Proof of Service with the court. If the debtor had an attorney, serve the attorney also (while this is not necessary, why take any chances). How to serve documents is covered in Chapter 21.

2. Find Out About Fees and Deposits

Most enforcement procedures require you to lay out money up front to cover costs, such as court fees, fees for serving papers and fees for levying on (seizing) property. We try to estimate the fees for particular enforcement methods to help you evaluate whether or not to use that remedy. You can get the exact fees from the levying officer, usually a sheriff or marshal, who has responsibility in a particular county for making levies. You should be able to add most of your enforcement costs on to the judgment (See Chapter 16).

If your income is low, you may qualify for a waiver of some or all court fees and levying fees. Check with the clerk of the court that issued the judgment.

3. Use the Correct Forms and Court Documents

The Appendix contains most of the forms you will need to use the procedures discussed in this book. We suggest that you always check the court's website for the most recent forms, but if you will be using the forms included in this book, make photocopies of any forms before you fill them in. Otherwise, you may find yourself empty handed if you need to use a particular form more than once. Most of the forms are issued by the California Judicial Council, and are available from the court clerk's office, a law library or at www.courts.ca.gov/forms.

4. Substitute Yourself for Your Attorney

If an attorney handled your case in court, you'll need to file a document called a Substitution of Attorney with the court (in Appendix). In this document, your attorney agrees to withdraw from the case so you can represent yourself. Your attorney will complete the form and then mail it back to you. You will then need to sign and date your portion. You will need to have the debtor served with a copy of the Substitution of Attorney. You can use service by mail or in person; see Chapter 21. Whoever serves the Substitution of Attorney must complete a proof of service. File the original substitution and proof of service with the court.

Blank Page

Chapter 2

Getting Started

A. How Long Must You Wait?	2/2
1. California Small Claims Judgments	2/2
2. California Superior Court Judgments	2/3
3. Federal Court Judgments	2/5
B. If You Can't Locate the Debtor	2/5
1. Internet	2/5
2. Telephone Directories	2/6
3. Directories of Unlisted Phone Numbers	2/6
4. Crisscross Directories	2/6
5. Voter Registration Records	2/6
6. U.S. Post Office	2/6
7. Credit Reports	2/7
8. Public Real Estate Records	2/8
9. Business Records	2/8

In Chapter 1, we reviewed the many methods available to you to enforce your judgment. You are probably anxious to get started, but don't move too fast. As odd as it may sound, just because you have a judgment in your hands doesn't mean you can, or even should, immediately start enforcing it. Delays are sometimes required by law. If you start before the law says it's okay for you to proceed, your enforcement efforts will be invalid. In extreme cases, the debtor might even be able to sue you for damages.

Other times, waiting can be a sound enforcement strategy. For example, let's say you obtained a default judgment, the defendant failed to respond to your complaint in the required time frame. A defendant might be able to file a motion to have a default judgment set aside and be given a chance to respond if they had a good reason for failing to respond in the first place. For this reason, it makes sense to hold off your enforcement efforts until the time to file a motion to set aside the default judgment has expired.

Sometimes delay is inevitable. If you can't find the debtor, for example, you'll need to do a bit of detective work before you start collecting.

This chapter explains some legal and practical reasons why you might want to delay your enforcement efforts. It also covers some basic information gathering techniques that you can use to track down the debtor.

A. How Long Must You Wait?

As mentioned, you must wait a certain number of days before you can begin enforcing your judgment. The length of the waiting period depends on which court awarded the judgment.

1. California Small Claims Judgments

If you have a judgment from a small claims court, the waiting periods for enforcing depend on how you won the case.

If the defendant showed up at the original small claims hearing and lost, you must wait at least 30 days from the date the verdict is issued before you can begin to enforce it. The debtor has 30 days to file an appeal in the superior court asking for a new trial, called a "trial de novo [CCP 116.750(b)]." You will be frustrated if you try to collect before this appeal period has passed. The court clerk will not provide you with a Writ of Execution or an abstract of judgment until the 30 days have elapsed [CCP 116.810(a)].

If you obtained a default judgment, because the defendant didn't show up at the hearing, you must also wait at least 30 days from the date the clerk mails the defendant notice of the judgment before you can begin to enforce [CCP 116.730(a)]. This is because the defendant might file a motion to set aside the judgment. If the debtor files a motion, you will be notified of the hearing date. You are not required to hold off on enforcement until the motion is decided unless the defendant files a bond with the court. But we suggest you hold off just in case they file and win.

Some judges almost always allow defendants to vacate a default judgment. If the judge does so in your case, they will either consider the merits of the dispute right then (so be prepared with your argument) or set another date for a hearing [CCP 116.730(d)]. If you win this contested small claims hearing, you must wait at least 30 days after the decision is issued to see if the debtor appeals before starting your enforcement.

Other judges vacate default judgments only if a defendant acts very quickly and has a very good excuse. If the defendant's motion is denied, you can begin enforcing. Although the debtor can theoretically appeal the denial of the motion, it is unlikely, and even less likely, for an appeal to succeed. If the defendant does file an appeal, stop enforcing your judgment until the appeal is resolved.

The defendant shows up six months later
If you obtained a default judgment, it is possible that the debtor will file a motion requesting a hearing, arguing that they were not served properly, that is, that they didn't attend the hearing because you didn't give them sufficient notice of the lawsuit. The debtor has 180 days after the judgment was entered to request this type of hearing [CCP 116.740]. Debtors rarely bring these motions, they are complicated and usually aren't granted, so we don't recommend that you wait six months before starting to enforce. But be warned that many courts will try to find a way to give a person their day in court if they really didn't know about a case. If the defendant requests a hearing, you may have to put your enforcement efforts on hold.

2. California Superior Court Judgments
If you received your judgment from a civil court (other than small claims) you must hold off your enforcement efforts until the clerk properly enters your judgment in the court records. Even after the judgment is entered, however, there are practical reasons why you might want to wait before starting.

a. Defendant Might File a Motion to Set Aside the Judgment
If the defendant didn't appear at the trial, the law gives them 180 days to file a motion to set aside the judgment. A court may very well grant the motion if the defendant has a good excuse, such as an unexpected serious emergency. In some very rare situations, a court may set aside a judgment up to two years after it is entered if the debtor can show that they weren't served with notice of the lawsuit and only recently learned of the judgment [CCP 473.5(a)].

If you believe that the debtor disputes your version of the facts, the most prudent course of action is to wait six months before starting to enforce your judgment. Otherwise, the debtor might find an attorney who will file a motion to set the default judgment aside.

Of course, there is a potential downside to waiting six months. If the debtor owes several people money, another creditor may move in quickly to grab the debtor's assets
or establish priority as a secured creditor. So in balancing whether or not to wait six months, consider the following:

- Consider waiting at least 30 days before starting to collect. As more time goes by, the defendant will have a harder time winning a motion to set aside the judgment.

- Make sure the defendant was served personally with the original court summons. Go back and ask the process server exactly what happened. Also, reread the proof of service filed with the court. The defendant will have a much harder time, setting aside a default, if they were personally served instead of if the summons and complaint were left at their place of business or with someone at their residence.

- Have the defendants served, personally, with a copy of the judgment. File a Proof of Service with the court clerk. Then wait 30 days to
see if the defendants do anything.

- Evaluate the defendant's financial situation. Does the defendant have lots of debts and few assets? Does the defendant have a steady job that provides a good income? The better off the defendant is financially, the less you have to worry about other creditors beating you to the punch if you postpone your enforcement efforts.

- Think about what the defendant is likely to do. If the defendant clearly owes you the money and is not likely to go to court unless forced to, it's probably safe to go ahead with collection efforts.

b. Defendant Might Appeal

Once you were declared the winner in your lawsuit, the court should have informed you and the defendant of the date the judgment was entered, or officially filed, in court records. You are then supposed to prepare a document called Notice of Entry of Judgment and serve it on the defendant to provide formal notice that the judgment has been entered [CCP 664.5].

If the debtor was present at the trial, they have 30 days to file a notice of appeal after they were served with a Notice of Entry of Judgment if Limited Civil Division [Calif. Rules of Court 8.822(a)] or 60 days if case was Unlimited, Family or Probate [Calif. Rules of Court 8.104(a)]. If you fail to prepare and serve the Notice of Entry of Judgment, they have 90 days, from the date the judgment was entered, to file a notice of appeal [California Rules of Court, Rule 8.822(a)(1)(c))] if Limited or 180 days for Unlimited, Family or Probate [Calif. Rules of Court 8.104(a)(1)(c)]. If the defendant wasn't present in court and a default judgment was taken against them, they are likely to file a motion to vacate the judgment [Calif. Rules of Court 8.104 (a) (2)] rather than appeal, if they choose to do anything to contest the situation.

Once the judgment is entered, you are legally entitled to start enforcement. You are not required to wait until the 30 or 90 day time periods expire. Nevertheless, we recommend that you do wait for these time periods to fully expire. If you start enforcement activities sooner, you may push the debtor into filing an appeal. On the other hand, if you have information that other creditors are seizing assets of the debtor or that the debtor is selling a house, you'll want to act immediately.

Even if the debtor does appeal, you can go ahead with your enforcement activities while the appeal is pending unless the debtor furnishes the court with something called an undertaking, a security similar to a bond, for an amount up to two times the amount of the judgment [CCP 917.1].

There are always both benefits and risks to enforcing while an appeal is pending. The benefit of grabbing assets now is that you eliminate the risk that the assets might no longer be available when the appeal ends, often several years down the road. The risk is that you might actually lose the appeal, which means you will have to pay back the money you recovered, plus interest and costs incurred by the debtor as a result of the enforcement.

Only you can decide if the benefit outweighs the risk. You may want to go ahead with enforcement if the appeal really lacks merit, you are concerned that assets might disappear or other creditors might grab all the assets if you delay. If none of these issues are concerns for you, we recommend that you wait until the appeal has run its course and your judgment is affirmed before you begin enforcement.

c. Defendant Has a Case Pending Against You

Let's say that not only did you win your case against the debtor, but that the debtor has a separate lawsuit pending against you. We agree that this is unusual, but it is not entirely unheard of. In that situation, the court that issued your judgment can issue an order called a Stay of Enforcement of the Judgment, which puts your right to enforce on hold. A court might do this only if it finds that the debtor is likely to prevail in the other action, the amount in dispute in the other action is comparable to the amount of your judgment and you might not be able to pay the judgment in the other case [CCP 918.5].

3. Federal Court Judgments

If your judgment was awarded by a federal court, the defendant has 30 days to file a notice of appeal after the judgment is entered, that is, signed by the judge or clerk and recorded in the clerk's docket [Fed. Rules of Appellate Procedure, Rule 4(a) (1) (A)]. If the United States or a federal officer or agency is the defendant, the appeal period is extended to 60 days [Fed. Rules of Appellate Procedure, Rule 4(a) (1) (B)].

As with state court judgments, you are legally entitled to start enforcing as soon as the judgment is entered, although you probably want to wait until the appeals period passes. Even if the debtor appeals, you can collect, but if the debtor posts a bond with the court and files a Motion for a Stay of Enforcement [Fed. Rules of Appellate Procedure, Rule 8(a) (1) (A)], you will need to cease your collection efforts. You will also have to pay back the debtor, with interest and costs, if the debtor wins the appeal. If you win the appeal, you may be able to enforce your judgment out of the bond [Fed. Rules of Appellate Procedure, Rule 8 (2) (E) (b)].

A defendant can file a motion to set aside a federal judgment. The defendant has several grounds to bring this motion, though the most common reason is "mistake, inadvertence, surprise or excusable neglect" [Fed. Rules of Civil Procedure, Rule 60(b) (1)]. The defendant has one year to file the motion, although winning this type of motion is a real uphill battle [Fed. Rules of Civil Procedure, Rule 60(c) (1)].

B. If You Can't Locate the Debtor

If you can't find the debtor, you may have to spend some time tracking them down before you can start collecting. This is called "skip tracing" in the legal trade. You have a number of resources at your disposal.

Massive amounts of information about virtually every person in this country have been collected by many public and private organizations. Data about addresses, phone numbers, employment, criminal convictions, real estate transfers, automobile registration, business or professional licenses, credit, banking and voting are stored in computer files. To obtain most of this information, you need only write, call or visit the appropriate office, or search the Internet. Some private records are obtainable by making a special request or by serving subpoenas (See Chapter 6).

This section describes resources likely to help you locate the debtor, not the debtor's assets. If you already know where the debtor is, Chapter 6 and the chapters that focus on seizing specific types of assets can help you figure out what the debtor owns.

1. Internet

Ask any regular Internet surfer how to find a long lost friend and he'll spout off several Internet sites that search for people. Admittedly, many of these records are out of date or incomplete, but they provide a good starting point for your search. Professional debt collectors use them all, with varying degrees of success, but mostly use professional search engines that are not available to the public.

If your debtor's name is not very common you may want to start by doing the simple searches such as Google, Yahoo, and Bing. You may also want to search to see if they have a Facebook page or any of the other social media sites.

- www.555-1212.com: Searches phone directories

- www.anywho.com: Searches white and yellow pages, toll-free directories and reverse directories (if you know the telephone number only).

- www.infospace.com: Searches white page directories, yellow page directories, reverse directories and email addresses.

- www.411locate.com: Searches white and yellow pages, email addresses and public records. Some searches are free, others cost money.

- www.bop.gov: Use the inmate locator to search the federal Bureau of Prisons to see if your missing debtor is an inmate in a federal penitentiary.

2. Telephone Directories

If you haven't already done so, call directory assistance (area code plus 555-1212) for all areas where the debtor might possibly live and ask if there is a listing. Again this is much easier if your debtor has an uncommon name, if their name is common then this will be a waste of time.

3. Directories of Unlisted Phone Numbers

The debtor may have an unlisted phone number. Calling it "unlisted" may be a misnomer, however. Unlisted numbers don't appear in the official phone company directories. But they often show up in directories of unlisted numbers, which are compiled surreptitiously and circulate among bill collectors. You may be able to gain access to one through an auto repossessor or other person who works in the collections industry. You'll be charged as much as $100 for a copy of a directory or for the information you need. If the information is good enough, it may be worth it.

4. Crisscross Directories

The idea behind crisscross directories is that if you know only certain information about the debtor, you can fill in the missing pieces. For example, if you know the street on which the debtor lives, you can locate the exact address. If you know the address, you can get the phone number. If you know just the phone number, you can find the address.

Some crisscross directories include a person's occupation and business name. You can also obtain the names, addresses and phone numbers of neighbors (or former neighbors), and these are often a good source of information about the debtor.

Crisscross directories are available for most major metropolitan areas. You can find them in public libraries, title companies or the county tax assessor's or recorder's office. Also, most Internet search services include a crisscross directory feature.

5. Voter Registration Records

Contact the registrar of voters for the county in which you suspect the debtor lives. If the debtor has registered to vote, the listing will include the debtor's name, address, phone number, birth date, party affiliation and date of registration. If the debtor has moved within the same county, the registrar will have the new address. Each county is different, has different requirements and provides all or some of this information.

Even if the debtor isn't a registered voter, you might find contact information for relatives with the same last name, assuming the name isn't too common.

6. U.S. Post Office

If the judgment debtor has moved and left a forwarding address, the post office will provide it to you. Send a request to the post office that serves the zip code where the debtor used to live. Even if an Internet search of change of address directories came up empty, this request might turn up something. Those directories are updated infrequently.

If you have a post office box number for the debtor, the post office will release the street address and phone number of the box holder only if the box is listed in the name of a business. Some post offices will give you this information over the phone, but usually you will have to request it in writing. You do not have to explain why you want the information.

The post office usually won't give out an individual box holder's address unless you provide a statement that the name, address and telephone number are needed to serve legal papers in a pending proceeding.

Here is an example of a Request for Post Office Change of Address information: Please google "coa or boxholder form 5-2" and use that form for your requests.

Whether this will work depends on the post office branch, and possibly on whether the person making the request is a registered process server. You may even need a court order, which is beyond the scope of this book (Chapter 19 covers court orders).

If the post office does not have the box holder's correct address on file, you can write a letter to the postmaster letting them know, and asking them to require the debtor to update this information. According to the Domestic Mail Manual, the postmaster can terminate post office box service for a variety of reasons, including a box holder's refusal to update information on the application for a post office box (Google "usps form 1093" and read "updating your information").

7. Credit Reports

A credit report includes a debtor's name, address, phone number, Social Security number and date of birth, as well as credit history and possibly employment information. A credit bureau might provide a copy of the debtor's credit report if you state that you need the information for a legitimate business purpose, such as collecting a debt [Civil Code 1785.11(a)(3)(F)].

Credit bureaus typically provide credit reports to banks, credit card issuers, finance companies, mortgage lenders, landlords, data vendors and other businesses that subscribe to their credit reporting services. Although credit bureaus often are unwilling to provide information to non-subscribers, it can't hurt to ask. Check your local phone book for the phone numbers of the "big three" credit bureaus, Experian, Equifax or TransUnion. If you can't find a listing, check their Internet sites (www.experian.com, www.equifax.com or www.transunion.com). Most of the information on the site is about ordering your own file or becoming a subscriber. However, the credit bureaus constantly update their pages, and you can email their customer service departments with your inquiry.

If a bureau will provide you with a copy of the debtor's credit report, you will probably have to provide a copy of your judgment or other documents showing that you're entitled to the report. You will probably also have to pay a fee of $50–$60.

Obtaining the debtor's credit report under false pretenses (such as pretending to be the debtor) is illegal. The debtor can sue you for at least $2,500 in compensatory damages, up to $5,000 in punitive damages plus costs and attorney fees [Civil Code 1785.31].

8. Public Real Estate Records

If the debtor owns real estate in California, the tax collector or assessor's office in the county where the property is located should have the debtor's current address. This is true even if the debtor lives outside of the county. The taxing authority needs the current address in order to send the property tax bill. In addition to showing the current property address, if the debtor owns more than one piece of property, the county recorder's office might also show another address (where the debtor might be now) if a recorded document regarding the property was ever sent there.

9. Business Records

If the debtor owns a business that sells taxable goods (the sale of most goods in California is taxed), the statistics unit of the Board of Equalization will probably have information on the business. You can contact the Board at (800) 400-7115 or www.boe.ca.gov.

If the debtor is one of the millions of Californians licensed by the Department of Consumer Affairs or another agency, location information may be easily available. Start with the Department of Consumer Affairs (800-952-5210 or www.dca.ca.gov). If another agency licenses the debtor, the Department of Consumer Affairs can provide a referral to the correct agency. Business addresses are usually listed in these records, and sometimes you'll get a home address as well.

If the debtor is a sole proprietor, California partnership or member of a California partnership, you can search the fictitious name records at the Recorder's office in the county in which the principal place of business is located. This lists the business's owners and their addresses.

If the debtor is, or owns, a California corporation, foreign corporation authorized to do business in California, a California limited liability company, a limited partnership or foreign general partnership authorized to do business in California, the debtor must register the business with the Secretary of State. You can get basic information from the Secretary of State's website, at http://ss.ca.gov. First select the search type of the business you want to find out more about. Then type in the name of the company in the entity name field and hit the search button or enter key. If you want more detailed information about any business that comes up in the business search results, simply click on the emboldened name of the company you are interested in. If you scroll down to the bottom of the next screen the website will take you to, you will see four bullet points. The second bullet point gives you a clickable link that will take you to the page on the Secretary of State's website dedicated to instructions for requesting information by mail, including order forms, fee schedules and mailing addresses.

Chapter 3

Enforcement Practices to Avoid

A. Debt Enforcement Laws (aka Collection Laws)	3/2
B. Common Sense	3/3
C. Communicating with the Debtor	3/3
D. Communicating with Others about the Debtor	3/4
E. Giving and Getting Information About the Debtor	3/5

State and federal laws protect debtors from unfair collection practices, including harassment and public embarrassment, by people who collect debts on behalf of others (collection agencies and collection lawyers) and by creditors collecting their own debts. Although some of these laws apply only to people collecting debts on behalf of others, we recommend that you follow them, or at least the provisions barring harassment and other unpleasant activities. Harassing a debtor is both unnecessary and counter-productive. Debtors have realized that new Debt Collection Laws grant certain protection from abusive collection practices. Further, there are an increasing number of law firms established to aggressively enforce these Debt Collection Laws and exact penalty fees from abusive collectors. The debtor might even sue you if your behavior turns outrageous. Why incur the ultimate irony of paying fees to a person who is not paying your judgment.

Most debt collection laws were designed to regulate collection activities before a creditor obtains a judgment. In fact, some of the laws bar a creditor or debt collector from threatening to sue someone unless the creditor or collector actually intends to pursue a lawsuit. You are well beyond that stage of collections. Fortunately for you, now that you have a judgment, there will be little reason to contact the debtor, except to request payments. Nevertheless, we suggest that you read this chapter, as you don't want to get sued for inadvertently violating the law.

A. Debt Collection Laws

The Federal Fair Debt Collection Practices Act (FDCPA) regulates only people who are paid to collect debts on behalf of others, collection agencies and collection attorneys [15 U.S.C. 1692 Title VIII of the Fair Debt Collection Practices Act and the sections that follow]. The FDCPA prohibits a collector from engaging in many kinds of behavior and also gives a debtor the right to tell a bill collector to cease communications. You are not bound by this law; however you still need to proceed with caution. While we suggest you not to harass the debtor, you are free to continue to contact the debtor even if the debtor asks you to stop. But before making yet another call or sending yet another letter, ask yourself why you want to contact the debtor again and whether you really expect to get anything from the additional communications.

You might be subject to the FDCPA if you knowingly and purposely mislead the debtor. Even though individual creditors are ordinarily not subject to the FDCPA, there is an exception for creditors who use a false name or other deception to lead the debtor to believe that they are dealing with a third party debt collector. For example, if you send letters to the debtor on collection agency letterhead, you could be liable for violating the FDCPA. This same issue comes up if you call and leave a message on a debtor's telephone answering machine depending upon what information you disclose on the message left and who listens to (or overhears) the message.

The California debt collection law [Civil Code 1788], otherwise known as the Rosenthal Fair Debt Collection Practices Act, and the sections that follow regulates not only those who collect debts on behalf of others, but also creditors collecting their own debts, which means this law may apply to you if your judgment is based on "consumer debt". Consumer Debts are defined as a credit transaction for personal, family or household purposes where the debtor is a natural person [Civil Code 1788.2(e) and 15 U.S.C. 1692a (5)]. We suggest that you assume it applies to you and avoid any problems. The law primarily prohibits a collector from engaging in certain kinds of behavior, most of the same activities that are barred by the federal law. The state law does not give the debtor the right to insist that you cease communications or collection activities.

If you're in doubt about a particular activity, you can look up the laws and decide for yourself whether or not it is permissible.

B. Common Sense

While this chapter lists specific activities prohibited by federal and state laws, don't assume you are free to do anything that isn't listed. Use these examples as a guide for the types of activities that are prohibited.

If you are honest, reasonably sensitive to the debtor's rights and interested solely in enforcing your judgment, there is little possibility that you will run afoul of these laws. But if you are seeking revenge, feeling vindictive or simply hoping to make the debtor's life miserable, your actions are apt to backfire. Remember the saying: "He who seeks revenge should first dig two graves."

C. Communicating With Debtor

If you want to contact the debtor to request payment or other information, whether in person, in writing or by phone, follow the guidelines listed here.

Phone calls. Here are some general rules if you are going to call the debtor:

- Do not call before 8 a.m. or after 9 p.m.
- Do not call the debtor directly, if they have an attorney.
- Do not call the debtor at work if you know that their employer prohibits them receiving collections calls at work.
- Do not place telephone calls without identifying yourself.
- Always disclose your identity in every telephone call to the debtor.
- Notify debtor in the initial communication that this is an attempt to collect a debt and any information obtained will be used for that purpose.
- Do not call repeatedly.
- Do not pretend you are different people on successive calls so you can call again and again.

Harassment or abuse

Do not engage in conduct meant to harass, oppress or abuse. Specifically:

- Do not use or threaten to use violence.
- Do not harm or threaten to harm the debtor, their reputation or their property.
- Do not use obscene or profane language.
- Do not threaten to publish the debtor's name as a person who doesn't pay bills.
- Do not visit the debtor and refuse to leave when asked.

False or misleading representations

Don't lie. Specifically:

- Do not claim to be a law enforcement officer or suggest that you are connected with the federal, state or local government.
- Do not falsely represent the amount owed.
- Do not claim to be an attorney or that a communication is from an attorney.
- Do not claim that you will have the debtor imprisoned or that their property will be seized, unless you intend to have the property seized.
- Do not claim that the debtor has committed a crime.
- Do not threaten to sell the debt to a third party, unless you truly intend to hire a collection agency.
- Do not send a document that looks like it's from a court or attorney or part of a legal process unless the document really is.
- Do not use a false business name.
- Do not claim to be employed by a credit bureau or collection agency.

If mailing something to the debtor, make sure the envelope states nothing that would inform any other person that it is regarding a debt. Write "Personal" and/or "Confidential" on the outside.

Sample "No-No" letter

August 22, 2015

Dear Jeff Isbad:

This letter is to advise you that my judgment against you will stand for the rest of your life, wherever you go and whatever you do, unless you pay it off within one week.

You owe me $6,000 plus interest at the rate of 25% per year, and you're obliged to pay me in full before you make mortgage payments, buy food for yourself or feed your cat.

This judgment gives me the right to talk to your boss about you, and to let him know what a deadbeat you are. In fact, I've even set up an appointment to meet with him at the end of next week if I don't hear from you.

Why not just pay up now, before anything happens to you or your family? I'm sure you'd hate to see your microwave, stereo, and car repossessed, or just happens to get smashed up.

I'm looking forward to talking with you soon, Jeff boy.

Sincerely,

Amy Right
Amy "call me knee-breaker" Right

Unfair practices

Don't use any unfair or outrageous method to collect the debt. Specifically:

- Do not add interest, fees or charges not authorized in the original agreement or by state law.
- Do not deposit a post-dated check prior to the date on the check.
- Do not solicit a post-dated check by threatening criminal prosecution.
- Do not call the debtor collect or otherwise cause them to incur communications charges.

D. Communicating With Others About the Debtor

In general, you cannot contact third parties about the debtor (except for the debtor's attorney or a credit bureau), unless you do so to obtain information that can help you locate the debtor.

This means that you cannot call the debtor's employer to inform them of your judgment or to ask them to put pressure on the debtor to pay. There are two exceptions to this rule however. First, you can contact the debtor's employer to verify employment or initiate legal collections, such as a wage garnishment. Also, if the debtor is on active military duty, you can contact the commanding officer and request assistance.

If you intend to contact a third person to obtain location information, you must give your name and only state that you are confirming or correcting location information. Here are some dos and don'ts for communications with third parties:

- Do not state that the debtor owes a debt.

- Do not contact a third party more than once unless the third party requests you to do so, or unless you believe the third party's response was wrong or incomplete and that the third party has correct or complete information.

- Do not send a postcard mentioning the judgment or indicate anything on the outside of an envelope about the debtor owing you money.

- If you write to a debtor at a place where another person is likely to open the mail, write PERSONAL or PERSONAL AND CONFIDENTIAL on the envelope.

- Do not harm or threaten to harm a person associated with the debtor, or that person's reputation or property.

- Do not tell the world how the debtor is a no good so and so.

- Do not distribute telegrams, pictures, photographs, cartoons, tapes or other materials to embarrass the debtor for not paying the judgment.

E. Giving and Getting Information About the Debtor

As a creditor of the debtor, you may be contacted by a financial or credit agency, such as a credit bureau, bank, finance company, credit interchange club or another creditor. You are free to provide these agencies with credit or financial information about the debtor. However, you are not obligated to do so if you don't want to. If the debtor asks you not to disclose information about your judgment, you have a decision to make. Your judgment is a matter of public record and the debtor cannot bar you from talking about it. At the same time, if you talk after the debtor asked you not to, the debtor isn't likely to come forward with payment.

If you decide to talk, state facts only, such as "I obtained a judgment against Shorty's Shoe Shop six months ago. I have asked for payment three times, but have received nothing." Avoid general negative assertions, such as "Jeff Isbad is a hopeless deadbeat and pathological liar and you would be nuts to do business with him." Similarly, don't make statements or conclusions you can't prove, like "Jeff Isbad doesn't have very good credit."

Blank Page

Chapter 4

Creating Liens on the Debtor's Property

A. Real Estate Liens	4/3
1. Limits of Real Estate Liens	4/3
2. How to Create a Real Estate Lien	4/4
B. Business Asset Liens	4/8
1. Limits of Business Asset Liens	4/9
2. How to Create a Business Asset Lien.	4/9
C. Personal Property Liens	4/10

Collection Factor

	High	Moderate	Low
Potential cost to you			✓
Potential for producing cash	✓		
Potential for settlement		✓	
Potential time and trouble			✓
Potential for bankruptcy			✓

 lien is a legal assertion that you have a claim of a specific value against certain property. A lien changes your general judgment against the debtor into a claim for a specific dollar amount against whatever property is subject to the lien. If the debtor sells or refinances the property, you are entitled to be paid out of the proceeds.

EXAMPLE 1: Amy obtains a judgment against Jeff and places a lien for $3,000 on Jeff's house. Jeff wants to sell his house to Frieda. To do so, however, he must clear up any liens. Thus, Amy will be paid out of the proceeds so that Frieda can take ownership of the house free of any claims against it.

EXAMPLE 2: Amy obtains a $3,000 judgment against Jeff's Rug Cleaning for damaging her Persian carpet. She places a lien against Jeff's business assets. Prospective purchasers of Jeff's Rug Cleaning or its assets, other than customers buying goods in the normal course of business, will require Jeff to pay off the lien as a condition of sale.

A lien is a passive enforcement device. It will not get you your money right away. Instead, it gives you standing as a creditor to be paid from proceeds if the property is sold or refinanced. Usually a lien will eventually produce enough cash to pay off your judgment, including post-judgment costs and interest.

Enforcing a judgment through liens involves little effort or expense, but it requires a lot of patience. If you think in terms of years rather than months, a lien can become, in the words of a former judge, a "little money machine."

Throughout this book, we caution against using overly-aggressive enforcement measures that may push the debtor into bankruptcy. Lien placement is a good way to minimize this risk. A lien does not affect the debtor's right to use and enjoy the property for the time being; it becomes effective only when the property is sold or refinanced. Of course, if you are looking for money right now, liens won't do you much good, unless interest rates are dropping and the debtor is likely to refinance their property soon.

If many creditors are trying to enforce their judgments by means of lien, you may find yourself at the end of a very long line. When the property owner sells or refinances, your pockets may be just as empty as they are today. When you record your lien, check to see whether other liens already exist on the property. If there are other liens, place yours anyway, but also give serious consideration to using some of the more aggressive strategies discussed in this book.

Property Can Be Transferred Without Removing Liens

No law requires that liens be removed before title to property is transferred. If a lien isn't paid off, it simply remains on the property, leaving the new owner to address it. This means that for transfers between relatives, the new owner may take title to the property, liens and all. If the new owner wants to transfer the property to someone who will need financing or who wants clear title, however, the lien will have to be paid.

Forcing the sale of property

Once a lien has been placed, you don't have to just sit and wait to get paid out of sales or the proceeds of a refinance proceeds. Theoretically, you can force a sale of property and get paid out of the proceeds. This is rarely cost effective, however, because of the time and expense involved.

The following types of liens are discussed in this chapter:

- real estate liens
- business property liens
- personal property liens.

Other Liens

Be aware of creditors with other types of liens who may stand in line to be paid ahead of you.

- **Tax lien**. A taxing authority, such as the IRS or Franchise Tax Board, creates this lien if the debtor makes no arrangement to pay back taxes.

- **Mechanic's lien**. This lien is created by someone who worked on or supplied materials to a real estate improvement project, and then was not paid.

- **Child support lien**. A parent owed child support can place a lien on the debtor's property.

- **Lien on pending legal action**. If the debtor is involved in a lawsuit (other than yours), the other party to that lawsuit might record a lien. If the other party wins the case, they would be entitled to pursue payment on their already recorded lien.

A. Real Estate Liens

You can create a lien on real estate owned by the debtor by registering your judgment with the recorder's office in any county in which the debtor currently owns real estate, or in which a judgment debtor might acquire it [CCP 697.340].

Once recorded, a lien applies to all of the debtor's interest in real property (real estate) in the county and to any real estate the debtor acquires after you create the lien. For example, assume that you register your judgment in Los Angeles County, even though the debtor owns no property in that county when you register the judgment. If the debtor later buys a house in Los Angeles (or in any other city in the county) your lien automatically will attach to the debtor's interest in the property.

It doesn't matter what California court issued your judgment, Small Claims, Federal, Superior or even a court from another state [CCP 697.060(a)]. You can even register a judgment obtained in a Worker's Compensation case [CCP 697.330].

Real estate liens won't work for every case. For example some may consider it a waste of time creating a real estate lien if the facts suggest that the judgment debtor is unlikely ever to own real estate. But keep in mind that liens last the statutory length of the judgment (ten years) and can be renewed if the judgment is renewed. Because fortunes can change, don't be too quick to write off the lien remedy as inapplicable.

1. Limits of Real Estate Liens

Your judgment will be paid if the owner of the real estate, on which you have placed a lien, sells or refinances their property, provided there is sufficient money (equity) available after payments to the mortgage lender and anyone who has recorded a lien ahead of you. As an example, if a judgment debtor falls behind on monthly mortgage payments and the lender forecloses on the property, the chances of collecting on the lien are low. A foreclosure sale rarely brings in enough to pay the amount owed to the mortgage lender, let alone to other creditors.

There is another potential limitation if your real estate lien attaches to the debtor's home. California law provides a Homestead Exemption, which provides homeowners with the right to exempt a portion of the equity in their residence [CCP 704.720] from enforcement of a judgment. At the writing of this book, the Homestead Exemption ranges from $75,000 for single owners to $100,000 for married couples (depending on the members of the family unit in whose name the property is titled), up to $175,000 for elderly and disabled homeowners [CCP 704.730].

Exemption laws apply to forced collections, not voluntary sales. If you force the sale of the property, which as noted earlier is rarely a good idea, you don't get paid until after the mortgage is paid off, the homeowner receives the exemption amount, and all parties who recorded liens ahead of you are paid. If there's enough equity in the property for you to get paid, you will. But don't count on it. Anyone with that much equity in their house isn't likely to let it be sold involuntarily.

You face another possible limitation if your debtor declares bankruptcy. The Bankruptcy Code gives debtors various ways to deal with liens in bankruptcy. One way, called "lien avoidance," allows a debtor to wipe out a lien completely. Lien avoidance is available on judgment liens to the extent the lien impairs the debtor's homestead exemption. This means that if no equity remains after the mortgage (including any second mortgage) and the homestead exemption are deducted, the debtor will likely be able to eliminate your judgment lien [11 U.S.C. 522(f)].

2. How to Create a Real Estate Lien

You create a real estate lien by completing a form called an Abstract of Judgment and having the court of jurisdiction certify its contents. You may then record it in any county you choose, typically, where the debtor owns real estate or might in the future (Chapters 6 gives tips on how to find out if and where the debtor owns real estate).

a. Complete an Abstract of Judgment

An Abstract of Judgment is a simple California court form that affirms that a judgment was entered against the debtor on a specific date for a specific amount. A completed sample is shown later in this chapter; a blank copy of the form is in the Appendix:

If your judgment is for child or spousal support, use the Abstract of Support Judgment form in the Appendix. The content is essentially the same as the form shown below.

Page 1 of California Judicial Council Form EJ-001; Abstract of Judgment Civil

Caption (top left area): Follow the format of your earlier court papers. Check the box labeled "Judgment Creditor." Don't check the box labeled "Amended" unless you are filing an amendment to your original abstract, (for that, see Section A2, below).

Item 1: Check the "judgment creditor" box.

Item 1a: Enter the name and last known address of the judgment debtor, as it is listed in the judgment.

Item 1b: Enter the last four digits of the judgment debtor's driver's license number. Check "unknown" if you don't know it.

Item 1c: Enter the last four digits of the judgment debtor's Social Security number. Check "unknown" if you don't know it.

NOTE: If you check "unknown" for Item 1b or Item1c, make sure you really don't know. Check any papers you have such as canceled checks, a lease or rental application, or a credit application in your possession, or call anyone you know who might have the information. If another creditor later establishes that you had this information or could easily have obtained it, your lien may be nullified (Keele v. Reich (1985) 169 Cal. App. 3d 1129). If you discover the information after recording the Abstract of Judgment, you can amend the abstract later [CCP 674(b)]. Also, in cases where your debtor's name is very common, not having the last four digits of their Social Security number will make it more probable that you will not be paid if they sell or refinance their home.

Item 1d: Enter the name and address at which you served the judgment debtor with the Summons and Complaint in the lawsuit in which you obtained the judgment. You, the County Sheriff, or your Registered Process Server writes this information on the Proof of Service and files it with the court file. If ever your copy of the Proof of Service is misplaced, check with the clerk of the court where it was filed.

If your judgment was obtained in another state, you must have it properly entered in California to enforce it here. In Item 1d, enter the name and address at which you served the debtor with a Notice of Entry of Sister State Judgment or the address you listed on the Statement for Registration of Foreign Support Order.

Item 2: If your judgment is against more than one defendant, and you want to impose a lien against real property owned by any of them, check the box. On the back of the form, enter the name, last known address and other requested information for each additional defendant. Be sure to fill out the caption on top of the back page.

Item 3: Include your name and address so you will be properly referenced in the recorder's office records and may be contacted in the event someone wants or needs to pay off the lien.

Item 4: Mark this box and include information on the second page if there are additional judgment creditors.

What If Debtor Goes By Different Name?

If the debtor uses a name that doesn't appear in the judgment, for example, the debtor goes by several different names or has an "aka," you will need to file a separate document, called an Affidavit of Identity. Ordinarily, you can only go after property held in the debtor's name as it appears in the judgment. By filing an Affidavit of Identity, you can go after property, using a writ of execution, which the debtor owns under a different name. Instructions for filing an Affidavit of Identity are in Chapter 1D.

Item 5: Leave this blank unless you're filing an amended Abstract, see Section A2, below.

Date and Signature: Enter the date and type your name. Do not sign yet.

Item 6: Enter the total amount of the judgment or renewed judgment as granted by the court.

Item 8a: Enter the date on which the clerk entered your judgment. This isn't the date it was filed or mailed, which may appear on the judgment. If you don't know the exact date of entry of judgment, call the court clerk.

Items 8b-8c: If you renewed your judgment prior to its expiration (see Chapter 20), put the renewal dates here.

Item 9: Check this box only if your judgment specifies that the debtor can pay it off in installments. You can still use an Abstract of Judgment to record a judgment lien. But your lien will be only for the amount of money then due and not yet paid under the installment judgment, not for the full amount of the judgment. If the debtor doesn't pay as required under the installment judgment, the lien will gradually increase.

Item 10: Leave this blank unless you, the judgment creditor, have a creditor who has

obtained a lien on you for this action.
Items 11a-11b: Check Item 11a unless you are in the very unusual situation in which the court has ordered a stay of enforcement. In that case, check Item 11b and enter the date the stay will expire.

Item 12a: Check this box.

Item 12b: Leave this blank.

This abstract issued on (date): Leave this box blank. It's for the clerk to complete.

Clerk, by: Leave this line blank. It's for the clerk to sign.

Page 2

You will complete Page 2 of form EJ-001 only if you indicated on page 1 that you want to impose a lien against real property owned by more than one defendant. If you do not complete Page 2, enter "DO NOT RECORD THIS SIDE" in the caption and leave the rest blank. When you record the Abstract of Judgment with the county recorder, you will be charged by the number of pages. You can save yourself a few dollars per abstract by indicating that you don't want Page 2 recorded.

b. Have Court Issue Abstract

Once you've completed your Form EJ-001 Abstract of Judgment, make as many copies as you need to record, i.e., one for each county in which the debtor owns or might own real property. After making copies, sign each one, which effectively turns these copies into "originals." Then take or mail them to the court clerk to be officially "issued." If you mail the Abstracts, you can use the cover letter in the Appendix. You'll have to pay a small fee of $ 25 for obtaining each issued Abstract of Judgment [Government Code 70626(a) (2)]. It is best to call the court clerk before mailing, or take your checkbook if you go in person.

The clerk will check the case file to make the information you wrote is accurate. Once the date and amount of the judgment is verified, the clerk will date and sign each Abstract form, stamp them with the official seal, and return them to you. Congratulations. Your Abstract of Judgment is officially issued.

c. Record Abstract of Judgment

Once you have your officially issued Abstract of Judgment, take or mail it to the county recorder's office for each county in which you want to create a lien. If you have reason to believe that the debtor is in the process of selling or refinancing the property, or that other creditors may also be in the process of creating liens, it may be to your benefit to go to the County Clerk in person in order to speed up the process. The cost of recording a judgment varies from county to county, and depends on the number of judgment debtors and the number of pages being recorded. Check with each County Recorder for the exact amount.

Record a Request for Notice

Make sure to complete and file a Request for Notice along with each of your abstracts. This will help in making sure that you are notified if the debtor's mortgages go into foreclosure. Record one per loan.

The County Recorder may first return a conformed copy stamped with recording information. Keep this copy until you receive back your original Abstract of Judgment back from the Recorder's office. This often takes several weeks.

Once your Abstract of Judgment is recorded, all of the judgment debtor's interest in real estate, in that county has a lien on it. If the debtor acquires property later on, the lien attaches to it, assuming the lien is still effective. Ordinarily, a lien remains effective as long as a judgment is valid, up to ten years from the date of entry of judgment and renewable for ten-year periods, or until you release it, which you must do when your judgment is satisfied (See Chapter 20).

The County Recorder is supposed to send the judgment debtor a copy of the Abstract of Judgment which informs them of the lien and gives them a chance to correct any mistakes on it.

Liens on Jointly Owned Property

How a lien on jointly owned real estate works depends on the form of joint ownership. To find out how property is owned, you can check the deed in the county recorder's office or hire a local title insurance company to check for you.

- **Tenancy in common**. A judgment lien attaches to the debtor's particular interest and remains attached even if the judgment debtor transfers, or leaves in a will, ownership to someone else. Property is held as a tenancy in common if the deed doesn't specify a particular type of joint ownership.

- **Joint tenancy.** A judgment lien attaches to the judgment debtor's share of the joint tenancy and remains enforceable if the debtor transfers their share to a third party. If the judgment debtor dies, however, your lien is wiped out. The surviving joint tenants automatically take the property without the lien.

- **Community property.** A judgment lien attaches to the entire property when it is held as community property by a married couple. The lien will be enforceable against the property even if it is transferred to a third party.

d. Your Continuing Responsibilities

As the holder of a judgment lien against the debtor's real estate, you have several ongoing responsibilities.

If you move - You must file any address change with the court that issued your judgment. The debtor will need to know how to reach you so you can be paid and remove the lien (See Chapter 1, Section E).

If you discover that you knew or had access to the debtor's Social Security Number or driver's license number - You must file an amendment to the Abstract of Judgment. Use the same form and check the box labeled "Amended" after the title. Complete the form again, adding the new or revised information. Be sure to complete Line 5; indicating the number of the original Abstract and the date you filed it. Each county will need its own prior information on line 5. Before you sign the form, make enough copies to record the Amendment in every county where you recorded the original Abstracts. Sign each form and record them in the counties where you recorded your original Abstracts. You will retain the lien priority of the earlier Abstract [CCP 674(b)].

If the judgment is satisfied - You must promptly release the lien if your judgment is paid or settled, in all counties where you filed an Abstract. Failure to promptly release liens can subject you to liability for damages that result (See Chapter 22 for instructions on how to release liens).

If the debtor has a common name - If your debtor has a common name like John Smith, you may be contacted by other people also named John Smith who own property. You need to clarify that you have put a lien on the property of "your" John Smith and not on any other John Smith. By law, you must immediately cooperate in clearing up the confusion, and upon request, you must provide the clarification in writing. If your lien was recorded against the property of the wrong person, that person may provide you with proof that they are not the judgment debtor and demand that you release the lien. You then have 15 days to provide that person with a release document suitable for recording [CCP 697.410(b)]. If you do not comply promptly with the wronged party's request, you could become liable for any damages, as well as a $100 fine. The wronged person can also request a court order to release the lien and can recover his legal fees, to do this, from you [CCP 697.410(d)].

B. Business Asset Liens

If the judgment debtor is a business, whether a sole proprietor, corporation, Limited Liability Company, or a partnership, you can create a lien against some of its assets. Simply register your judgment with the California Secretary of State. This type of lien lasts for five years, until the judgment is satisfied or until the judgment creditor removes it, whichever happens first. As with a judgment, this lien may be extended.

EXAMPLE: Nathan owned and operated a business in which he built and sold small business computer systems. Lucinda bought a lemon of a system from Nathan for $8,000, and she sued him when he refused to give her a refund. By the time Lucinda got a judgment against Nathan, Nathan had liquidated the business. Lucinda knew that Nathan had been an independent businessperson and had not worked for anyone else for over 20 years. Figuring that Nathan would soon open another business, Lucinda created a judgment lien against Nathan's (future) business assets. If Nathan had not had this long history as a businessperson, Lucinda might have waited until Nathan actually went back into business before creating the lien.

A judgment lien on business assets attaches to any of the following assets that the debtor currently owns or acquires while the lien is in effect. Note that for some items the judgment debtor must be located in California and for other items the actual property needs to be located in California (remember, the lien lasts as long as five years) [CCP 697.530(a) and 697.510(b)]:

- **Accounts Receivable**, money owed to the debtor from a transaction involving their business (judgment debtor must be located in California)

- **Tangible chattel paper**, a document showing evidence of a monetary obligation and security interest in specific goods, such as an automobile lease (judgment debtor must be located in California)

- **Business equipment and furniture**, such as machines, tools, computers, bookcases and cash registers. If the judgment debtor is a sole proprietor, they may be able to claim some of them as exempt tools of their trade and prevent you from getting them (equipment must be located in California)

- **Farm products**, crops that have been harvested (crops must be located in California)

- **Items of inventory worth $500 or more**. Most of the inventory of a car dealership would qualify, but rarely would items in a book store (items must be located in California)

- **Negotiable documents of title**, such as a negotiable bill of lading or warehouse receipts (documents must be located in California).

The Business Asset Lien does not attach to the debtor's cars, boats or other vehicles registered with the Department of Motor Vehicles [CCP 697.530(d) (1)]. It also does not apply to business fixtures that have been permanently attached to the office or building, such as a lighting system; these become part of the real estate [CCP 697.530(e)].

1. Limits of Business Asset Liens

As with other liens, a business asset lien is most likely to pay off when the business itself is sold, not when business assets are sold. Few business property assets carry title documents, so it is easy for a debtor to sell business assets without either you learning of the sale or the purchaser knowing of the lien. When assets are transferred in the ordinary course of business (bought and sold for a reasonable amount in a method acceptable within the industry), any lien on them is extinguished, meaning the buyer gets it free and clear of the lien. If assets of $500 or more are transferred not in the course business, the lien will remain, but you will likely need the help of an attorney to enforce it.

Even a lien on the business itself may not yield money. Your lien has priority only over those judgment liens that are filed after you file your lien. If the debtor used the business as security when purchasing the property, or for other loans made prior to you filing your lien, those earlier lenders have priority when the business sells, as long as the lenders have taken the steps necessary to "perfect" their security interests. They do this by filing a financing statement, called a UCC1, with the California Secretary of State. To find out if other liens have been filed, contact the Secretary of State's office to obtain Form UCC11, the Information Request Form for California. The Secretary of State's UCC division can be reached at 916-653-3516, or you can download the form and instructions from the Secretary of State's website at www.ss.ca.gov. From the Secretary's home page, click on the "California Business Portal," then go to the UCC page and click on "Forms & Fees" to find the UCC11. You may ask for a general search, or you can limit your search by street address or time period. The fee for each search is $10, but the Secretary of State's office will also charge you copying costs for any documents uncovered by the search. Be sure to follow the instructions that accompany the form referencing how to submit fees that will cover these costs.

You cannot create a business asset lien if you have a superior court installment judgment, unless all of the installments under the judgment have come due and the debtor has not paid them, per [CCP 697.510(a)]. You can, however, avail yourself of this type of lien if you have a small claims installment judgment, but only for the amount that is delinquent unless a court orders otherwise [CCP 697.540].

Still, it can make sense to create a business asset lien if the judgment debtor is a relatively large business with valuable assets or inventory. If the business goes bankrupt, you will be treated as a secured creditor. Furthermore, if the business needs a loan or sells, the lender or buyer will probably require the business to pay off the lien.

2. How to Create a Business Asset Lien

You create a business asset lien by completing a form called a Notice of Judgment Lien, (Form JL1) serving a copy of it on the debtor, and filing it with the California Secretary of State. If five years pass and you still have not collected your judgment, the lien will expire. You can continue the lien by filing a continuation statement in the six months prior to the expiration of the five-year lien [CCP 697.510(c) & (d)]. You can file continuations indefinitely [CCP 697.510(e)]. If the lien expires, you can obtain another lien, however, you won't get the benefit (priority) of the earlier filing date. The effective date of the second lien will be the new filing date [CCP 697.510(c)].

a. Complete Notice of Judgment Lien

A blank copy of the Notice of Judgment Lien and instructions for filling it out are in the Appendix. The instructions are printed on the back of the form, but two items require further explanation or from the Secretary of State's website at www.sos.ca.gov. A sample completed form is available later in this chapter.

Item 3F: Enter the total of your judgment, plus accrued interest and any post-judgment costs you have incurred less credit for payments received (See Chapter 16 to figure out these amounts).

Item 3G: Put the date you will mail the Notice of Judgment Lien, and then make sure you actually mail it that day. If the Notice gets to the Secretary of State's office more than ten days after the date on the form, the Secretary of State will likely reject the form, and you'll have to refile it.

b. Serve and File the Notice of Judgment Lien

After you complete the Notice of Judgment Lien, you must serve the judgment debtor with a copy. Service by first class mail is sufficient (See Chapter 21 for information on how to have documents served by mail). Make sure the person who serves the Notice completes a Proof of Service form. Mail the original and one copy of the Notice of Judgment Lien to the address on page 2 of the form. Enclose a check made out to the Secretary of State for $10 for two pages, and an additional $10 for any filing in excess of 2 pages. If you file in person, you'll have to pay an additional $10 fee.

C. Personal Property Liens

It is possible to create a short-term lien against a judgment debtor's personal property, that is, all property that isn't real estate, e.g. jewelry, stocks, pianos, precious metals and computers. A personal property type of lien is created primarily to prevent the property from being transferred to avoid enforcement of your judgment, but also to protect you if the debtor files for bankruptcy.

Chapter 6 describes a procedure called a debtor's examination. This is a process in which you serve papers on the judgment debtor ordering them to come to court and answer questions about their income and assets [CCP 708.110]. As soon as the papers are served on your debtor, a "silent" lien attaches to the debtor's non-exempt personal property and remains in place for a year [CCP 708.110(d)]. For information on what property is exempt, see Chapter 13. You can renew the lien by serving a new set of debtor's examination papers. Remember that a judgment debtor examination can only be done every 120 days. The lien is valid for one year.

If the debtor sells or gives away personal property subject to this lien, you may be able to take it from the new owner, if you can track it down. If a third party bought the property at or near its fair market value, and had no knowledge of your lien, you may be out of luck [CCP 697.610 (a)]. The lien may also give you an advantage over other creditors if the judgment debtor files for bankruptcy more than 90 days after the lien takes effect (See Chapter 17).

If the Debtor Appeals

If your debtor files an appeal, you should wait until the appeal is decided, by the court, before creating liens. You are prohibited from recording an Abstract of Judgment of 30 days after judgment is entered and while a small claims appeal is pending [CCP 116.810(a)]. And for other judgments, creating liens while an appeal is pending could mean that you'll be stuck with significant costs later on if the defendant wins. See a lawyer before creating liens while an appeal is pending.

NOTICE OF JUDGMENT LIEN

FOLLOW INSTRUCTIONS CAREFULLY (front and back of form)

A. NAME & PHONE OF FILER'S CONTACT (optional)
Amy Right 310-555-5555

B. SEND ACKNOWLEDGMENT TO: (NAME AND ADDRESS)
Amy Right
1000 My st
Mytown, Ca 90000

THIS SPACE FOR FILING OFFICE USE ONLY

1. JUDGMENT DEBTOR'S EXACT LEGAL NAME - Insert only one name, either 1a or 1b. Do not abbreviate or combine names.

1a. ORGANIZATION'S NAME

1b. INDIVIDUAL'S LAST NAME	FIRST NAME	MIDDLE NAME	SUFFIX
Isbad	Jeff		

1c. MAILING ADDRESS	CITY	STATE	POSTAL CODE	COUNTRY
666 e Cra P st	Helltown	Ca	90000	US

2. JUDGMENT CREDITOR'S NAME - Do not abbreviate or combine names.

2a. ORGANIZATION'S NAME

2b. INDIVIDUAL'S LAST NAME	FIRST NAME	MIDDLE	SUFFIX
Right	Amy		

2c. MAILING ADDRESS	CITY	STATE	POSTAL CODE	COUNTRY
1000 My st	Mytown	Ca	90000	US

3. ALL PROPERTY SUBJECT TO ENFORCEMENT OF A MONEY JUDGMENT AGAINST THE JUDGMENT DEBTOR TO WHICH A JUDGMENT LIEN ON PERSONAL PROPERTY MAY ATTACH UNDER SECTION 697.530 OF THE CODE OF CIVIL PROCEDURE IS SUBJECT TO THIS JUDGMENT LIEN.

A. Title of court where judgment was entered: Superior Cout of Calibrnia
Stanley Mosk Courthouse

B. Title of the action: Right v. Isbad

C. Number of this action: 14K5000

D. Date judgment was entered: 01/01/2014

E. Date of subsequent renewals of judgment (if any): n/a

F. Amount required to satisfy judgment at date of this notice: $ 3,025.00

G. Date of this notice: 02/01/2014

4. I declare under penalty of perjury under the laws of the State of California that the foregoing is true and correct:

Dated: 02/01/2014
(If not indicated, use same as date in item 3G.)

SIGNATURE - SEE INSTRUCTION NO. 4

FOR: Amy Right

FILING OFFICE COPY

NOTICE OF JUDGMENT LIEN (FORM JL1) (Rev. 6/01)
Approved by the Secretary of State

EJ-001

ATTORNEY OR PARTY WITHOUT ATTORNEY *(Name, address, and State Bar number):*
After recording, return to:

Amy Right
1000 My st
Mytown, Ca 90000

TEL NO.: 310-555-5555   FAX NO. (optional):
E-MAIL ADDRESS *(Optional):*
[ ] ATTORNEY FOR   [X] JUDGMENT CREDITOR   [ ] ASSIGNEE OF RECORD

SUPERIOR COURT OF CALIFORNIA, COUNTY OF Los Angeles
STREET ADDRESS: 111 Hill st
MAILING ADDRESS:
CITY AND ZIP CODE: Los Angeles, Ca 90012
BRANCH NAME: Stanley Mosk Courthouse

PLAINTIFF: Amy Right
DEFENDANT: Jeff Isbad

ABSTRACT OF JUDGMENT—CIVIL AND SMALL CLAIMS   [ ] Amended

FOR RECORDER'S USE ONLY

CASE NUMBER: 14K5000

FOR COURT USE ONLY

1. The [X] judgment creditor [ ] assignee of record
   applies for an abstract of judgment and represents the following:
   a. Judgment debtor's
      Name and last known address

      Jeff Isbad
      666 e Cra P st
      Helltown, Ca 90666

   b. Driver's license no. [last 4 digits] and state: [ ] Unknown
   c. Social security no. [last 4 digits]:   1234   [X] Unknown
   d. Summons or notice of entry of sister-state judgment was personally served or mailed to *(name and address):*
      Jeff Isbad - 666 e Cra P st, Helltown, Ca 90666

2. [ ] Information on additional judgment debtors is shown on page 2.
3. Judgment creditor *(name and address):*
   Amy Right
   1000 My st
   Mytown, Ca 90000
   Date: 02/01/2014

   Amy Right
   _____
   (TYPE OR PRINT NAME)

4. [ ] Information on additional judgment creditors is shown on page 2.
5. [ ] Original abstract recorded in this county:
   a. Date:
   b. Instrument No.:

   ▶
   _____
   (SIGNATURE OF APPLICANT OR ATTORNEY)

6. Total amount of judgment as entered or last renewed: $ 3,000.00
7. All judgment creditors and debtors are listed on this abstract.
8. a. Judgment entered on *(date):* 01/01/2014
   b. Renewal entered on *(date):*

9. [ ] This judgment is an installment judgment.

[SEAL]

This abstract issued on *(date):*

10. [ ] An [ ] execution lien [ ] attachment lien
    is endorsed on the judgment as follows:
    a. Amount: $
    b. In favor of *(name and address):*

11. A stay of enforcement has
    a. [X] not been ordered by the court.
    b. [ ] been ordered by the court effective until *(date):*

12. a. [ ] I certify that this is a true and correct abstract of the judgment entered in this action.
    b. [ ] A certified copy of the judgment is attached.

Clerk, by _____, Deputy

Form Adopted for Mandatory Use
Judicial Council of California
EJ-001 [Rev. July 1, 2014]

ABSTRACT OF JUDGMENT—CIVIL AND SMALL CLAIMS

Page 1 of 2
Code of Civil Procedure, §§ 488.480, 674, 700.190

PLAINTIFF: Amy Right	COURT CASE NO.:
DEFENDANT: Jeff Isbad	14K5000

NAMES AND ADDRESSES OF ADDITIONAL JUDGMENT CREDITORS:

13. Judgment creditor *(name and address):*

14. Judgment creditor *(name and address):*

15. ☐ Continued on Attachment 15.

INFORMATION ON ADDITIONAL JUDGMENT DEBTORS:

16. Name and last known address

Driver's license no. [last 4 digits] and state: ☐ Unknown
Social security no. [last 4 digits]: ☐ Unknown
Summons was personally served at or mailed to *(address):*

17. Name and last known address

Driver's license no. [last 4 digits] and state: ☐ Unknown
Social security no. [last 4 digits]: ☐ Unknown
Summons was personally served at or mailed to *(address):*

18. Name and last known address

Driver's license no. [last 4 digits] and state: ☐ Unknown
Social security no. [last 4 digits]: ☐ Unknown
Summons was personally served at or mailed to *(address):*

19. Name and last known address

Driver's license no. [last 4 digits] and state: ☐ Unknown
Social security no. [last 4 digits]: ☐ Unknown
Summons was personally served at or mailed to *(address):*

20. ☐ Continued on Attachment 20.

ABSTRACT OF JUDGMENT—CIVIL AND SMALL CLAIMS

RECORDING REQUESTED BY:

Amy Right

AND WHEN RECORDED MAIL TO:

Amy Right
1000 My st
Mytown, Ca 90000

SPACE ABOVE THIS LINE IS FOR RECORDER'S USE

A.P.N.: _____ Order No.: _____ Escrow No.: _____

REQUEST FOR NOTICE UNDER §2924b CIVIL CODE

In accordance with Section 2924b, Civil Code, request is hereby made that a copy of any NOTICE OF DEFAULT and a copy of any NOTICE OF SALE under the DEED OF TRUST recorded as Instrument No. __123456__, on __May 1__, __2000__, in Book __12__, Page __36__, Official Records of __Los Angeles__ County, California, and describing land therein as:

Lot 22 of Tract 65

executed by __Jeff Isbad__
as Trustor, in which __get from recorder's office__
is named as Beneficiary, and __get from recorder's office__
as Trustee, be mailed to __Amy Right__
at __1000 My st__
 (Number and street)
Mytown, Ca 90000
 (City and state)

NOTICE: A COPY OF ANY NOTICE OF DEFAULT AND OF ANY NOTICE OF SALE WILL BE SENT ONLY TO THE ADDRESS CONTAINED IN THIS RECORDED REQUEST. IF YOUR ADDRESS CHANGES, A NEW REQUEST MUST BE RECORDED.

Dated: _____
02/01/2014
STATE OF CALIFORNIA
COUNTY OF _____

On _____ before me, _____

Personally appeared _____

who proved to me on the basis of satisfactory evidence to be the person(s) whose name(s) is/are subscribed to the within instrument and acknowledged to me that he/she/they executed the same in his/her/their authorized capacity(ies), and that by his/her/their signature(s) on the instrument the person(s), or the entity upon behalf of which the person(s) acted, executed the instrument.

I certify under the PENALTY OF PERJURY under the laws of the State of California that the foregoing paragraph is true and correct.

WITNESS my hand and official seal.

Amy Right

_____ (Notary seal)
Signature

Chapter 5

Getting the Debtor to Pay Voluntarily

A. Ask for Your Money	5/2
B. Send a Final Demand Letter	5/3
C. Negotiate an Installment Plan.	5/5
1. Installment Payment Agreement	5/6
2. Income and Expense Statement	5/6
D. Accept Less than the Judgment as Full Payment	5/7
1. Four Considerations	5/7
2. How a Partial Payment Offer is Made	5/7
E. Respond to the Debtor's Claims of "No Money"	5/8
1. Help the Debtor Find Money	5/8
2. Barter for Goods or Services	5/10

Collection Factor

	High	Moderate	Low
Potential cost to you			✓
Potential for producing $$$		✓	
Potential for settlement	✓	✓	
Potential time and trouble		✓	
Potential for bankruptcy			✓

You might be able to skip this chapter

This chapter focuses on steps you can take to try to get the debtor to pay voluntarily in cash or kind. People whose goal is to preserve a personal, business or family relationship with the debtor often take this approach, resorting to forced collection methods only if absolutely necessary. You might also read this chapter if you know the debtor has no money and you want to explore alternatives to cash payment. However, if neither of these is true for you and your gut tells you that getting the debtor to pay voluntarily is highly unlikely, you can probably skip ahead to Chapter 6.

At first glance, it may seem hopelessly optimistic to think that the debtor you have sued will now pay you without further legal struggle. But it is a real possibility.

Before you obtained your judgment, you had only your own conviction that you were entitled to money. The debtor may have disputed the amount or even the existence of the obligation. Or, the debtor might have known that they owed you money, but also known that you couldn't force collection until you had a judgment. Now you have that judgment. You can subject the debtor to forced enforcement remedies for at least ten years from the date you obtained your judgment (in California, but all Judgment term lengths differ from State to State; this information can be looked up online) and ten years expire. Imagine what this will do to the debtor's credit rating and what a powerful incentive it can provide for voluntary payments.

A. Ask for Your Money

Once the debtor's time to appeal has expired (see Chapter 2), remind the debtor that the judgment is due. Depending on your relationship with the debtor and your own comfort level, you can do this in a letter or a phone call. If the debtor is likely to greet a phone call angrily or is a business with which you have no personal contact, send a letter. If you do call, note down the date, time and content of the conversation. This type of documentation can be valuable if the debtor later accuses you of harassment.

The debtor should already know about the judgment, even if you obtained it by default. But the debtor might not know about it, or at least might not know the exact amount. The debtor may be ignoring the situation, including the court papers. So when you contact the debtor, have these three goals in mind:

- to let the debtor know you are serious about collecting

- to inform the debtor exactly what they owe you, and

- to leave the channels of communication open so you can try to work something out without resorting to forced enforcement methods.

Your first contact is not likely to produce immediate payment unless you are dealing with a reputable business or individual who refused to pay before your lawsuit because of a genuine dispute concerning the merits of your claim. Instead, most debtors who have ignored your previous efforts to work things out or have reneged on promises to pay will probably continue the pattern. So view your call or letter as an opening to negotiate. Your tone should be firm, yet polite.

For example, let's say that you obtained a judgment against a local grocer. You call and say something like this: "Hello, Ms. Aquino? This is Robert Bridge … I am the man who obtained the judgment against you in small claims court for $800. I'm calling to find out when I can expect to receive payment."

If the debtor is willing to talk to you, try to pin them down to specifics—for example, full payment by a specified date, eight equal payments on the 15th of each month, payment in goods or services or some other arrangement satisfactory to you. If the debtor tries to put you off, come back with a counteroffer, such as, "I will accept part now and the rest in a post-dated check that I can cash in two weeks," or "How about a $200 payment each month, with the first check dropped by my office today?" Except in unusual circumstances, insist on being paid at least some money now, even if the debtor gives you a song and dance about having no money. Even a small payment starts the process and gets the debtor thinking in terms of paying you what they owe. Getting a debtor over this psychological hump is very important.

You may wish to ruffle the debtor's feathers a little and suggest that you "really don't want to start formal enforcement remedies", but it's usually better, during your first contact, to stick to a softer approach. There will be time for a heavier touch later, if necessary.

If you write rather than call, include a statement that you'd like to settle the matter amicably. If you know that the debtor is having financial problems that make immediate payment in full difficult, let the debtor know that you can be flexible if the debtor gets in touch with you promptly to work out a payment plan in good faith. Also include a copy of the judgment with your letter.

Below are two sample letters. The first is a brief reminder to a small businessperson who lost a judgment to another small businessperson in a relatively routine matter. It is the sort of letter you might send if a debtor hasn't paid but has obvious assets and will probably cooperate. The second letter assumes the same situation; with the very important difference that the creditor knows the judgment debtor is experiencing significant financial difficulties.

Sample Reminder that Payment is Due

July 9, 2014

Mr. Jeff Isbad
Franklin Printing Company
666 e. Cra P st
Helltown, Ca 90666

Re: Papers-by-Amy v. Jeff Isbad dba

Franklin.... Dear Jeff,
This is a reminder that I have not yet received payment of the final judgment of $ 3,000 which I was awarded on January 1, 2014, in small claims court case # 14K5000 in Los Angeles. Can you please send your payment now, so I can close this matter?
I appreciate your prompt attention to this matter, and look forward to receiving your payment within the next ten days. Please feel free to contact me about arranging a schedule for payments if you cannot pay the judgment in full at this time.

Sincerely
Amy Right

B. Send a Final Demand Letter

If your first call or letter doesn't produce a satisfactory response within ten days, follow up with a more formal, written demand. Face up to the fact that your initial goodwill and positive rewards approach didn't work, and emphasize the arsenal of legal weapons you have available to collect if voluntary payment isn't promptly forthcoming. Your detailed knowledge about your legal rights may convince a debtor to pay rather than avoid you. For example, you can share knowledge of the debtor's and their spouse's employer and the risk of embarrassment from a wage garnishment action. To demonstrate your seriousness to enforce the judgment, send a Final Demand Letter after taking an initial enforcement action (i.e. a Bank Levy). Sending a Final Demand Letter referencing the Bank Levy validates your explicit intention to get paid in full.

To emphasize your tougher stance, start your formal demand letter with the words "Final Notice." Then be forceful, but don't violate any collection laws (See Chapter 3). Let the debtor know generally that you can make their life unpleasant. Don't mention that you might deplete cash assets, such as a bank account; this is apt to prompt the debtor to change banks and hide their money.

Below is a sample (Legal citations tell the debtor that you know what you're talking about).

After you send a letter like this, the debtor may contact you. Sometimes the debtor mainly wants to tell you why they haven't paid. Even if you believe you are being fed a line, it normally pays to be patient enough to open up communications. If you hear a debtor out, you sometimes get paid sooner.

Example: Janice didn't appear in court when Jim sued her for refusing to pay for work he had done. After Jim got the judgment, he wrote asking for payment. Janice called Jim to explain in a long-winded way that she hadn't paid because she has had some objections to how Jim had done the project, and also because one of her big clients hadn't paid her, which was probably the real reason. Jim listened sympathetically but reminded Janice that she had never raised any objections about his work, either personally or in court, and that he was entitled to be paid under the judgment. After complaining a bit more, Janice finally admitted it, and paid up. Jim is convinced that listening patiently to Janice's face-saving explanation for the delay speeded up the collection process.

Sample Reminder that Payment is Due When Debtor Has Financial Problems

July 9, 2014

Mr. Jeff Isbad
Franklin Printing Company
666 e. Cra P st
Helltown, Ca 90666
Re: Papers-by-Amy v. Jeff Isbad dba Franklin...

Dear Jeff:

As you know, I have a judgment against you for $ 3,000 in Small Claims Court case # 14K5000 in Los Angeles for goods supplied. This is a legal debt and I expect payment in full.

I understand that you have recently experienced some difficult financial times. While my strong preference is to collect the judgment promptly, I am willing to do so in a way that will leave you in the best financial condition possible under the circumstances. Accordingly, I am open to a regular payment plan to take care of this matter over the next few months.

In addition, let me say that I honestly feel our difficulty in getting together to resolve this matter, prior to this judgment, was due in part to your financial pressures. For this reason, I am open to discussing working together on future projects, once the judgment is paid.

I hope we can work out a plan for you to pay off the judgment amicably. I look forward to hearing from you within the next ten days.

Sincerely
Amy Right

C. Negotiate an Installment Plan

The debtor may try to work out an installment payment arrangement, claiming that they can't afford to pay the full amount now. You will need to use your best judgment in assessing what the debtor tells you. Do you think they really have financial difficulties? Or are they simply trying to delay paying you? You can ask the Judgment Debtor to produce six to twelve months' worth of their Bank Statements voluntarily for your review in order to work-out a more convenient, flexible plan.

Final Notice

July 19, 2014
Mr. Jeff Isbad
666 e Cra P St
Helltown, Ca 90666

Dear Mr. Isbad,

As you know, I received a judgment against you for $ 3,000 in the Los Angeles Municipal Court on January 1, 2014. I wrote to you on July 1, 2014 requesting payment and offering to set up a payment schedule. I have not heard from you.

This judgment is final. Accordingly, I hereby request that you pay it in full immediately. When I receive full payment, I will file a Satisfaction of Judgment with the court, which will close the matter.

I have the right to garnish your wages [CCP 706.021], seize your car [CCP 700.090], put a lien on your home [CCP 697.310(a)], and more. If I am forced to undertake any further efforts to get my money, you will be liable for the costs, in addition to the judgment.

I will begin forced collections in 10 days unless I receive your full payment.

Sincerely

The Debtor's Credit Rating

Credit reporting agencies have employees who comb legal filings looking for information to add to consumers' files, such as judgments, divorces and convictions. Under federal law, negative information, including court judgments, can stay on a credit report for up to seven years. The debtor may not realize this. It behooves you to let the debtor know, and we include such information in the sample "final notice."

Some debtors may not care because their rating is already so bad that your judgment won't make much difference. But most people know that bad credit can affect their ability to get a credit card, take out a loan, rent an apartment or buy a house or car.

Let the debtor know that credit bureaus hire companies that routinely check public records, including court records, and add that information to their database. Also let the debtor know that as soon as the judgment is paid, you will file notice with the court, and that their credit report may be updated to show that the judgment has been satisfied.

Take the initiative. Suggest a payment plan that works for you. How do you know what that might look like? Start by assessing the likelihood of success if you start aggressive enforcement. For example, if the debtor is working at a decent job and you could easily garnish their wages, you have the leverage to insist on fairly rapid and substantial payments. Another method to incentivize a debtor to pay in installments is to offer to freeze accrued interest if installment payments are timely made by a specific date.

Be wary of a debtor who proposes to pay nothing now, with the first payment to start in a few weeks or months. You are not apt to see a cent. Also, the debtor probably expects you to be a fairly tough bargainer and may make a first offer they think you will reject. Start your bargaining from the high end and give yourself room to move down.

Of course, there are exceptions to every rule. If you feel the debtor is sincere and has some financial problems that will clear up soon, consider waiting a short but reasonable time. For example, if the debtor is paid infrequently, such as an inventor who receives patent royalties, you may agree to wait until they expect their next payment.

1. Installment Payment Agreement

If the debtor agrees to make installment payments, draw up an agreement. A letter can do the trick, for example, "If you pay $325 per month for seven months beginning February 1, 2014, I will not actively seek to execute on the judgment except for recording an Abstract of Judgment." Send two signed copies of your letter to the debtor; ask that they sign one and return it to you and keep the other copy for their records. Keep the signed letter in your files, but don't file it with the court. If the debtor defaults on the agreement, immediately proceed to forced enforcement of your judgment. Below is a sample letter.

Another, more legalistic, approach involves getting something called a Stipulation of Payment to the Judgment. Formal stipulations need to be approved by the judge and, if the debtor fails to keep their word, you must obtain court approval to end the stipulation and initiate formal enforcement activities. This is too much work and of no benefit to you.

Sample Installment Agreement Letter

September 3, 2014
Jeff Isbad
666 e. Cra P st
Helltown, Ca 90666

Dear Mr. Isbad,
This letter confirms your agreement to pay me $ 250 per month by the first of each month, starting on October 1, 2014, until you fully pay off the $ 3,000 judgment, plus post-judgment costs an interest, which I obtained against you on January 1, 2014 in Small Claims Court, case # 14K5000.

As long as you make these payments, I will not undertake the enforcement remedies available to me under California law, other than recording an Abstract of Judgment, against your real estate, and filing a JL1 lien with the State of California. If you fail to make a payment within 5 days of the due date, however, this agreement will immediately become null and void, and I will proceed with my legally available enforcement options. Please sign and return this agreement to me within 5 days, or it will be void.

Sincerely
Amy Right

2. Income and Expense Statement

A collection agency usually requires a debtor who wants to make installment payments to fill out a form indicating the debtor's assets, income and expenses. The agency uses the information to decide whether or not to accept the proposal to pay in installments and if so, in what amount. You can ask for the same information as a condition of any settlement, but don't insist on it. Many debtors will pay your debt, but don't want to give you all that private information. However, if the debtor returns the completed form and later defaults on the agreement, you will have information you can use to collect. We would use form EJ-165, a copy is included in the Appendix.

D. Accept Less Than the Judgment as Full Payment

Suppose the debtor offers to pay you a portion of the judgment immediately if you agree to waive the rest. Your first response may be "no way." You went to the trouble of getting your judgment, and you want to be paid in full. But think again. Collections experts can tell you that taking a hard line may get you nothing. A better approach is to always consider a reasonable offer from the debtor. "A bird in the hand is better than two in the bush".

1. Four Considerations

Before rejecting or accepting partial payment, consider these four factors.

a. Likelihood of Collecting the Full Judgment

If the debtor has income or assets you believe can satisfy your judgment, don't compromise. On the other hand, you aren't likely to collect on your own from a financially strapped debtor with no visible means of support. In that situation, it probably makes more sense to take the proverbial bird in the hand than to try to catch the two in the bush.

b. Value of Your Time

When comparing a partial payment to the full amount, remember that recovering the full judgment will take time, and that time is money. For instance, assume you are self-employed and value your time at $40 an hour. If it will take you 30 hours to fully enforce your judgment, you have to subtract $1,200 from your judgment to determine its actual value to you. Under this approach, you should reject an offer by the debtor to pay you $1,000 on a $3,000 judgment. You'd have to spend 50 hours collecting, 20 hours more than you think it would take, before the offer would pay out. On the other hand, an offer of $2,000 on the judgment makes sense. It translates into 25 hours of collecting, five hours fewer than you think it would take to collect the full amount.

c. Possibility of Losing More Money

Consider the debtor's assets and income. Could you easily enforce the full judgment, or will it be tough to get your hands on the debtor's property? If you spend money on futile enforcement techniques, going after empty bank accounts and cars with no value, you're just throwing good money after bad. In this situation, it's probably better to take a reduced amount than to risk coming up empty-handed.

d. Your Desire to Get the Last Dime

Remember the prayer that asks for the vision to seek what is possible, the courage to accept what isn't and the wisdom to know the difference? That's the strategy we suggest you use in enforcing your judgment. On the other hand, you may be just so angry at the judgment debtor that you will do whatever it takes to collect every penny owed. You have that right, and it's up to you to weigh how much time and trouble you are willing to expend to achieve it. But keep in mind the words of one collection professional: "You'll have two choices. Either learn to take what you can with a smile, or go after every last nickel and be upset when you come up short."

2. How a Partial Payment Offer Is Made

In California, if you receive a partial payment check containing the language "cashing this check constitutes payment in full," you can cross out the language and collect the balance [Civil Code 1526(a)]. When enacting this law, the legislature also created a procedure allowing debtors to settle debts for less than the full amount. Here's how.

    a. The debtor must send you a letter stating that they intend to send you a partial payment check, also called a restrictive endorsement, to cover the full amount.

b. You have 15 days to state any objection.
c. If you don't object, the debtor can send you a check for the partial payment with a letter stating that the check constitutes payment in full.

E. Respond to the Debtor's Claims of "No Money"

What if the debtor really doesn't have the means to pay your judgment? You have three ways of approaching this problem. The first is to try to help the debtor find money. The second is to see if the debtor can offer something besides money that you will accept as payment. The third is simply to forget about ever collecting and to expend your energy in a more creative way.

1. Help the Debtor Find Money

Debtors often have more ways to pay than they originally think. You can help them identify potential resources. Most of the sources listed below apply to debtors with personal or small business debts, though some are more appropriate to one than the other. Some resources may be adequate to pay you in full, while others will help the debtor pay in installments.

When you mention some sources of cash, the debtor may resist. They may not want to touch a particular asset. Or they may not want to ask friends, relatives or their boss for a loan because they don't want to take on another obligation or are reluctant to talk about their financial problems. But you have a judgment and are in a fairly strong position to persuade them to tap one or more of these resources. If you hit resistance in one area, suggest an alternative. If they repeatedly turn you down, ask them to suggest sources for payment. The trick is to get the debtor involved in the problem-solving process, on the theory that if they really want to find the money to pay you, they will.

This process can have an important side benefit. Even if you don't get cash, you might collect valuable information about the debtor's assets that you can use if you have to resort to aggressive enforcement.

Some of our suggestions may seem inappropriate or naive. They are neither. There is no way to predict which suggestion will touch a nerve with a particular debtor. So suspend your disbelief; do not reject any suggestion out of hand. Go through each one with the debtor until you find one that works.

Deposit accounts - This may seem too obvious. After all, if the debtor has money in the bank, they wouldn't claim to be broke, would he? Leaving aside the fact that some debtors lie, others simply don't think of funds that they have earmarked for special purposes. You are entitled to be paid before the debtor's family goes on its next vacation, buy Christmas presents or spend other nonessential money.

Retirement accounts - Many people have thousands of dollars in retirement accounts—IRAs, Keoghs or 401(k) plans—which can be withdrawn, although subject to penalties and the loss of interest. Because of the cost involved, the debtor may not consider these funds available. If you offer to take slightly less than the full amount to help offset the penalty for early withdrawal, you may get paid.

Investments - The debtor may not think of securities as a source of ready cash. In fact, debtors sometimes conveniently forget they have these resources. Even a debtor who remembers their investments may resist selling because they provide a feeling of security. Suggest that the debtor keep the securities and use them as collateral to take out a bank loan, or better yet, a margin loan from the broker to pay you.

People who actively play the stock market often have large cash reserves on deposit with their broker so that stock transactions can be instantly carried out with a telephone call. This is a source of money for payment.

Income tax refunds - The debtor may be awaiting a tax refund, which can be given to you as a relatively painless way of satisfying all or part of the judgment.
This approach works best in the first several months of the calendar year, just before the refund comes from the IRS or California Franchise Tax Board.

Personal loans - Ask the debtor to borrow the money to pay you. If he's a member of a credit union, suggest they check there first. Credit union loans tend to have good terms (low interest rates). Credit unions may also be more willing to lend money because they usually insist that the loan be repaid through paycheck withholding.

Another source for a personal loan is a bank or savings and loan. Even a debtor with financial problems may qualify, especially if they have a car they can pledge as collateral or has a longtime relationship with a particular bank.

Home equity loans - If the debtor owns real estate, they may qualify for an equity loan. This suggestion is most appropriate if the debtor owes you a substantial amount of money and hasn't already encumbered the property with second or third deeds of trust.

Credit card cash advance - Virtually everyone, even destitute debtors, have credit cards. So suggest that the debtor take a cash advance on a MasterCard, Visa or other account.

Insurance policies - Whole life insurance policies have a cash value. Usually, a debtor can borrow against this value. In addition, if your judgment is based on a tort (personal injury) claim, the debtor's homeowner's or renter's policy may cover it.

Pay advance - Sometimes, the debtor's employer will advance money against a salary or other money the debtor is entitled to receive, such as a bonus or extra pay for overtime. Even a debtor who doesn't want others to know about the judgment may be willing to request an advance if the alternative is a wage garnishment. But be careful not to threaten a wage garnishment if you don't intend to, or cannot, implement one.

Loans from friends or relatives - Family or close friends may make a loan to the debtor, although many debtors resist the idea, out of pride or shame. But this reaction often doesn't make much sense. Wouldn't you want to help a good friend or relative who truly needs it? If the answer is yes, perhaps you can think of a way to help the debtor overcome their reluctance to ask.

Selling personal possessions - Selling unwanted household or office items can be an excellent and often painless way for the debtor to raise funds. A successful garage sale can raise several hundred dollars or more. Ask the debtor about items they might not need and can sell. For instance, you might say something like, "Is there some older office equipment you aren't using very much, since you bought the new computer?" Or "Why don't you put your video camera up for sale? You aren't using it anymore anyway. If you sell it now, you'll still get good value, but if you hold it a year or two, it will lose most of its value."

Investors or new business partners - If the debtor has a basically sound business that is struggling, bringing in an investor is an obvious way to raise funds. The additional capital might even give the business an infusion of management skill.

If the debtor is receptive and you know something about their business, suggest ways for them to do this. For example, personal friends or others in the same type of business who might not agree to make a simple loan might be willing to extend an investment, if they think the business has a chance of making them some money.

Hobbies - If the debtor has a hobby, they may be able to get money from it. For example, a person who is a whiz with cameras might get jobs photographing parties or weddings. Someone who has a way with dogs might offer a dog sitting service. The possibilities are almost endless.

Rental income - Can the debtor rent out part of their house or business building?

Help the debtor find work - If the debtor is unemployed, a good way to get paid is to help them find work. If you have a business, you may even hire them in exchange for a promise to pay. This is viable only if you and the debtor have a decent relationship and the debtor has skills you can use. If you hire the debtor, pay them what you'd pay anyone else doing that job, but insist that you be given a reasonable amount each pay period as an installment payment against the judgment, 10% to 20% of the total pay is a fair amount. If the debtor is self-employed and you can make use of their services, negotiate to pay a lower than normal rate. Keep track of the difference until the judgment is paid off.

Sometimes, just keeping in touch with the debtor is a way to help them find work.

Example: Amy Right got a judgment against Jeff Isbad, a former business associate, who was having financial difficulties. Amy agreed to accept a small payment each month. After Jeff made one payment and missed one, Amy ran into him at a business event, spoke to him privately and reminded him of their agreement. Amy reconfirmed the agreement, paid for several months and then dropped out of sight. When he resurfaced, Amy reminded him of the debt. Jeff explained that his consulting business was kaput and he had no income. Amy got an idea about a job he might bid on and called him. Jeff made the bid, got the job, thanked Amy and resumed making payments. We think the moral of this story is not only that it often produces better results to help people who are down on their luck rather than simply shunning them, but that it almost always pays in the long run to stay in touch with people who owe you significant amounts of money.

Another possible source of money is an extra part-time job. If the debtor is receptive but needs help finding a job, be ready to offer suggestions.

2. Barter for Goods or Services
If the debtor is not likely to have enough money to pay you a meaningful amount any time soon, think of non-monetary ways they can satisfy your judgment. One way is to accept goods or services instead of money. Although it's rare today, not too long ago entire communities operated on a barter, rather than cash, basis. A carpenter might have little cash but could trade carpentry work for food, shelter and even medical care. There is no reason why you can't encourage the debtor to embrace barter.

Perhaps the debtor owns equipment or furniture that you could use, or you know someone you could give it to.

Example: Amy was owed money by a former client, Jeff. Jeff had to move several thousand miles away, and suggested that Amy take his furniture as full payment. At first Amy refused, not having any use for somewhat battered furniture. Then, realizing her daughter was planning to move into her first apartment and had nothing, she agreed. It wasn't as good as full payment, but it was much better than getting nothing from a person who was likely to be judgment-proof for years to come.

We don't suggest that you take the debtor's property with the idea of selling it and crediting the debtor with the proceeds. The price you get will probably be far less than the debtor expects, which may mean another hassle. Either agree to accept specific property in exchange for a specific credit, or insist that the debtor sell the property and give you the proceeds.

If you consider barter, be flexible. What can the debtor reasonably offer you? What are you willing to accept? Agricultural produce, canned goods, artworks, handicrafts, camping gear, furniture, sports equipment, electronic equipment or photographic equipment are among the items a debtor may offer you. If the debtor has a business, maybe they have a conference table and chairs, desk, file cabinet or computer.

If the judgment debtor has nothing tangible to give you, they may be able to provide some service. These could be anything from lessons, such as music, art, computer repair or tennis, to home or car repairs. We are suggesting specific, finite services. We are not suggesting that the judgment debtor work for you on an ongoing basis without pay.

Any agreement you come up with needs to be spelled out in writing. Be precise on what the debtor will do in order to satisfy all or part of the judgment. Clearly describe the goods or services to be rendered and received as barter. Also, specify what happens if the debtor doesn't fulfill their end of the agreement so they understand that you will force collections if they don't comply. Make sure the debtor is credited with partial payment for any partial performance. Finally, be sure the debtor states that they have entered into the agreement knowingly and freely, and fully understands what it says. A sample agreement is included here. When the debtor fulfills their part of the bargain, it's your legal obligation to file a Satisfaction of Judgment with the court (See Chapter 22).

Sample Agreement for Payment by Barter

Judgment Creditor Amy Right ("Judgment Creditor") and Judgment Jeff Isbad ("Judgment Debtor") agree as follows:

1. The judgment referred to in this agreement was obtained by Judgment Creditor against Judgment Debtor, entered in the Los Angeles County Small Claims Court on January 1, 2014, Case # 14K5000, plus post-judgment costs which have been incurred, and accrued interest.

2. Judgment Debtor agrees to provide the following goods and services to Judgment Creditor, valued at a total of $3,000, toward satisfaction of the judgment, costs and interest:
   a. One hour-long jujitsu lesson per week for ten consecutive weeks, beginning September 6, 2014 ($250, or $25 per lesson).
   b. One used 2005 Kawasaki Vulcan motorcycle ($2,500).
   c. One used oak computer workstation ($250).

3. In consideration for this agreement, Judgment Debtor understands that this judgment held against him by Judgment Creditor will be considered fully satisfied, or satisfied (circle one) for the amount described in paragraph 2.

4. Judgment Debtor understands that if he fails to 1) deliver the goods and/or services described in paragraph 2 (b) & (c) within one week of the date Judgment Debtor signs this agreement, this agreement and 2) deliver the services as described in paragraph 2(a) on time, agreement will immediately become null and void at the Judgment Creditor's option, and the judgment can be enforced against Judgment Debtor to obtain the balance due on the judgment, less the value of any item or part of any item described in paragraph 2 that Judgment Debtor has already paid or provided to Judgment Creditor.

Judgment Debtor and Judgment Creditor have entered into this agreement knowingly and freely, and fully agree to its terms.

Agreed to by:

_____

Date	Judgment Creditor

_____

Date	Judgment Debtor

Chapter 5B

Default in Payment Agreement

A. Payment Plan Categories.. 5B/2

B. Debtor Defaulted 5B/2

C. Default in Small Claims.. 5B/3

    1. Complete the "Declaration of Default in Payment of Judgment"..................... 5B/3

    2. Complete the "Order on Declaration of Default in Payments"......................... 5B/3

    3. General Instructions.. 5B/3

D. Default in Civil Court 5B/4

    1. Judgment entered.. 5B/8

    2. Judgment NOT entered... 5B/9

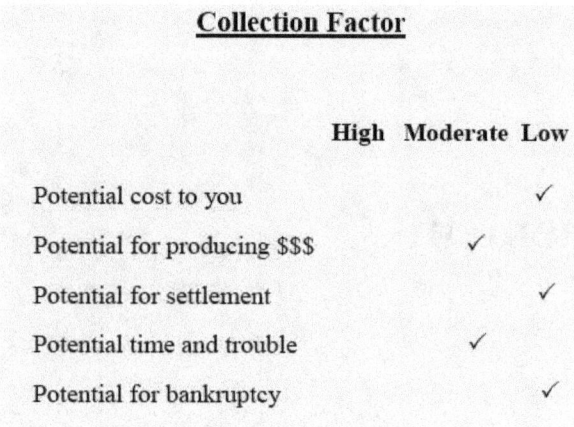

Collection Factor

	High	Moderate	Low
Potential cost to you			✓
Potential for producing $$$		✓	
Potential for settlement			✓
Potential time and trouble		✓	
Potential for bankruptcy			✓

You might be able to skip this chapter

This chapter focuses on steps you must take when a court is involved in a payment plan that the debtor defaults on. If you set up a payment plan with the debtor voluntarily, meaning that the court is not aware of it, then you can skip this chapter. But read section A first. If the court knows about the payment plan, then read on.

The debtor agreed to monthly payments, and you thoughts your work was over. And then they stopped making the payments (or never made the first one). What do you do?

There are four ways that a debtor may be allowed to make monthly payments to you and therefore forcing you to accept these payments instead of trying to enforce your full judgment.

1) You could have set up a payment agreement after you won the case (voluntary), outside the court's realm.

2. The debtor, and yourself, could have agreed to the payments in a stipulated agreement. A stipulated agreement is when all parties agree to terms and the Judge confirms the terms at the trial hearing.

3. The Judge could have ordered a payment plan, after ruling in your favor at the trial.

4. The debtor could have asked the court to approve a payment plan at a hearing after the trial. This could be as a response to a wage garnishment, bank levy, or some other enforcement action that you took, which the debtor will state that they cannot afford.

A. Payment plan categories

First, let's separate the four possibilities into two distinct categories. There are voluntary payment plans and court ordered payment plans.

The first category is the Voluntary Payment Plan. This means that you and the debtor came up with some agreement AND the court was not involved. Item # 1 on list. You can skip this chapter and move forward with enforcing your judgment. If you did get some payments from the debtor, you should report the payments, additional post-judgment costs, and interest prior to trying to enforce the remainder of the judgment (see Chapter 16).

The second category is the court ordered payment plans (involuntary). This means that the court was involved in setting up or approving the payment plan. This category would include when the payment plan is part of a stipulated agreement between you and the debtor, because the court confirmed it. Items # 2-4 on previous list.

B. Debtor Defaulted on # 2-4

When the court is involved, only the court can make a determination. If the debtor defaulted on the payment arrangement, you and the debtor know that the payment agreement has been defaulted on.

This is not enough. You need the court to determine that the payment agreement is in default. The court ordered the payments and now the court must end the payment agreement.

We will deal with defaults in Small Claims court and Civil court.

C. Defaults in Small Claims

If your case is in small claims court, then you will need to file a "Declaration of Default in Payment of Judgment" form (SC-223) and an "Order on Declaration of Default in Payments" form (SC-225) with the court. You can find these forms at www.courts.ca.gov/forms. A completed sample of the form is at the end of this chapter. You will need a separate set of forms for each debtor.

1. Complete the "Declaration of Default in Payment of Judgment" form (SC-223)

a. Complete the information in the "Superior Court of California, County of" box

This box is on the upper-right side of the page. You will enter the county where your court is located first, then the name and address of the court.

b. Complete the information in the "Case Number" box.

This box is just below the "Superior Court" box. Fill in your complete case number and the short title of your case. Example: "Right v. IsBad".

Item 1: Enter your full name, exactly as it appears on your judgment. Then enter your mailing address, including apartment number and zip code. Now enter your phone number and e-mail address (optional). If there was more than one plaintiff, then enter all names.

Item 2: Enter the full name of the debtor, exactly as it appears on your judgment. Then enter their mailing address, phone number, and e-mail (optional).

Item 3: Enter the date that the judgment was entered in the court and the original amount of the judgment. If your judgment was for $ 4,000.00 plus $ 65 in court costs, then your judgment amount is for the total $ 4,065.00. Do not add any additional costs or interest here.

Item 4: Enter the date when the court approved the payment plan (this may or may not be the same date as the judgment date). Then complete section a or b depending on what the court ordered.

Item 5: Complete this section if the debtor has made some payments to you after the court judgment. So, if the debtor made a payment in January and February and then defaulted, you would enter the dates and amounts for those two payments. If the debtor has made more than 8 payments then check the box, and make a list of the dates and amounts of each payment on a separate paper named "SC-223, Item 5" and attach that document to this form.

Item 6: Enter the total amount the debtor paid you. Enter the difference between the original judgment and the amount paid. Example: Original judgment was $ 4,065.00 and debtor paid $ 1,065.00, therefore you enter $ 3,000.00.

Item 7: Enter the interest due as of the date of this form. You can calculate this at ijcalc.sdcourt.ca.gov (no www.). Print out the completed form from this site and attach it. After "calculated as follows:" enter "attached".

Now date, sign, and print your name on this form. If there was more than one plaintiff then all plaintiffs should sign.

2. Complete the "Order on Declaration of Default in Payments" form (SC-225)

a. Complete the information in the "Superior Court of California, County of" box

This box is on the upper-right side of the page. You will enter the county where your court is located first, then the name and address of the court.

b. Complete the information in the "Case Number" box.

This box is just below the "Superior Court" box. Fill in your complete case number and the short title of your case. Example: "Right v. IsBad".

Item 1: Enter the date that the judgment was entered (may not be the same date as the payment plan was approved) and the name of one of the debtors. Remember you need a separate form for each debtor.

Item 2: Enter this information, it should be the same as Item 4 of form SC-223.

Item 3: Enter the date you signed form SC-223 and then enter your full name as shown on the judgment. Include the names of all plaintiffs.

Leave the rest of this form blank.

Some courts may not take this form from you, they may choose to complete it themselves. Do not risk wasting time. Offer it to the court clerk.

3. General instructions

There may not be a charge for filing these forms, but take your checkbook with you, in case the clerk believes that they should charge as if this is a motion (which it kind of is).

The small claims clerk will mail you and the debtors a copy of your forms. They will also mail the debtor a blank form for their response. The debtor will have 10 days to file their response from the date they receive the court form. Since the court is mailing the form, I would wait 20 days for a court decision, but it could be sooner. Once that time has passed, the court will mail all parties a 1) decision, or 2) a notice that there will be a hearing on the matter. If you are given a hearing date, you will need to attend and explain to the judge why they should rule that the debtor is in default and the full amount is now due.

D. Defaults in Civil Court

If your case is in civil court, then which form you will use will depend on several factors;

1) If the judgment was already entered at trial

2) If the judgment will be entered upon default of payment agreement

SC-223 Declaration of Default in Payment of Judgment

Clerk stamps here when form is filed.

Important: Read the other side before you fill out this form or if it was mailed to you. If you are the judgment debtor named in ② and you disagree with this *Declaration of Default in Payment of Judgment*, you may file *Response to Declaration of Default in Payment of Judgment* (Form SC-224) within 10 days after the declaration was mailed to you.

① I am asking the court to order that the remaining balance of a small claims judgment is now due and collectible because payments were not made as the court ordered.
My name is: Amy Right
Mailing address: 1000 My st
Mytown, Ca 90000
Phone: 310-555-5555 E-mail *(optional)*: _____

Fill in the court name and street address:
Superior Court of California, County of
Los Angeles
Stanley Mosk Courthouse
111 Hill st
Los Angeles, Ca 90012

② The judgment debtor who has not made payments as the court ordered is *(complete a separate form for each judgment debtor who has not paid as ordered)*:
Name: Jeff Isbad
Mailing address: 666 e Cra P st
Helltown, Ca 90666
Phone: 310-666-6666 E-mail *(optional)*: _____

Fill in your case number and case name:
Case Number:
14K5000
Case Name:
Right v Isbad

③ On *(date)*: 01/01/2014 the court ordered that the judgment debtor named in ② must pay me, or someone who assigned the judgment to me, principal, prejudgment interest, and costs in the total amount of $3,000.00.

④ On *(date)*: 02/01/2014 the court ordered that the judgment debtor named in ② may pay the judgment described in ③ as follows:
  a. [x] Payments of $100.00 on the 1st day of each *(month, week, other)*: month starting *(date)*: 03/01/2014, until *(date of final payment)*: 8/01/2016; amount of final payment: $100.00
  b. [ ] Other payment schedule *(specify)*: _____

⑤ The payments listed below, and no others, have been made on the judgment described in ③.
  [ ] Check here if there is not enough space below. List the date and amount of each payment on a separate page and write "SC-223, Item 5" at the top.

Date	Amount	Date	Amount	Date	Amount	Date	Amount

⑥ The total amount of the payments that have been made on the judgment described in ③ is $0.00, and the balance due, without adding any interest after the judgment, is $3,000.00.

⑦ I request interest on the judgment, in the amount of $50.00, calculated as follows:
  [ ] Check here if there is not enough space below. Explain how you calculated interest on a separate page and write "SC-223, Item 7" at the top.

I declare under penalty of perjury under the laws of the State of California that the information above is true and correct.
Date: 04/01/2014

Amy Right
Type or print your name ▶ *Sign here*

Declaration of Default in Payment of Judgment
(Small Claims)

Default in Payments on Small Claims Judgment
General Information

If the court ordered that another plaintiff or defendant (judgment debtor) may pay a small claims judgment in payments, and that judgment debtor has not made the payments as ordered, you can ask the court to order that the full balance of the judgment is due and collectible. Here's how:

- Read this form.
- Fill out page 1 of Form SC-223, *Declaration of Default in Payment of Judgment*. Fill out a separate form for each judgment debtor who did not make payments as ordered.
- File your completed form(s) with the small claims court clerk.

The court will mail all other plaintiffs and defendants in the case copies of the *Declaration* and a blank Form SC-224, *Response to Declaration of Default in Payment of Judgment*.

The judgment debtor will have 10 days to file a *Response*. Then the court will mail all plaintiffs and defendants in the case:

- A decision, or
- A notice to go to a hearing.

If the court ordered that you may make payments on a judgment, and another plaintiff, defendant, or person to whom the judgment has been assigned (judgment creditor) has filed Form SC-223, *Declaration of Default in Payment of Judgment*, asking the court to order that the full balance is now due and collectible because you did not make the payments:

- Read this form and the *Declaration*.
- If you agree with the court ordering that the amounts claimed in the *Declaration* are now due in full, you do not need to do anything.
- **If you do not agree with the *Declaration* or with the court ordering that the amounts it claims are now due in full, file a *Response* within 10 calendar days after the court clerk mailed the *Declaration* to you.** (This date is on the *Clerk's Certificate of Mailing*.)

To file your *Response*:

- Fill out Form SC-224, *Response to Declaration of Default in Payment of Judgment*.
- Have your *Response* served on the judgment creditor and all other plaintiffs and defendants in your case. (See Form SC-112A, *Proof of Service by Mail*.)
- File your *Response* and *Proof of Service* with the small claims court clerk.

Answers to Common Questions

When is the judgment due?
Unless the court orders otherwise, small claims judgments are due immediately. If the judgment is not paid in full within 30 days, the judgment creditor (person to whom the money is owed) can take legal steps to collect any unpaid amount. (Collection may be postponed if an appeal or a request to vacate (cancel) or correct the judgment is filed.)

When can the judgment debtor make payments?
A plaintiff or defendant who was ordered to pay a small claims judgment (judgment debtor) can ask the court for permission to make payments. If the court agrees, the plaintiff or defendant who is owed money (the judgment creditor) cannot take any other steps to collect the money as long as the payments are made on time. If payments are not made on time, the judgment creditor can ask the court to order that the remaining balance of the judgment is due and collectible.

Is interest added after the judgment?
Interest (10 percent per year) is usually added to the unpaid amount of the judgment from the date the judgment is entered until it is paid in full. Interest can only be charged on the unpaid amount of the judgment (the principal); interest cannot be charged on any unpaid interest. If a partial payment is received, the money is applied first to unpaid interest and then to unpaid principal.

When the court allows payments, the court often does not order any interest, as long as all payments are made in full and on time. Unless the judgment creditor asks for interest to be included in the order allowing payments, the judgment creditor may lose any claims for interest. But if the judgment debtor does not make full payments on time, interest on the missed payment or the entire unpaid balance might become due and collectible.

How do I calculate interest?
If you are asking for interest or disagreeing with a request for interest, you need to explain your interest calculation. Interest, at the rate of 10 percent per year (.0274 percent per day), may be added to the full unpaid balance of the judgment or only to payments that were not made on time. To calculate interest, show the unpaid principal balance, the dates and number of days you want the court to allow interest on that amount, and the total interest for that period. If payments were made, you will need to make separate calculations for the reduced principal balance after each payment.

Need help?
For free help, contact your county's small claims advisor:
[local info here]

Or go to *www.courts.ca.gov/smallclaims/advisor*

New July 1, 2013   **Declaration of Default in Payment of Judgment**   SC-223, Page 2 of 2
(Small Claims)

SC-225	**Order on Declaration of Default in Payments**	*Clerk stamps here when form is filed.*

① A judgment was entered in this case on *(date)*: 01/01/2014
against *(name of judgment debtor)*: Jeff Isbad

② On *(date)*: 02/01/2014, the court ordered that the judgment debtor named in ① may pay the judgment as follows:

   a. [x] Payments of $ 100.00, on the 1st day of each *(month, week, other)*: month
      starting *(date)*: 03/01/2014
      until *(date of final payment)*: 08/01/2016,
      amount of final payment: $ 100.00

   b. ☐ The payment schedule is stated on Form SC-225A, item ①.

③ On *(date)*: April 1, 2014 the judgment creditor *(name)*: Amy Right
informed the court that the judgment debtor had not made one or more payments as provided in ② and asked the court to order that the remaining balance of the judgment is due and collectible.

④ ☐ On *(date)*: _____ the judgment debtor filed a response to the judgment creditor's request.

Fill in the court name and street address:
Superior Court of California, County of
Los Angeles
Stanley Mosk Courthouse
111 Hill st
Los Angeles, Ca 90012

Fill in your case number and case name:
Case Number:
14K5000
Case Name:
Right v Isbad

The court orders:

⑤ ☐ **The payment order referred to in ②** *(check one)*:
   a. ☐ is terminated and the balance of the judgment is collectible.
   b. ☐ remains in effect, without modification.
   c. ☐ is modified as stated on Form SC-225A, item ②.

⑥ ☐ **The following amounts are owing on the judgment as of** *(date)*: _____
   a. ☐ Principal balance of judgment and costs included in judgment *(amount)*: $ _____
   b. ☐ Interest *(amount)*: $ _____

⑦ ☐ **Other orders are stated on Form SC-225A, item ③.**

⑧ ☐ **The court will make orders on the matter after a hearing,** which will take place on:

Hearing Date → _____ Time: _____ Dept. _____
Name and address of court if different than address above:
_____
_____

Request for Accommodations Assistive listening systems, computer-assisted real-time captioning, or sign language interpreter services are available if you ask at least five days before the hearing. Contact the clerk's office or go to *www.courts.ca.gov/forms* for *Request for Accommodations by Persons With Disabilities and Response* (Form MC-410). (Civil Code, § 54.8)

Date: _____

Judicial officer

? Need help?
For free help, contact your county's small claims advisor:
[local info here]

Or go to *www.courts.ca.gov/smallclaims/advisor*

Judicial Council of California, www.courts.ca.gov
New July 1, 2013, Optional Form
Code of Civil Procedure, § 116.620

Order on Declaration of Default in Payments
(Small Claims)

SC-225

Unfortunately, the State of California's Judicial Council has not set up an official form to deal with this matter. Many courts have their own local forms, so check your court's website to see if they have a form they prefer you use. In this book we will use the local forms provided by the county of San Diego. If your court does not provide a form, you can use the ones we provide, just change the court information on the form. If your court will not allow you to file the forms we provide, then you can copy these forms onto legal paper (also known as Numbered Pleading Paper), a sample is provided in the Appendix. Just complete the caption (see Chapter A, page 1).

1. Judgment entered

If the judgment was already entered, then you will use the "Declaration re: Default in Installment Payments and Order Thereon". A completed sample is provided at the end of this chapter. You do not need a separate form for each debtor, just include all names everywhere the debtor's name is asked for.

a. Complete the top, left hand, box with your name, address, telephone number, and e-mail address (optional). Where it says "attorney for", you will enter "Pro-Per" if you are representing yourself.

b. In the box just below, delete the name of the county and enter your county's name. Delete the name and address of the court and enter your court's name and address.

c. Enter the full name of the Plaintiffs, as shown on the judgment

d. Enter the full name of the Defendants, as shown on the judgment

e. Enter the full case number, as shown on the judgment

Line 1: Enter the name(s) of all debtors, as shown on the judgment

Line 2: Enter the date the judgment was entered in court (this may not be the date that the payment plan was ordered)

Line 3: Enter the full amount of the judgment

Line 4: Enter the monthly payment that the court ordered

Line 5: Enter the date when the first payment was due, per the court order

Line 6: Enter on which day of the month, each following payment was to be due. Example: 1st

Line 7: Enter the amount the debtor has paid until now. If no payments have been made, then enter 0.

Line 8: Enter the date the payment was due, that the debtor defaulted on

Sign and date the form. Have a copy of the form served on the debtor, by mail, and have the server complete a Proof of Service form. File all forms with the court clerk. Now we wait for a response from the court. If you do not hear anything within 30 days, contact the court clerk for more information.

2. Judgment NOT entered

If the judgment will be entered upon default in payments, then we will use the "Declaration of Default re: Stipulated Agreement and Judgment Thereon" form. A completed sample is provided at the end of this chapter. You do not need a separate form for each debtor, just include all names everywhere the debtor's name is asked for.

a. Complete the top, left hand, box with your name, address, telephone number, and e-mail address (optional). Where it says "attorney for", you will enter "Pro-Per" if you are representing yourself.

b. In the box just below, delete the name of the county and enter your county's name. Delete the name and address of the court and enter your court's name and address.

c. Enter the full name of the Plaintiffs, as shown on the judgment

d. Enter the full name of the Defendants, as shown on the judgment

e. Enter the full case number, as shown on the judgment

Line 1: Enter the date that the stipulation was entered in court.

Line 2: Enter the names of all the parties that agreed to the stipulation. Enter the names in the same order as the judgment title. (See Chapter A)

Line 3: Enter the terms of the stipulation.

Item 1: Check the "Defendant" box

Item 2: Leave blank, unless you want a hearing

Item 3: Check the "Plaintiff" box. On the line below, check the "Plaintiff" and enter the amounts you are requesting. The "stipulated" amount should be the same as on the stipulation. The "costs of filing and service" is in regards to any costs that were waived previously by the court (you or the debtor filed for financial hardship to avoid paying a court fee). You will probably not have any attorney fees to add. You can calculate the interest at ijcalc.sdcourt.ca.gov (no www.). Leave the total blank and fill out with the clerk.

Line 4: Check and complete if you are asking for possession of a property. This is for unlawful detainers (landlord evictions).

Sign and date the form. Have a copy of the form served on the debtor, by mail, and have the server complete a Proof of Service form. File all forms with the court clerk. Now we wait for a response from the court. If you do not hear anything within 30 days, contact the court clerk for more information.

ATTORNEY OR PARTY WITHOUT ATTORNEY (Name, State Bar number, and address): Amy Right 1000 My st Mytown, Ca 90000 TELEPHONE NO.: 310-555-5555 FAX NO.(Optional): EMAIL ADDRESS (Optional): ATTORNEY FOR (Name): In Pro Per	FOR COURT USE ONLY

SUPERIOR COURT OF CALIFORNIA, COUNTY OF

PLAINTIFF(S)
Amy Right

DEFENDANT(S)
Jeff Isbad

DECLARATION RE: DEFAULT IN INSTALLMENT PAYMENTS AND ORDER THEREON	CASE NUMBER 14K5000

The undersigned judgment creditor in the above-entitled action declares:

Judgment was entered against judgment debtor Jeff Isbad _____ on

___January 1, 2014___ for $ ___3,000.00___ ; the court ordered the judgment paid in installments of

$ ___100.00___ per month commencing on ___March 1, 2014___ and on the ___1st___ day of

each month thereafter until paid in full. $0.00_____ has been paid on the judgment.

Debtor has failed to comply with the terms of the judgment by failing to make the payment due and payable on or before

March 1, 2014_____.

Therefore, judgment creditor requests that writ of execution be issued for the balance due.

I declare under penalty of perjury under the laws of the State of California that the foregoing is true and correct.

Date: April 1, 2014_____   _____

IT IS SO ORDERED.

Date: _____   _____

DECLARATION RE: DEFAULT IN INSTALLMENT
PAYMENTS AND ORDER THEREON

ATTORNEY OR PARTY WITHOUT ATTORNEY (Name, State Bar number, and address):	FOR COURT USE ONLY
Amy Right 1000 My st Mytown, Ca 90000 TELEPHONE NO.: 310-555-5555 FAX NO.(Optional): EMAIL ADDRESS (Optional): ATTORNEY FOR (Name): In Pro Per	

SUPERIOR COURT OF CALIFORNIA, COUNTY OF

PLAINTIFF(S)
Amy Right

DEFENDANT(S)
Jeff Isbad

DECLARATION OF DEFAULT RE: STIPULATED AGREEMENT AND JUDGMENT THEREON	CASE NUMBER 14K5000

The undersigned states that on <u>February 1, 2014</u>, a Stipulated Agreement was entered into by <u>Amy Right and Jeff Isbad</u>. The Stipulated Agreement was as follows: <u>Jeff Isbad was to make payments of $ 100.00 per month, starting on March 1, 2014 and ending on August 1, 2016.</u>

1. [X] Plaintiff [X] Defendant has failed to comply with the terms of the Stipulated Agreement signed by both parties.
2. [ ] Plaintiff [ ] Defendant hereby requests that the dismissal be set aside and the matter be set for hearing.
3. [X] Plaintiff [ ] Defendant hereby requests that the dismissal be set aside and judgment be entered in favor of the
   [X] Plaintiff [ ] Defendant as follows:

   $ 3,000.00 _____ Stipulated amount (not including court costs)
   $ _____ Costs of filing and service*
   $ 0.00 _____ Attorney fees
   $ 50.00 _____ Interest
   $ (0.00 _____) Less payments received
   $ _____ Total

4. [ ] Possession of the premises located at _____

I declare under penalty of perjury under the laws of the State of California that the foregoing is true and correct.

Date: April 1, 2014

_____
Signature of Declarant

NOTE: If this is a Small Claims case, you must attach the original contract, check, or documents to support your claim.

FOR COURT USE ONLY

* REIMBURSEMENT FOR WAIVED COSTS
[ ] Plaintiff(s) [ ] Defendant(s) _____
[ ] to pay costs of $_____ to the San Diego Superior Court [ ] to pay costs of $_____ to the San Diego County Sheriff.
Pursuant to Gov. Code § 68637(b)(1), the court may refuse to enter satisfaction of judgment until the order requiring payment of waived fees and costs has been satisfied.

IT IS SO ORDERED.

Date: _____

_____
Judge/Commissioner of the Superior Court

SDSC CIV-243 (Rev. 12/14)
Mandatory Form

DECLARATION OF DEFAULT RE: STIPULATED AGREEMENT AND JUDGMENT THEREON

Chapter 6

Determining What the Debtor Owns

A. Debtor's Statement of Assets	6/2
B. Family Court Records	6/2
C. Schedule a Debtor's Exam	6/3
1. Determine the Proper Court for Debtor's Examination	6/4
2. Schedule the Examination	6/4
3. Complete the Form: Application and Order for Appearance and Examination	6/5
4. Have Court Issue Order	6/6
D. Obtain a Subpoena Duces Tecum	6/6
1. Complete the Form	6/7
2. Complete the Declaration for the Subpoena	6/7
3. Have Court Issue the Subpoena.	6/8
E. Have the Documents Served	6/9
1. Who Can Serve the Papers	6/11
2. Type of Service Required	6/11
3. Witness Fees	6/11
4. Complete a Proof of Service and File Forms	6/11
F. Prepare for the Examination	6/12
G. Conduct the Examination	6/12
H. If the Debtor Doesn't Show	6/13

Unless the debtor agrees to pay you voluntarily (see Chapter 5), the enforcement method that is most likely to yield money quickly is seizing the debtor's assets. This isn't hard to do as long as you know what assets the debtor has and where to find them.

If you have no idea what the debtor owns, you may be able to find out by using one or more of the procedures described in this chapter. They are designed to help you discover general information about the debtor's assets, income and expenses. Later chapters provide methods for locating specific types of assets.

If You Want to Find	Go To:
Bank and Deposit accounts	Chapter 8
Where the Debtor works	Chapter 9
Debts owed Debtor by others	Chapter 10
Motor Vehicles	Chapter 12
Real Estate	Chapter 14

A. Debtor's Statement of Assets

If your judgment was issued by a small claims court, a special information gathering method is available to you. Once the judgment is entered, the clerk must mail the debtor a form called a Statement of Assets [CCP 16.830(a)], which the debtor has to complete and return to you within 30 days [CCP 116.830(b)]. What if your judgment is a default judgment and the debtor files a motion to vacate or an appeal, they don't have to return the form to you until 30 days after losing their motion or appeal [CCP 116.830(c)]. Check with the small claims advisor or clerk about the procedure.

Unfortunately, few judgment debtors complete the form. If that happens to you, you can file a motion asking the small claims court judge to hold the debtor in contempt of court for failing to complete and return the form [CCP 116.830(d)].

If you received a completed Judgment Debtor's Statement of Assets, you'll have information about the debtor's occupation, employer, income, bank accounts, vehicles and other personal property.

B. Family Court Records

If the debtor has been involved in any sort of prior litigation, whether it be having been sued or suing someone else , or is or has been involved in a divorce proceeding, the court files in those cases probably contain valuable information about the debtor including their assets, employment history and general whereabouts. If you know little or nothing about your debtor this is the place to start. In most divorce and support cases, parties must submit detailed income and expense statements giving information about their finances. In addition, a divorce judgment often specifies which items of property each spouse gets in the divorce (Pointer: Keep in mind when looking at any filings regarding a debtor's separation or divorce, that debtors are known to fake a separation in order to hide/ shield their community property assets) In other words, if a debtor files for divorce or separation around the time a claim has been filed against them, always suspect a fraudulent divorce to evade their creditors.

These court files are public records. To review a particular file, all you have to do is go to the records office, or court clerk's office of the court house in which the case was heard, fill out their request form and have them pull the records for your review. You need to find out the case number of the legal proceeding, which can be done online in many counties. Once you find the right case, write down the case number. Give it to the court clerk and request to see the case file. Review and copy down information about bank account numbers, retirement plans, employment, real estate, cars and whatever else looks helpful. Ask the clerk how you can make copies if there's too much information to write down. You cannot take the court file or any documents in the file out of the clerk's office, any sealed envelopes are generally not public records and should not be opened but most everything else is, and you are entitled to them. Also, don't take individual documents from the file most courts have a manner to mark the pages you want "them" to copy, such as a paperclip or similar.

C. Schedule a Debtor's Exam

As a judgment creditor, you can require the judgment debtor to appear in court and answer questions about their income and assets [CCP 116.820(a) & 708.110(a)]. This procedure is called a "debtor's examination", "ORAP", or "OEX." The purpose is to provide you a manner to ask the debtor questions about their assets that could be used to satisfy your judgment.

This is a fairly simple procedure but requires a great deal of preparation to be done effectively especially against an experienced debtor. You fill out a form, have a copy personally served on the judgment debtor by a registered process server and file the original with the court. The judgment debtor must then show up in court and answer your questions. You can also require the debtor to bring documents for your examination, such as bank statements, stock certificates, deeds, and pay stubs, by serving the debtor with an additional form called a Subpoena Duces Tecum.

If the debtor doesn't cooperate, you can ask the supervising official (typically a judge or discovery commissioner) to order the debtor to appear. If they still don't show up, the supervising official can issue a bench warrant, if the Order for Examination was served by a Registered Process Server or the Sheriff [CCP 708.170(a) and CCP 1993] or order them to court to explain why they shouldn't be held in contempt of court [CCP 1209(a)(5)]. Since the debtor's appearance is ordered by the court, many courts will issue a warrant for the debtors arrest if they fail to appear which would be for contempt of court for violation of a court order, but with some courts it may take two or three no shows and other courts are often too busy to care. If you schedule an OEX be prepared to spend some money, anywhere from a few hundred dollars to many thousands, and that's if you do it yourself. A court reporter is not required by law but is a must if you want your examination (OEX) to have any teeth in your enforcement efforts. Experienced debtors rarely tell the truth in court and without the evidence of their testimony at the OEX in writing; you won't have any evidence of their lies to show the Judge.

You can also order third parties such as business partners or spouses to appear, at a debtor's examination, to answer questions or provide documents for you to review, by submitting a declaration that you believe those third parties possess personal property belonging to the judgment debtor or owe the debtor at least $250 [CCP 708.120 (a) & CCP 708.130].

Another Option is to examine the debtor in writing

Instead of conducting a debtor's exam, you can send written questions called interrogatories to the debtor [CCP 708.020]. The procedure costs very little and is easier than conducting a debtor's examination. As a general rule you can only do one or the other in a 120 day period [see CCP 708.020 (b)]. So, your choices as a creditor are either do a full blown Examination or sending written interrogatories as stated here. Again, be careful you can't do both within 120 days of each other (unless you can show the courts good cause). Enforcement professionals almost never use interrogatories and we recommend against them, unless it is a small, Small Claims judgment. If the debtor is willing to give you information, send an income and expense statement for them to complete and return to you instead and then do an examination if necessary (See Chapter 5, Section C2).

1. Determine the Proper Court for Debtor's Examination

The proper court for conducting the debtor's examination is usually, but not always, the court in which the money judgment was entered—called the "judgment court." You can use the judgment court if the judgment debtor:

- lives or has a place of business in the same county as the judgment court, or

- lives or has a place of business within 150 miles of the judgment court.

If neither of these conditions applies, you must move the examination to a court in the same county as the debtor's residence or place of business [CCP 708.160].

To conduct a debtor's examination in a different county from the judgment court, follow these steps [CCP 708.160(d)]:

1. Find the court in the county where the debtor lives or has a place of business.

2. Fill out the debtor examination form (See Section C3, below).

3. Obtain an Abstract of Judgment from the judgment court (See Chapter 4)

4. Prepare a declaration showing that the judgment debtor lives or has a place of business in the county where examination is being sought.

5. Mail or take all of these papers to the new court along with the appropriate filing fee $60 [CCP 708.160(d) (4) & Government Code 70617(a)].

2. Schedule the Examination

Before you complete the examination form, contact the court clerk to find out their procedure to set up a date. The clerk will tell you when debtors' examinations are scheduled at that courthouse and will let you know the next available date. Do not set the date until you have prepared all of the documents.

Some courts let you select the date; others assign you a particular date. Either way, make sure the date is far enough in the future to allow you to get the form issued from the court and get the debtor personally served at least 10 days before the examination [CCP 708.110(d)]. As a general rule, you should allow at least 20 days for service, which means that you shouldn't schedule the debtor's examination sooner

> **If the debtor lives far away**
>
> It is often too burdensome to conduct an examination if you have to travel a long way to do it. As mentioned, debtors often don't show up, and courts are often too busy with other matters to protect your right to conduct the exam. If the judgment is large enough one option is to find an attorney close to the court where the debtor lives and hire them to appear on your behalf and if necessary to conduct the exam. This generally only works on the larger judgments and generally only produces general information about the debtor unless it's worth paying the attorney to prepare for the exam. Or you can consider doing your own investigation along the lines suggested in subsequent chapters on specific types of assets, or hiring an investigation agency if again, the judgment is large enough to warrant the cost.

than 30 days from when you start the process. It isn't uncommon to have an examination date set for six to eight weeks after the process is initiated.

Timing is everything

Before scheduling the examination do the following:

1) Make sure you know where the debtor will be served and by whom (current address)

2) Make a discovery plan – know what you will ask for (documents), from whom, will it need a subpoena, where will you serve that subpoena, etc.

3) Prepare all documents (examination, subpoenas, declarations, etc.) prior to scheduling the examination.

If subpoenas will be used then you will need much more time for that information to be sent back to the court. Give yourself an additional 60 - 75 days.

3. Complete the Form: Application and Order for Appearance and Examination

Use the Judicial Council's Application and Order for Appearance and Examination form (Form EJ-125 for both small claims and civil court). We will call this form an "OEX" from now on since the name is so long. A sample completed form and instructions follow.

Page 1

Caption: Follow the format of your earlier court papers. Check the box labeled "Enforcement of Judgment." Check the appropriate box to indicate whether you want the judgment debtor or a third person to appear.

Item 1: Enter the name of the person you want to appear.

Item 2a or 2b: Check the correct box depending on whether you want the debtor to appear or you want a third party to appear. If you want both, you must complete two separate forms.

Item 2c: Leave this box blank.

Rectangular box: Leave blank until your examination is scheduled.

Item 3: Unless the court specifically allows otherwise, it is required that you have a professional (sheriff, marshal or registered process server) carry out the service, in which case you'd leave this blank. If you use someone else, put their name here (See Section E, below, for more on service).

Item 4: Check "judgment creditor" and insert the same name you put in Item 1, above.

Item 5: Check "judgment debtor" if you want to examine the debtor. If you want to examine a third party, check "third person" and attach a declaration showing that the third party possesses property worth more than $250 belonging to the debtor. You need not specify how you learned this; you can state that your knowledge is based on information and belief, although we suggest that you provide as much detail as you can [CCP 708.120(a)]. Below is a sample declaration. Type it up, double-spaced, on numbered pleading paper.

> **Debtor's Exam Creates Personal Lien**
> An important added benefit to ordering the judgment debtor in for a debtor's exam is that you automatically create a lien on the debtor's personal property the instant the Application and Order for Appearance and Examination is served on them (for more information, see Chapter 4C). The lien attaches to the debtor's non-exempt personal property and lasts for a year. You can renew the lien by personally serving a new Application and Order for Appearance and Examination. The lien attaches to the debtor's personal property whether they show up to court or not.

> **Sample Information & Belief Declaration**
>
> I, Amy Right, declare as follows:
>
> 1. I obtained a judgment against Jeff Isbad from the Los Angeles County Superior Court on January 1, 2014, in case #14K5000.
>
> 2. The balance due on the judgment is $3,000, plus accrued interest and post-judgment costs.
>
> 3. My neighbor, Roscoe Kline, is a former business associate of Jeff Isbad. On several occasions, Jeff Isbad and I attended social functions given by Mr. Kline. At these functions, Mr. Isbad told me several times that he owns a variety of original paintings, valued at approximately $12,000. I am informed and believe that these paintings are in the possession of his agent, Arnold Florsheim.
>
> 4. Mr. Isbad also told me that these paintings are the primary items of value he owns.
>
> I declare under penalty of perjury under the laws of the State of California that the foregoing is true and correct.
>
> 6/2/2014   (sign your name)
> Date   Amy Right
>
> DECLARATION OF AMY RIGHT

Item 6: Read it to make sure you are filing in the right court.

Item 7: Check this box only if the court where you want the examination conducted is not the one that issued the judgment. In that situation, go back and read Section 2, above.

Item 8: Leave this blank if this is the first time you have tried to examine the judgment debtor or if you examined them more than 120 days ago. If you examined them within the last 120 days, check this box and attach a declaration stating your good reason for another examination [CCP 708.110 (c)]. A sample follows.

Page 2

If you want to examine a third party, complete Item 2 in the box titled "Appearance of a Third Person." In capital letters, fill in the amount of money you think the person owes the debtor, or describe the property you believe is in the third party's possession and it's estimated value.

Serving this Order on the third party creates a personal lien (Chapter 4), for one year, on the money or property if it is adequately described on page 2 [CCP 708.120(c)]

4. Have Court Issue Order

Take or send the completed Application and Order for Appearance and Examination to the court to be signed by a judge. Once the form is signed, the court clerk will return either the original form or a certified copy to you to be served on the judgment debtor. Make four photocopies of the original. Send the original and three photocopies (keep one for yourself) to the clerk of the court along with a self-addressed stamped envelope and a cover letter explaining that you want the order issued and returned to you. You will find a generic cover letter in the Appendix. Call first to confirm the filing fee.

D. Obtain a Subpoena Duces Tecum

A Subpoena Duces Tecum is a form you can serve on the debtor or a third party if you want them to bring certain documents to the court for you to examine. If you do this, the judgment debtor or third party will have pertinent documents with them at the examination, which makes it much harder for them to repeatedly answer "I don't know" to your questions. You can serve as many a Subpoena to as many third parties as you consider necessary.

If you decide to obtain a Subpoena Duces Tecum, do it at the same time as you get the

Application and Order for Appearance and Examination and request that the examination be scheduled an additional 60 days later than previously considered.

1. Complete the Form

Call the court to find out if the court pre-issues subpoenas, that is, provides blank forms with the court's seal on them (often photocopied). If the court uses pre-issues them, obtain the form from your court otherwise use form SUBP-002. A completed sample and instructions follow.

Caption : Follow the format of your earlier court papers. Check the box labeled "Duces Tecum."

The People of the State of California, to (Name): Enter the name of the judgment debtor or the third party you are examining. Do not enter their address or phone number.

Item 1: Enter the date, time and place of your scheduled debtor's examination, listed on the Application and Order for Appearance and Examination.

Item 3: If you are subpoenaing the debtor, or a third party which you want to be present at the hearing then check "a". If you are subpoenaing a third party that you are willing to have them just send the documents to the court then check "b".

Item 4: Enter your name and telephone number.

Item 5: Subpoenas to third parties, where you checked box 3a, require you to pay them a witness and mileage fee. At this time the witness fee is $ 35 per day and the mileage (both ways) is $ 0.20 per mile. Check Government Code 68093 to confirm that it is still correct.

Leave the bottom section blank. It will be completed by the court clerk.

Sample Declaration for Exam Within 120 Days

I, Amy Right, declare as follows:

1. I obtained a judgment against Jeff Isbad from the Los Angeles County Superior Court on January 1, 2014, in case # 14K5000.

2. The balance due on the judgment is $3,000, plus accrued interest and post- judgment costs.

3. My neighbor, Roscoe Kline, is a former business associate of Jeff Isbad. On several occasions, Jeff Isbad and I attended social functions given by Mr. Kline. Several times Mr. Isbad told me that he owns a variety of original paintings, valued at approximately $12,000. I am informed and believe that these paintings are in the possession of his agent, Arnold Florsheim.

4. Mr. Isbad also told me that these paintings are the primary items of value he owns.

5. On May 15, 2014, I conducted a third party debtor's examination of Arnold Florsheim to discover more about Jeff Isbad's paintings. Mr. Florsheim told me that he returned the paintings to Jeff Isbad in February 2014.

6. Although fewer than 120 days have elapsed since my last examination of Jeff Isbad, I need to conduct another examination to discover the location of the paintings.

I declare under penalty of perjury under the laws of the State of California that the foregoing is true and correct.

6/2/2014	(sign your name)
Date	Amy Right

DECLARATION OF AMY RIGHT

2. Complete the Declaration for the Subpoena

A Subpoena Duces Tecum is not valid unless it is accompanied by a declaration, or affidavit, in which you state that you believe the records you want are in the possession of the person you are subpoenaing, and that the records are material to your efforts to collect your judgment [CCP 1985(b)].

You have two options to deal with this declaration. The first option, also the simplest, is to check "the following declaration" on the top of page 2.

Item 1: Check which title you hold. Most of the time you will be the "plaintiff".

Item 2: Check the box and attach the list of items requested from this witness (or debtor). A sample "Attachment 2" is provided.

Sign and date the bottom. You are the "subpoenaing party"

The second option is to prepare a Declaration (check "the attached affidavit" on the top of page 2), use lined paper with numbers down the left side (called pleading paper). In your declaration, you must state why you want the person to produce these materials and why you think they are relevant to your case. A sample is included.

Attach to your declaration an "Exhibit A", a list of the documents you want the person to bring to court. You can assume that they possess any document that would normally be in their possession. For instance, you can request that the judgment debtor bring ledgers and statements for their bank accounts, stock certificates issued in their name, bonds owned by them, deeds to real estate they own and certificates of title to their automobiles.

A sample "Exhibit A" containing a basic list of documents you might want to request, follows.

There's no court charge for issuing a Subpoena Duces Tecum unless you have to transfer the examination to another court (See Section C1, above).

Sample Declaration for Subpoena Duces Tecum

I, Amy Right, declare as follows:

1. I obtained a judgment against Jeff Isbad from the Los Angeles County Superior Court on January 1, 2014, in case #14K5000

2. The balance due on the judgment is $3,000, plus accrued interest and post-judgment costs.

3. I am scheduling a debtor's examination of Jeff Isbad for August 1, 2015, at 9 am in Dept. 1 of this Court so that Jeff Isbad can provide information I need to levy on his property, he will need to bring certain materials with him to the debtor's examination.

4. I believe that Jeff Isbad has in his possession or under his control the documents or copies of the documents listed in the attached, "Attachment 2", as well as any other documents which provide information about his assets.

5. These materials are needed to enforce this judgment.

6. These materials are relevant to this case because they contain information which I need to levy on the judgment debtor's property in order to satisfy this judgment.

I declare under penalty of perjury under the laws of the State of California that the foregoing is true and correct.

6/2/2014   (sign here)   D
DECLARATION OF AMY RIGHT

3. Have Court Issue Subpoena
Unless you are using a form that already has the court's seal on it, follow the procedures described in Section C4, above, for obtaining an OEX from the court, but instead of the OEX, request that a Subpoena Duces Tecum be issued. If you're obtaining the subpoena at the same time as the OEX, you can send or bring these to the court together.

4. Mail a copy of the Subpoena to the debtor

Before you can request a third party to provide you with any information about someone else (debtor or others), you must notify the party whose information you are trying to obtain about your request so that they can have the opportunity to oppose it [CCP 1985.3 & 1985.6].

You do this by completing a Notice to Consumer or Employee and Objection (form Subp-025, we will call "Notice" from now on) for each subpoena you plan on serving (is not needed for a subpoena to the debtor themselves). Once you complete the Notice, you will have the Notice and a copy of that Subpoena served on the party whose information is being requested. This service can be done by mail but must be sent out by someone allowed to serve documents (see Chapter 21).

We suggest that you have the OEX, Notice and Subpoenas all served at the same time. If you are serving the Notice on the individual by personal service, then the subpoenas can be served on the third party 10 days after (wait 11 days just to be sure). If the Notices are being served by mail, then add an additional 5 days to the waiting period.

E. Have the Documents Served

You must now find someone to serve the OEX, any Subpoena Duces Tecum, and the Notice, on the judgment debtor or third party. All documents must be served at least ten days before the hearing date. And the documents must be served correctly to establish a personal property lien.

Sample Exhibit A (If you are using option 1, then name document "Attachment 2")

Documents Requested in Subpoena Duces Tecum

1. Passbook, ledger and statements for bank, credit union and savings and loan checking, savings, money market and mutual fund accounts for previous 12 months.
2. Stock certificates, certificates of deposit and bonds for investments held currently or during previous year.
3. IRA, Keogh, 401(k) or other pension fund statements.
4. Pay stubs of judgment debtor and judgment debtor's spouse.
5. Receipts for property owned by judgment debtor or judgment debtor's spouse but held by third parties.
6. Insurance policies.
7. Any trust instrument under which judgment debtor is trustee or beneficiary.
8. Copies of child or spousal support order, if judgment debtor pays or receives support.
9. Deeds to real estate; deeds of trust.
10. Title certificates to motor vehicles.
11. Title certificates to personal property other than motor vehicles.
12. General ledger for business debtor or independent contractor.
13. Promissory notes payable to judgment debtor or judgment debtor's spouse evidencing debts owed by others.
14. Invoices for goods and services delivered by judgment debtor or judgment debtor's business to third parties.
15. Bills of sale for property sold within previous three months.
16. Patents, copyright certificates, trademark registration certificates, royalty contracts for books, music, film, computer software, art, etc.
17. Leases signed by judgment debtor as a landlord or a tenant.
18. Copies of canceled checks paid by tenants (if judgment debtor is landlord).
19. Copies of current occupational licenses or certifications.
20. Applications for credit made within previous three years.
21. Receipts for funds placed in escrow.
22. Bankruptcy papers, if petition filed within previous six years.
23. Pawnbroker receipts.
24. Determination of eligibility and award for Social Security, disability, unemployment, workers' compensation or other public benefit.
25. Copies of judgments against judgment debtor, copies of judgments that judgment debtor has against another party, copies of recent court papers filed in any cases in which judgment debtor or judgment debtor's business or spouse is a party.

Serving papers is covered in Chapter 21. This section provides a few additional details.

> **Serving the Subpoenas on a 3rd party**
>
> Along with a copy of the Subpoena (you always keep the originals) you must serve the third party with a copy of the Notice, a completed Proof of Service for the Notice, and all attachments to the Subpoena.
>
> Always give third parties plenty of time to respond to your subpoena. We would suggest serving the third party at least 45 days prior to the hearing date.

1. Who Can Serve the Papers?

Unless a judge signs an order allowing service by an individual, the OEX **must** be served by a sheriff, marshal or registered process server. An individual may serve the Subpoena Duces Tecum and Notices without the court's permission. If you want to move quickly, hire a registered process server. The debtor will not be happy to be served with these documents; we suggest having everything served at the same time (See Chapter 21).

2. Type of Service Required

An OEX and any Subpoena Duces Tecum must be personally served on either the debtor or a third party. If you have a third party served, you must also serve the debtor with a copy by mail [CCP 708.120(b) (2)]. The Notice and Subpoena can be served by mail on the debtor.

3. Witness Fees

Any person is entitled to be paid a witness fee for appearing at an examination. The fee includes both mileage (currently 20¢ a mile) and an appearance fee of $35 per day [Government Code § 68093].

Your server must offer to pay the party at the time of service. If the party doesn't take the money, be ready to pay them at the hearing. Also be prepared to reimburse them for photocopying the documents requested in the Subpoena Duces Tecum, at the rate of 10¢ per page plus $ 24 per hour [Evidence Code 1563(b)].

When doing a third party OEX, the third party must be paid the mileage fee in order for the OEX to be effective [CCP 708.120(f)]. Make sure that your Proof of Services includes the fact that these fees were paid.

Witness Fees for the Judgment Debtor?
Some judges have held that, because the judgment debtor is not really a witness to the proceeding (instead, they are a party), you don't have to pay the debtor witness fees. But be prepared to pay them in case your judge does not see things this way.

4. Complete a Proof of Service and File Forms

After the debtor or third party is served but before the examination, whoever served the documents must complete a Proof of Service form indicating how and when the debtor or third party was served. A Proof of Service for the OEX form appears in the Appendix. The Proof of Service for the Subpoena Duces Tecum is on the back of that form.

Make sure it includes the amount paid to parties for Witness and Mileage.

After you receive the completed Proof of Service forms, file them, along with the original or certified copy of the OEX, the original Subpoena Duces Tecum, and the Notices with the court clerk. If the court clerk will not accept them, then keep them in your file and bring the originals, and a copy, to court with you on the date of the exam.

F. Prepare for the Examination

Before you appear at the examination, check online or call the court clerk to make sure it is still scheduled. The examination may have been taken off the court calendar if the proof of service wasn't filed on time, or if the judgment debtor or third party wasn't

> **File the forms on time**
>
> The documents usually must be filed with the court at least five business days before the examination is scheduled, although some courts require only three days and a few will accept the forms the day of the examination. Whatever the deadline is, make sure you meet it otherwise the clerk may cancel the examination and you will have to start over.

personally served at least ten days before the scheduled date. Either way, you'll have to start over. If your sole purpose was to establish a lien (Chapter 4, Section C), you don't need to refile and serve the documents if the debtor was served properly.

In planning for the examination, make a list of questions to ask. Confine yourself to questions that you really need answered; don't rattle off a list of irrelevant or unnecessary questions. If you unnecessarily repeat yourself or waste time, the debtor or third party may walk out or ask the supervising official to cut the examination short. Make each question count.

We provide a checklist of possible questions in the Appendix. Before the examination, review your list, crossing out questions that don't apply or to which you already know the answer.

One question you should always ask the debtor is how much cash they have on them, because you can ask the judge to order the debtor to turn the cash over to you right on the spot. By having served the debtor with the OEX, you created a lien on all personal property of the debtor [CCP 708.110(d), 708.205] and all property of the debtor is subject to enforcement of a judgment unless that property is exempt [CCP 695.010(a)]. It is up to the debtor to prove, to the judge, that the money in their pocket is exempt. The judge won't necessarily order it verbally; you need to prepare a written order for the judge to sign. A completed sample follows.

G. Conduct the Examination

It is common for judgment debtors not to show up for an examination (See Section H, below). For the moment, however, let's assume that your debtor does appear.

The examination is usually scheduled for a courtroom and then moved elsewhere. When you arrive at the actual courtroom, you'll find a commissioner, referee or judge present, along with a bailiff. The court clerk will announce how that court handles checking in and the rest of the hearings. When your name is called, the debtor is briefly sworn in and agrees, under penalty of perjury, to answer your questions truthfully. If you have subpoenaed any third parties, ask the clerk for the documents. You and the debtor are then directed to an area where you can conduct the examination. If a problem occurs such as the debtor refusing to answer a question in which they have asserted no applicable privilege you can return to the judge or referee and ask them to order the debtor to answer.

If you served a Subpoena Duces Tecum, ask the debtor for the documents. Examine each document before you begin asking your questions; some of your questions will be answered by the documents, and other questions will be suggested by them. Then ask your unanswered questions.

If the debtor failed to bring the documents, won't answer your questions or isn't responding honestly or thoroughly, ask the supervising official for help. If necessary, the official (if they aren't a judge) can ask the judge to take action. Usually, a little assistance of this type will get the debtor to cooperate. But if they still refuse when ordered by the judge, the judge can cite them for contempt of court, fine them and even jail them [CCP 1209 & 1993].

Whatever the debtor says, don't come off like a hostile adversary maliciously asking embarrassing and personal questions. Present yourself as someone trying to help the debtor find money to pay you. The debtor may not be paying you because they don't have the money or has put other obligations first (Chapter 5 suggests ways that the debtor can come up with money to pay your judgment). If you explain that you need to ask some questions to work out a reasonable payment plan, they may open up. Another reason not to be pushy during this examination is that it could nudge the judgment debtor into declaring bankruptcy.

H. If the Debtor Doesn't Show

If a debtor fails to show up, most judges simply set another date for the debtor's examination. Usually, the court will notify the debtor of the new date. But ask about this; sometimes, you are responsible for serving the notice. If the debtor doesn't show up the second time, you can apply and pay for the court to issue a bench warrant. Ask the court clerk to provide you with an application form. The fee may be $50 or more [Government Code 26744 & 26744.5].

Timeline for Examination

1. Prepare a plan – who will you examine, who will you subpoena, what information will you ask for, will they need to appear in court?

2. Prepare all the documents – type up the OEX, Subpoenas, Notices, Declarations, Exhibits (Attachments). Leave the court hearing schedule blank and do not sign or date yet.

3. How much time will you need? – This will depend on what you will be including and who will be serving the documents.

Add time, court issuance to hearing date
Sheriff service – add 35 days
Process Server – add 15 days
Subpoena to third party – add 60 days (includes Notices)
Subpoena to debtor – add 30 days (included in subpoena to third party)
If debtor will be hard to serve – add????

4. Schedule the OEX – go to the court, or mail, and have the court schedule the OEX and issue the subpoena. If you do this by mail, then add 30 days to hearing date. Request date or "not prior to X number of days from issuance" from the court.

5. If you are examining the debtor;
5a. Serve all documents asap, including all Notices (to third parties). The Proof of Services will be blank.
5b. Complete proof of services.
5c. Wait 15 days. Now serve all third party Subpoenas, attachments, and Notices (with completed proof of services that debtor was served with Notices and copies of subpoenas).

6. If examining a third party (always use a subpoena)
6a. Serve debtor with a copy of the OEX, subpoenas, and Notices.
6b. Wait 15 days. Now serve third party with OEX, attachments, their Subpoena, their Notice (with completed proof of service), witness and mileage fees.
6c. Serve all other Subpoenas, with Notices (after same 15 day wait).

7. Complete all Proof of Services.

8. File with the Court – Original OEX, Subpoenas, Notices, and Proofs of Services. Get filed copies for your record.
Some courts do not file Subpoenas & Notices. Keep in file.

File with Court ASAP, Things happen, don't wait

If the Judgment Debtor Brings an Attorney

Don't be concerned if the debtor shows up with an attorney. Simply explain that you want to arrange a voluntary payment plan that the debtor can honor. In other words, approach the attorney in the same way you would approach the debtor to get answers to your questions. Then, proceed to ask your questions.

The attorney will let the debtor know whether or not they should respond. As long as your questions are reasonable, there is no reason the debtor shouldn't answer. If the attorney puts up resistance that seems unreasonable, ask the supervising official to explain your situation to the judge. The judge may ask the attorney to direct the debtor to answer questions that the judge feels are appropriate.

Facing an attorney gives you one benefit: if you do work out a settlement and the debtor reneges, you can nag the attorney rather than the debtor. Attorneys tend to be easier to find and less emotionally involved in the situation than their debtor clients.

Debtor's Property is in the name of a Trust

Many times a debtor will place their Real Estate or other valuables in a trust. A trust may go by many names; Family Trust, Living Trust, Revocable Trust, Irrevocable Trust, and Land Trust, etc.

If a Trust is Irrevocable then going after the property will be harder and we will not be able to cover it in this book. You may need an attorney's assistance. But start thinking Fraudulent Transfer (not covered in book). If you are going after Secured Property (see chapter 4), which was transferred to the Trust after your lien was filed/recorded, then transfer is subject to your lien. Notify Trust of your "senior" lien and demand payment.

If the Trust is Revocable then you can move against it as if the property were still in your debtor's name [Probate Code 18200 & 18201]. You will need to use an Affidavit of Identity (Chapter 1).

How do you know if a trust is revocable or not? You request a copy of the trust when you do an Examination of the debtor. The difference between a Revocable and Irrevocable Trust is that, in a Revocable Trust, the settlor (person who put the property into the trust) can revoke, or modify the trust and take the property back at any time. In an Irrevocable Trust, once the property is in the Trust, it belongs to the trust and not the settlor.

		AT-138/EJ-125
ATTORNEY OR PARTY WITHOUT ATTORNEY: STATE BAR NO.: NAME: Amy Right FIRM NAME: STREET ADDRESS: 1000 My st CITY: Mytown STATE: Ca ZIP CODE: 90000 TELEPHONE NO.: 310-555-5555 FAX NO.: E-MAIL ADDRESS: ATTORNEY FOR (name): In Pro Per		FOR COURT USE ONLY

SUPERIOR COURT OF CALIFORNIA, COUNTY OF LOS ANGELES
STREET ADDRESS: 111 Hill st
MAILING ADDRESS:
CITY AND ZIP CODE: Los Angeles, Ca 90012
BRANCH NAME: Stanley Mosk Courthouse

PLAINTIFF Amy Right
DEFENDANT Jeff Isbad

APPLICATION AND ORDER FOR APPEARANCE AND EXAMINATION [X] ENFORCEMENT OF JUDGMENT [ ] ATTACHMENT (Third Person) [X] Judgment Debtor [ ] Third Person	CASE NUMBER: 14K5000

ORDER TO APPEAR FOR EXAMINATION

1. TO (name): Jeff Isbad
2. YOU ARE ORDERED TO APPEAR personally before this court, or before a referee appointed by the court, to
   a. [X] furnish information to aid in enforcement of a money judgment against you.
   b. [ ] answer concerning property of the judgment debtor in your possession or control or concerning a debt you owe the judgment debtor.
   c. [ ] answer concerning property of the defendant in your possession or control or concerning a debt you owe the defendant that is subject to attachment.

Date: May 1, 2016   Time: 8:30 am   Dept. or Div.: 11   Rm.: 450
Address of court [X] is shown above [ ] is:

3. This order may be served by a sheriff, marshal, registered process server, **or** the following specially appointed person (name):

Date: _____
                                                JUDGE

This order must be served not less than 10 days before the date set for the examination.
IMPORTANT NOTICES ON REVERSE

APPLICATION FOR ORDER TO APPEAR FOR EXAMINATION

4. [X] Original judgment creditor   [ ] Assignee of record   [ ] Plaintiff who has a right to attach order
   applies for an order requiring (name):
   to appear and furnish information to aid in enforcement of the money judgment or to answer concerning property or debt.
5. The person to be examined is
   a. [X] the judgment debtor.
   b. [ ] a third person (1) who has possession or control of property belonging to the judgment debtor or the defendant or (2) who owes the judgment debtor or the defendant more than $250. An affidavit supporting this application under Code of Civil Procedure section 491.110 or 708.120 is attached.
6. The person to be examined resides or has a place of business in this county or within 150 miles of the place of examination.
7. [ ] This court is **not** the court in which the money judgment is entered or (attachment only) the court that issued the writ of attachment. An affidavit supporting an application under Code of Civil Procedure section 491.150 or 708.160 is attached.
8. [ ] The judgment debtor has been examined within the past 120 days. An affidavit showing good cause for another examination is attached.

I declare under penalty of perjury under the laws of the State of California that the foregoing is true and correct.
Date: 02/15/2016

Amy Right   ▶
(TYPE OR PRINT NAME)   (SIGNATURE OF DECLARANT)

Form Adopted for Mandatory Use   **APPLICATION AND ORDER FOR**   Code of Civil Procedure,
Judicial Council of California   **APPEARANCE AND EXAMINATION**   §§ 491.110, 708.110, 708.120, 708.170
AT-138/EJ-125 [Rev. January 1, 2017]   (Attachment—Enforcement of Judgment)   www.courts.ca.gov

AT-138/EJ-125

Information for Judgment Creditor Regarding Service
If you want to be able to ask the court to enforce the order on the judgment debtor or any third party, you must have a copy of the order personally served on the judgment debtor by a sheriff, marshal, registered process server, or the person appointed in item 3 of the order at least 10 calendar days before the date of the hearing, and have a proof of service filed with the court.

IMPORTANT NOTICES ABOUT THE ORDER

APPEARANCE OF JUDGMENT DEBTOR (ENFORCEMENT OF JUDGMENT)
NOTICE TO JUDGMENT DEBTOR If you fail to appear at the time and place specified in this order, you may be subject to arrest and punishment for contempt of court, and the court may make an order requiring you to pay the reasonable attorney fees incurred by the judgment creditor in this proceeding.

APPEARANCE OF A THIRD PERSON (ENFORCEMENT OF JUDGMENT)
(1) NOTICE TO PERSON SERVED If you fail to appear at the time and place specified in this order, you may be subject to arrest and punishment for contempt of court, and the court may make an order requiring you to pay the reasonable attorney fees incurred by the judgment creditor in this proceeding.

(2) NOTICE TO JUDGMENT DEBTOR The person in whose favor the judgment was entered in this action claims that the person to be examined under this order has possession or control of property that is yours or owes you a debt. This property or debt is as follows *(describe the property or debt)*:
 If you are examining a third party, you would type in; *
1) how much money the third party a) owes the debtor, or b) is holding on behalf of the debtor

 OR
2) a description, and estimated value, of any property (of the debtor's) the third party holds

If you claim that all or any portion of this property or debt is exempt from enforcement of the money judgment, you must file your exemption claim in writing with the court and have a copy personally served on the judgment creditor not later than three days before the date set for the examination. You must appear at the time and place set for the examination to establish your claim of exemption or your exemption may be waived.

APPEARANCE OF A THIRD PERSON (ATTACHMENT)
NOTICE TO PERSON SERVED If you fail to appear at the time and place specified in this order, you may be subject to arrest and punishment for contempt of court, and the court may make an order requiring you to pay the reasonable attorney fees incurred by the plaintiff in this proceeding.

APPEARANCE OF A CORPORATION, PARTNERSHIP, ASSOCIATION, TRUST, OR OTHER ORGANIZATION
It is your duty to designate one or more of the following to appear and be examined: officers, directors, managing agents, or other persons who are familiar with your property and debts.

 **Request for Accommodations.** Assistive listening systems, computer-assisted real-time captioning, or sign language interpreter services are available if you ask at least 5 days before your hearing. Contact the clerk's office for *Request for Accommodation* (form MC-410). (Civil Code, § 54.8.)

SUBP-002

ATTORNEY OR PARTY WITHOUT ATTORNEY *(Name, State Bar number, and address)*:	FOR COURT USE ONLY
Amy Right 1000 My st, Mytown, Ca 90000 TELEPHONE NO.: 310-555-5555 FAX NO.: E-MAIL ADDRESS: ATTORNEY FOR *(Name)*: In Pro Per	

NAME OF COURT: Superior Court of California
STREET ADDRESS: 111 Hill st
MAILING ADDRESS:
CITY AND ZIP CODE: Los Angeles, Ca 90000
BRANCH NAME: Stanley Mosk Courthouse

PLAINTIFF/PETITIONER: Amy Right
DEFENDANT/RESPONDENT: Jeff Isbad

CIVIL SUBPOENA (DUCES TECUM) for Personal Appearance and Production of Documents, Electronically Stored Information, and Things at Trial or Hearing and DECLARATION

CASE NUMBER: 14K5000

THE PEOPLE OF THE STATE OF CALIFORNIA, TO *(name, address, and telephone number of witness, if known)*:

Jeff Isbad - 666 e Cra P st, Helltown, Ca 90666

1. **YOU ARE ORDERED TO APPEAR AS A WITNESS** in this action at the date, time, and place shown in the box below UNLESS your appearance is excused as indicated in box 3b below or you make an agreement with the person named in item 4 below.

   a. Date: May 1, 2016   Time: 8:30 am   ✓ Dept.: 11   ☐ Div.:   ✓ Room: 450
   b. Address: court address is shown above

2. **IF YOU HAVE BEEN SERVED WITH THIS SUBPOENA AS A CUSTODIAN OF CONSUMER OR EMPLOYEE RECORDS UNDER CODE OF CIVIL PROCEDURE SECTION 1985.3 OR 1985.6 AND A MOTION TO QUASH OR AN OBJECTION HAS BEEN SERVED ON YOU, A COURT ORDER OR AGREEMENT OF THE PARTIES, WITNESSES, *AND* CONSUMER OR EMPLOYEE AFFECTED MUST BE OBTAINED BEFORE YOU ARE REQUIRED TO PRODUCE CONSUMER OR EMPLOYEE RECORDS.**

3. **YOU ARE** *(item a or b must be checked)*:
   a. ✓ Ordered to appear in person and to produce the records described in the declaration on page two or the attached declaration or affidavit. The personal attendance of the custodian or other qualified witness and the production of the original records are required by this subpoena. The procedure authorized by Evidence Code sections 1560(b), 1561, and 1562 will not be deemed sufficient compliance with this subpoena.
   b. ☐ Not required to appear in person if you produce (i) the records described in the declaration on page two or the attached declaration or affidavit and (ii) a completed declaration of custodian of records in compliance with Evidence Code sections 1560, 1561, 1562, and 1271. (1) Place a copy of the records in an envelope (or other wrapper). Enclose the original declaration of the custodian with the records. Seal the envelope. (2) Attach a copy of this subpoena to the envelope or write on the envelope the case name and number; your name; and the date, time, and place from item 1 in the box above. (3) Place this first envelope in an outer envelope, seal it, and mail it to the clerk of the court at the address in item 1. (4) Mail a copy of your declaration to the attorney or party listed at the top of this form.

4. **IF YOU HAVE ANY QUESTIONS ABOUT THE TIME OR DATE YOU ARE TO APPEAR, OR IF YOU WANT TO BE CERTAIN THAT YOUR PRESENCE IS REQUIRED, CONTACT THE FOLLOWING PERSON BEFORE THE DATE ON WHICH YOU ARE TO APPEAR:**
   a. Name of subpoenaing party or attorney: Amy Right   b. Telephone number: 310-555-5555

5. **Witness Fees:** You are entitled to witness fees and mileage actually traveled both ways, as provided by law, if you request them at the time of service. You may request them before your scheduled appearance from the person named in item 4.

DISOBEDIENCE OF THIS SUBPOENA MAY BE PUNISHED AS CONTEMPT BY THIS COURT. YOU WILL ALSO BE LIABLE FOR THE SUM OF FIVE HUNDRED DOLLARS AND ALL DAMAGES RESULTING FROM YOUR FAILURE TO OBEY.

Date issued:

_____   ▶   _____
(TYPE OR PRINT NAME)   (SIGNATURE OF PERSON ISSUING SUBPOENA)

(Declaration in support of subpoena on reverse)   (TITLE)

Form Adopted for Mandatory Use
Judicial Council of California
SUBP-002 [Rev. January 1, 2012]

CIVIL SUBPOENA (DUCES TECUM) for Personal Appearance and Production of Documents, Electronically Stored Information, and Things at Trial or Hearing and DECLARATION

Code of Civil Procedure,
§ 1985 et seq.
www.courts.ca.gov

PLAINTIFF/PETITIONER: Amy Right	CASE NUMBER:
DEFENDANT/RESPONDENT: Jeff Isbad	14K5000

SUBP-002

The production of the documents, electronically stored information, or other things sought by the subpoena on page one is supported by *(check one)*:

☐ the attached affidavit or   ☐ the following declaration:

DECLARATION IN SUPPORT OF CIVIL SUBPOENA (DUCES TECUM) FOR PERSONAL APPEARANCE AND PRODUCTION OF DOCUMENTS, ELECTRONICALLY STORED INFORMATION, AND THINGS AT TRIAL OR HEARING
(Code Civ. Proc., §§ 1985, 1987.5)

1. I, the undersigned, declare I am the ☐ plaintiff ☐ defendant ☐ petitioner ☐ respondent
   ☐ attorney for *(specify)*:   ☐ other *(specify)*:
   in the above-entitled action.

2. The witness has possession or control of the documents, electronically stored information, or other things listed below, and shall produce them at the time and place specified in the Civil Subpoena for Personal Appearance and Production of Records at Trial or Hearing on page one of this form *(specify the exact documents or other things to be produce; if electronically stored information is demanded, the form or forms in which each type of information is to be produced may be specified)*:

   ☐ Continued on Attachment 2.

3. Good cause exists for the production of the documents, electronically stored information, or other things described in paragraph 2 for the following reasons:

   ☐ Continued on Attachment 3.

4. The documents, electronically stored information, or other things described in paragraph 2 are material to the issues involved in this case for the following reasons:

   ☐ Continued on Attachment 4.

I declare under penalty of perjury under the laws of the State of California that the foregoing is true and correct.

Date:

_____   ▶ _____
(TYPE OR PRINT NAME)   (SIGNATURE OF ☐ SUBPOENAING PARTY ☐ ATTORNEY FOR SUBPOENAING PARTY)

Request for Accommodations

Assistive listening systems, computer-assisted real-time captioning, or sign language interpreter services are available if you ask at least five days before the date on which you are to appear. Contact the clerk's office or go to www.courts.ca.gov/forms for *Request for Accommodations by Persons With Disabilities and Response* (form MC-410). (Civil Code, § 54.8.)

(Proof of service on page 3)

CIVIL SUBPOENA (DUCES TECUM) for Personal Appearance and Production of Documents, Electronically Stored Information, and Things at Trial or Hearing and DECLARATION

SUBP-025

ATTORNEY OR PARTY WITHOUT ATTORNEY *(Name, State Bar number, and address)*:	FOR COURT USE ONLY
Amy Right 1000 My st Mytown, Ca 90000 TELEPHONE NO.: 310-555-5555 FAX NO. *(Optional)*: E-MAIL ADDRESS *(Optional)*: ATTORNEY FOR *(Name)*: In Pro Per	

SUPERIOR COURT OF CALIFORNIA, COUNTY OF Los Angeles
STREET ADDRESS: 111 Hill st
MAILING ADDRESS:
CITY AND ZIP CODE: Los Angeles, Ca 90000
BRANCH NAME: Stanley Mosk Courthouse

PLAINTIFF/PETITIONER: Amy Right
DEFENDANT/RESPONDENT: Jeff Isbad

CASE NUMBER: 14K5000

NOTICE TO CONSUMER OR EMPLOYEE AND OBJECTION
(Code Civ. Proc., §§ 1985.3, 1985.6)

NOTICE TO CONSUMER OR EMPLOYEE

TO *(name)*: Jeff Isbad

1. PLEASE TAKE NOTICE THAT **REQUESTING PARTY** *(name)*: Amy Right
   SEEKS YOUR RECORDS FOR EXAMINATION by the parties to this action on *(specify date)*: May 1, 2016
   The records are described in the subpoena directed to **witness** *(specify name and address of person or entity from whom records are sought)*: Your Bank, NA 1234 Main st, Los Angeles, Ca 90019
   A copy of the subpoena is attached.

2. IF YOU OBJECT to the production of these records, YOU MUST DO ONE OF THE FOLLOWING BEFORE THE DATE SPECIFIED, IN ITEM a. OR b. BELOW:

   a. If you are a party to the above-entitled action, you must file a motion pursuant to Code of Civil Procedure section 1987.1 to quash or modify the subpoena and give notice of that motion to the **witness** and the **deposition officer** named in the subpoena at least five days before the date set for production of the records.

   b. If you are not a party to this action, you must serve on the **requesting party** and on the **witness,** before the date set for production of the records, a written objection that states the specific grounds on which production of such records should be prohibited. You may use the form below to object and state the grounds for your objection. You must complete the Proof of Service on the reverse side indicating whether you personally served or mailed the objection. The objection should **not** be filed with the court. **WARNING:** IF YOUR OBJECTION IS NOT RECEIVED BEFORE THE DATE SPECIFIED IN ITEM 1, YOUR RECORDS MAY BE PRODUCED AND MAY BE AVAILABLE TO ALL PARTIES.

3. YOU OR YOUR ATTORNEY MAY CONTACT THE UNDERSIGNED to determine whether an agreement can be reached in writing to cancel or limit the scope of the subpoena. If no such agreement is reached, and if you are not otherwise represented by an attorney in this action, YOU SHOULD CONSULT AN ATTORNEY TO ADVISE YOU OF YOUR RIGHTS OF PRIVACY.

Date: 02/15/2016

Amy Right
_____
(TYPE OR PRINT NAME)

▶ _____
(SIGNATURE OF ☐ REQUESTING PARTY ☐ ATTORNEY)

OBJECTION BY NON-PARTY TO PRODUCTION OF RECORDS

1. ☐ I object to the production of all of my records specified in the subpoena.
2. ☐ I object only to the production of the following specified records:

3. The specific grounds for my objection are as follows:

Date:

_____
(TYPE OR PRINT NAME)

▶ _____
(SIGNATURE)

(Proof of service on reverse)

Form Adopted for Mandatory Use
Judicial Council of California
SUBP-025 [Rev. January 1, 2008]

NOTICE TO CONSUMER OR EMPLOYEE AND OBJECTION

Code of Civil Procedure,
§§ 1985.3, 1985.6,
2020.010–2020.510
www.courtinfo.ca.gov

PLAINTIFF/PETITIONER:	CASE NUMBER:
DEFENDANT/RESPONDENT:	

PROOF OF SERVICE OF NOTICE TO CONSUMER OR EMPLOYEE AND OBJECTION
(Code Civ. Proc., §§ 1985.3, 1985.6)

☐ Personal Service ☐ Mail

1. At the time of service I was at least 18 years of age and **not a party to this legal action.**
2. I served a copy of the *Notice to Consumer or Employee and Objection* as follows *(check either a or b)*:
   a. ☐ **Personal service.** I personally delivered the *Notice to Consumer or Employee and Objection* as follows:
      (1) Name of person served: (3) Date served:
      (2) Address where served: (4) Time served:

   b. ☐ **Mail.** I deposited the *Notice to Consumer or Employee and Objection* in the United States mail, in a sealed envelope with postage fully prepaid. The envelope was addressed as follows:
      (1) Name of person served: (3) Date of mailing:
      (2) Address: (4) Place of mailing *(city and state)*:

      (5) I am a resident of or employed in the county where the *Notice to Consumer or Employee and Objection* was mailed.
   c. My residence or business address is *(specify)*:
   d. My phone number is *(specify)*:

I declare under penalty of perjury under the laws of the State of California that the foregoing is true and correct.
Date:

▶

(TYPE OR PRINT NAME OF PERSON WHO SERVED)   (SIGNATURE OF PERSON WHO SERVED)

PROOF OF SERVICE OF OBJECTION TO PRODUCTION OF RECORDS
(Code Civ. Proc., §§ 1985.3, 1985.6)

☐ Personal Service ☐ Mail

1. At the time of service I was at least 18 years of age and **not a party to this legal action.**
2. I served a copy of the *Objection to Production of Records* as follows *(complete either a or b)*:
   a. ON THE REQUESTING PARTY
      (1) ☐ **Personal service.** I personally delivered the *Objection to Production of Records* as follows:
         (i) Name of person served: (iii) Date served:
         (ii) Address where served: (iv) Time served:

      (2) ☐ **Mail.** I deposited the *Objection to Production of Records in* the United States mail, in a sealed envelope with postage fully prepaid. The envelope was addressed as follows:
         (i) Name of person served: (iii) Date of mailing:
         (ii) Address: (iv) Place of mailing *(city and state)*:

         (v) I am a resident of or employed in the county where the *Objection to Production of Records* was mailed.
   b. ON THE WITNESS
      (1) ☐ **Personal service.** I personally delivered the *Objection to Production of Records* as follows:
         (i) Name of person served: (iii) Date served:
         (ii) Address where served: (iv) Time served:

      (2) ☐ **Mail.** I deposited the *Objection to Production of Records* in the United States mail, in a sealed envelope with postage fully prepaid. The envelope was addressed as follows:
         (i) Name of person served: (iii) Date of mailing:
         (ii) Address: (iv) Place of mailing *(city and state)*:

         (v) I am a resident of or employed in the county where the *Objection to Production of Records* was mailed.
3. My residence or business address is *(specify)*:
4. My phone number is *(specify)*:

I declare under penalty of perjury under the laws of the State of California that the foregoing is true and correct.
Date:

▶

(TYPE OR PRINT NAME OF PERSON WHO SERVED)   (SIGNATURE OF PERSON WHO SERVED)

Amy Right
1000 My st
Mytown, Ca 90000
Tel : 310-555-5555

SUPERIOR COURT OF CALIFORNIA
COUNTY OF LOS ANGELES

Amy Right

    Plaintiff,

vs.

Jeff Isbad

    Defendant

Case No.: 14K5000

Turn over order

CCP 708.205

Date: **May 1, 2016**
Time: **8:30 AM**
Dept: **11**

The examination of Jeff Isbad, judgment debtor and defendant herein, was conducted on the date and at the time set forth above. It appearing from said examination that the judgment debtor has in his possession or under his control the following property which is not exempt form enforcement of a money judgment:

1)

2)

3)

4)

TURNOVER ORDER

IT IS ORDERED that the judgment debtor shall immediately deliver to the Creditor the above-described property which shall be applied toward the satisfaction of the judgment.

DATED: _____   _____
                                   Judge of the Superior Court

Points and Authorities

CCP 708.205: (a) Except as provided in subdivision (b), at the conclusion of the proceeding pursuant to this article, the court may order the judgment debtor's interest in the property in the possession or under the control of the judgment debtor or the third person or a debt owed by the third person to the judgment debtor to be applied toward the satisfaction of the money judgment if the property is not exempt from enforcement of a money judgment. Such an order creates a lien on the property or debt.

(b) If a third person examined pursuant to 708.120 claims an interest in the property adverse to the judgment debtor or denies the debt and the court does not determine the matter as provided in subdivision (a) of Section 108.180, the court may not order the property or debt to be applied toward the satisfaction of the money judgment but may make an order pursuant to subdivision (c) or (d) of Section 708.180 forbidding transfer or payment to the extent authorized by that section.

TURNOVER ORDER

Chapter 7

Obtaining a Writ of Execution

A. Complete the Writ of Execution Form	7/2
B. Have Court Issue Writ	7/5
C. What to Do With Your Writ.	7/5

A Writ of Execution (or simply a Writ) is a key tool for enforcing judgments. The phrase "Writ of Execution" conjures up visions of black hooded hangmen presiding over medieval scaffolds. But today's Writs take a completely different form and could probably benefit from a name change. A Writ is simply authorization from the court to seize the debtor's income (wage garnishment) or assets (levy). Most property subject to enforcement of a money judgment is subject to levy under a Writ [CCP 699.710], but certain property is not and may be seized with different enforcement methods [CCP 699.720].

Obtaining a Writ of Execution is easy. The debtor won't even know you've done so, until you actually use it to seize the debtor's income or assets.

As explained in Chapter 2, you'll want to wait until certain periods expire before initiating enforcement of your judgment. For instance, if you are seeking a Writ of Execution on an out-of-state judgment, you usually can't obtain a Writ until 30 days after the debtor is served with the Notice of Entry of Sister-State Judgment. Once all time periods have passed, however, it doesn't mean you should run to court to get your Writ. A Writ of Execution is valid for only 180 days from the date of issuance [CCP 699.530(b) & 699.560(a) (4)]. While you could wait to find assets first, and then get the Writ, some courts are backlogged and those assets may be gone by the time you finally get the court to issue you the Writ.

Know the local rules
Some courts require you to file an extra form with your Writ of Execution, a Memorandum of Cost. Contact the clerk of your court to find out.

A. Complete the Writ of Execution Form

A Writ of Execution form is in the Appendix. You will need a separate Writ for each county in which you are going after assets [CCP 699.510(a)].

A court will issue only one Writ per county at a given time. However, if the debtor has assets in multiple counties, it is more convenient to have the court issue all of the various county Writs at the same time.

Writs can be used for more than one asset at a time within the same county. For instance, you can ask the levying officer to sequentially levy against a debtor's bank account and then execute a wage garnishment against the debtor's employer for the remaining amount due on the judgment.

After the levying officer seizes (or attempts to seize) asset X, they may return the Writ to the court. As a general rule, you should always ask the levying officer to hold the Writ for the full duration until the 180 days expire. Then you can request that they pursue asset Y, using the same Writ. If the Writ expires (remember, it lasts only 180 days), you will need a new one to go after assets in that county.

If you anticipate needing more than one Writ, you can save yourself some time by taking the following steps:

1. Complete page 1, except for Items 1, 17, & 18

2. Make one photocopy of the partially completed form for as many Writs as are needed.

3. Complete Item 1 and Items 11–20 for each Writ.

4. Follow the rest of our instructions for each Writ. A sample is attached.

Caption: Follow the format of your other court papers. Check the Execution (Money Judgment) box.

Other Kinds of Writs

A Writ of Possession is normally obtained in eviction actions, when a landlord sues to recover possession of the premises from the tenant. It is also used in actions where a secured creditor seeks judicial authority to repossess personal property.

Just below the box where the case number is written, you are asked to check a box(es) stating what type of case you have [CCP 699.520(k)]. A small claims case would mean you check "limited" and "small claims". Other cases may be "limited", "unlimited", or "other" (possibly Probate or Family case).

Item 1: Enter the name of the county in which the assets are located.

Item 3: Enter your name exactly as it appears on the judgment and check the judgment creditor box.

Item 4: Enter the judgment debtor's name exactly as it appears in the judgment, and the debtor's last known address. If there are more than one debtors, check the additional judgment debtors box, turn over the sheet, check box # 21 on Page 2 and enter the additional judgment debtors' names and addresses. If any debtor Alias names are added to the judgment via an Affidavit of Identity, these debtor Alias Names have to be added to the Writ. Insert these debtor Alias Names as "AKA debtor Alias Name #1 AKA debtor Alias Name #2". You must list all judgment debtors and all Alias Names in each Writ, even if those other judgment debtors own no property in this county, except if a debtor has received a discharge in bankruptcy [CCP 699.510(c)(1)(A)] or if you already filed a Satisfaction of Judgment for that debtor [CCP 699.510(c)(1)(B)].

Item 5: Enter the date on which your judgment was entered [CCP 699.520(d)]; you'll find it on the judgment or the Notice of Entry of Judgment. If you don't know the date, call the court clerk or look in the court file. If you converted a sister-state judgment to a California judgment, enter the date the California judgment was entered.

Item 6: Check this box only if you have renewed your judgment before its ten-year expiration. If so, fill in the renewal dates (See Chapter 20).

Item 7: If you contacted a third party who has a security interest in the debtor's property such as a dealer who is still owed money under a car loan that third party may have requested that you send them a notice of sale if you decide to seize and sell that property. If so, check box 7b, turn over the sheet, check box 22 on page 2 and enter the third party's name and address. Otherwise, check box 7a.

Item 8: Skip this unless you have amended your judgment to add additional judgment debtors [CCP 989-994]. If you have, check box 8, turn over the sheet, check box 23 on Page 2 and enter the new debtors' names and addresses. If you *originally* obtained judgment against more than one defendant, this item does not apply unless you've added even more defendants since obtaining your judgment.

Item 9: Skip this item unless you are doing an eviction.

Item 10: Check this box only if you obtained a judgment against someone in another state and turned it into a California judgment (We don't cover this procedure in this book).

Items 11 thru 19 involve numbers. Do not leave any line empty. If you will enter nothing then enter "0.00"

Item 11: Enter the full amount of the judgment, including court costs and interest accrued before judgment. This sum is on the judgment or the Notice of Entry of Judgment [CCP 699.250(e)].

Item 12: To ensure the Writ includes accrued interest due; always file a Memorandum of Costs ("Memo of Costs", covered in Chapter 16) when you submit the Writ to the court. Some courts will not proceed with your request and may reject your documents unless you include a Memo of Costs form with your submission. If you are only adding accrued interest on the Memo of Costs, the Writ can be issued immediately without notice to the debtor. Filing a Memo of Costs that includes allowable collection costs, other than accrued interest, may alert the judgment debtor that you are planning to actively enforce the judgment, because you must send them a copy of the Memo of Costs prior to filing it with the court [CCP 685.070(c), 685.070(f), 1013(a)]. If you want to surprise the debtor, plan on claiming enforcement costs later, you can do so up to two years after they were incurred [CCP 685.070(b)]. If you decide to file the Memo of Costs now to add collection costs, you usually must do so at least two weeks before a Writ is issued, unless the costs are less than $ 100 [CCP 685.070(e)]. If you previously filed a Memo of Costs, enter any statutory enforcement costs and accrued interest recorded on that form. If you've filed more than one, enter the cumulative collection costs total [CCP 699.520(e)].

Item 13: Add Items 11 and 12 and enter the sum here.

Item 14: Enter the total amount of principal reductions (credits) you have received toward the judgment (See Chapter 16 for a worksheet to keep track of payments). Also credit the value of services, or goods, you have received under any barter agreement (See Chapter 5). This is not the total money you have received from the debtor. It should not include any money received before the judgment was entered by the court. When you receive money belonging to the debtor, you would use it in the following order 1) allowed costs after judgment 2) accrued interest 3) principal reduction. This will require you to file a Memo of Cost (line 4 on Memo).

Example: Jeff paid Amy $ 100 toward the judgment. Amy had $ 35 in approved costs and $ 30 in accrued interest. The principal of the judgment is reduced by $ 35 ($100 - 35 – 30 = 35).

Item 15: Subtract Item 14 from Item 13 and enter the difference.

Item 16: File a Memo of Costs and enter the post judgment accrued interest amount here from Line 5 on Page 1 of the Memo of Costs. If debtor paid some money, interest paid for is not included here.

Item 17: Enter the fee for issuance of the Writ of Execution. The amount is currently $ 25 per Writ but you can verify by looking up Government Code 70626(a) (1).

Item 18: Total up Items 15, 16 and 17 and enter it here.

Item 19a: Multiply the amount in Item 15 by 0.0002739 to get the daily interest rate and enter it here (round off to two decimal points (must be $ 2.14, not $ 2.1411523) [CCP 699.520(g)].

Item 19b: Leave this item blank unless either of the following is true:

- you work for a public agency trying to recover costs that a court waived because of the agency's public status, or

- the court originally waived your filing fee or other court costs because of your indigency, and the judgment states that the waived fees are to be recovered from the judgment debtor.

If Item 19b applies, enter the amount waived [CCP 699.520(i)].

Item 20: Check this box only if you plan to

ask the levying officer to collect different amounts from more than one debtor. If so, get out a blank piece of paper, type

"Attachment 20" at the top and state the amounts for each debtor or use form MC-025 (copy is in the Appendix).

Back of Form: If you checked the boxes in Item 4, 7b or 8 then you will need to fill out the corresponding items on page 2.

B. Have Court Issue Writ

Once you have prepared the Memo of Costs and all of the Writs that you need (only one Memo is needed even if you are asking for a Writ for each of 50 counties), you are ready to go to the court and have them issue the Writs. For each Writ, make five photocopies, plus one copy for each additional judgment debtor. Copy both sides, even if page two is blank. Make two copies of the Memo of Costs. Put one copy, of each, away for safekeeping.

Take the original and remaining copies of the Writ and Memorandum of Costs to the court clerk's office. You will give all of them to the clerk; the clerk will affix the official seal of the court and put the date of issuance on the Writ. Many courts will not issue the Writ at the time that you bring it in. So whether you take it to the court, or mail it in, also submit a self-addressed, stamped envelope and a cover letter asking the clerk to mail everything back to you. Enclose a check for the amount of the Writ Fee required to issue the Writ in each county (there is no fee for the Memo of Costs).

C. What to Do With Your Writ

After you obtain your Writ, you must decide which assets you want to go after. Chapter 1 has a chart listing the types of assets typically available for enforcement. Remember that the Writ lasts only 180 days.

Next you will need to determine which County Sheriff's office you will have to work with. Please review the chapter that pertains to the type of asset you will be going after.

Check with that Sheriff's office, that you will be using, if they are backlogged with work. Each office is different. You don't want to ask them to levy on a bank account and then find out that they are behind by two months and do not release funds for six months (after receiving the money). If the Sheriff is too busy you may want to consider hiring an **Experienced** Registered Process Server to do the work.

Although specific counties and levying officers work differently, the general procedure is the same. You contact a levying officer (County Sheriff, Court Services Division), give them the original Writ, plus three copies, and complete their local "creditor instructions" form where you will indicate which assets you would like them to go after. Once they seize (or are unsuccessful at seizing) the asset, they will hold onto the Writ until the 180 days expire or return the original Writ to the court instead. Your preference is that they keep the Writ and you can ask them to do so if they don't (In your cover letter, state that you want the Writ held for its entire life, absent a 100% successful levy). Why do you want them to keep it? So they can use it again against other assets before the 180 days expire. If, however, they prematurely return the Writ, you can obtain a new one (for an additional fee) [CCP 699.080(g)].

If the levy satisfies your judgment, the levying officer will automatically return the Writ to the court.

As soon as the levying officer serves a levy, a personal property lien automatically applies against the asset the officer is to seize and remains in effect for two years [CCP 697.710 & 706.029] (See Chapter 4, Section C).

What if you over collect?

If you limit your enforcement efforts to one county, you don't have to worry about over-collecting. The levying officer should make sure that you receive no more than you are entitled to under the Writ. If, however, you give Writs to levying officers in two or more counties, there is a risk that you'll be overpaid. It is important to let each levying officer know who the other officers are and how to contact them. Rather than holding off on enforcing in more than one county, notify all officers of money recovered by the other officers.

If you are enforcing in more than one county, make sure to notify all officers once you have been paid in full.

EJ-130

ATTORNEY OR PARTY WITHOUT ATTORNEY *(Name, State Bar number and address):*
Amy Right
1000 My st
Mytown, Ca 90000

TELEPHONE NO.: 310-555-5555 FAX NO.:
E-MAIL ADDRESS:
ATTORNEY FOR *(Name):*
[ ] ATTORNEY FOR [✔] JUDGMENT CREDITOR [ ] ASSIGNEE OF RECORD

SUPERIOR COURT OF CALIFORNIA, COUNTY OF Los Angeles
STREET ADDRESS: 111 Hill st
MAILING ADDRESS:
CITY AND ZIP CODE: Los Angeles, Ca 90012
BRANCH NAME: Stanley Mosk Courthouse

PLAINTIFF: Amy Right

DEFENDANT: Jeff Isbad

FOR COURT USE ONLY

WRIT OF	[✔] EXECUTION (Money Judgment) [ ] POSSESSION OF [ ] Personal Property [ ] Real Property [ ] SALE

[✔] Limited Civil Case [✔] Small Claims Case
[ ] Unlimited Civil Case [ ] Other_____

CASE NUMBER: 14K5000

1. **To the Sheriff or Marshal of the County of:** Los Angeles
   You are directed to enforce the judgment described below with daily interest and your costs as provided by law.
2. **To any registered process server:** You are authorized to serve this writ only in accord with CCP 699.080 or CCP 715.040.
3. *(Name):* Amy Right
   is the [✔] judgment creditor [ ] assignee of record whose address is shown on this form above the court's name.
4. **Judgment debtor** *(name, type of legal entity stated in judgment if not a natural person, and last known address):*

   Jeff Isbad
   666 e Cra P st
   Helltown, Ca 90666

   [ ] Additional judgment debtors on next page
5. **Judgment entered** on *(date):* 01/01/2014
6. [ ] **Judgment renewed** on *(dates):*
7. **Notice of sale** under this writ
   a. [✔] has not been requested.
   b. [ ] has been requested *(see next page).*
8. [ ] Joint debtor information on next page.

[SEAL]

9. [ ] See next page for information on real or personal property to be delivered under a writ of possession or sold under a writ of sale.
10. [ ] This writ is issued on a sister-state judgment.
11. Total judgment .... $ 3,000.00
12. Costs after judgment (per filed order or memo CCP 685.090) .... $ 0.00
13. Subtotal *(add 11 and 12)* .... $ 3,000.00
14. Credits .... $ 0.00
15. Subtotal *(subtract 14 from 13)* ...... $ 3,000.00
16. Interest after judgment (per filed affidavit CCP 685.050) (not on GC 6103.5 fees)... $ 0.82
17. Fee for issuance of writ .... $ 25.00
18. **Total** *(add 15, 16, and 17)* .... $ 3,025.82
19. Levying officer:
    (a) Add daily interest from date of writ *(at the legal rate on 15)* (not on GC 6103.5 fees) of .... $ 0.82
    (b) Pay directly to court costs included in 11 and 17 (GC 6103.5, 68637; CCP 699.520(i)) .... $
20. [ ] The amounts called for in items 11–19 are different for each debtor. These amounts are stated for each debtor on Attachment 20.

Issued on *(date):* _____ Clerk, by _____, Deputy

NOTICE TO PERSON SERVED: SEE NEXT PAGE FOR IMPORTANT INFORMATION.

Page 1 of 2

Form Approved for Optional Use
Judicial Council of California
EJ-130 [Rev. January 1, 2012]

WRIT OF EXECUTION

Code of Civil Procedure, §§ 699.520, 712.010, 715.010
Government Code, § 6103.5
www.courts.ca.gov

PLAINTIFF: Amy Right	CASE NUMBER:	EJ-130
DEFENDANT: Jeff Isbad	14K5000	

— Items continued from page 1—

21. ☐ **Additional judgment debtor** *(name, type of legal entity stated in judgment if not a natural person, and last known address):*

22. ☐ **Notice of sale** has been requested by *(name and address):*

23. ☐ **Joint debtor** was declared bound by the judgment (CCP 989–994)
    a. on *(date):*
    b. name, type of legal entity stated in judgment if not a natural person, and last known address of joint debtor:

    a. on *(date):*
    b. name, type of legal entity stated in judgment if not a natural person, and last known address of joint debtor:

    c. ☐ additional costs against certain joint debtors *(itemize):*

24. ☐ *(Writ of Possession* or *Writ of Sale)* **Judgment** was entered for the following:
    a. ☐ Possession of real property: The complaint was filed on *(date):*
        (Check (1) or (2)):
        (1) ☐ The Prejudgment Claim of Right to Possession was served in compliance with CCP 415.46. The judgment includes all tenants, subtenants, named claimants, and other occupants of the premises.
        (2) ☐ The Prejudgment Claim of Right to Possession was NOT served in compliance with CCP 415.46.
            (a) $ was the daily rental value on the date the complaint was filed.
            (b) The court will hear objections to enforcement of the judgment under CCP 1174.3 on the following dates *(specify):*
    b. ☐ Possession of personal property.
        ☐ If delivery cannot be had, then for the value *(itemize in 24e)* specified in the judgment or supplemental order.
    c. ☐ Sale of personal property.
    d. ☐ Sale of real property.
    e. Description of property:

NOTICE TO PERSON SERVED

WRIT OF EXECUTION OR SALE. Your rights and duties are indicated on the accompanying *Notice of Levy* (Form EJ-150).
WRIT OF POSSESSION OF PERSONAL PROPERTY. If the levying officer is not able to take custody of the property, the levying officer will make a demand upon you for the property. If custody is not obtained following demand, the judgment may be enforced as a money judgment for the value of the property specified in the judgment or in a supplemental order.
WRIT OF POSSESSION OF REAL PROPERTY. If the premises are not vacated within five days after the date of service on the occupant or, if service is by posting, within five days after service on you, the levying officer will remove the occupants from the real property and place the judgment creditor in possession of the property. Except for a mobile home, personal property remaining on the premises will be sold or otherwise disposed of in accordance with CCP 1174 unless you or the owner of the property pays the judgment creditor the reasonable cost of storage and takes possession of the personal property not later than 15 days after the time the judgment creditor takes possession of the premises.
► *A Claim of Right to Possession* form accompanies this writ (unless the Summons was served in compliance with CCP 415.46).

WRIT OF EXECUTION

MC-012

ATTORNEY OR PARTY WITHOUT ATTORNEY *(Name, State Bar number, and address):*
Amy Right
1000 My st
Mytown, Ca 90000

TELEPHONE NO.: 310-555-5555 FAX NO.:
ATTORNEY FOR *(Name):* In Pro Per

NAME OF COURT: Superior Court of California
STREET ADDRESS: 111 Hill st
MAILING ADDRESS:
CITY AND ZIP CODE: Los Angeles, Ca 90012
BRANCH NAME: Stanley Mosk Courthouse

PLAINTIFF: Amy Right

DEFENDANT: Jeff Isbad

FOR COURT USE ONLY

MEMORANDUM OF COSTS AFTER JUDGMENT, ACKNOWLEDGMENT OF CREDIT, AND DECLARATION OF ACCRUED INTEREST	CASE NUMBER: 14K5000

1. I claim the following costs after judgment incurred within the last two years *(indicate if there are multiple items in any category)*:

		Dates Incurred	Amount
a	Preparing and issuing abstract of judgment		$
b	Recording and indexing abstract of judgment		$
c	Filing notice of judgment lien on personal property		$
d	Issuing writ of execution, to extent not satisfied by Code Civ. Proc., § 685.050 *(specify county):*		$
e	Levying officers fees, to extent not satisfied by Code Civ. Proc., § 685.050 or wage garnishment		$
f	Approved fee on application for order for appearance of judgment debtor, or other approved costs under Code Civ. Proc., § 708.110 et seq.		$
g	Attorney fees, if allowed by Code Civ. Proc., § 685.040		$
h	Other: *(Statute authorizing cost):*		$
i	Total of claimed costs for current memorandum of costs *(add items a-h)*		$

2. All previously allowed postjudgment costs: . . . . $

3. **Total** of all postjudgment costs (add items 1 and 2): . . . . **TOTAL** $

4. **Acknowledgment of Credit.** I acknowledge total credit to date (including returns on levy process and direct payments) in the amount of: $

5. **Declaration of Accrued Interest.** Interest on the judgment accruing at the legal rate from the date of entry on balances due after partial satisfactions and other credits in the amount of: $ 0.82

6. I am the ✔ judgment creditor ☐ agent for the judgment creditor ☐ attorney for the judgment creditor.
I have knowledge of the facts concerning the costs claimed above. To the best of my knowledge and belief, the costs claimed are correct, reasonable, and necessary, and have not been satisfied.

I declare under penalty of perjury under the laws of the State of California that the foregoing is true and correct.

Date: 02/01/2014

Amy Right
(TYPE OR PRINT NAME) ▶ (SIGNATURE OF DECLARANT)

NOTICE TO THE JUDGMENT DEBTOR
If this memorandum of costs is filed at the same time as an application for a writ of execution, any statutory costs, *not exceeding $100 in aggregate* and not already allowed by the court, may be included in the writ of execution. *The fees sought under this memorandum may be disallowed by the court upon a motion to tax filed by the debtor, notwithstanding the fees having been included in the writ of execution.* (Code Civ. Proc., § 685.070(e).) A motion to tax costs claimed in this memorandum must be filed within 10 days after service of the memorandum. (Code Civ. Proc., § 685.070(c).)

(Proof of service on reverse)

Form Adopted for Mandatory Use
Judicial Council of California
MC-012 [Rev. January 1, 2011]

MEMORANDUM OF COSTS AFTER JUDGMENT, ACKNOWLEDGMENT OF CREDIT, AND DECLARATION OF ACCRUED INTEREST

Code of Civil Procedure
§ 685.070
www.courts.ca.gov

SHORT TITLE: Right v Isbad	CASE NUMBER: 14K5000

MC-012

PROOF OF SERVICE
☐ Mail ☐ Personal Service

1. At the time of service I was at least 18 years of age and not a party to this legal action.

2. My residence or business address is *(specify)*:

3. I mailed or personally delivered a copy of the *Memorandum of Costs After Judgment, Acknowledgment of Credit, and Declaration of Accrued Interest* as follows *(complete either a or b)*:

   a. ☐ **Mail.** I am a resident of or employed in the county where the mailing occurred.
      (1) I enclosed a copy in an envelope AND
         (a) ☐ **deposited** the sealed envelope with the United States Postal Service with the postage fully prepaid.
         (b) ☐ **placed** the envelope for collection and mailing on the date and at the place shown in items below following our ordinary business practices. I am readily familiar with this business's practice for collecting and processing correspondence for mailing. On the same day that correspondence is placed for collection and mailing, it is deposited in the ordinary course of business with the United States Postal Service in a sealed envelope with postage fully prepaid.
      (2) The envelope was addressed and mailed as follows:
         (a) Name of person served:
         (b) Address on envelope:

         (c) Date of mailing:
         (d) Place of mailing *(city and state)*:

   b. ☐ **Personal delivery.** I personally delivered a copy as follows:
      (1) Name of person served:
      (2) Address where delivered:

      (3) Date delivered:
      (4) Time delivered:

I declare under penalty of perjury under the laws of the State of California that the foregoing is true and correct.

Date:

....
(TYPE OR PRINT NAME)

▶ _____
(SIGNATURE OF DECLARANT)

MC-012 [Rev. January 1, 2011] **MEMORANDUM OF COSTS AFTER JUDGMENT, ACKNOWLEDGMENT OF CREDIT, AND DECLARATION OF ACCRUED INTEREST** Page two

Chapter 8

Enforcement from Deposit Accounts

A. Finding Deposit Accounts.	8/2
1. Check Your Papers	8/2
2. Ask the Debtor	8/2
3. Check Government Records	8/2
4. Trash Run	8/3
5. Divorce Records	8/3
6. Bankruptcy Records	8/3
7. Subpoena Vehicle Records	8/3
8. Subpoena Rental or Mortgage Records	8/3
9. Subpoena Information from Employer	8/4
10. Third Party Examination	8/4
11. Shotgun Levy of 5 Banks in Immediate Area	8/4
12. Subpoena the top 10 banks in the Area	8/4
13. Property Records at the County	8/4
14. Subpoena Utility Companies	8/4
B. Figuring Out if the Funds are Exempt	8/4
C. Levying on Joint and Business Accounts	8/6
D. How to Levy on Bank Accounts and Safe-Deposit Boxes	8/6
1. Determine Your Timing	8/7
2. Provide Instructions for Levying Officer	8/7
3. Serve Notice of Levy.	8/8
4. Distribute Proceeds	8/9

Collection Factor	High	Moderate	Low
Potential cost to you		✓	✓
Potential for producing $$$	✓		
Potential for settlement		✓	
Potential time & trouble		✓	
Potential for bankruptcy		✓	

This chapter shows you how to locate and recover money from deposit accounts: savings, checking, money market and mutual fund accounts in banks, savings and loans or credit unions. We also show you how to look for cash or other liquid assets, such as securities and gems, in safe deposit boxes. For convenience, we use the term "bank" to refer to banks, savings and loans and credit unions.

If you can find this kind of asset, and it is not exempt under California's debtor protection laws, you are miles ahead in the collection game. What do we mean by exempt? Legally, the judgment debtor is allowed to keep cash that they received from certain sources, such as Social Security. No matter how large your judgment, if the debtor can prove that the money came from exempt sources, you cannot take it. But the debtor must file a form called a Claim of Exemption with the levying officer, who collected the money, and debtors rarely do so. If they don't file the form, the levying officer will release the funds, to you, without worrying about where they came from. If they file a Claim of Exemption and the court rules that the money is exempt, the levying officer will return the money to the debtor.

> **You might be able to skip Section A**
> If you know the judgment debtor's bank account number or the institution where they bank, skip to Section B, below. If you need to find deposit accounts, read Section A.

A. Finding Deposit Accounts

A levying officer cannot seize the money in a bank account, or the contents of a safe deposit box, unless they have the name and the address of where to serve the documents. Once you have the name of the bank you can serve any branch of that bank unless the bank has listed a specific address to serve the levy at. You can look up if there is an exclusion, by going to the California Department of Financial Institutions website and searching by the name of the bank. The website will also give you any other restriction that the levying officer will need to know.
http://www.dbo.ca.gov/Laws_&_Regs/legislation/service_of_legal_process/

Be discreet - If the debtor gets a whiff that you are closing in on a deposit account, they will surely move the money out of the account. Then you'll have to start from scratch.

1. Check Your Papers

You can easily find the debtor's bank if you have a copy of a check written by the debtor, which may be the case if, you had a business relationship with them. You may also have this information on a credit application or other form you had the debtor complete.

2. Ask the Debtor

If you haven't done so already, schedule a Debtor's Examination, following the procedures described in Chapter 6. At the exam, you can ask the debtor about their bank accounts and you can ask the debtor to bring copies of bank statements, using a Subpoena Duces Tecum.

3. Check Government Records

If the debtor runs a business, you may be able to find bank account information from public records. For example, if the debtor has applied for a Seller's Permit, they were required to list banks and account numbers on the application. To access these records, contact the Board of Equalization at 800-

400-7115. And if the debtor has been

involved in other lawsuits, court records and filings in those cases may include banking information.

4. Trash Run or Dumpster Dive

This is a two-step process:

1) Call the city and find out when the trash, on the debtor's particular street, is picked up. Also check to make sure that there are no laws against taking items out of someone else's trash cans. Make sure you explain that the cans will be on the sidewalk or street (you will not be trespassing), you are not stealing recyclables, and that you collect things that others throw away to give to charity (don't mention you are looking for bank statements).

2) Late at night, on the day before trash day, go to the debtor's home and bring trash bags filled with newspaper. The idea is not just to take the trash, but to take it and then replace it with new trash. This way the debtor is not aware that anything is missing. The information found in trash cans is invaluable. You may find a lot of things that will help you enforce the judgment.

5. Divorce Records

Divorce Records are a treasure trove of information. In most cases, divorce records are public information. The added benefits are that you learn what assets each spouse got to keep and how much each party has to pay the other party.

6. Bankruptcy Records

A lot of debtors have filed for bankruptcy, and they don't know the wealth of information they have left behind. Bankruptcy is a public proceeding. Debtors have to give the court their social security numbers and list all assets, including bank accounts, on the Bankruptcy Petition. Viewing the debtors Bankruptcy schedules provide a significant amount of information on assets and income sources. But there is more Good news! Bankruptcy petitions are online!

Go to **http://pacer.psc.uscourts.gov/** and set up an account. It's free to set up with minimal charges for copy fees. Then spend a little time seeing how the site works, navigate to Bankruptcy Courts, and search for the debtor's bankruptcy filing. Even if your debtor filed Bankruptcy eight years ago, the records may still be online. And even if the Bank information is old, a lot of debtors have trouble switching to a new bank. If the Bankruptcy information is relatively old, you can ask the Bankruptcy Court where you can view archived records.

7. Subpoena Vehicle Records

Does your debtor own, rent, or lease a vehicle? The license plate will often tell you where they purchased it. Then subpoena the loan or lease applications, purchase contract, and copies of the down payment checks from the dealer. To get the best auto deal, the debtor was probably quite liberal in stating their assets and income. You may also find out where the debtor works. Bank accounts will also be listed. Loan or Lease Applications are tremendous sources of information. Accessing the debtor's credit report will also provide the name of the lender that financed their vehicle. Subpoena them for the loan application, income documentation, and copies of the checks used to make the monthly payment.

8. Subpoena Rental or Mortgage Applications

Whether your debtor rents or owns a home, there is an available paper trail. If the debtor rents, serve the manager, owner or landlord a subpoena for "full application and all other records relating to the rental of properties, as well as any copies of debtor's rental checks".

If the debtor owns a home, you can probably go online a get a copy of the "deed of trust." Then you'll know who the mortgage holder is, and you can immediately subpoena the mortgage application. Again, the debtor will have made a very positive assessment of their assets.

9. Subpoena Information from Employer

Some employee information is confidential. However, which bank the debtor's wages are sent for direct deposit is fair game to request. Subpoena Employer records with a Notice to Consumer.

10. Third Party Examination

In many states you can require that someone who owes the debtor money or who even "knows" about debtor's assets can be required to appear in court and answers questions. Check with your court, and check the codes of your state online. If it's doable, do it. Bring the person in and ask the questions you want, including where does the debtor bank. In California it is possible to bring in the landlord of the debtor, and even their employer, but it varies by court.

11. Shotgun Levy of 5 Banks in Area

Most people bank within a 2 mile radius of where they live or work. So go to Yahoo Maps or Map Quest, put in the debtor's address, and check to see what banks are in the immediate area. Choose the five main ones, get a writ and have the Sheriff, or Marshall, levy on all five of them. You will need a Writ of Execution and you will have
to pay for 5 levies. But you may get a 'hit' on one or more bank accounts!

12. Subpoena the top 10 banks in the area

On the subpoena you might request "Any and all checking and savings statements of the debtor over the past year". Most of the banks will simply write back saying there are no accounts there. That's fine. But then one day you may get a phone call from the bank's business department who tells you that there is a copy fee that has to be paid. Bingo! You may then ask whether that will include last month's statement. Bingo! The account or accounts are still open! Now you might want to 'levy' the bank right away. If the debtor objects to a subpoena at a particular bank, levy that bank.

13. Property Records at the County

If your debtor owns real property they will pay property taxes. In some states and in some counties the check you write is part of the public record at the Assessor's Office. More and more these records are user friendly. What used to be on microfiche and microfilm is in many cases on the county computer, and even online. Check the records at the county. See if it applies to you.

14. Subpoena Utility Company

Whether the debtor rents an apartment or owns a home, they need utilities (electricity, water, gas, cable TV, etc.). Find out what companies service the debtor's neighborhood and subpoena copies of the payment checks that the debtor used to pay their bill.

B. Figuring Out if the Funds Are Exempt

As mentioned, some of the money in a deposit account may be exempt. If you try to levy on an account containing exempt cash, it is up to the debtor to file a Claim of Exemption with the court and prove that the money came from an exempt source. Few debtors file such a claim. Even if the debtor does, it's possible that the debtor has some exempt money but mixes it with non-exempt money and cannot prove that the money grabbed by the levying officer came from the exempt source. In such a situation, you can oppose the debtor's Claim of Exemption. Also, if your judgment is for child support, most exemptions won't apply (See Chapter 15 for information on opposing a Claim of Exemption). There are some sources of income that are exempt without filing a Claim of Exemption, like Social Security and Public Benefit payments [CCP 708.080(b) & 703.030(b)]. In these cases the banks themselves will sometimes reject the levy for those reasons.

The following is a list of sources of cash deposited in bank accounts that the debtor may claim as exempt. The debtor can exempt these monies only if they are held in personal, not business accounts.

• Wages: The debtor may exempt up to 75% of their wages. If the debtor's wages were garnished prior to the deposit, the ungarnished amount is fully exempt [CCP 704.070(b)].

• Social Security and Disability: The debtor may exempt 100% of their Social Security and Disability income, up to $ 2,425 for one account owner [CCP 704.080(b)(2)] or $ 3,650 for two account owners [CCP 04.080(b)(4)] (if both receive the benefit). If by direct deposit then exemption is automatic.

• **Public benefits**: The debtor may exempt 100% of Veterans', welfare, unemployment and workers' compensation benefits. Funds of up to $1,225 for one depositor [CCP 704.080(b) (1)] or $1,825 for two, or more, depositor [CCP 704.030(b) (3)] (if both receive the benefit). If by direct deposit then exemption is automatic. Excess amounts may also be exempt, but if there is an amount, in the account, in excess of the automatically exempt amount, then the bank will freeze the excess, notify the levying officer, who in turn will notify you. You must then file a Notice of Opposition [CCP 703.560 & 708.080(e)] (see Chapter 15), set a hearing date, provide the levying officer a copy, and serve the debtor with the Notice, all within 5 days. Otherwise the levying officer will release the money back to the debtor. At the hearing, it is up to the debtor to prove that all funds are exempt [CCP 708.080(e) (4)].

• **Retirement plans:** The debtor may exempt public and private retirement benefits, including IRAs and Keoghs, with one exception. If the debtor periodically receives the proceeds of a private retirement plan, those proceeds are exempt only to the same extent as wages [CCP 704.110(d) & 704.115(b)].

• **Insurance proceeds:** The debtor may claim as exempt 100% of disability and health insurance benefits, matured (paid out) life insurance proceeds needed to support the debtor and the debtor's family and loan proceeds of up to $9,700 for an unmarried debtor and $19,400 for a married couple on an unmatured life insurance policy. The debtor may generally claim as exempt homeowner's insurance proceeds up to six months after received or up to $1,900 on an auto insurance policy, if the vehicle was lost or stolen [CCP 704.100(a) & (b), 704.130(a) &704.720(b)].

• **Personal injury awards:** The debtor may claim as exempt personal injury and wrongful death awards to the extent they are necessary to support the judgment debtor and the judgment debtor's family, with one exception. If you are a healthcare provider with a judgment for services rendered in connection with the injury or death, the funds may not be claimed as exempt [CCP 704.140 & 704.150].

• **Financial aid:** The debtor may exempt funds received for financial aid to attend an institution of higher learning [CCP 704.190(b)].

• **Miscellaneous:** Other sources of income a debtor may claim as exempt: up to $1,225 paid to an inmate [CCP 704.090(a)], benefits paid in order to relocate [CCP 704.180] and union benefits paid during a labor dispute [CCP 704.120].

C. Levying on Joint and Business Accounts

If the account is in the debtor's name alone, whether the debtor is a business entity or an individual, the entire account will be subject to your levy. If the account belongs to the judgment debtor and their spouse, the entire account will be subject to your levy, but the spouse will have an opportunity to object to the levy.

EXAMPLE 1: The judgment is against Stewart Kingfish. The account is in the name of Stewart Kingfish. You may levy against the entire account.

EXAMPLE 2: The judgment is against Stewart Kingfish, Inc., a California corporation. You may levy against any account carrying the name of Stewart Kingfish, Inc. You may not levy against an account belonging to Stewart Kingfish unless you amend the judgment to name them as an individual.

EXAMPLE 3: The judgment is against Stewart Kingfish as an individual. The account is in the name of Stewart Kingfish, Inc., a solely owned corporation. You may not levy against the corporate account unless you amend the judgment to name the corporation as a defendant.

EXAMPLE 4: The judgment is against Stewart Kingfish and Kingfish, a California partnership. You may levy against a Stewart Kingfish and Kingfish partnership account. If your judgment is against Stewart Kingfish, one of the partners, you may not levy against the account without a special order of the court called a "charging" order. This book does not cover charging orders.

EXAMPLE 5: The judgment is against Stewart Kingfish as an individual. The account is in the name of Kingfish Consultants, an individual proprietorship owned by Stewart Kingfish. You may levy against the Kingfish Consultants account if you provide the levying officer with a certified copy of the fictitious business name statement filed by Stewart Kingfish [CCP 700.160(b)(3)].

If the account is in the name of the judgment debtor's spouse, either alone or with others, you may levy on it. But you must provide the levying officer with a declaration showing that the parties are married [CCP 700.160(b) (2)]. A sample declaration appears in Section D, below. The spouse and any third parties will have the opportunity to object to the levy.

If the account is in the name of the debtor and someone else, not their spouse, you may not be able to levy on the other person's share of the funds. Most deposit accounts are presumed to be held in joint tenancy. However the law provides that an account belongs to the parties in proportion to the net contribution of each party [Probate Code 5301(a)]. In some cases, the bank will turn over an entire joint account, figuring it is up to the non-debtor to object.

Because of the need to protect the rights of non- debtors, you may be required to post an undertaking for twice the amount on which you are seeking to levy, or $ 10,000 (whichever is less) [CCP 720.160(b) & 720.260(b)]. If so, check with a title insurance company or bonding company. The bond normally costs between 2% and 4% of its face amount. This cost is not recoverable from the bonding company, but you can recover it from the judgment debtor by claiming the amount on a Memo of Costs (See Chapter 16).

D. How to Levy on Bank Accounts and Safe Deposit Boxes

To levy on an account, you must first obtain a Writ of Execution (See Chapter 7). If there are accounts (based on where the bank must be served, see section A page 1) in more than one county, you will need a Writ for each county. Once you have your Writ, follow these steps.

1. Determine Your Timing

If you plan to levy on a checking account, timing is important. The amount of money in it probably fluctuates a lot during the month. Unless you time the levy carefully, the account may not have enough funds to make your efforts cost effective. If you plan on levying on a savings account or the contents of a safe deposit box, timing is less of an issue. The balances are usually highest around the 1st of the month, especially now that many paychecks are direct deposited into accounts.

If you move to levy when the account balance is low, you not only collect little money, but also alert the debtor to your efforts. They will almost certainly move the account. There is an old saying: "If you shoot at the Emperor, don't miss." In the same manner, when you levy on a bank account, count on doing it only once.

The levying officer will normally need a little lead time before making the levy. Therefore, you will want to deliver your instructions well in advance of when you want the actual levy to occur. Check with the levying officer to find out how far in advance they will need your papers; some may have a backlog.

Large judgments normally can't be satisfied in full by levying on a checking account. The best you can do is to get as large a portion as possible of the money you are owed. If you have a $2,500 judgment and levy on $800 in a checking account, you'll probably need to use other enforcement efforts to go after the rest.

Although more expensive than using sheriffs as levying officers, Registered Process Servers (RPS's) provide maximum flexibility for bank levies. RPS's can be directed to levy on bank accounts on specific days, i.e. Fridays when most businesses make payroll distributions or on the first day of the month when many governmental agencies send out disbursement checks. RPS's can also be directed to levy against multiple banks on the same day to minimize the risk of the debtor attempting to close accounts or change banks.

2. Provide Instructions for Levying Officer

To find the levying officer for a given county, call the sheriff's Court Services office and ask if it levies on civil money judgments. You can find their number by looking up "sheriff civil process (name of county) county". If not, ask if another public official does. If the local levying officer doesn't levy on bank accounts, is backlogged or has a reputation for inefficiency, consider hiring an <u>experienced</u> registered process server (See Chapter 21). Using a process server is more expensive, you still have to pay the levying officer and the server, but they can be faster, more experienced, and more flexible for those times when you need the bank served on a particular day. Fees paid to a registered process server are usually fully coverable as a statutory cost and can be added on the Memo of Cost [CCP 685.095, 699.080(f), & 1033.5(a) (4) (B)].

When you find the right person, call and find out the fee, how many copies of the Writ are needed and whether the office has local instruction forms for you to use. Prepare your instructions for the levying officer using their form or the "Instructions to Levying Officer" form letter in the Appendix. Provide as much of the following information as possible:

- name, branch and street address of the financial institution

- account number (if known, but add "and all other accounts")

- debtor's social security number

- a statement that you are seeking personal property

- name or names in which the account is held

If you want the levying officer to seize from more than one bank, prepare separate instructions and provide separate copies of the Writ for each seizure. For example, if you want the levying officer to grab the debtor's savings account in bank X and the debtor's checking account in bank Y, prepare two sets of instructions and be prepared to pay separate fees for each. Remember, if you collect more than the total balance due on your judgment, you must return the surplus.

If the account is held under the name of the debtor's spouse, you will have to complete a declaration to that effect so that the levying officer can seize the account. A sample declaration is provided here.

A sample Instructions to Levying Officer form letter is provided. Make the necessary copies of the Writ and your instructions (and your declaration, if the account is held in a spouse's name), keeping one set for your records. Then mail or bring the documents and fee to the levying officer.

Sample Declaration to Levy on Bank Account Held in Spouse's Name

I, Amy Right, declare as follows:

I obtained a judgment against Jeff Isbad from the Los Angeles County California Superior Court on January 1, 2014, in Case Number 14K5000.

I have knowledge of and believe to be true that Judgment Debtor Jeff Isbad is married to, and was married, to Cruela Isbad, SSN# 555-55-5555, at the time the judgment was awarded. CCP 700.160(b) (2) allows levies against deposit accounts in the name of a spouse.

I swear under penalty of perjury under the laws of the state of California that the foregoing is true and correct.

10/19/2014   (sign your name)
DATE   Amy Right

Sample Instructions to Levying Officer

October 19, 2014

Sheriff, Los Angeles County:

Enclosed please find an original and three copies of a Writ of Execution and a check for $40.

Please serve the Writ of Execution and levy against any bank accounts and safe deposit boxes belonging to Jeff Isbad at National Bank of Commerce, 567 Andrews Avenue, Santa Cruz. One known account number is: 034-731078. The debtor's social security number is 555-55-1234. Please collect from any other accounts owned by Jeff Isbad at that bank. Please send any funds collected to me at 1000 My st, Mytown, CA 90000.

Please hold this Writ until I notify you by phone that I want it served, and then levy that same day or as soon thereafter as possible. [Or, please perform this levy between the third and sixth day of the month]. Please do not return this writ, to the court until it expires or is paid off.

If you levy on a safe deposit box, ask the judgment debtor to open it voluntarily. If the box contains personal property other than cash that must be stored and sold, contact me first for further instructions. Contact me for further instructions before using force to open any safe deposit box. All property being sought in this Writ is personal property.

Sincerely,
Amy Right

3. Serve Notice of Levy

The levying officer uses the Writ and your written instructions to fill out a Notice of Levy, which they serve on the person in the institution in charge of the debtor's account. The debtor gets a copy by mail. Any other debtor listed in the judgment should also receive a copy by mail.

The Notice of Levy includes the amount necessary to satisfy the judgment. It also advises the institution that it has up to ten days to claim priority over the levy and that the funds must be frozen in the interim. If the bank objects, which is unlikely unless the account is virtually empty, we suggest that you drop the matter or consult a lawyer. If the debtor files a Claim of Exemption opposing the levy, you must set a court hearing where the merits of the levy can be decided by a judge (See Chapter 15).

4. Distribute Proceeds

The bank should mail a notice (called a Memorandum of Garnishee) to the levying officer within 10 days of the date of the levy and the levying officer, in turn, should mail a copy of the notice to you [CCP 701.030(a) & (c)]. This notice will state 1) what amount of money the bank is holding/sending to the levying officer 2) if there is another person named on the account, and their name. Once the levying officer receives the proceeds of the levy, they will disburse them to you. There will be a 30+ day delay, it shouldn't be too long but it depends on the backlog at that sheriff's branch. If you're concerned that you've fallen through the cracks, call the levying officer.

Safe-Deposit Boxes

When levying on a safe deposit box, the levying officer is faced with several choices. They can:
• ask the judgment debtor to voluntarily open the box
• forcibly open the box if the judgment debtor refuses to cooperate, or
• require you to obtain a seizure order from the court allowing the box to be opened (see Chapter 19, Section A1).

If the safe deposit box must be forcibly opened, the bank will require you to post a deposit (usually $100-$300) to cover the costs. Before paying this large fee, ask the Bank when was the last time the debtor accessed the Safe Deposit Box? If this date is not recent, the Safe Deposit Box may not contain liquid assets that can be used to pay down the judgment.

A safe deposit box typically contains items such as insurance policies, stock certificates, bonds, title certificates, jewelry and/or cash. Some or all will be seized by the levying officer. Cash and bonds can be given to you outright; tangible items such as jewelry must be stored and sold by the levying officer. For this, you will need to post a large deposit to cover storage and sales costs. If you don't want this property sold, it may not be worth it, the levying officer will return it to the judgment debtor.

Blank Page

Chapter 9

Collecting from Wages

A. Limits on Wage Garnishments	9/3
1. Debtor is Already Subject to Another Garnishment	9/3
2. Debtor Needs the Money for Basic Support	9/3
3. Debtor is a Federal Employee or in the Military	9/3
4. Debtor Receives Public Benefits or Payments from Pension Plan	9/4
B. How to Garnish Wages	9/4
1. Locate Debtor's Workplace	9/5
2. Complete Application for Earnings Withholding Order	9/5
3. Provide Instructions for Levying Officer	9/6
4. Wait for Employer to Complete Return	9/6
5. If Employer Does Not Cooperate.	9/7
6. If Debtor Files Claim of Exemption	9/8
7. Get Your Money	9/8

Collection Factor	High	Moderate	Low
Potential cost to you			✓
Potential for producing $$$	✓		
Potential for settlement	✓		
Potential time and trouble		✓	
Potential for bankruptcy		✓	

If the debtor is working, you may be able to intercept up to 25% of their wages (up to 50% for child or spousal support) to satisfy your judgment. This process is called a wage garnishment. You can garnish wages relatively quickly and cheaply if:

- the debtor receives a regular wage, that is, they are not self-employed

- the debtor's pay is above the poverty line

- other wage garnishments aren't already in effect, unless your wage garnishment is for child or spousal support, and

- the debtor does not quit the job, contest the garnishment or file for bankruptcy.

A wage garnishment requires little effort on your part. You give the levying officer information about where the judgment debtor works, provide a Writ of Execution (Chapter 7) and pay a modest fee of $ 35 [Government Code 26750]. Then you simply wait; the levying officer collects money from the employer and gives it to you. You can end the wage garnishment if you and the judgment debtor make an agreement about payment of the judgment. If the judgment debtor is married you can garnish their spouse's wages, but you need a court order [CCP 706.109].

A wage garnishment is often a strong incentive for a debtor to make arrangements to pay off a judgment; many people want to avoid the embarrassment and inconvenience of having their salary reduced. Also, despite a federal law that bars an employer from firing an employee whose wages are garnished due to a single judgment [15 U.S.C. 1674], most employees believe that a garnishment won't win them brownie points with their bosses. And the law does not bar an employer from firing an employee whose wages are garnished to pay more than one judgment.

Oftentimes, debtors may be willing to voluntarily pay off the judgment in installment payments in order to avoid the embarrassment of the wage garnishment. In this instance, you can negotiate significantly shorter repayment terms than the wage garnishment repayment schedule. Many debtors will sincerely appreciate this voluntary repayment option versus the embarrassment from the wage garnishment

But instead of inducing the debtor to settle, a wage garnishment could have the opposite effect, pushing a debtor to quit their job or worse, file for bankruptcy. The loss of part of a paycheck, coupled with having an employer know about their financial problems, may cause a debtor to look for a quick solution to relieve the pressure. If you choose to garnish wages, remember that you walk a fine line between making great progress on enforcing your judgment and closing off any possibility of satisfying your judgment.

The debtor probably won't go bankrupt or quit their job if the judgment isn't for very much, they are a well-established member of the community without other debt problems, they own their own well-established business or they own real estate with significant equity.

A. Limits on Wage Garnishments

Under federal law, you cannot garnish more than 25% of the debtor's disposable income. There is an additional protection for low income people. A wage earner must be left with a weekly wage equal to 40 times the current California's minimum wage in effect at the time the earnings are payable [CCP 706.050(a)(2) & 15 U.S.C. 1673(a)(1)]. This means that the debtor gets to keep the first $400, per week, of their take home pay; you can garnish 25% of the excess.

If your judgment is for child or spousal support, you can garnish at least 50% of the judgment debtor's take home pay after the first $400.00 per week. A judge has the discretion to increase that to as much as 60% if the debtor is not currently supporting a child or spouse [15 U.S.C. § 1673(b)(2)(B) & CCP 706.052(c)].

You may face some additional limitations, or at least potential obstacles, in a few situations.

1. Debtor Is Already Subject to Another Garnishment

You cannot garnish wages if they are already being garnished by another creditor [CCP 706.023(c)], unless you have a judgment for alimony or child support [CCP 706.030(b) (2)] or you have a judgment for elder abuse or dependent adult financial abuse {CCP 706.023(d)}. Support judgments receive first wage garnishment priority, and as mentioned, can be used to grab up to 60% of the judgment debtor's net earnings. If neither exception applies, the employer will reject your garnishment and you will have to apply again when the previous creditor's garnishment ends.

2. Debtor Needs the Money for Basic Support

The debtor has the right to object to your garnishment on the ground that they need the money for their own support or the support of a spouse or children [CCP 706.051(b)], except if the judgment is for 1) some types of legal fees, wages owed an employee, 3) support. The debtor makes this objection by filing a Claim of Exemption (Chapter 15).

3. Debtor Is a Federal Employee or in the Military

You can garnish the wages of most federal employees, but the process may prove cumbersome [5 U.S.C. 5520a] (You can't garnish the wages of a seaman, longshoreman or harbor worker [33 U.S.C. 902(3) & 916]. But see Chapter 19 for possible use of an assignment order).

To garnish the wages of a Federal Employee you must complete the form titled "Application for Federal Employee Commercial Garnishment", a copy of which is in the Appendix. Attached is a completed sample copy of the Application for Federal Employee Commercial Garnishment and instructions on how to complete it. A blank copy is in the Appendix and available at www.opm.gov/forms.

Title and address of employing agency's designated agent: Enter the name and address of the director of personnel for the agency where the debtor works. This is where you will send the documents. A government publication called the Code of Federal Regulations (CFR) contains a listing the address and phone number for every federal agency, indicating the appropriate official to receive your papers. The CFR is available at a law library or large public library, you want to look at 5 CFR 581.501, Appendix A (most employees), or 5 CFR 582.501 (certain military employees). You can also look up the CFR at www.access.gpo.gov/nara/cfr/cfr-retrieve.html. You'll be asked to enter the Year (most recent), Title (5), Part (581 or 582) and Section (501). If the debtor works for the 1) Department of Defense, 2) Health and Human Services, 3) Dept. of Veterans Affairs, 4) Broadcast Board of Governors or 5) Department of Energy, then the Director of Personnel will be:

Defense Finance and Accounting Service
Cleveland DFAS-HGA/CL PO Box 998002
Cleveland, OH 44199-8002
Tel: 888-332-7411
Fax: 877-622-5930
http://www.dfas.mil/garnishment/civgarnishment/faqs

Once you have the address and phone number, call the office to verify the address and to find out exactly what forms, and how many copies, the agency needs.

Item A1: Enter the debtor's name.

Item A2: Enter the debtor's birth date. If you don't know, write "unknown". You should include it.

Item A3: Enter the debtor's Social Security number. If you don't know, write "unknown". You should include.

Item A4: Enter the name of the federal agency for which the debtor works, the debtor's title (or job description) if you know it and the address, including zip code, where the debtor actually works.

Item A5: Enter the debtor's last known home address.

Item A6: Leave this blank.

Item B1: Enter the name of the court that issued your Writ of Execution, such as "Superior Court of California – Los Angeles," and the case number.

Item B2: Cross off the dollar sign and enter "25% of net earnings until judgment is satisfied."

Item B3: Enter 180 days from the date the Writ was issued.

Item B4: Check the "no" box.

Item B5: Check the "yes" box.

Item B6: Check the "yes" box.

Items C1-C4: Enter the requested information about yourself.

Items D1-D5: If you would like the money directly deposited into your bank account, rather than mailed to you, enter the requested information. Otherwise, leave these blank.

Once you send the form, the agency is supposed to begin the garnishment within 30 days, but your garnishment will be subject to all other garnishments served before that date. Child and spousal support garnishments always get first priority.

To garnish the wages of a person on active military duty you need to complete a "Involuntary Allotment Application" (Form DD2653. You can find the form and instructions at http://www.dfas.mil/garnishment/milcommdebt/debtcollect.html. You will need to attach a certified copy of your judgment with the application.

4. Debtor Receives Public Benefits or Payments from Pension Plan

Social Security benefits can never be garnished. Unless your judgment is for child or spousal support, you can't garnish unemployment insurance, workers' compensation awards, relocation benefits or disability or health insurance benefits. Garnishing payments made from a retirement plan also are very difficult. Most retirement plans contain "anti-alienation" provisions barring the plan administrator from paying anyone except the plan holder or beneficiary, such as a spouse. If the debtor receives these benefits, you may be better off looking elsewhere for payment.

B. How to Garnish Wages

Before you can garnish wages, you must obtain a Writ of Execution directed to the county where you will be serving the garnishment documents (See Chapter 7). Once you have the Writ, follow the steps below.

1. Locate Debtor's Workplace

To garnish the debtor's wages, you need their employer's name and address. Skip to Section B2, below, if you have this information and have called to verify it. If you don't have a clue about the debtor's employment, here are some suggestions for tracking it down.

- Don't **violate the debt collection laws.** When speaking with others, avoid mentioning your judgment (Chapter 3).

- Debtor's **examination:** You can request that the debtor appear in court and answer questions concerning their employment at a debtor's examination (Chapter 6).

- Debtor's **statement:** If you are collecting a small claims judgment, the debtor is supposed to file a debtor's statement within 30 days, this should include the name of their employer (Chapter 6).

- **State employment:** If you think the debtor may work for the state, go to the website of California's Dept. of General Services, Telecommunications Division, at www.cold.ca.gov/state_employees.asp. Here, you can type in someone's name and find out whether they work for a government agency. If the person works for the state, this site will give you contact information. You can also get this information over the phone, by calling 800-807-6755.

- **Unions:** The debtor may belong to a union; check with a local branch. You'll find a list of labor unions in your phone book under "Labor Organizations."

- **Debtor's friends and neighbors:** The debtor's friends or neighbors may provide you with information about where the debtor works.

When you believe you have located the debtor's place of employment, verify it by calling that work number. You can either ask if the debtor works there or ask to speak to the debtor. Or, if you don't want to speak to the debtor, call when they may not be there (lunchtime) and ask to speak with them. You should either be told, "he's out to lunch" or "no one by that name works here."

2. Complete Application for Earnings Withholding Order

You must give the levying officer instructions for serving the wage garnishment papers on the debtor's employer. A sample completed form and instructions follow. A blank copy is in the Appendix.

Caption: Follow the format of your previous court papers. Leave the box for the levying officer's file number blank if you haven't levied, on this debtor, in this county before. If you have, the number is on those papers. Put that number in the box.

To the sheriff or any marshal or constable of the county of: Enter the county where the debtor is employed.

Item 1: First, enter your name as it appears in the judgment. Then in the box on the left, enter the name and street address of the debtor's employer. In the box on the right, enter the debtor's name exactly as it appears in the judgment and the debtor's home address (or last known address). If you know the debtor's Social Security number, you will complete form WG-035 (in Appendix).

Item 2: Check 2a if you want the money paid to you. If you want the money paid to someone else, check 2b and enter that person's name, address and telephone number.

Item 3a: Enter the date the judgment was entered.

Item 3b: Leave this blank unless you have

agreed with the debtor that they can pay less than the full judgment. If so, put the amount you agreed to here. Also, if you have received any money toward the judgment since you obtained the Writ, subtract that amount from the total shown in Item 18 of the Writ of Execution and put the difference here.

Item 4: Check any box that applies to you.

Item 5: If you have special instructions to the levying officer, check this box and enter the instructions. Attach an additional page if you need more space. Example of special instructions includes the following:

- At work, the debtor uses a name different than what is on the judgment.
- You are seeking less than 25% of the debtor's net income. You might garnish less if you previously garnished the debtor's wages, they filed a Claim of Exemption and the court determined a certain amount to be exempt.

Item 6: Check "a" if you have not previously garnished the wages of the debtor. Check "b" if you previously obtained an order to garnish the judgment debtor's wages from this employer. Then check the first box if you attempted a wage garnishment before, but it was terminated by a court order (You cannot serve another Earnings Withholding Order until 100 days after service of the first one or 60 days after it was terminated, whichever is later)[CCP 706.105(h)]. Check the second box if your wage levy was ineffective, for example, another wage garnishment had priority over yours.

Type or print your name and sign the form twice. Also, enter the date you sign the form.

3. Provide Instructions for Levying Officer

To find the levying officer for a county, call the sheriff's office and ask if it levies on civil money judgments for the particular address of the employer. If not, find out who does and call to find out the fees and how many copies of the Writ and Application are required.

Make the necessary copies, keeping a set for your records, and mail or take the documents and correct fee to the levying officer. A letter of instructions to the levying officer is provided in the Appendix. If you go in person, take your checkbook or cash for payment.

Based on the information in your instructions, the levying officer prepares an Earnings Withholding Order. They then serve it and an Employer's Return form on the employer or an agent in charge of the office or payroll along with notice documents for the employee [CCP 706.103(a)]. The employer then gives the debtor/employee the necessary documents about the garnishment [CCP 706.104(a)].

Sample Letter of Instructions

December 19, 2014
To the Sheriff, County of Los Angeles: Enclosed please find an original and three
copies of a Writ of Execution, an original Application for Earnings Withholding Order and a check in the amount of $ 40.00 to cover your fees.

Please proceed with a wage garnishment according to the Application for Earnings Withholding Order.

Please hold the original Writ of Execution for its entire 180-day duration or until the judgment has been satisfied, unless I contact you and instruct you differently.

Sincerely,
Amy Right

---

4. Wait for Employer to Complete Return

The employer is legally required to complete an "Employer's Return" and mail it back to the levying officer within 15 days [CCP 706.104(b)]. The levying officer will forward it to you. Note on your calendar to watch for a copy of the Employer's Return about four to six weeks after you send instructions to the levying officer. If you don't get a copy of the "Employer's Return", ask the levying officer what is happening with your garnishment.

On the Employer's Return, the employer:

- corrects any wrong information about the debtor's name and address

- indicates whether the debtor is still employed and if so, the earnings in the last pay period, and

- states when the debtor is paid, such as, every two weeks or monthly.

In addition, the employer must notify the debtor of the Earnings Withholding Order at least ten days before the garnishment is to begin so the debtor can:

- see an attorney

- work out an agreement with you, or

- file a Claim of Exemption.

If the debtor doesn't file a Claim of Exemption or work out an arrangement with you, the employer will begin sending a portion of the debtor's wages to the levying officer each pay period. The employer is required to send all monies, withheld from the employee's wages, to the levying officer no less than monthly, not later than the 15th of each month [CCP 706.025(a)]. The levying officer in turn forwards the payments to you.

If you decide to lift or modify the garnishment before your judgment is paid in full, you must complete and send a Notice of Termination or Modification of Earnings Withholding Order (form WG-012) to the employer, the debtor and the levying officer instructing them how to proceed.

5. If Employer Does Not Cooperate

If the employer doesn't return the Employer's Return form and carry out the order, you can sue the employer to recover the amount that should have been withheld, as well as any attorney's fees you spend in this effort [CCP 706.154(a)]. You can also sue an employer who interferes with a wage garnishment, for example by accelerating or deferring payments to the judgment debtor. An employer could even be subject to criminal prosecution if they don't comply [CCP 706.152].

Fortunately, it is seldom necessary to go this far. After you double-check with the levying officer to make sure they have not received the Employer's Return, call or write the employer and find out what's wrong. Let them know that you have the right to sue them. This usually produces the form. See the sample letter.

If the employer still doesn't cooperate and you don't want to sue, you can bring them in for a debtor's exam (See Chapter 6, Section C).

It is possible that an employer will send back the Employer's Return, but object to the wage garnishment. If this happens, the levying officer will send you a copy and ask you for further instructions. Common objections include:

- the debtor does not work there any more
- the debtor's wages are already being garnished by someone else, or
- the debtor works as an independent contractor, not an employee.

If the debtor no longer works for that employer, and you can find a current employer located in the same county as the former employer, you can send another Application for Earnings Withholding Order to the levying officer along with a new fee. The levying officer can use the same Writ of Execution. If the debtor's wages are already being garnished, you have to wait for that garnishment to end before yours take effect. If the other one lasts more than six months (180 days), you'll have to get a new Writ. If the debtor is an independent contractor, instead of a wage garnishment, you can do a third-party levy (Chapter 10) or assignment (Chapter 19).

6. If Debtor Files Claim of Exemption

The debtor can contest your wage garnishment by filing something called a Claim of Exemption with the levying officer. In this form, the debtor states that they are contesting the wage garnishment and gives their reasons for doing so. When the levying officer receives the Claim of Exemption, they will mail you a copy, along with a financial statement completed by the debtor and a document called Notice of Filing of Claim of Exemption [CCP 706.105(c)] (Claims of Exemption are covered in Chapter 15).

7. Get Your Money

If the debtor doesn't object to your wage garnishment or you win the Claim of Exemption hearing, the employer sends the money to the levying officer, who disburses it to you. Don't expect your money right away, delay is common. While you can call the levying officer to make sure your case hasn't fallen through the cracks, be patient. Levying officers often transmit collected funds in lump sums, rather than distributing them as they are collected.

Make sure you keep track of all money collected, as well as any costs incurred by you. We discuss this in Chapter 16.

If the employer receives an order of higher priority, such as for child or spousal support, your wage garnishment will be put on hold for up to two years; after that it will automatically terminate [CCP 706.032(a)(2)].

If your judgment is satisfied except for costs and interest, you can seek a final Earnings Withholding Order to recover those costs and interest [CCP 706.028].

If the debtor leaves their job, the order will automatically terminate after a 180-day period during which no money is withheld [CCP 706.032(a) (1)]. If the debtor changes jobs, you can file for another garnishment with the new employer.

Sample Letter to Uncooperative Employer

January 29, 2016

Nina Hart
Downlow Corporation
1000 Industrial Street
Yolo, CA 95000

Re: Amy Right v. Jeff Isbad
Los Angeles Court Case No. 14K5000

Dear Ms. Hart:

On December 19, 2015, I sent instructions to the Los Angeles County sheriff to proceed with a wage garnishment in the above-referenced case. They have informed me that they served you at Downlow Corporation with an Earnings Withholding Order on January 2, 2016. By law, you were required to complete and forward the Employer's Return to the sheriff within 15 days after service, and to comply with the wage garnishment unless you filed a formal objection.

There are serious legal penalties for refusing to comply with a wage garnishment. You could be found liable for the amount due and owing on the judgment, and you could be subject to a separate lawsuit.

Rather than taking more formal steps at this time, I would appreciate it if you would immediately complete and return the Employer's Return to the sheriff, and comply with the wage garnishment as required by law.

Sincerely,

Amy Right

cc: Sheriff, Los Angeles County (File No. 1000)

WG-001

ATTORNEY OR PARTY WITHOUT ATTORNEY (Name, State Bar number, and address):	LEVYING OFFICER (Name and Address):
Amy Right 1000 My st, Mytown, Ca 90000 TELEPHONE NO.: 310-555-5555 FAX NO.: E-MAIL ADDRESS: ATTORNEY FOR (Name): In Pro Per	Los Angeles County Sheriff 123 s Main st Helpful, Ca 90001 323-555-6666

SUPERIOR COURT OF CALIFORNIA, COUNTY OF Los Angeles
STREET ADDRESS: 111 Hill st
MAILING ADDRESS:
CITY AND ZIP CODE: Los Angeles, Ca 90012
BRANCH NAME: Stanley Mosk Courthouse

PLAINTIFF/PETITIONER: Amy Right
DEFENDANT/RESPONDENT: Jeff Isbad

APPLICATION FOR EARNINGS WITHHOLDING ORDER (Wage Garnishment)	COURT CASE NUMBER: 14K5000
	LEVYING OFFICER FILE NUMBER:

TO THE SHERIFF OR ANY MARSHAL OR CONSTABLE OF THE COUNTY OF: Los Angeles
OR ANY REGISTERED PROCESS SERVER

1. The judgment creditor (name): Amy Right   requests
   issuance of an Earnings Withholding Order directing the employer to withhold the earnings of the judgment debtor (employee).

   Name and address of employer

   ```
   Department of Defense
   422 Jefferson st
   Santa Monica, Ca 90044
   ```

   Name and address of employee

   ```
   Jeff Isbad
   666 e Cra P st
   Helltown, Ca 90666
   ```

2. The amounts withheld are to be paid to   Social Security no. [✓] on form WG-035 [ ] unknown
   a. [✓] The attorney (or party without an attorney)   b. [ ] Other (name, address, and telephone):
          named at the top of this page.

3. a. Judgment was entered on (date): 01/01/2014
   b. Collect the amount directed by the Writ of Execution unless a lesser amount is specified here: $

4. Check any that apply:
   a. [ ] The Writ of Execution was issued to collect delinquent amounts payable for the **support** of a child, former spouse, or spouse of the employee.
   b. [ ] The Writ of Execution was issued to collect a judgment based entirely on a claim for elder or dependent adult financial abuse.
   c. [ ] The Writ of Execution was issued to collect a judgment based in part on a claim for elder or dependent adult financial abuse. The amount that arises from the claim for elder or dependent adult financial abuse is (state amount): $

5. [ ] Special instructions (specify):

6. Check a or b:
   a. [✓] I have not previously obtained an order directing this employer to withhold the earnings of this employee.
      —OR—
   b. [ ] I have previously obtained such an order, but that order (check one):
      [ ] was terminated by a court order, but I am entitled to apply for another Earnings Withholding Order under the provisions of Code of Civil Procedure section 706.105(h).
      [ ] was ineffective.

Amy Right
_____   ▶ _____
(TYPE OR PRINT NAME)   (SIGNATURE OF ATTORNEY OR PARTY WITHOUT ATTORNEY)

I declare under penalty of perjury under the laws of the State of California that the foregoing is true and correct.
Date: 03/10/2014

Amy Right
_____   ▶ _____
(TYPE OR PRINT NAME)   (SIGNATURE OF DECLARANT)

Form Adopted for Mandatory Use
Judicial Council of California
WG-001 [Rev. January 1, 2012]

APPLICATION FOR EARNINGS WITHHOLDING ORDER
(Wage Garnishment)

Code Civ. Procedure, § 706.121
www.courts.ca.gov

CONFIDENTIAL WG-035

ATTORNEY OR PARTY WITHOUT ATTORNEY *(Name, State Bar number, and address)*: Amy Right 1000 My st Mytown, Ca 90000 TELEPHONE NO.: 310-555-5555 FAX NO.: E-MAIL ADDRESS: ATTORNEY FOR *(Name)*: In Pro Per	DATE RECEIVED BY COURT *(Do not file in public court file.)*
SUPERIOR COURT OF CALIFORNIA, COUNTY OF Los Angeles STREET ADDRESS: 111 Hill st MAILING ADDRESS: CITY AND ZIP CODE: Los Angeles, Ca 90012 BRANCH NAME: Stanley Mosk Courthouse	
PLAINTIFF/PETITIONER: Amy Right DEFENDANT/RESPONDENT: Jeff Isbad	COURT CASE NUMBER: 14K5000
CONFIDENTIAL STATEMENT OF JUDGMENT DEBTOR'S SOCIAL SECURITY NUMBER (Supplement to Wage Garnishment Forms WG-001, WG-002, WG-004, WG-005, WG-009, WG-012, and WG-030)	LEVYING OFFICER FILE NUMBER:

(Do not attach to forms.)

This separate *Confidential Statement of Judgment Debtor's Social Security Number* contains the Social Security number of the judgment debtor for whom an earnings withholding order is being sought or has issued in the case referenced above. **This supplement must be kept separate from any applications or orders filed in this case, and should not be a public record.**

INFORMATION ON JUDGMENT DEBTOR:

1. Name: Jeff Isbad

2. Social Security Number: 555-55-1234

TO COURT CLERK
THIS STATEMENT IS **CONFIDENTIAL**.
DO NOT FILE THIS CONFIDENTIAL STATEMENT IN A PUBLIC COURT FILE.

Form Adopted for Mandatory Use
Judicial Council of California
WG-035 [New January 1, 2012]

CONFIDENTIAL STATEMENT OF JUDGMENT DEBTOR'S SOCIAL SECURITY NUMBER
Wage Garnishment

www.courts.ca.gov

APPLICATION FOR FEDERAL EMPLOYEE COMMERCIAL GARNISHMENT

Approved by OMB 3206-0229

Date Received in Office of Designated Agent

INSTRUCTIONS

1. Federal law, 5 U.S.C. § 5520a, provides for the commercial garnishment of the pay of Federal employees.
2. Each garnishment order or similar legal process in the nature of garnishment must be delivered to the agency's Designated Agent. (See 5 CFR Part 582 Appendix A and 5 CFR Part 581 Appendix A for the lists of Designated Agents to receive legal process.)
3. Employing agencies will generally begin to disburse amounts withheld from employee-obligor's pay within 30 days of receipt by Designated Agent.
4. Employing agencies will **not** modify compensation schedules or pay disbursement cycles in responding to legal process.
5. 31 CFR Part 210 governs funds remitted by Electronic Funds Transfer.
6. See reverse side for Public Burden Statement.

Title and Address of Employing Agency's Designated Agent
Defense Finance and Accounting Service
Cleveland DFAS-HGA/CL
PO Box 998002
Cleveland, OH 44199-8002

Note: Service of legal process **may** be accomplished by certified or registered mail, return receipt requested, or by personal service only upon the agent to receive process as explained in 5 CFR 582.201, or if no agent has been designated, then upon the head of the employee-obligor's employing agency.

A. EMPLOYEE IDENTIFICATION
5 U.S.C. § 5520a requires sufficient information to enable the employing agency to identify the employee-obligor. Please provide as much of the information in items 1 through 5 as possible.

1. **Full Name of Employee-Obligor**
   Jeff Isbad
2. **Date of Birth**
   04/01/1963
3. **Employee/Social Security Number**
   555-55-1234
4. **Employing Agency, Component, and Employee's Official Duty Station/Worksite Address and ZIP Code**
   Department of Defense
   422 Jefferson st
   Santa Monica, Ca 90044
5. **Home Address or Current Mailing Address and ZIP Code**
   666 e Cra P st
   Helltown, Ca 90666
6. For Agency Use

B. CASE INFORMATION

1. **Name of Court and Case Number in Garnishment Order**
   Superior Court of California - Los Angeles county # 14K5000
2. **Garnishment Amount**
   $3,000.00
3. **Legal process expiration date (if time limited)**
   06/01/2016

4. Is there a dollar amount or percentage limitation under the applicable law of the jurisdiction where the order has been issued that will result in a lower amount to be garnished than would otherwise be applicable under the Consumer Credit Protection Act, 15 U.S.C. § 1673? ☐ Yes ☒ No   If Yes, provide a citation and a copy of the applicable provision: _____

5. Does the law of the jurisdiction where this legal process is issued have a "one order at a time" rule that precludes employers from garnishing more than one order at a time?
   ☒ Yes ☐ No

6. Does the law of the jurisdiction where this legal process is issued provide for the garnishment of interest amounts that are not reflected on the order or in item number B2?
   ☒ Yes ☐ No

C. AUTHORIZED PAYEE IDENTIFICATION

1. **Full Name of Person Authorized to Receive Payment, as it appears on Court Order**
   Amy Right
2. **Address of Authorized Payee, including ZIP Code**
   1000 My st
   Mytown, Ca 90000
3. **Daytime Telephone - Area Code and Number**
   310-555-5555
4. **Signature of Authorized Payee, Creditor, or Creditor's Representative, and Date Signed**

D. ELECTRONIC FUNDS TRANSFER (if available)

If you wish to request that the funds be remitted by electronic funds transfer rather than by paper check, please complete items D1 through D5.

1. **Name and Address of Authorized Payee's Financial Institution**
   Bank of America
   155 Main st, Mytown, Ca 90000
2. **Depositor (Payee) Account No. and Title**
   Amy Right
   Type of Account: ☒ Checking ☐ Savings
3. **9-Digit Routing Transit No. of Authorized Payee's Financial Institution (Verify with Financial Institution)**
   123456789
4. **Name and Title of Authorized Payee's Representative**
   Amy Right
5. **Signature of Authorized Payee's Representative and Date Signed**

U. S. Office of Personnel Management

Optional Form 311 (March 1997)

Blank Page

Chapter 10

Collecting from Money / Property Owed Debtor

A. Locating Money or Property Owed Debtor	10/2
1. Independent Contractor Receipts	10/3
2. Accounts Receivable - Businesses	10/3
3. Accounts Receivable - Professional Services	10/3
4. Security Deposit	10/4
5. Rent Payments	10/4
6. Debtor's Securities	10/4
7. Debtor's Property or Money	10/4
B. How to Levy on Money or Property held by Third Party	10/5
1. Prepare Levying Instructions	10/5
2. Provide Instructions for Levying Officer	10/6
3. Get Proceeds from Levy	10/7

Collection Factor	High	Moderate	Low
Potential cost to you		✓	
Potential for producing $$$		✓	
Potential for settlement		✓	
Potential time and trouble	✓		
Potential for bankruptcy			✓

One potential source of funds for satisfying your judgment is money that other parties owe your debtor. You can demand that these funds be paid directly to you instead of to the debtor [CCP 700.170]. There are a few exceptions, however. For example, unless you have a judgment for child or spousal support, you can't go after debts owed the judgment debtor by the government, including tax refunds [CCP 699.720(a) (5)].

Common types of debts third parties may owe a debtor include:

- accounts receivable, if the debtor is a business

- money due for services rendered, for example, if the debtor is a professional, consultant or independent contractor or works on commission

- judgments obtained by the debtor against a third party, and

- loans made by the debtor to a third party.

Third parties may also have, at least temporarily, property that belongs to the judgment debtor. For instance, a gallery may have a craftsperson's works on consignment.

Generally, for a levying officer to levy on property held by a third party, the property must be someplace that is open to the public. If it isn't, you must obtain a Seizure Order from a court to let the levying officer enter a private place to get the property (Seizure Orders are covered in Chapter 19). Getting a Seizure Order can be a bit complicated; we generally don't recommend it unless the amount of your judgment justifies the effort, and your other attempts to enforce your judgment have not been successful.

To enforce your judgment against money or property owed the debtor; the levying officer sends a levy notice to the third party, directing that person to pay the levying officer instead of the debtor [CCP 700.170]. This kind of levy can capture a future stream of payments to the judgment debtor [CCP 701.050(a) & 701.010(b) (2) (B)]. So if you know that the debtor is an independent contractor working mainly for Curry Company, you can levy on the money due the debtor from Curry Company and you can intercept any money payable to the debtor. be sure to include reference to CCP 701.050(a) so the garnishee knows they have an ongoing duty.

There is another way to maintain an ongoing "levy." If the debtor receives regular payments from a third party, such as royalty payments or certain government benefits, you can request a court order for something called an "Assignment Order", in which the debtor assigns their right to receive these payments to you. The upside is that you don't have to levy the money owed the debtor each month, it's automatically paid to you through the assignment. The downside is that you must obtain a court order (Assignment Orders are covered in Chapter 19).

A. Locating Money or Property Owed Debtor

To initiate a levy on money or property held by third parties, you first need to figure out who owes the debtor, where they are, and what they owe the debtor. Below are common types of money or property others might owe the debtor. If you contact anyone directly, follow the collection guidelines in Chapter 3.

1. Independent Contractor Receipts

For our purposes, an independent contractor is someone who works for themselves and does not have a formal employer/ employee relationship, with the person for whom they do projects or other work. If the debtor has a steady income as an independent contractor, it can be a great source for enforcing your judgment.

Independent contractors include people who:

- work for a business as outside salespersons on commission

- are artists or writers who do projects on contract

- freelance their work for larger companies, such as consultants, or

- do home repair or garden maintenance on a regular or semi-regular basis.

Carpenters, stoneworkers, plumbers, painters, pool service companies, roofers, electricians, housecleaners, writers and many others fall into the category of independent contractors. Some of them, especially consultants, may be incorporated, in which case you would have to levy on the business instead (See Chapter 11).

It may be obvious for whom the debtor does work. A commissioned sales rep may have a business card identifying a principal supplier; a writer or artist may list major accounts on a publicity brochure. Look the debtor up on social media and the internet. There is a wealth of information out there on most people.

In other situations, you may have to do some searching. You could ask people you know and who also know the debtor. They may give you this information in the course of a casual conversation. You might even follow the debtor a few mornings to see where they go.

A more formal way to get this information is to conduct a debtor's examination, along with a Subpoena Duces Tecum, asking for copies of statements and books showing accounts receivable (See Chapter 6). If these methods fail, consider hiring an investigator.

2. Accounts Receivable—Businesses

"Accounts receivables" means a right to payment of a monetary obligation [CCP 680.130 & Commercial Code 9102(a) (2)] and usually represents money that customers owe a business for goods or services provided. For instance, a printing business is often owed large sums for printing jobs, a wholesaler for goods supplied a retailer and a clothing manufacturer for goods distributed to stores. Or, the debtor may work out of their home selling mail-order products. While you cannot use a levy to collect from the business itself (see Chapter 11 on how to collect from a business), if you know the names of customers who have made purchases but haven't yet paid, you can levy on the money due. In many businesses, payment is not expected until 30 to 90 days from the date of the invoice.

3. Accounts Receivable - Professional Services

If the debtor provides professional services as a lawyer, accountant, financial planner, doctor, acupuncturist, therapist, dentist or other professional, their clients or patients may be good sources of money. You'll want to find clients or patients with whom the debtor has a regular and ongoing relationship. If you find someone who sees the professional regularly (such as a therapist's patient), you may possibly get a steady stream of money. If the client or patient is a major and steady source of income for the debtor, intercepting one payment may quickly lead the debtor to pay the debt in full or negotiate a payment plan.

If the payments are steady and large enough, consider obtaining an Assignment

Order from a court (See Chapter 19). Under an Assignment Order, you will receive the payments from the third party as they become due until your judgment is satisfied or you cancel the assignment.

If you know the name of a regular, major client of the judgment debtor, levying on that person's payments may make sense. But don't invade anyone's privacy to find out the names of patients or clients.

4. Security Deposit

If the debtor is a renter, their landlord probably holds a security deposit. While no specific statute authorizes a levy on a tenant's security deposit and no court of appeals has reviewed the issue yet, several statutes read together may been interpreted as providing that authority: See CCP 695.010 and 699.710 and Civil Code 1950.5(d). Some judges will not allow it.

5. Rent Payments

If the debtor is a landlord of either commercial or residential property, finding out the names of renters is usually not difficult. You can ask the debtor in a debtor's examination (Chapter 6). You could use a reverse directory, which lists the names of people who have phone numbers at a particular address (See Chapter 2, Section B4). You could visit the property and read the tenants' names on the mailboxes or business signs.

Several California communities have rent control ordinances that require landlords of covered units to register their units and provide information about the tenants. If the debtor owns residential property in a community with rent control laws, the rent control agency should have information about the debtor's building.

6. Debtor's Securities

If the debtor owns stock, how you get it depends on how the stock ownership is physically represented. If a stockbroker holds the certificates for the debtor, you can use the levy described in this chapter against the branch office of the stock brokerage firm [CCP 700.130 & Commercial Code 8112]. If ownership is manifested in stock certificates held by the debtor, you can levy against the certificates themselves as tangible personal property (See Chapter 13). If the stock ownership is represented only in the computer database of the company issuing the stock, you can use the levy procedure outlined in this chapter against the company's California headquarters. If the headquarters are out of state, you will need to obtain an Assignment Order directed to the judgment debtor (See Chapter 19).

7. Debtor's Property or Money

Finding out who has possession of the debtor's property or money can be difficult. If you know the debtor or their associates well, however, you may be able to get this information through casual conversation. Or you might be able to track down some potential third parties from what you know about the debtor. For example, if the debtor has appointed a money manager to handle their funds, that person could be reached through a third-party levy. The same goes for a friend who is keeping personal property for a debtor.

Furthermore, if the debtor is a craftsperson, artist or small publisher, they might have some books or artworks on consignment with a bookstore or gallery. A third party would be legally responsible for turning over to you any payments due the debtor at the time of the levy. You could also levy against the property itself, but the fees, storage costs and sales costs associated with levies on tangible personal property usually make a levy counterproductive (See Chapter 13).

If you suspect that the debtor has hidden valuable assets by transferring them to third parties, and your attempt to levy against this property fails because the third party claims ownership, you still may be able to get the assets. However, you'll have to bring a separate lawsuit against the third party, a process well beyond the scope of this book.

B. How to Levy on Money or Property Held by Third Parties

Before you can levy on money or property held by a third party, you must obtain a Writ of Execution directed to the county in which the third party is located (See Chapter 7). Once you have the Writ, follow the steps below. If the business headquarters are in another state, you will not be able to levy against it and instead will have to obtain an Assignment Order directed to the judgment debtor (See Chapter 19).

1. Prepare Levying Instructions

To find the levying officer for a county, call the sheriff's office and ask if it levies on civil money judgments. Find out the fees, if they have a local form they require, and how many copies of the Writ are required. If you are levying against money only, you could use a process server to speed up the process (See Chapter 21).

a. Money Owed to Debtor

To levy on money owed to the debtor by a third party, include the following in your instructions:

- the third party's name and address

- the amount of money you believe the third party will owe the debtor at the time the levy is made,

- when you want the levy to be made, near the end of the month is often good, as it is likely to be when the maximum amount will be owed.

Sample Instructions to Levying Officer for Money Owed

June 6, 2015
Re: Amy Right v Jeff Isbad

To the Sheriff, County of Los Angeles:

Enclosed please find an original and copies of a Writ of Execution and a check in the amount of $ 40.00 to cover your fee. Please serve the Writ of Execution and levy against any money due and owing judgment debtor Jeff Isbad by the third party, Careful Cat Catering, 100 Siamese Street, Compton, CA 90028.

Jeff Isbad should be owed approximately $1,100 by Careful Cat Catering for deli items delivered but not yet paid for. Please execute this levy sometime during the week of June 23, 2015.

Please call me if you have any

questions. Sincerely,

Amy Right

b. Tangible Personal Property Held by Third Party

Tangible personal property is all property, except real estate, of a physical nature, that is, property that you can actually touch. Examples are pianos, jewelry, cameras, computers, stereos, furniture, and stamp collections. Examples of intangible personal property are copyrights and trademarks.

> **Sample Instructions to Levying Officer for Property Held**
>
> June 6, 2015
> Re: Amy Right v. Jeff Isbad
> To the Sheriff, County of Los Angeles:
> Enclosed please find an original and copies of a Writ of Execution and a check in the amount of $ 500 to cover your fee. Please proceed to levy on (remove, store and sell) the following tangible personal property belonging to Jeff Isbad, which is in the possession of Miguel Fast:
>
> • One Steinway baby grand piano, and
> • Full set of 12 crystal goblets.
>
> This property is located at the Space Studio of Miguel Fast, 2001 Space Street, Torrance, CA 90105. The Space Studio is generally open to the public.
>
> Please keep me informed as to the status of this levy. I would like to attend the sale, so let me know when that will be.
>
> Please call me if you have any questions.
>
> Sincerely,
> Amy Right

To levy on tangible property held by a third party, you must instruct the levying officer to take, store, and sell the property [CCP 700.040]. You will have to pay the regular levy fee as well as a substantial deposit, probably several hundred dollars, to cover the associated costs.

2. Provide Instructions to Levying Officer

Send the fee, your instructions and the original and copies of your Writ to the levying officer. The levying officer will serve the third party with copies of your papers, a Notice of Levy and a form called a Memorandum of Garnishee. The judgment debtor will be mailed a Notice of Levy.

Unless the third party has a good reason for refusing to turn over the money or property, they must give the levying officer what is due or belongs to the debtor at the time of the levy [CCP 701.010]. They must also complete and return the Memorandum of Garnishee to the levying officer within ten days of receiving it [CCP 701.030(a)].

a. If Third Party Doesn't Comply

A third party who does not turn over the money or property sought in the Writ must explain in the Memorandum why they won't or cannot comply. One common reason is that someone else already served a levy and has rights to the money ahead of you. Or the third party might state that they don't owe anything to the debtor or don't hold property for the debtor. Or the obligation might be due but not yet payable. If the levying officer receives a Memorandum of Garnishee, you will be sent a copy. We generally don't recommend pursuing the matter if the third party objects, unless the amount at stake justifies hiring a lawyer.

There are penalties for failing to comply with a levy, assuming the third party is able to comply and simply does not. If you sue the third party, they may be ordered to pay you the lesser of the following:

- the value of the judgment debtor's interest in the property or the amount of the payments you are seeking to levy, or

- the amount required to satisfy the judgment.

The court can also require the third party to pay your attorney's fees [CCP 701.020].

Fortunately, it is seldom necessary to go this far. An informed third-party debtor commonly pays after being reminded of their obligation to do so. You can help this process along with a letter along the lines of the sample provided.

Sample Letter Reminding Third Party of Levy

July 10, 2015

Re: Amy Right v Jeff Isbad
Los Angeles County Municipal Court Case # 14K5000

Miguel Fast
2001 Space Street
Torrance, CA 90105

Dear Mr. Fast:

On June 6, 2015, I sent instructions to the Los Angeles County sheriff to proceed with a levy on property that you have in your possession belonging to Jeff Isbad. The specific property in question is a Steinway baby grand piano and a full set of 12 crystal goblets.

The sheriff has informed me that you were personally served with levying papers on June 13, 2015, but you have not stated any objection on the Garnishee's Memorandum or turned the property over to the sheriff by law, you were required to complete and forward the Garnishee's Memorandum to the sheriff within ten days after receiving it, and to comply with the levy unless you filed a formal objection.

For refusing to comply with a sheriff's levy, you could be sued and found personally liable for the amount due on the judgment. I do not want to take such steps. I would appreciate it if you would immediately complete and return the Garnishee's Memorandum to the levying officer, and comply with the levy as required by law.

Sincerely,

Amy Right
cc: Sheriff, Los Angeles
    (Officer's File No. 1000)

b. If Debtor Objects

The judgment debtor might file a Claim of Exemption. If this happens, see Chapter 15.

3. Get Proceeds From Levy

The levying officer ultimately disburses the money or sales proceeds to you. Don't expect the money right away, delay is common. While you can call the levying officer to make sure your case hasn't fallen through the cracks, be patient. Levying officers often transmit collected funds in lump sums, rather than distributing them as they are collected.

Make sure you keep track of all money collected, as well as any collection costs you incurred. We discuss how to do this in Chapter 16.

Blank Page

Chapter 11

Collecting from a Business

A. Levying Against Cash Receipts or Business Assets	11/2
1. Levying Against Cash Receipts.	11/2
2. Levying Against Business Assets.	11/3
B. How to Levy Against Cash Receipts	11/4
1. Obtain Till Tap and Keeper Information	11/4
2. Provide Instructions for Levying Officer	11/4
3. Get Your Money	11/5
C. How to Levy Against Business Assets	11/5
1. Obtain Levying Information	11/6
2. Provide Levying Officer with Instructions	11/6
3. Get Your Money	11/6
4. If Inappropriate Property is Seized	11/7

Collection Factor
Levying on Cash Coming into Business

	High	Moderate	Low
Potential cost to you			✓
Potential for producing $$$	✓		
Potential for settlement	✓		
Potential time and trouble		✓	
Potential for bankruptcy			✓

Collection Factor
Levying on Assets of Business

	High	Moderate	Low
Potential cost to you		✓	✓
Potential for producing $$$	✓		
Potential for settlement	✓		
Potential time and trouble		✓	
Potential for bankruptcy			✓

If you have a judgment against an ongoing business, whether it's a Limited Liability company, corporation, partnership, or sole proprietorship, you can have the levying officer enforce your judgment using any of the following methods:

- make a one-time seizure of cash and checks in the cash register, called a till tap

- stay at the business for a day or longer, collecting cash and checks as they come in, called a keeper, or

- seize personal assets of the business and sell them.

These procedures are available only if the business entity is a named defendant in the judgment. If your judgment is against the debtor as an individual, you probably will need a court order to levy on the business, even if the individual owns it lock, stock and barrel.

These procedures have a coercive effect: Most business owners would rather pay your judgment than face the prospect of a sheriff standing by the cash register or seizing business assets. In most cases, business owners facing these types of enforcement efforts find a way to pay the judgment voluntarily.

A. Levying Against Cash Receipts or Business Assets?

Most judgment creditors opt to levy against cash receipts rather than going for business assets. Before you make a choice, however, you should understand how each method works.

1. Levying Against Cash Receipts

As we mentioned, you can seize cash and checks on a one-time basis (till tap) or by having a sheriff stand at the cash register all day (keeper). There are some restrictions, however:

- You cannot levy against receipts received by a home based business without a court order (See Chapter 19).

- You cannot levy against credit card receipts or receipts for sales that are not yet final, such as a down payment or layaway deposit.

- Some levying officers refuse to collect checks because of the problems involved in getting them cashed. You might deal with this by asking the levying officer to have the debtor endorse the checks over to you.

a. Till Tap

If you request a till tap, the levying officer makes a single trip to the business and picks up all the cash and checks in the cash register or cash box [CCP 700.030]. This is a quick way of going after business receipts and you can request one as often as you want, but you have to prepare new levy forms each time. If the business owner keeps their money in their wallet or a locked safe, a till tap probably won't work.

You must pay fees in advance, currently, sheriffs charge about $200, as a deposit, for a till tap [Government Code 26722 & 26748]. If the levying officer can't tap the till, for example, because the business is closed, you may get some of the deposit back. You are entitled to apply the levying officer's fee, as well as the judgment, out of the till tap.

b. Keeper

If you request a keeper, the levying officer (usually a deputy sheriff) shows up at the business with another person, who is not a sheriff, a Keeper. The Keeper remains at the business and collects all cash and checks that come in. This is a great way to enforce your judgment against a retail establishment. A keeper is also a good way for you to find out about the assets of the business, because you can instruct the levying officer to inventory the equipment, furniture and merchandise.

A keeper can be authorized to remain on a business's premises in daily increments, up to ten days. After that, the assets or inventory must be seized and sold. In the real world, a keeper stays until they have collected the balance specified in your Writ, plus the amount needed to cover the levying officer's costs. A keeper may choose not to stay if the debtor expressly objects. In that case, however, the levying officer is permitted to immediately seize, store and sell business assets [CCP 700.070].

You have three choices when you request a keeper.

- **An eight-hour keeper.** This is your least expensive option.

- **A 24 or 48-hour keeper.** The longer the keeper stays, the more it will cost you. A 24 or 48-hour keeper makes sense if you're dealing with a business that has unusually long hours or operates around the clock, such as a convenience store.

- **An open-ended keeper (up to ten days).** If your judgment is fairly large and the business does not take in enough cash each day to satisfy the judgment in a day or two, be prepared for a long-term keeper, if you can afford it. But be aware that with an open-ended keeper, you run a greater risk of driving the debtor out of business or into bankruptcy.

The levying officer has a right to collect potential costs in advance; you will probably have to deposit as much as $ 300 to $ 1,000 for an eight-hour keeper, and much more than that for a ten-day keeper. Part of this deposit may be refunded if the costs don't run that high. And these costs may be recovered by the keeper or in a subsequent levy [Government Code 26726(a)].

2. Levying Against Business Assets

Having business assets seized and sold is expensive, time consuming and economically risky. The forced sale of property typically brings only a small percentage of its true market value. You must pay substantial costs up front for conducting an inventory, transporting and storing the assets and holding the sale [Government Code 26720.9, 26722, 26729, 26730, and 26748]. Also, the property you try to seize and sell may already be serving as security for other debts (which get paid before you), or may be exempt from sale. Therefore, we don't recommend levying against business assets unless:

- you have a hefty judgment and are certain that the sale will bring in significantly more than the cost of having the property seized, stored and sold, or

- you want to acquire the property for your own use.

B. How to Levy Against Cash Receipts

Before you can levy against cash receipts, you must obtain a Writ of Execution directed to the county where the business is located (See Chapter 7). Once you have the Writ, follow the steps below.

1. Obtain Till Tap and Keeper Information

To find the levying officer for a county, call the sheriff's office and ask if it levies on civil money judgments. Find out the fees for a till tap versus the different kinds of keepers, whether the levying officer has their own form and how many copies of the Writ are required.

Once you speak to the levying officer, decide which type of levy you want to use, till tap, eight-hour keeper, 24-hour keeper or open-ended keeper.

Sample Letter of Instructions - Till Tap

March 24, 2015

Re: Amy Right v Jeff Isbad

To the Sheriff, County of Los Angeles: Enclosed please find an original and 3 copies of a Writ of Execution and a check for your fee in the amount of $ 300.00. You are hereby instructed to seize cash and checks, ask the judgment debtor to endorse the checks over to me, in the possession of the following business to satisfy the sum specified in the accompanying Writ of Execution.

Jeff Isbad dba Jeff's Crazy Cakes
234 West Street
Los Angeles, CA 90008
310-333-3333

Please levy on or before 3 p.m. on a Friday, Jeff Isbad makes weekly deposits at approximately 3:30 p.m. on Friday afternoons. Thank you.

Sincerely, Amy Right

2. Provide Levying Officer with Instructions

If the levying officer does not provide a form, use the samples below as guides. A blank "Instructions to Levying Officer" form letter is in the Appendix. If you believe the business is likely to have a substantial amount of cash on hand at a certain time, instruct the levying officer to visit then.

Here are sample instructions for an eight-hour keeper. If you want a longer keeper, modify this sample to change the time the keeper is to last. Be sure to direct the levying officer to inventory the premises.

Sample Letter of Instructions - Keeper

March 24, 2015

Re: Amy Right v Jeff Isbad

To the Sheriff, County of Los Angeles: Enclosed please find an original and 3 copies of a Writ of Execution and a check for your fee in the amount of $ 600.00. You are hereby instructed to place an eight-hour keeper at the following business by virtue of the accompanying Writ of Execution.

Jeff Isbad dba Jeff's Crazy Cakes
234 West Street
Los Angeles, CA 90008
310-333-3333

In addition, please make an inventory of the personal property in Isbad's bakery, including all equipment, appliances, machinery and utensils used for food preparation, and all other personal/business property on the premises.

Please call me if you have any questions.
Sincerely,

Amy Right

After you type up the instructions, make the necessary copies of the Writ and instructions for the levying officer, plus one set for your file. Send the original and copies of the Writ along with your instructions and fees to the levying officer for the county where the debtor's business is located. It is always best to personally take the documents, but if the Sheriff is too far, call a week later to confirm receipt.

3. Get Your Money

The levying officer will proceed with your instructions. They may advise you about the outcome of the levy. If there was any problem with the levy, for example, the business is in a private home or has moved. They should contact you.

Once the levying officer has collected the proceeds of the levy, they will disburse them to you. Don't expect your money right away, delay is common. While you can call the levying officer to make sure your case hasn't fallen through the cracks, be patient. Levying officers often transmit collected funds in lump sums, rather than distributing them as they are collected.

Make sure you keep track of all money collected, as well as any costs incurred by you. We discuss how to do this in Chapter 16.

C. How to Levy Against Business Assets

If you decide to seize the assets of a business, the levying officer will hire a moving company, at your expense, to pick up the property, store it and conduct a sale. As costly and time consuming as it is, seizing business assets has extreme coercive value, the debtor may pay all or part of the judgment just to avoid the seizure.

Not all business property can be seized to pay off your judgment; some is off-limits. But that's the business owner's concern, not yours. You should instruct the levying officer to seize everything. The levying officer might decide not to take certain property. You have little practical alternative but to rely on their judgment.

The levying officer is likely to steer clear of the following kinds of property:

- Property found on the business premises that is not a part of the business, that is, property that is owned by the debtor as an individual, and is exempt by law. For example, the business owner's personal motorcycle is at the business when the levying officer arrives. The motorcycle cannot be seized as a business asset, and the owner may claim it as an exempt motor vehicle (See Chapter 12).

- Exempt business assets, the debtor can claim up to $6,075 of tools, materials or equipment [CCP 704.060]. Exemptions can only be claimed by natural persons [CCP 703.020(a)], so if your judgment is against a corporation you are safe.

- Property that doesn't belong to the business, that is, items borrowed or leased from a third party, such as computers and copying machines.

- Inventory held on consignment, such as works by local artists.

- Partnership property, unless it actually belongs to the debtor. If it does not, you will need a Charging Order from the court to seize it. Such orders are beyond the scope of this book.

- Inventory, furnishings, equipment and other items subject to a security interest that has been perfected through filing a financing statement with the Secretary of State (See Chapter 4, Section B).

- Property located in a private home, unless the debtor consents to, or a court issues an order permitting, the entry or seizure [CCP 699.030]. Judges are reluctant to issue such an order unless you have exhausted other methods of collection, the judgment is big enough to justify your reaching a little further than is normally permitted or the debtor conducts a substantial business out of their home. If you feel you have a basis for collecting from a business in a private home, you must obtain a Seizure Order from the court where you obtained your judgment (See Chapter 19).

EXAMPLE: If Jeff, the debtor, does some professional writing out of a room in his house, this would not justify a court order allowing you to enter and seize property. On the other hand, if Jeff uses a substantial part of his home for a suite of offices, has clients coming and going on a regular basis, and has several employees, a court might allow a levying officer to enter. This might also hold true if you could show that the debtor is conducting a substantial mail order business from his home.

If you decide to go after the assets of a business, you must obtain a Writ of Execution directed to the county where the business is located (See Chapter 7). Once you have the Writ, follow the steps below.

1. Obtain Levying Information

To find the levying officer for a county, call the sheriff's office and ask if it levies on civil money judgments. Ask about the procedure for seizing and selling personal assets of a business, whether the levying officer has their own form, any deposit required and how many copies of the Writ are required.

2. Provide Levying Officer with Instructions

If the levying officer does not provide a form, use the below sample as a guide. A blank Instructions to Levying Officer form letter is in the Appendix. These instructions require the levying officer to give you an estimate of the potential cost of seizing the assets. This gives you a chance to back away from this remedy if it appears too expensive.

They also let the levying officer seize less than all of the assets if, in their opinion, the amount seized will be sufficient to satisfy your judgment.

After you type up the instructions, make the necessary copies of the Writ and instructions for the levying officer, plus one set for your file. Take, or send the original and copies of the Writ along with your instructions and fees to the levying officer for the county where the debtor's business is located.

3. Get Your Money

The levying officer will follow your instructions and proceed with a keeper or the seizure and sale of business property. They may contact you to ask you to post further fee deposits, to let you know the outcome of the levy or to tell you about any problem with the levy, for example, that the business lacks siezable assets or has moved.

If the debtor wants to object, they can file a Claim of Exemption (See Section C4, below). You must oppose it if you want the sale of the seized property to proceed. If the debtor doesn't file a Claim of Exemption or loses at the hearing, the levying officer will sell the property. They will notify the debtor at least ten days in advance and post other notices in the city or district, telling where and when the sale will take place.

Sample Letter of Instructions

March 24, 2015

Re: Amy Right v Jeff Isbad
To the Sheriff, County of Los Angeles: Enclosed please find an original Writ of Execution and 3 copies and a check for your fee in the amount of $ 1,000.00. You are hereby instructed to seize, advertise for sale and sell by virtue of the accompanying Writ of Execution the following business personal property: all money, debts, credits and effects, all goods, wares, merchandise, stock in trade, equipment, inventory, fixtures and furniture in possession or under the control of the following:

Jeff Isbad dba Jeff's Crazy Cakes
234 West Street
Los Angeles, CA 90008
310-333-3333

Please place a keeper in charge for a 48- hour period. As soon as possible, please inventory the premises, obtain an estimate of the moving and storage costs, and contact me at the telephone number below before taking further action. If I desire to continue with the levy, and no settlement with the judgment debtor has been made, this is your authority to remove enough property or merchandise from the premises to satisfy the amount of the claim specified in the Writ of Execution.

Finally, if a sale will be held, please advise me in advance so I can attend.

Sincerely,
Amy Right

Such sales are rare, because they are expensive to conduct and produce so little money. At this stage, the debtor is likely to work out a settlement to get the property back. Up until the actual sale, the debtor can settle with you, paying you the balance owed on the judgment, all enforcement costs and interest [CCP 695.210].

If the levying officer proceeds with a sale, you can attend. You can even buy the business assets without affecting your judgment. The levying officer will pay you out of the money you spend on the business. You might also use your judgment as credit in the bidding process (ask the levying officer about this). In this case, you would have to put up cash only if you bid higher than the unsatisfied amount of your judgment.

After the sale, the levying officer will turn over the proceeds to you, up to the balance of your judgment, less any fees and costs you still owe the levying officer for conducting the sale. If anything is left over, it goes back to the debtor.

4. If Inappropriate Property is Seized
If the business is open to the public and not located in the debtor's home, the levying officer can seize just about anything they find there. The levying officer can assume the debtor owns or is in charge of everything present, unless the debtor shows them evidence to the contrary. The officer will use their judgment in deciding if the evidence is convincing.

A debtor who wants to get back any seized property or protest the levy must file a Claim of Exemption with the levying officer within ten days, giving a reason why this property should not have been taken, for example, because the property belongs to someone else or is exempt. If a third party wants to claim ownership of property seized in the levy, they can object to the levy by filing a claim of ownership or a security interest [CCP 720.110 & 720.210]. If either the debtor or a third party objects to your levy, you will be notified and given an opportunity to oppose the objection (See Chapter 15).

Blank Page

Chapter 12

Seizing a Motor Vehicle

A. Limitations on Vehicle Levies	12/2
1. Debtor May Not Own Vehicle	12/2
2. Vehicle May Not Be Worth Much	12/2
3. Vehicle May Be Partially Exempt	12/2
4. Vehicle Will Sell for Far Less Than Value	12/3
5. Vehicle Levies Are Expensive	12/3
6. You May Need a Court Order	12/3
B. How to Levy on a Vehicle	12/3
1. Get Vehicle Information	12/4
2. Determine Debtor's Ownership in Vehicle	12/4
3. Provide Levying Officer With Instructions	12/6
4. If Debtor or Third Party Objects	12/6
5. Attend the Sale if You Want	12/7
6. Get Your Money	12/7

Collection Factor			
	High	Moderate	Low
Potential cost to you	✓		
Potential for producing $$$			✓
Potential for settlement		✓	
Potential time and trouble		✓	
Potential for bankruptcy			✓

You are permitted to go after a debtor's motor vehicle to satisfy a judgment. This includes a debtor's car, truck, motorcycle, boat, plane, or recreational vehicle.

Motor Home Versus Mobile Home

Motor homes are considered vehicles, and can be seized using the methods in this chapter. But mobile homes are considered real property, not vehicles (see Chapter 14 for information on seizing real property). How can you tell the difference? Generally, a motor home is capable of routinely traveling the roads (it has wheels) and must be registered with the Department of Motor Vehicles (DMV). By contrast, a mobile home is usually attached to the ground permanently or semi-permanently and does not travel the roads unless it is being moved. A mobile home need not be registered with the DMV, instead the owner will probably have to pay property taxes in the county where the home sits (unless the home is situated in a mobile home park where the debtor may not own the land and any taxes may be part of the park's fees).

To the uninitiated, going after a debtor's motor vehicle to satisfy a judgment might sound like a good idea. In reality, however, forcing the sale of a motor vehicle usually nets little or no cash for the judgment creditor unless one of the following is true:

- the vehicle is valuable and the debtor has substantial equity in it, that is, the debtor owns it pretty much free and clear from loans

- you want the vehicle for your own use. If so, you can force a sale and buy the vehicle yourself, or

- you think that going after the vehicle will coerce the debtor into settling with you.

A. Limitations on Vehicle Levies

As mentioned, going after a debtor's vehicle is often fruitless. This section outlines some of the reasons why.

1. Debtor May Not Own Vehicle

If the vehicle is relatively new and in good condition, there's a good chance that the debtor still owes a bundle to a lender, such as a car dealer or bank. If so, that lender must be paid off before you receive any money. Because forced vehicle sales rarely net what the vehicle is worth, don't expect any money to be left over for you. If the debtor doesn't owe a lender on their car, it may be because they're leasing it, which means they don't own it. In that case, you are out of luck.

2. Vehicle May Not Be Worth Much

If the judgment debtor owns the vehicle free and clear, it's paid off and not leased, it may be an older model worth too little to warrant the cost of sale. You can check the value of a vehicle by checking the Kelley Blue Book. You can find a Kelly Blue Book in a library, bookstore, AAA office, or online at www.kbb.com.

3. Vehicle May Be Partially Exempt

If you seize a debtor's only motor vehicle, the debtor is automatically entitled to an exemption of $3,050 [review Judicial Council Form EJ-156, page 2, and use CCP 704.010]. This means that after the sale, the debtor will receive $3,050 of the proceeds before you get a penny. If the debtor owns more than one vehicle, he may still be entitled to the $3,050 exemption, but he must come forward and claim it. The Sheriff is responsible for checking the Department of Motor Vehicle records to confirm how many vehicles the debtor owns. If the debtor uses the motor vehicle in their business (for more than just commuting,) they may be entitled to exempt $4,850 – 9,700 [review Judicial Council Form EJ-156, page 2, and use CCP 704.060]. In short, you will receive cash from the sale of a motor vehicle only if the debtor's equity in the vehicle is substantially over the applicable exemption amount plus your costs.

If you want to seize a boat or RV that is the debtor's principal residence, they may be entitled to claim a homestead exemption (See Chapter 14). If so, your chances of realizing any proceeds from a forced sale are almost nil.

4. Vehicle Will Sell for Far Less Than Value

Anyone who has sold a used vehicle knows that what it fetches depends greatly on how it is sold. For example, a car that can be sold for $5,000 through a newspaper may bring in only $2,500 as a trade-in.

Cars seized to satisfy a judgment are sold by the levying officer at an auction, which tends to bring in even less than a trade-in does. As a general rule, auctioned vehicles sell for about half (or less) of their Blue Book value.

5. Vehicle Levies Are Expensive

In order to sell a debtor's vehicle, the Sheriff must seize the vehicle and put it into storage. Then, the Sheriff has to advertise the sale well in advance. When the vehicle is finally sold at the Sheriff's auction, the selling price will most likely depend on how many people show up at the auction. This process can take 2-3 months. Seizing, storing and selling a vehicle can cost up to $2,500 or more. These costs must be deposited with the levying officer in advance of the levy. If the levy is unsuccessful or doesn't produce any money, you will have thrown a lot of good money after bad, although you may be able to recover these costs if you satisfy your judgment from other assets.

EXAMPLE 1: Amy obtained a $2,100 small claims judgment against Jeff. Amy had Jeff's Honda Prelude seized and sold after paying the levying officer a $1,100 deposit. At auction, the car sold for $11,000, even though its market value was probably closer to $18,000. Out of the $11,000, the legal owner of the Honda, Gulp Bank, was paid the amount still due on the note, or $7,300. Next, Jeff received his $3,050 exemption, leaving $650. After deducting the costs of seizure, storage and sale ($800), the sheriff gave Amy $950 ($ 300 of her deposit back plus $650 from the sale). Amy ended up losing $150 out of pocket as a result of the levy.

EXAMPLE 2: Amy obtained a $5,000 judgment against Jeff. Jeff owned an RV which he kept at his mother's house except when he used it for vacations (not his only vehicle). Amy did a little asking around and determined that the RV had a market value of $5,000. She had it seized and sold by the sheriff. It sold for $2,500 and the costs of seizure, storage and sale amounted to $1,000. Amy realized $1,500 from the sale.

6. You May Need a Court Order

Normally, a vehicle can be seized only if it is in a public place, such as a street. If the debtor keeps it in a garage or other private place, you must first get a Seizure Order from the court (See Chapter 19).

B. How to Levy on a Vehicle

Before you can levy on a vehicle, you must obtain a Writ of Execution directed to the county where the vehicle is located (See Chapter 7). Don't assume that a vehicle is in the same county as the debtor's residence. Rather, find out where the vehicle is physically located, for instance, it might be in a public parking garage near where the debtor works. Once you have the Writ, follow the steps below.

1. Get Vehicle Information

To initiate a levy, you will have to provide the levying officer with a description of the vehicle, the license plate or vehicle ID number (VIN), and the approximate location of the vehicle. You will also need to make sure that the debtor is the legal owner or co- owner so you don't initiate a levy on a leased vehicle.

Here are some ways to get vehicle information:

- Debtor's Examination and Subpoena Duces Tecum (Chapter 6) - to avoid arousing the debtor's suspicion, try to ask questions about the vehicle in a routine manner, not as though you are seeking to levy on it

- Debtor's Statement of Assets (Chapter 6, Section A)

- court records (Chapter 6, Section B)

- data search firms, asset tracing firms and investigators.

Another source of information is the Department of Motor Vehicles (DMV), which maintains information on all vehicles registered in California. If you send a request to the DMV for information on a registered motor vehicle, DMV will send a copy of your request to the vehicle's owner, who will have ten days to object to your request. Unless you are planning to serve the debtor with legal papers, the debtor's objection is likely to be upheld. (If you are planning to serve the debtor, see Chapter 21.)

If you decide to contact the DMV anyway, you need to complete Form INF-70 Request for Record Information. You can use it to request information about what cars, boats, trucks, RVs and motor homes are registered under the name of the debtor. You can also find out information about the legal owners of vehicles. This search currently costs $5.

To obtain a copy of form INF-70, visit https://dmv.ca.gov (search for forms, INF-70). Send the completed form and fee to DMV, Public Operations, Unit G-199, and P.O. Box 944247, Sacramento, CA, 94244-2470. You can find more information at the DMV's website at www.ca.dmv.gov.

As you complete the form, keep in mind that the DMV checks for an exact match of the name you provide. If you specify John Markford, but the judgment debtor's vehicles are registered under Jon Markford, the DMV search may turn up a blank. If the name is very common, you may want to submit several requests with variations of the debtor's full name (John P. Markford, John Paul Markford, J.P. Markford, J. Paul Markford). You must pay for each name search, however.

2. Determine Debtor's Ownership in Vehicle

Once your DMV information request is sent back to you, look on the printout for the legal owner, or L/O. The registered owner is indicated by the code R/O. If the debtor is neither the legal owner nor the registered neither the legal owner nor the registered owner, you have probably reached a dead end.

If you discover that the vehicle was very recently transferred, you may be able to seize the car from the new registered or legal owner, but only if the debtor did this to hide their assets from you. To do this you will need the help of an attorney.

Legal Owners, Registered Owners and Lienholders

People typically purchase new vehicles by making a down payment and obtaining a loan for the balance. The lender retains legal title to the vehicle until the loan is paid off. Accordingly, when the vehicle is registered with DMV, the registration shows the purchaser as the registered owner and the lender as the legal owner. DMV records remain this way until the legal owner files a release after full payment of the loan.

Until the vehicle is paid off, the legal owner is normally entitled to repossess the vehicle if the registered owner defaults on payments. If the vehicle is sold to satisfy other debts, the legal owner is entitled to be paid the full value of the outstanding loan first. The legal owner can also ask the court to prevent the vehicle from being sold and have the property released to the registered owner.

Certain liens may have been placed on the vehicle, such as tax liens and attachment liens. These liens entitle their lienholders to be paid before anyone else if the car is sold, except for the legal owner, who is always paid first.

When a motor vehicle is levied on, the levying officer must send a Notice of Levy to all legal owners (if different than the judgment debtor) and to all lienholders. This notice gives the others an opportunity to protect their interests in the vehicle.

If you discover that the vehicle was very recently transferred, you may be able to seize the car from the new registered or legal owner, but only if the debtor did this to hide their assets from you. To do this you will need the help of an attorney.

a. If Debtor Isn't the Legal Owner

Often, the debtor is the registered owner of a vehicle but a bank or financing company is the legal owner. In this situation, it is extremely unlikely that you will get anything in a forced sale. The vehicle will sell for less than its value and the legal owner must be paid before you. In addition, the debtor may be entitled to an exemption. To get a rough estimate of your chances of collecting any money, start by figuring out the low value of the car by checking the Kelley Blue Book. (See Section A2). If you are going after a boat or plane, you can get the same type of information from dealers. If you are unable to obtain access to a used vehicles price guide, check advertised prices on the internet and use the lowest sales price listed for the year and type of vehicle. Now take half of the amount you came up with using either method, this represents what you can actually expect the car to go for in a forced sale.

Next, subtract the amount the debtor owes on the vehicle. You can get this information from the legal owner or from the debtor in a Debtor's Examination. (See Chapter 6). If you have difficulty getting this information, you probably should give up right here.

If there's anything left over, subtract $3,050, the judgment debtor's personal exemption in the vehicle, and another $1,500 (estimate) to cover the cost of a vehicle levy. If there is still money left over and no other liens have been placed on the vehicle, you may be one of the rare creditors who get something from a vehicle seizure.

If there's no money to be had, you still might want to pursue this levy if you think beginning the process will force the judgment debtor into settlement, or if you want to purchase the car for yourself at a forced sale. Otherwise, don't bother.

b. If Judgment Debtor Is the Legal Owner

If the judgment debtor is the legal owner, the vehicle is paid off. Figure out the low value, take 50% of the amount, subtract any other liens, subtract the $3,050 exemption and $1,500 levy costs and see what's left over. If it's a positive number, you may be able to get some cash from a forced sale. Otherwise, forget it, unless you want the car for yourself or are willing to spend $1,500 in hopes of inducing a settlement.

If the legal owner is a business owned by the debtor as a sole proprietor, ask the levying officer how to proceed. Similarly, if the vehicle is jointly owned, ask the levying officer what additional documentation he needs to levy on the vehicle.

3. Provide Levying Officer with Instructions

To find the levying officer for a county, call the sheriff's office and ask if it levies on civil money judgments. Find out the deposit amount required for a vehicle levy, whether the levying officer has his own instruction form, whether the vehicle must be worth a certain minimum amount and how many copies of the Writ are required.

For a car, you will need the license plate number, make and year. The vehicle identification number (VIN) helps provide positive identification, in case the license plates have been put on a different car, but it isn't required. Include the car's color and known identifying factors, such as a dent in the right rear fender, two-tone or convertible.

You also want to provide as much detail as you can about where and when the levying officer is likely to find the car. An officer can't go into a private garage unless the owner invites him in. But a vehicle on the street or in a public place is fair game. Most people park within a four block radius of their home. If you know when the debtor is likely to be home, say so in your instructions. If the debtor takes his car to work and parks it in a public parking lot, advise the officer accordingly, and give him the times when the debtor is at work.

For boats, planes, motorcycles and RVs, give the same type of identifying information, including the manufacturer, license number, color and type of vehicle or craft.

If someone other than the debtor is the legal owner or a lienholder, the Sheriff, as levying officer, will determine from the appropriate department the name and address of the legal owner and each lienholder of the property levied upon. The Sheriff will then serve that person or entity with a copy of the Writ of Execution and Notice of Levy [CCP 700.090].

If the levying officer does not provide a form, use the below sample as a guide. A blank Instructions to Levying Officer form letter is in the Appendix.

If it becomes clear that the debtor is keeping his car on property that a levying officer is not permitted to enter, your only alternative is to seek a court Seizure Order permitting an officer to enter this property. (See Chapter 19).

4. If Debtor or Third Party Objects

After the debtor is notified of your levy, he can file a Claim of Exemption [CCP 703.520(a)]. They don't have to if the levy is on their only motor vehicle; they are automatically entitled to a $3,050 exemption. If they own more than one motor vehicle, they must file a Claim of Exemption to receive the $3,050 motor vehicle or $4,850 – 9,700 tool of the trade exemption. The tool of the trade exemption is likely to be denied if the debtor has two cars, unless one is totally unfit for his business purposes; for example, they have a VW beetle as a second car, but need to haul pipe for their plumbing business.

If the debtor files a Claim of Exemption, follow the procedure outlined in Chapter 15 to oppose it. There is little you can do to contest the $3,050 exemption, but that's not the case if they claim a $4,850-9,700 tool of the trade exemption and their other car is reasonably adequate for use in the business.

Sample Letter of Instructions

May 23, 2014

Re: Amy Right v Jeff Isbad

To the Sheriff, County of Mendocino:

Enclosed please find an original and 3 copies of a Writ of Execution and a check in the amount of $1,500.

Please proceed to levy on (seize, store and sell) the following vehicle belonging to Jeff Isbad:
2009 Saab 900 Turbo Silver with black interior KGOF bumper sticker License Number 1111ZZZZ
Vehicle ID No. DUUUUUUUUH999
The vehicle is almost always parked in the street in front of Jeff Isbad's place of business between the hours of 9:00 a.m. and 5:00 p.m., located at:
Highlighter Haven
666 Coastal Highway
Gualala, CA

Please keep me up updated as to the status of this levy. I would like to attend the sale, so let me know when that will be.

Sincerely,
Amy Right

Third-party owners can object to the sale. If a third-party owner files a claim, and you don't oppose it by posting a deposit equal to the approximate worth of the car, the car will be released back to the debtor. As a general rule, you should oppose a third-party claim only if you are convinced you can prevail legally. You'll probably need a lawyer.

5. Attend the Sale If You Want

After you send your papers and fees to the levying officer, he will follow your instructions and proceed to seize and sell the vehicle. He may contact you to get further fee deposits, to let you know the outcome of the levy or to tell you about any problems with the levy.

Sales of vehicles and the distribution of the proceeds are governed by CCP 701.510-701.830. If you are contemplating buying the vehicle yourself, read these statutes to get an idea of what is involved and ask the levying officer about the specific procedures used in that county.

You and the debtor will be given notice of the time and place of the sale. The sale is conducted like an auction, with the vehicle sold to the highest bidder. As mentioned, the price normally obtained for vehicles in these auctions is far below their value. Attend if there's any chance you could use the vehicle. You may be better off buying it yourself than letting it go for an amount that most likely will get you little or nothing in satisfaction of your judgment.

If you buy the vehicle, the levying officer will pay you out of the money you spend on the vehicle. You might also use your judgment as credit in the bidding process (ask the levying officer about this) and have to put up cash only if you bid higher than the unsatisfied amount of your judgment.

6. Get Your Money

If you did not attend the sale and the levying officer has collected the proceeds of the levy, she will disburse them to you. Don't expect your money right away, delay is common. While you can call the levying officer to make sure your case hasn't fallen through the cracks, be patient. Levying officers often transmit collected funds in lump sums, rather than distributing them as they are collected.

Make sure you keep track of all money collected, as well as any costs incurred by you. We discuss how to do this in Chapter 16.

Blank Page

Chapter 13

Seizing Tangible Personal Property

A. Limitations on Personal Property Levies	13/2
1. Locating Assets to Pursue	13/2
2. Property May be Claimed as Exempt	13/3
3. Property May Secure a Third-Party Debt	13/4
4. Property May be Subject to an Examination Lien	13/4
5. Property May be Owned with Spouse	13/5
B. How to Levy on Personal Property	13/5
1. Obtain Seizure Order for Assets in Debtor's Home	13/5
2. Provide Levying Officer With Instructions	13/5
3. If Debtor or Third Party Objects	13/5
4. Attend the Sale if You Want	13/6
5. Get Your Money	13/6

Collection Factor	High	Moderate	Low
Potential cost to you	✓		
Potential for producing $$$			✓
Potential for Settlement			✓
Potential time and trouble		✓	
Potential for bankruptcy			✓

Information on levying types of property

Not all personal property is covered in this chapter. You might also want to look at Chapter 10 (money held by third parties on behalf of the debtor), Chapter 11 (personal property owned by a business) or Chapter 12 (motor vehicles).

On all items, use the exemption limits on Judicial Council Form EJ-156 instead of the CCP codes. The Judicial Council form is updated more frequently than the CCPs.

Items of tangible personal property are physical objects of value, such as stock certificates, bonds, cameras, stamps, coins, computers, expensive musical instruments, video equipment, stereos, jewelry, tools, recreational equipment, weapons, luxury clothing (such as a mink coat), animals, pets, art and precious metals. In theory, you may be able to satisfy your judgment by seizing personal property that the debtor owns and has in their possession.

But it's often in theory only. Prying personal property loose from a debtor is difficult and often not worthwhile. You face several possible obstacles, most fundamentally that the amount you'll realize from a forced sale is rarely worth the effort and expense, unless you seize items with a ready market value, such as securities, precious metals and pianos.

But if you can identify a possible source to satisfy your judgment and have tried other methods of collection without success, keep reading.

A. Limitations on Personal Property Levies

As mentioned, enforcing your judgment against personal property is rarely successful. But if you are going to pursue this possibility, here are some of the problems you might face.

1. Locating Assets to Pursue

To begin, you must find out if the debtor has tangible personal property that might make this procedure worthwhile. If you don't know, you'll have to do some investigating.

Here are a few suggestions:

- schedule a debtor's examination and serve a Subpoena Duces Tecum (Chapter 6, Sections C and D)

- review the Judgment Debtor's Statement of Assets (Chapter 6, Section A)

- examine court records (Chapter 6, Section B), or

- hire a data search firm, asset tracing firm or investigators.

Once you learn what the debtor owns, you must evaluate whether it's worth pursuing. Consider two factors:

Value at forced sale - Most personal property brings in a small fraction of its fair market value at a sale by a levying officer. For example, a dining room table that might bring $1,000 in an antique store could fetch only $250–$300 in a forced sale. The only exceptions are assets that can easily be liquidated, such as gold, gemstones, coin collections, pianos and securities (stocks, bonds, etc.).

Cost of storage and sale - The levying officer must store seized assets to give the debtor a chance to file a claim of exemption and to give notice of the sale. If a sale does occur, the cost of conducting it is substantial. In short, the costs associated with levies on personal property are significant. When these costs are deducted from the artificially low proceeds, there may be little or nothing left over to put toward the judgment.

2. Property May Be Claimed as Exempt

Debtors are allowed to keep certain items of property, called exemptions. Exemption laws attempt to strike a balance between the creditor's right to enforce their judgment and the debtor's right to avoid sinking to the level of the many homeless people who haunt American cities.

Exemptions apply to property owned by individuals, not businesses. They take one of two forms: property that is fully exempt and therefore cannot be sold at all, and property that is partially exempt, so that if it is sold, the debtor is entitled to a specific amount of the proceeds before you can put the money toward your judgment. For a debtor to claim certain property as exempt, they must file a Claim of Exemption (See Chapter 15).

Below we list some of the exemptions for tangible personal property. Cash exemptions are covered in Chapter 8, wage exemptions in Chapter 9 and motor vehicle exemptions in Chapter 12.

Household furnishings and personal effects: The debtor is entitled to exempt all household furnishings and personal effects located at their principal residence and reasonably necessary for personal use by them or their dependents [CCP 704.020]. There is no dollar limitation, however "reasonably necessary" is subject to a court's discretion. A court could determine that a debtor is entitled to keep a certain item. If the court decides that a particular item is too valuable, it can allow the item to be sold and require that the debtor receive a reasonable amount from the sale to buy a replacement item. If the debtor doesn't purchase the replacement item within 90 days of the sale, the proceeds are available for the creditor to seize [CCP 704.020(c)].

Jewelry, heirlooms and works of art: The debtor is entitled to exempt up to $8,000 worth of jewelry, heirlooms and works of art [CCP 704.040]. It makes little sense to seize these types of assets unless the sale will bring in considerably more than $8,000. Even then, the debtor may claim that some items of jewelry or heirlooms are personal effects, which are exempt without regard to value if they are ordinarily and reasonably necessary.

Health aids: The debtor is entitled to exempt all health aids necessary to help them work or live comfortably, such as a wheelchair [CCP 704.050].

Building materials: The debtor is entitled to exempt up to $3,200 in building supplies if they were purchased to repair their home [CCP 704.030].

Tools of the trade: The debtor is entitled to exempt up to $8,000 of tools of their trade. A tool of the trade is anything the debtor or a spouse uses to carry out a business activity, including:

- business-related equipment, such as musical instruments or cooking implements

- materials, such as paper, cloth, wood and hardware

- uniforms

- office furnishings

- books and manuals

- one commercial motor vehicle (see Chapter 12, Section A), and

- one fishing boat or other vessel used in the business.

Computer equipment needed to do desktop publishing, word processing or research also probably fits within the tools of the trade exemption. If the debtor and their spouse are in the same trade, business or profession which is also their livelihood, they are entitled to a $15,975 tools-of-the-trade exemption [CCP 704.060].

3. Property May Secure a Third-Party Debt

You can't, as a practical matter, reach property that is subject to a perfected security interest or to liens that have priority over yours. Chapter 4 explains liens and lien priorities.

We recommend that you check to see whether property is subject to a security interest before instructing a levying officer to seize and sell it. You can find out by checking with the Secretary of State, who keeps a record of all perfected security interests. We discuss this in Chapter 4, Section B2. Or, you can pay a data search firm to do it for you.

What's a Perfected Security Interest?

A security interest in property is created when the purchaser of the property borrows money for the purchase and gives the lender title to the property until the loan is paid off. This arrangement is common in purchases of expensive equipment, jewelry and household furniture.

For the lender to assert their rights to the property as title owner, they must "perfect" their title by registering it with the California Secretary of State [Commercial Code 9310]. Once a security interest is perfected, the security interest owner can prevent others (including you as a judgment creditor) from seizing the property until the loan has been paid and the security interest released.

What happens if you levy on property that is subject to a third-party security interest? If the third party learns of the proposed sale before it happens, they can file a third-party claim of ownership to stop the sale. If they learn of the sale after it has occurred, they can file a claim to get paid what the debtor owes them out of the proceeds of the sale. If you have spent the proceeds, they can sue you for the value of the property or try to have the property seized, in which case the purchaser would come after you. And you could be liable for any costs the third party spent in their efforts to collect the money owe to them.

4. Property May Be Subject to an Examination Lien

If another judgment creditor has served the debtor with notice of a debtor's examination, all their personal property is automatically subject to a one-year examination lien (See Chapter 4, Section C). If you attempt to levy on property subject to such a lien, the fruits of your effort may end up in the lienholder's basket.

If you think that other creditors have judgments against the debtor, check the court records for each county in which a creditor may have conducted a debtor's examination (See Chapter 4, Section C). If you locate a judgment against the debtor, examine the file for a Proof of Service for an Application and Order for Appearance and Examination. If you find one that was served within the past year, all of the judgment debtor's personal property is subject to that lien until one year from the date of the order [CCP 708.110(d)]. In such a situation, you can proceed with your levy, and hope that the other lienholder won't find out about it, or you can wait until the lien expires to go after the assets.

Checking for Other Creditors Records from other court cases may give you an idea of which previous attempts to enforce those judgments have worked and which have not. These records can steer you away from an asset that a previous creditor couldn't reach because it was exempt or because it was subject to a perfected security interest held by a third party.

You might also find out about other creditors' enforcement attempts from the levying officer where the debtor or their assets are located. It makes sense to find out if there are other active creditors, because levying officers must levy on writs in the order received.

5. Property May Be Owned With Spouse

In general, you can seize a married debtor's separate property and the couple's community property, but you usually cannot go after the separate property of a non- debtor spouse (See Chapter 1, Section D).

Without a complete history of a how an item of property was obtained, for example, by one spouse before the marriage, by the couple during the marriage or by one spouse during the marriage through inheritance, you have no idea which partner owns the property or if it's owned by both. So how should you proceed? Go after the property and force the debtor or their spouse to prove that the property is the separate property of the non-debtor spouse.

B. How to Levy on Personal Property

Before you can levy on personal property, you must obtain a Writ of Execution directed to the county where the property is located, that is, where the debtor lives (See Chapter 7). Then follow these steps.

1. Obtain Seizure Order for Assets in Debtor's Home

For property located inside the debtor's house or another private location, such as the back yard, you'll need a court order permitting the levying officer to enter. To obtain such a Seizure Order, you must tell the judge what you expect to find (See Chapter 19). The judge will not allow the levying officer to go on a fishing expedition in search of any and all property that's not nailed down.

Even if the levying officer is willing attempt a levy without a court order, and knows to stop if the debtor refuses to allow them inside, we recommend that you get the court order first [CCP 699.030(b)]. If the debtor refuses to let the officer in, the debtor will have time to move their property while you're busy getting the Seizure Order.

2. Provide Levying Officer with Instructions

To find the levying officer for a county, call the sheriff's office and ask if it levies on civil money judgments. Find out the deposit amount required for a personal property levy (you may have to put down a few hundred dollars as deposit), if they have their own instructions form and how many copies of the Writ are required.

If the levying officer does not provide a form, use the sample below as a guide. A blank "Instructions to Levying Officer" form letter is in the Appendix.

After receiving your instructions, the levying officer fills out a Notice of Levy, which they serve personally on the judgment debtor. The Notice of Levy identifies the property to be levied on and the amount necessary to satisfy the judgment.

3. If Debtor or Third Party Objects

When the debtor receives a Notice of Levy, they have ten days to challenge the levy (if they were served personally [CCP 703.520(a)]. If the debtor was served by mail, they get an additional 5 days to file the claim [CCP 1013(a)]. To do so, they must file a Claim of Exemption explaining why they believe that certain items identified in the Notice of Levy are exempt. They must also cite (specify in writing) the section of the Code of Civil Procedure that permits the exemption.

If the debtor files a Claim of Exemption,

Sample Letter of Instructions

May 30, 2014

Re: Amy Right v. Jeff Isbad
To the Sheriff, County of Los Angeles:
Enclosed please find an original and 3 copies of a Writ of Execution, a certified copy of a Seizure Order and a check in the amount of $ 600.

Please proceed to levy on (seize, store and sell) the following tangible personal property of Jeff Isbad, located in his home at 666 e Cra P st, Helltown, California, 90666:

a. Original signed lithograph set by artist Cha-Ching
b. Camera equipment
c. Mink coat (kept in hall closet)
d. Antique bedroom set (in guest bedroom)
e. Coin collection (kept in Jeff Isbad's study)
f. Steinway baby grand piano.

Please keep me updated as to the status of this levy. I would like to attend the sale, so let me know when it will be. Thank you.

Sincerely,
Amy Right

---

the levying officer will serve you with a copy of it and a Notice of Claim of Exemption [CCP703.540]. Unless you oppose the Claim of Exemption, the debtor's property will be returned to them. Instructions for opposing a Claim of Exemption are in Chapter 15.

A third party who learns about the levy may object on any of the following grounds:

- the debtor is storing the property for them
- the debtor has the property on consignment
- the debtor borrowed the property from them
- the debtor has already sold or signed over the property to them, or
- the debtor pledged the property as security for a loan.

If a third party files a claim [CCP 720.110 & 720.210], the procedure for opposing it is similar to opposing a debtor's Claim of Exemption [CCP 720.310]. If the amount of your judgment justifies getting legal help to pursue this, by all means do so. Usually, however, you are better off dropping the matter.

4. Attend Sale If You Want

The levying officer posts a notice of sale and serves the notice on the debtor either personally or by mail. The notice states the date, time and place of the sale and describes the property. The notice must be posted in three public places in the city or judicial district where the property is to be sold [CCP 701.530].

The property is sold at an auction to the highest bidder [CCP 701.570(b) & (d)]. If you want the property yourself, you can use the judgment as a credit against your bid [CCP 701.590(b)], but you'll need cash or a certified check to pay for a bid higher than the amount of your judgment. Call the levying officer and find out more about the auction and your options as a judgment creditor.

The levying officer distributes the sale proceeds as required by law. Your share of these proceeds depends on the total fees due the levying officer [CCP 687.050], applicable exemptions, and the claims of third-party owners who must be paid and the priorities of any other creditors with claims.

5. Get Your Money

If you did not attend the sale and the levying officer has collected the proceeds of the levy, they will disburse them to you. Don't expect your money right away, delay is common. While you can call the levying officer to make sure your case hasn't fallen through the cracks, be patient. Levying officers often transmit collected funds in lump sums, rather than distributing them as they are collected.

Make sure you keep track of all money collected, as well as any costs incurred by you. We discuss how to do this in Chapter 16.

Blank Page

Chapter 14

Seizing Real Estate

A. Limitations on Real Estate Levies	14/2
B. Finding Debtor's Real Estate	14/3
1. County Tax Assessor's Records	14/3
2. County Recorder's Office	14/3
3. Title Companies	14/3
4. Data Search Firms	14/4
C. Forcing a Sale of Property	14/5
1. Is It Economically Worthwhile?	14/5
2. Does a Homestead Exemption Apply?	14/5
3. Sale Procedures	14/6

Collection Factor	High	Moderate	Low
Potential cost to you	✓		
Potential for producing $$$		✓	
Potential for settlement	✓		
Potential time and trouble	✓		
Potential for bankruptcy			✓

In Chapter 4, we explained liens, what they are, and how to obtain them. As soon as you get your judgment, you should record a lien in any county in which the debtor owns or is likely to own real estate.

Collecting on a real estate lien is often a passive act, most people wait until the debtor (owner of the real estate) refinances or sells the property, and then the lien is paid out of escrow.

You can also take a more active approach, by forcing the sale of the debtor's real estate in order to get paid out of the proceeds, but few judgment debtors undertake this procedure. Seizing real estate is expensive, time consuming and cumbersome, and usually requires a lawyer's help.

This chapter does not take you step by step through the process. It does give you a broad overview of what's involved, as well as guidance to get you started. If you decide to force the sale of the property, you should certainly consider hiring a lawyer. By initiating the process, however, you may get the debtor's attention, and get them to pay your judgment before you have to do anything drastic.

A. Limitations on Real Estate Levies

In addition to the expense, time and burden of the process, you may face several other obstacles in seizing real estate.

- The debtor probably owes a first mortgage and possibly a second or third. These debts may have to be paid out of the sale before you get anything.

- If the real estate is the debtor's home, exemption laws entitle them to keep between $75,000, to $175,000, of the proceeds of the sale, before you get a penny.

- The property may be subject to liens ahead of your lien, such as tax liens, mechanics' liens or other judgment liens. These creditors may have to be paid before you.

- In a forced sale, real estate usually sells for less than its market value. Partly because of the scavenging nature of the process, forced sales often bring in less than what the property would fetch if sold conventionally, but also because the bidders do not usually have an opportunity to view the inside of the premise nor to conduct a formal inspection.

- If the real estate is a dwelling, for example, a twenty unit building, you must obtain a special order of sale, which is a fairly complex court proceeding.

- The cost and possible attorney fees of selling real estate may eat up a chunk of the eventual proceeds.

Do You Want to Own the Debtor's Property?

Forcing the sale of the debtor's real estate might make sense if you want to buy the property for yourself. You may be able to get it cheaply by forcing a sale and bidding on it yourself through the 'creditors bid' process. While you may not realize any cash from the sale to satisfy your judgment, you may get a good deal on the property and still be eligible to collect your judgment against other income streams or assets of the debtor.

B. Finding Debtor's Real Estate

If you don't know what real estate the debtor owns, the methods outlined in Chapter 6 may help you find out. In addition, you may be able to use the following sources to get that information.

1. County Tax Assessor's Records

Each county tax assessor's office has records of the owner of every piece of real estate in the county. You can look up the debtor, check under the spouse's name and any business names as well. The records won't usually tell you whether the debtor owns the property alone or with someone else, but it's easy to find that out by looking at the deed (Section B2, below).

You can also use the records to discover the name of the owner of a certain piece of property, if you have the property's address. If the debtor rents, you can find out the name of his landlord, who may give you useful information.

The tax assessor's records also include the address where the assessor mails the owner's tax bills. If it's different from the property address, it may help you serve the debtor with court papers, and lead you to another piece of property to satisfy your judgment.

Some assessors' offices give out information by phone, though in these budget constrained times, such assistance is becoming less common. If not, you can visit or write the office. If you write, you can use a letter similar to the sample below. There should be no fee for this information, but enclose a self-addressed, stamped envelope with your request.

2. County Recorder's Office

The County Recorder's Office is where the deed and other security interests are recorded. When you obtained your real estate lien (Chapter 4), you recorded it at the county recorder's office. These are public records that you'll have to search in person. Here's what you'll find.

- The names of all the owners of the property. If the debtor owns the property with someone else, your judgment lien might attach only to the debtor's share. But if the debtor and a spouse own the home as community property or in joint tenancy, you may be entitled to reach both spouses' shares (See Chapter 1, Section D6)

- Whether the debtor owes money to a bank, mortgage lender, the seller or anyone else who provided the funding to purchase the property.

- Other creditors and lienholders who have an interest in the property, lenders with a second or third mortgage or home equity loan, other judgment creditors, taxing authorities and the like.

- Any filed Declaration of Homestead, which might provide the debtor with a substantial exemption, even if they are not currently living in the house. (See Section C2.)

Deeds are usually indexed by the name of the owners. The indexes are generally alphabetical, and cover a certain number of years. So you may need to check several printouts or microfiche cards to locate all property listings for a debtor for a given 20 year period. When you visit the County Recorder's Office, ask for help finding the information you need.

3. Title Companies

Another way to find out where the judgment debtor owns property is to contact a title company. Title companies provide a large range of services to buyers and sellers of real estate, such as title searches, title insurance and escrow transactions.

Sample Letter to Assessor

July 24, 2014

Assessor's Office, County of Los Angeles

Dear Assessor:

Please provide me with the following information:
1. Regarding the property located at 666 E Cra P st, Helltown, California 90666: the names and addresses of the current owners of record, the Assessor's Parcel Number and the date the property was acquired.
2. Whether or not Jeff Isbad owns any property in Los Angeles. If so, please indicate, for each property, the date the property was acquired, the property address and the Assessor's Parcel Number.

Enclosed is a self-addressed, stamped envelope for the return of this information. Thank you for your assistance.

Sincerely,

Amy Right

Many title companies have an alphabetical listing of property owners. While some title companies have access to the entire list, including listings in every county, many have listings only for their area. This means you may have to check with title companies in several counties if you suspect the debtor has property in more than one place.

Title companies may have more detailed information, often called a property profile, on a particular piece of property. Besides listing the owner of record, a profile may include additional information of use to you, such as:

- the year the deed was recorded

- the owner's mailing address

- the assessed value of the property

- the estimated total value of the property

- the original amount of any existing mortgage

- the amount of taxes assessed, whether taxes have been paid and to whom the tax bill was sent, and

- a copy of the last deed and latest open deed of trust.

Title companies vary in their willingness to give out information. Some let you come in and look through their records. Others give out some information over the phone if you give them an address or the name of a property owner. Still others don't give any information to the public. Check with title companies in your area; you can find them listed in the Yellow Pages. When you call, ask to speak to customer service or an escrow officer. Note that even where a title company is willing to provide a complimentary "property profile" which will often include deeds of trust, they usually will not reflect involuntary liens such as those created by Abstracts of Judgments, which, if recorded and senior to your lien, must be paid off prior to the sale of a dwelling. Some title companies will provide a limited title report, sometimes called a Litigation Guarantee Report, for a few hundred dollars, but the insurance provided by such reports is usually limited to about $25,000.

4. Data Search Firms

For less than a few hundred dollars, you can also usually find a data search firm to conduct a statewide search for real estate owned by the judgment debtor. In many instances, it is worth your while to have one of these companies do your search rather than do it yourself.

C. Forcing a Sale of Property

As mentioned, forcing the sale of real estate is time consuming and expensive, and will probably require the help of a lawyer. Here is some information to help you determine whether a forced sale appears worthwhile and, if so, how to start the process on your own.

1. Is It Economically Worthwhile?

Before levying against real estate, you want to figure out whether there is sufficient equity in the property to justify the effort. Equity is the amount of the debtor's share left over after all mortgages, liens and security interests are subtracted from the property's likely sales price. If the likely sales price is $270,000 and the debtor owes $210,000, their equity is $60,000. Remember that when calculating these amounts, where the debtor is only a joint tenant or tenant in common, and, unless the other owner is a spouse where that interest can be sold as community property, the creditor can only execute against the debtor's interest, and all senior liens and exemptions discussed below, must be satisfied from only that fractional portion. The second important factor in determining economic feasibility is the determination of a homestead exemption discussed below.

2. Does a Homestead Exemption Apply?

Next, find out whether the property is covered by the California homestead exemption. The exemption covers primary residences only [CCP 704.710(a)]. But a primary residence could be anywhere the debtor can live legally. So a debtor could claim that their 10 story apartment building is their primary residence, because they live in unit 2B, but cannot claim that they live in a hardware store because it is not zoned as a "residential unit". In some counties, a tent on a piece of land could be considered a primary residence. It depends on the judge. Usually the homestead exemption does not need to be in writing, the court can grant the exemption upon evidence provided by the debtor, that they or their spouse reside in the property.

It makes no sense to force a sale unless the sale would yield an amount above the exemption and liens, in fact, the court will not even allow it. In a forced sale, the homeowner (judgment debtor) receives the amount of the homestead exemption before the judgment creditor gets anything. So after you figure out the equity (Section C1, above) and subtract the cost of sale, subtract the appropriate homestead exemption amount (rules are simplified here, confirm by reviewing CCP 704.730), as follows:

- $75,000 if the debtor is unmarried,

- $100,000 if the debtor is married or has dependents at the home

- $175,000 if the debtor is 65 or older or disabled, or

- $175,000 if the debtor is 55 or older, and either single and earning under $15,000 per year, or married and earning under $20,000 per year.

If a homestead applies then the property must be sold at a minimum of 90% of the value approved by the court. This is very rare since the buyers will have no opportunity to view the home prior to making a bid. Also, all liens ahead of yours must be paid in full at the sale.

Even if the debtor does not live in the property, only the court can rule that the property is not a homestead. This means that you will need to file a motion with the court to allow the sale and rule that there is no homestead (if the property is a commercial property, this is not necessary).

Example: Amy wants to seize Jeff's home and force a sale. The property is homesteaded at $75,000. The court decided that the home was worth $850,000. Jeff has a first mortgage of $626,000 and a tax lien of $70,000. Because the home qualifies for the exemption, the Sheriff cannot sell if for less than $765,000. Once it sells the Sheriff must pay off the first mortgage and tax lien first ($696,000) and then apply the balance to Jeff's homestead exemption ($75,000). In this case there is no money left for Amy and therefore the court would have never allowed the home to go to sell in the first place.

If the homestead does not apply, then the property can be sold for the highest bid and will be subject to all senior liens, meaning they do not have to be paid off at the sale but will become the responsibility of the new buyer.

You could lose a lot of money

If you attempt to force a sale but no bid comes in that is sufficient to pay off the mortgages, liens, costs of sale and homestead exemption, you will not be able to recover your costs from the judgment debtor. In short, you will lose money if you unsuccessfully levy on property covered by a homestead exemption [CCP 704.840], and, you will be prohibited from even trying to sell it again for another year.

3. Sale Procedures

As mentioned earlier, you will probably need a lawyer's help if you really want to force the sale of the debtor's real estate. Before calling a lawyer, you might want to become familiar with the laws governing real estate levies. In a law library or on the Internet, you'll want to read California CCP 700.015 and 701.540 through 701.680. If the real estate is a dwelling, you also will want to read 704.710 through 704.850.

Here are the basic steps you'll have to take to force a sale when the property is a dwelling. If the property is not a dwelling, court hearings are not required.

Step 1: Obtain a Writ of Execution. (See Chapter 7.)

Step 2: Prepare written instructions for the levying officer. To find the levying officer for a county, call the sheriff's office and ask if it levies on civil money judgments. Find out the deposit amount required for a real estate levy, whether the levying officer has his own instruction form, what documents you must provide with your levy instructions and how many copies of each document are required.

Step 3: Deliver the required papers and deposit to the levying officer.

Step 4: The levying officer serves the Writ of Execution and Notice of Levy on the judgment debtor.

Step 5: Within 30 days after Notice of Levy is served on judgment debtor, you must give the levying officer a list of all those holding a mortgage, lien or security interest on the property. (See Section B above.)

Step 6: You must file a formal motion in the county where the property is located, post notice of the motion and obtain an Order of Sale within 20 days after the Notice of Levy was served on the debtor (if property is a dwelling).

Step 7: The court sets a hearing date within 45 days after the motion is filed and issues an Order to Show Cause, which requires the debtor to explain why the property shouldn't be sold.

How to Obtain an Order of Sale

Before you obtain an Order of Sale, you must get the property independently appraised, obtain a title report that reflects all mortgages, liens and other security interests and determine whether the home is subject to a homestead exemption.

Senior liens are those that were created before yours or receive priority by law, such as tax liens. Junior liens are liens created after yours. When property subject to liens is forcibly sold, senior liens are paid off first; junior liens are only paid if there is enough left over. After the forced sale, all liens are extinguished except for federal and state tax liens if property is homesteaded. If not homesteaded, a buyer can buy property subject to senior liens.

Step 8: Have the Order to Show Cause and certain other papers served on the debtor and occupants of the dwelling within 30 days of the scheduled hearing.

Step 9: If the debtor doesn't attend the hearing, they are entitled to request a second hearing.

Step 10: At the hearing, the court determines and issues an order stating the amount of any homestead exemption, the fair market value of the property and the amount of sale proceeds that must be distributed to cover all mortgages, liens and other security interests.

Step 11: The levying officer holds a sale no sooner than 120 days after the Notice of Levy was served, after giving notice to the judgment debtor, occupants of the dwelling, and all mortgage, lien and other security interest holders at least 20 days before the sale. The notice states the date, time and place of sale and the address and a description of the property. IF the property is homesteaded then the property may be sold only if the winning bid is at least 90% of the property's fair market value. If no adequate bid is received, the court can order a new sale one year or more later.

Blank Page

Chapter 15

Opposing a Claim of Exemption

A. Wage Garnishment	15/2
1. Opposing a Claim of Exemption	15/3
2. Completing the Notice of Opposition to Claim of Exemption	15/3
3. Completing the Notice of Hearing on Claim of Exemption	15/4
4. Serve and File the Opposition Papers	15/4
5. Attend Hearing	15/7
B. Property Seizure	15/8
1. Opposing a Claim of Exemption	15/8
2. Completing the Notice of Opposition to Claim of Exemption	15/11
3. Completing the Notice of Hearing on Claim of Exemption	15/11
4. Serve and File the Opposition Papers	15/12
5. Attend Hearing	15/13
6. Wait for the Ruling	15/13

If you seek to empty the debtor's bank accounts, garnish their wages, seize money or property owed them, seize their motor vehicle, or other personal property, the debtor can formally protest by filing a Claim of Exemption. A third party, who claims to have interest in the property, may also file a Claim of Exemption. You can object to the Claim of Exemption if you feel that the property is not exempt or is not necessary for the debtor's support.

There are two different procedures to object to a Claim of Exemption. One is used to garnish wages, the other to seize money (other than wages) or property.

FREQUENT REASONS TO SEEK DENIAL OF CLAIM OF EXEMPTION

Exclusion of Financial Statements - Financial statement are required when the debtor claim is that property taken is necessary for the support of the debtor and/or family. This is a direct violation of CCP 703.520 & 703.530.

Without a valid Financial Statement, signed by the debtor and spouse, the Claim of Exemption is not valid and void its face. Without a Financial Statement, neither the Creditor nor the Court can properly evaluate the debtor's financial condition. The Court should be asked to deny the Claim of Exemption for inadequate information to base the decision on and for violation of CCP 703.520 & 703.530.

Fraudulent Assertions in Financial Statement - Upon receipt of the Claim of Exemption Notice from the Sheriff's Office, immediately update your due diligence on the debtor's financial status. This due diligence provides insight into the accuracy of the debtor's submitted Financial Statement.

A. Wage Garnishment

The debtor can contest your wage garnishment by filing a Claim of Exemption form with the levying officer. On the form, the debtor must state that they are contesting the wage garnishment and give their reasons. When the officer receives the Claim of Exemption, he will mail you a copy, along with a financial statement completed

Realize that Debtors are very innovative in the ways they falsify financial statements. Key income sources may be totally excluded to minimize reported income. Excess, or inflated, costs may also be included to minimize net income.

Debtor's frequently exclude income from a business in their Financial Statement. This fragrant omission should always be highlighted with supporting Exhibits to the Court and should be the basis for the denial of the Claim of Exemption.

Most debtors include 401(K) payments and other optional payments as valid expenses in the Financial Statements. Because these payments are optional, they should not be allowed as legitimate expenses in the Financial Statement. Highlighting and quantifying these "optional" payments to the Court lowers the debtor's credibility in requesting the Claim of Exemption.

In Attachment 6 attached to the Notice of Opposition to Claim of Exemption (Form EJ-170), individually highlight and dispute each fraudulent submission based on your due diligence facts. When the debtor condescends to include fraudulent assertions in the Financial Statements, respectfully ask the Court to disregard the falsified Financial Statements and deny the Claim of Exemption.

In summary, the more items that can be disputed with substantiating facts, the higher the odds the Claim of Exemption will be denied by the Court.

by the debtor and a document called Notice of Filing of Claim of Exemption (Wage Garnishment).

Only about 15% of all debtors file a Claim of Exemption to protest a wage garnishment. If your debtor decides to join this minority, however, the ball is in your court. Unless you oppose the claim, your Earnings Withholding Order (see Chapter 9) will automatically terminate or be modified to reflect any amount the debtor indicated they could pay.

1. Opposing a Claim of Exemption

You must file your notice of opposition to the Claim of Exemption with the levying officer and the court within **ten days** of when the Notice of Filing of Claim of Exemption [form WG-008] was mailed [CCP 706.105(c)(3) & 706.105(d)]. That date is on the form. This means you may have only a few days to respond to the Notice after you receive it.

People in the judgment enforcement business quickly learn whether or not it makes sense to oppose a Claim of Exemption. They examine the financial statement for any of the following items:

- an expense that seems out of line, such as $400 for utilities

- an expense that should not be as high a priority as your judgment, for example, large payments on an expensive or second car, or

- omitted income or assets.

If you find any of these, your opposition to the debtor's Claim of Exemption may very well succeed. Similarly, if the debtor's income is well above the poverty level, the Claim of Exemption is not likely to win. On the other hand, if the debtor's financial statement appears reasonable and the debt does not fall into one of exceptions listed under the instructions for item 5 in Section 2, below, you may want to think compromise.

If you decide to oppose the debtor's Claim of Exemption, first read the "Instructions to Judgment Creditor" on the Notice of Filing of Claim of Exemption form.

Next, fill out the Notice of Opposition to Claim of Exemption (Wage Garnishment form WG-009) and Notice of Hearing on Claim of Exemption (form WG-010) forms (see Sections A2 and A3, below), which are in the Appendix. Make five copies of, and file them with the clerk of the court and with the levying officer within ten days of the mailing date listed on the Notice. If you miss this deadline, your wage garnishment will be terminated, or modified, if the debtor asked only for a modification.

2. Completing the Notice of Opposition to Claim of Exemption

A completed sample and instructions are below; a blank copy is in the Appendix.

Caption: Follow the format of your previous court papers. Be sure to enter the levying officer's file number, which is on the Claim of Exemption you received.

Item 1: Enter your name and address.

Item 2: Enter the name and address of the debtor. If you know the debtor's Social Security number, check the box under item 2 and complete form WG-035

Item 3: Enter the date the Notice of Filing of Claim of Exemption was mailed. It should be in Item 1 on that form.

Item 4: Check "a" if you think none of the debtor's wages are exempt. Check "b" if you think only a portion of the wages is exempt.

Item 5: Check "a", "b", and/or "c" and elaborate as follows:

Item 5a: The debtor can claim that their wages are exempt from enforcing a judgment if the debtor proves they need the money to support their family [CCP 706.051(c) (1)]. However you may be able to prove that all of the income is not necessary.

Item 5b: If the judgment is for the award of attorney fees under Family Code 2030, 3121 or 3557, the exemption is not available to the debtor. Check this box [CCP 706.051(c) (1)].

Item 5c: The debtor cannot claim that their wages are exempt from enforcing a judgment based on personal services you rendered the debtor as their employee [CCP 706.051(c) (2)]. For instance, if you worked in the debtor's shop and obtained a judgment against them for back pay, they cannot exempt their wages from you. Nor can the debtor exempt their wages if your judgment is for child or spousal support [706.051(c) (3)]. Other possible grounds to oppose include the debtor lying about their financial obligations or assets. If you need more room, add an attachment sheet.

Item 6: Put the amount of payment per pay period (listed on the Employer's Return) you are willing to accept.

At the end, enter the date and your name, and then sign the form.

3. Completing the Notice of Hearing on Claim of Exemption

A completed sample and instructions are below; a blank copy is in the Appendix.

Caption: Follow the format of your previous court papers. Be sure to enter the levying officer's file number.

Item 1: Enter the levying officer's name and address. Then enter the name and address of the debtor. Below the Sheriff's information, check the box if you garnished the wages of the debtor's spouse, and fill in their information below the check box. Check the last box and fill in the name and address if the judgment debtor has an attorney representing them.

Item 2: Check appropriate box

Item 2a: Call the court clerk for a hearing date, time and location, and enter them here. The hearing must be held within 30 days of the date you file your papers with the court [CCP 706.105(e)]. The clerk is likely to give you several alternative dates within the 30-day period. If the court cannot accommodate the time-frame required, because they are too busy, don't worry they know the legal requirements.

Item 2b: Enter the address of the court.

Item 3: Check this box only if you don't intend to be at the hearing in person. We recommend that you do attend. If you can't be there, prepare a declaration on lined paper and attach it to your opposition forms. Explain why you won't be there and why you believe the Claim of Exemption should be denied, for instance, you know the debtor has other sources of income which they didn't state on their form. An example of a declaration is shown below.

Finally, enter the date and your name, and sign the form. Leave the Proof of Service on the back blank for now.

4. Serve and File the Opposition Papers

You must serve the papers on the debtor and file them with the court. Your response must be served on the debtor at least 16 court days before the hearing date, add 5 days if service is by mail [CCP 1005(b) & 706.105(e)]. You can have these papers served on the judgment debtor by mail or personally. In most cases, mail is the easiest and least expensive approach, as long as it allows the debtor enough notice of the hearing date.

Either way, don't delay in serving the forms. Once they are served, you must file the forms with the court, and that filing must take place within ten days from the mailing date of the Notice of Filing of Claim of Exemption [CCP 706.105(e)]. Here's how to proceed:

1. Make at least five copies of your documents. One is for your records, another is for the levying officer, a third is for the court and a fourth is for the judgment debtor. If there is an

WG-009

ATTORNEY OR PARTY WITHOUT ATTORNEY *(Name, State Bar number, and address)*:	LEVYING OFFICER *(Name and Address)*:
Amy Right 1000 My st, Mytown, Ca 90000 TELEPHONE NO.: 310-555-5555 FAX NO.: E-MAIL ADDRESS: ATTORNEY FOR *(Name)*: In Pro Per	Los Angeles County Sheriff 123 Main st Los Angeles, Ca 90012

SUPERIOR COURT OF CALIFORNIA, COUNTY OF Los Angeles
STREET ADDRESS: 111 Hill st
MAILING ADDRESS:
CITY AND ZIP CODE: Los Angeles, Ca 90012
BRANCH NAME: Stanley Mosk Courthouse

PLAINTIFF/PETITIONER: Amy Right
DEFENDANT/RESPONDENT: Jeff Isbad

NOTICE OF OPPOSITION TO CLAIM OF EXEMPTION (Wage Garnishment)	COURT CASE NUMBER: 14K5000
	LEVYING OFFICER FILE NUMBER.:

TO THE LEVYING OFFICER:

1. Name and address of judgment creditor

   Amy Right
   1000 My st
   Mytown, Ca 90000

2. Name and address of employee

   Jeff Isbad
   666 e Cra P st
   Helltown, Ca 90666

   Social Security No. [✔] on form WG-035   [ ] unknown

3. The Notice of Filing Claim of Exemption states it was mailed on
   (date): 03/22/2015

4. The earnings claimed as exempt are
   a. [ ] not exempt.
   b. [✔] partially exempt. The amount not exempt per month is: $ 900.00

5. The judgment creditor opposes the claim of exemption because
   a. [✔] the following expenses of the debtor are not necessary for the support of the debtor or the debtor's family *(specify)*:
      $ 250 clothing expense is excessive (should be limited to $ 50)
      $ 300 entertainment expense is excessive (should be limited to $ 25)
      $ 350 gasoline expense is excessive (should be limited to $100)
      $ 250 cable TV expense is excessive (should be limited to $75)

   b. [ ] the debt was for attorney's fees based on a court order under Family Code section 2030, 3121, or 3557.

   c. [ ] other *(specify)*:

6. [✔] The judgment creditor will accept: $ 500.00   per pay period for payment on account of this debt.

I declare under penalty of perjury under the laws of the State of California that the foregoing is true and correct.

Date: 03/22/2015

Amy Right
(TYPE OR PRINT NAME)   ▶   (SIGNATURE OF DECLARANT)

Form Adopted for Mandatory Use
Judicial Council of California
WG-009 [Rev. January 2, 2012]

NOTICE OF OPPOSITION TO CLAIM OF EXEMPTION
(Wage Garnishment)

Code of Civil Procedure, § 706.128
www.courts.ca.gov

WG-010/EJ-175

ATTORNEY OR PARTY WITHOUT ATTORNEY *(Name, State Bar number, and address):*
Amy Right
1000 My st
Mytown, Ca 90000

TELEPHONE NO.:

FOR COURT USE ONLY

ATTORNEY FOR *(Name):* In Pro Per

NAME OF COURT, JUDICIAL DISTRICT OR BRANCH COURT, IF ANY
Superior Court of California - Stanley Mosk Courthouse

PLAINTIFF: Amy Right

DEFENDANT: Jeff Isbad

NOTICE OF HEARING ON CLAIM OF EXEMPTION
(Wage Garnishment—Enforcement of Judgment)

LEVYING OFFICER FILE NO.: 123456

COURT CASE NO.: 14K5000

---

1. **TO:**

   Name and address of levying officer
   Los Angeles County Sheriff
   123 Main st
   Los Angeles, Ca 90012

   Name and address of judgment debtor
   Jeff Isbad
   666 e Cra P st
   Helltown, Ca 90666

   ☐ Claimant, if other than judgment debtor *(name and address):*

   ☐ Judgment debtor's attorney *(name and address):*

2. **A hearing to determine the claim of exemption of**
   ☑ judgment debtor
   ☐ other claimant
   will be held as follows:

   a. date: April 10, 2015   time: 8:30 am   ☑ dept.: 13   ☐ div.:   ☑ rm.: 410

   b. address of court:
   111 Hill st
   Los Angeles, Ca 90012

3. ☐ The judgment creditor will not appear at the hearing and submits the issue on the papers filed with the court.

Date: 03/22/2015

Amy Right
(TYPE OR PRINT NAME)

▶

(SIGNATURE OF JUDGMENT CREDITOR OR ATTORNEY)

If you do not attend the hearing, the court may determine your claim based on the Claim of Exemption, Financial Statement (when one is required), Notice of Opposition to Claim of Exemption, and other evidence that may be presented.

Form Approved by the Judicial Council of California
WG-010/EJ-175 [Rev. January 1, 2007]

NOTICE OF HEARING ON CLAIM OF EXEMPTION
(Wage Garnishment—Enforcement of Judgment)

Code of Civil Procedure, § 703.550, 706.107
www.courtinfo.ca.gov

additional claimant (such as the debtor's employer), make an extra copy.

Sample Declaration Opposing Claim of Exemption

I, Amy Right, declare as follows:

1. I obtained a judgment against Jeff Isbad from the Los Angeles Superior Court on January 1, 2014, in case #14K5000.

2. The balance due on the judgment is $3,000, plus accrued interest and post-judgment costs.

3. On March 1, 2015, I sent instructions to the Los Angeles Sheriff for a wage garnishment of Jeff Isbad. On March 22, 2015, a Notice of Filing of Claim of Exemption was sent to me.

4. I cannot attend the Hearing on Claim of Exemption which is scheduled for April 10, 2015. I will be in Washington, D.C. for business during the second half of April.

5. In Jeff Isbad's Financial Statement, he indicates that he pays $1,500 in house payments. I am informed and believe that this is not true, but that he personally only pays $500 in house payments and receives $1,000 from two tenants each month. Jeff Isbad did not claim this $1,000 per month income in his Financial Statement.

6. Jeff Isbad claims that he needs $250 per month for clothing, $85 per month for laundry and cleaning, and $125 per month for entertainment. I believe that these expenses are excessive and unnecessary, and he should use those sums to pay off the judgment in this case. I declare under penalty of perjury under the laws of the State of California that the foregoing is true and correct.

Dated:
Amy Right

2. Have a set served on the judgment debtor, and their attorney if they have one. Service by mail and personal service are explained in Chapter 21. Be sure whoever serves the papers completes the Proof of Service form on the back of the Notice of Hearing form.

3. Within the ten day deadline, give or send (by overnight mail) the levying officer the original Notice of Opposition to Claim of Exemption (the one with your original signature) and a copy of the Notice of Hearing on Claim of Exemption.

4. Also within the ten-day deadline, file with the clerk of the court the original Notice of Hearing on Claim of Exemption form, a copy of the Notice of Opposition to Claim of Exemption stapled to Notice form and the original Proof of Service.

5. Attend Hearing

If you attend the hearing, review your argument the day before. On the day of the hearing, try to get to the courtroom a little early. At the entrance, there may be a bulletin board with a list of the cases to be heard that day. If your case isn't listed, check with the clerk.

Step forward when your case is called. Be prepared to answer the judge's questions. Call the judge "Your Honor" and don't interrupt the debtor, even if you disagree with what they say. The judge will give you a chance to state your disagreement. Be prepared for the judge to try to get you and the debtor to compromise. While you are entitled to remain adamant and go for it all, that attitude may lead the judge to decide for the debtor.

Understand that judges have almost complete discretion in deciding when a debtor is entitled to exempt their wages, and how much. Many judges sympathize with debtors and take their side if a creditor comes across as hard-nosed. So if the debtor offers to have less than 25% withheld, whatever the reason, it might be worthwhile to accept their offer.

Judges often persuade the parties to compromise. Some judges take this opportunity to pressure the judgment debtor to agree to voluntarily pay a substantial portion of the judgment in installments. Then, the judge amends the judgment to make it an installment judgment [CCP 582.5].

If the court decides in your favor, the wage garnishment will go forward. If the judge decides that your Earnings Withholding Order should be modified or terminated, the clerk will send the judge's order to the levying officer, who will notify the employer. In either instance, you will soon receive a notice, called an Order Determining Claim of Exemption [form WG-011], of what the court has decided.

If you lose the hearing on the Claim of Exemption, you can try another wage garnishment as soon as you can establish a material change of circumstance in the debtor's situation. For example, you could try again if the debtor gets a new and job or a promotion. If the debtor's situation - remains the same, you can try again either 60 days after the termination of the previous garnishment order or 100 days after the previous garnishment order was first served, whichever date is later [CCP 706.105(h)].

Either you or the debtor can appeal the judge's decision on the Claim of Exemption [CCP 706.105(j)]. In the meantime, the judge's order is in effect. If you lose and appeal, the exemption is allowed while your appeal is pending. If the debtor loses appeals and wins on appeal, any money you have collected from the garnishment will have to be returned to the debtor.

Appeals are time consuming, and few are granted. We recommend against appealing if you lose. It is much easier to simply wait a while and try again. Similarly, the debtor is unlikely to appeal.

B. Property Seizure

The debtor can contest your property (bank accounts, piano, stock, etc.) seizure by filing a Claim of Exemption form [form EJ-160] with the levying officer. On the form, the debtor must state that they are contesting the seizure because they believe the property is exempt. When the officer receives the Claim of Exemption, he will mail you a copy along with a document called Notice of Filing of Claim of Exemption.

Only about 15% of all debtors file a Claim of Exemption to protest a property seizure. If your debtor does, however, the burden is on you to oppose it. If you don't oppose the claim, your Writ of Execution will automatically terminate.

1. Opposing a Claim of Exemption

You must file your Notice of Opposition to the Claim of Exemption (Enforcement of Judgment – form EJ-170) with the levying officer and the court within ten days after the Notice of Claim of Exemption was personally served on you, or within 15 days after the Notice of Claim of Exemption was mailed to you, if notice was sent by mail to an address in California. This means you may have only a few days to respond to the Notice after you receive it [CCP 703.550 & 684.120(b) (1)].

If you decide to oppose the debtor's Claim of Exemption, first read the "Instructions to Judgment Creditor" on the Notice of Filing of Claim of Exemption form.

Next, fill out the Notice of Opposition to Claim of Exemption (form EJ-170) and Notice of Hearing on Claim of Exemption (form EJ-175) forms (see Sections A2 and A3, below), which are in the Appendix. Make five copies of, and file them with the clerk of the court and with the levying officer within ten days of the mailing date listed on the Notice. If you miss this deadline, your levy will be terminated.

ATTORNEY OR PARTY WITHOUT ATTORNEY (Name and Address):	TELEPHONE NO.:	FOR COURT USE ONLY
Amy Right 1000 My st Mytown, Ca 90000	310-555-5555	
ATTORNEY FOR (Name): In Pro Per		
NAME OF COURT: Superior Court of California STREET ADDRESS: 111 Hill st MAILING ADDRESS: CITY AND ZIP CODE: Los Angeles, Ca 90012 BRANCH NAME: Stanley Mosk Courthouse		
PLAINTIFF: Amy Right		
DEFENDANT: Jeff Isbad		

	LEVYING OFFICER FILE NO.:	COURT CASE NO.:
NOTICE OF OPPOSITION TO CLAIM OF EXEMPTION (Enforcement of Judgment)	123456	14K5000

— DO NOT USE THIS FORM FOR WAGE GARNISHMENTS —

The original of this form and a Notice of Hearing on Claim of Exemption must be filed with the court.
A copy of this Notice of Opposition and the Notice of Hearing *must* be filed with the levying officer.
A copy of this Notice of Opposition and the Notice of Hearing must be served on the judgment debtor and other claimant at least 10 days *before* the hearing.

TO THE LEVYING OFFICER:

1. Name and address of judgment creditor

   Amy Right
   1000 My st
   Mytown, Ca 90000

2. Name and address of judgment debtor

   Jeff Isbad
   666 e Cra P st
   Helltown, Ca 90666

   Social Security Number (if known): xxx-xx-1234

3. ☐ Name and address of claimant (if other than judgment debtor)

4. The notice of filing claim of exemption states it was mailed on (date): 03/22/2015
5. The item or items claimed as exempt are
   a. ☑ not exempt under the statutes relied upon in the Claim of Exemption.
   b. ☑ not exempt because the judgment debtor's equity is greater than the amount provided in the exemption.
   c. ☑ other (specify): because piano belongs to debtor, not his spouse

6. The facts necessary to support item 5 are
   ☑ continued on the attachment labeled Attachment 6.
   ☐ as follows:

I declare under penalty of perjury under the laws of the State of California that the foregoing is true and correct.

Date: 03/22/2015

Amy Right
(TYPE OR PRINT NAME)   (SIGNATURE OF DECLARANT)

Form Approved by the
Judicial Council of California
EJ-170 [New July 1, 1983]

NOTICE OF OPPOSITION TO CLAIM OF EXEMPTION
(Enforcement of Judgment)

CCP 703.550

WG-010/EJ-175

ATTORNEY OR PARTY WITHOUT ATTORNEY (Name, State Bar number, and address):	TELEPHONE NO.:	FOR COURT USE ONLY
Amy Right 1000 My st Mytown, Ca 90000 ATTORNEY FOR (Name): In Pro Per		

NAME OF COURT, JUDICIAL DISTRICT OR BRANCH COURT, IF ANY

Superior Court of California - Stanley Mosk Courthouse

PLAINTIFF: Amy Right

DEFENDANT: Jeff Isbad

NOTICE OF HEARING ON CLAIM OF EXEMPTION (Wage Garnishment—Enforcement of Judgment)	LEVYING OFFICER FILE NO.: 123456	COURT CASE NO.: 14K5000

1. TO:

   Name and address of levying officer:
   Los Angeles County Sheriff
   123 Main st
   Los Angeles, Ca 90012

   Name and address of judgment debtor:
   Jeff Isbad
   666 e Cra P st
   Helltown, Ca 90666

   ☐ Claimant, if other than judgment debtor (name and address):

   ☐ Judgment debtor's attorney (name and address):

2. A hearing to determine the claim of exemption of
   ☑ judgment debtor
   ☐ other claimant
   will be held as follows:

   a. date: April 10, 2015   time: 8:30 am   ☑ dept.: 13   ☐ div.:   ☑ rm.: 410

   b. address of court:
   111 Hill st
   Los Angeles, Ca 90012

3. ☐ The judgment creditor will not appear at the hearing and submits the issue on the papers filed with the court.

Date: 03/22/2015

Amy Right
(TYPE OR PRINT NAME)   ▶ _____
                                                                  (SIGNATURE OF JUDGMENT CREDITOR OR ATTORNEY)

If you do not attend the hearing, the court may determine your claim based on the Claim of Exemption, Financial Statement (when one is required), Notice of Opposition to Claim of Exemption, and other evidence that may be presented.

Form Approved by the Judicial Council of California
WG-010/EJ-175 [Rev. January 1, 2007]

NOTICE OF HEARING ON CLAIM OF EXEMPTION
(Wage Garnishment—Enforcement of Judgment)

Code of Civil Procedure, § 703.550, 706.107
www.courtinfo.ca.gov

2. Completing the Notice of Opposition to Claim of Exemption

A completed sample and instructions are below; a blank copy is in the Appendix.

Caption: Follow the format of your previous court papers. Be sure to enter the levying officer's file number, which you can find on the Claim of Exemption you received.

Item 1: Enter your name and address.

Item 2: Enter the name and address of the debtor, and the last four digits of their Social Security number if you know it [Civil Code 1798.85(a) (1) & 1798.85(a) (5) & California Rules of Court 1.20(b) (2) (A)].

Item 3: Skip this unless someone other than the debtor made the Claim of Exemption. This might occur if you have levied on property in the debtor's possession that belongs to someone else.

Item 4: Enter the date the Notice of Filing of Claim of Exemption was mailed. You can find it on the form that the Sheriff mailed you.

Item 5: Check a, b, and/or c and elaborate as follows:

Item 5a: The debtor cannot claim an exemption to which they are not entitled. (See Chapter 13, Section A2, for information on exemptions.) For instance, assume the debtor is claiming that their camera equipment is exempt as tools of the trade. You can object if they are employed full-time in another capacity and photography is only a hobby.

Item 5b: The debtor cannot claim an exemption if the equity in the property is greater than the amount allowed by the exemption. For example, let's say the debtor claims their works of art as exempt for the allowable amount of $5,000. You know they have paintings in their home and office and believe they are worth much more. Obviously, it is difficult to contradict a debtor's statement as to the value of their property. Your argument is likely to prevail only if the property's value is obviously much greater than the amount claimed.

Item 5c: Add any other reasons you believe the debtor's claim of exemption should be denied, such as the debtor's false statements

Item 6: Check the first box if you need extra room to elaborate on your reasons in Item 5. Then attach a signed declaration, setting out your reasons. (We've included a sample declaration, below.) Check the second box if you can set out your facts in the space provided. Then add whatever information supports your position from Item 5.

Finally, date the form, type or print your name and sign it.

3. Completing the Notice of Hearing on Claim of Exemption

Use the instructions for Section A3, above, with the following modifications:

Item 1: Fill in any third-party claimant.

Item 2a: The hearing must be held within 30 days of the date you file your opposition papers with the court [CCP 703.570(a)]. You must have the debtor served at least 15 days before the hearing, if service is by mail, or ten days before, if service is personal [CCP 703.570(b)].

Item 3: If you do not plan on attending the hearing, see the sample declaration below to attach to your papers.

Sample Declaration Opposing Claim of Exemption
ATTACHMENT 6

I, Amy Right, declare as follows:

1. I obtained a judgment against Jeff Isbad from the Los Angeles Superior Court on January 1, 2014, in case #14K5000.

2. The balance due on the judgment is $3,000, plus accrued interest and post-judgment costs.

3. On March 1, 2015, I sent instructions to the Los Angeles Sheriff for a levy against tangible personal property owned by and in the possession of Jeff Isbad. On March 22, 2015, a Notice of Filing of Claim of Exemption was sent to me.

4. I cannot attend the Hearing on Claim of Exemption which is scheduled for April 10, 2015. I will be in Boston for my sister's wedding from March 28 through April 26, and the claim of exemption must be heard during this time.

5. Jeff Isbad states in his claim of exemption that the lithograph set by artist DeChing is worth less than $5,000 and therefore is exempt pursuant to Code of Civil Procedure § 704.040. I am informed and believe that the lithograph set is worth more than $7,000. A similar lithograph set by artist DeChing was recently sold by the 20th Street Art Gallery for the sum of $8,500. The owner of the art gallery told me over the the phone that all of DeChing's lithograph sets are worth "at least $7,000 and probably much more."

6. Jeff Isbad states in his claim of exemption that the camera equipment is exempt pursuant to Code of Civil Procedure § 704.060 inasmuch as he uses it as a tool of the trade. I am informed and believe that this is not true since Jeff Isbad works for his father at Ping-Pong Game Shop.

7. Jeff Isbad states, in his claim of exemption, that the Steinway baby grand piano belongs solely to his spouse. I am informed and believe that this is not true because Jeff Isbad received it as an inheritance from his mother.

I declare under penalty of perjury under the laws of the State of California that the foregoing is true and correct.

Dated: March 30, 2015

Amy Right

4. Serve and File the Opposition Papers

You must serve the papers on the debtor, and then file them with the court. Your response must be served on the debtor at least 10 days before the hearing date, 15 days if service is by mail. You can have these papers served on the debtor by mail or personally. In most cases, mail is the easiest and least expensive approach, as long as it allows the debtor at least 15 calendar days' notice of the hearing date.

Either way, don't delay in serving the forms. Once they are served, you must file the forms with the court, and that filing must take place within ten days of the mailing date of the Notice of Filing of Claim of Exemption. Here's how to proceed:

1. Make at least five copies of your documents. One is for your records, another is for the levying officer, a third is for the court and a fourth is for the debtor. If there is an additional claimant (such as a third party who contests your levy), make an extra copy.

2. Have a set served on the debtor, and their attorney if they have one, at the address indicated on Item 2 of the Claim of Exemption. Service by mail and personal service is explained in Chapter 21. Be sure whoever serves the papers completes the Proof of Service form on the back of the Notice of Hearing form.

3. Within the ten or 15 day deadline, file with the clerk of the court the original Notice of Opposition to Claim of Exemption form, the original Notice of Hearing on Claim of Exemption and the original Proof of Service, which is on the back of the Notice of Hearing form.

4. Also within the ten or 15 day deadline, give or send (by overnight mail) the levying officer a copy of the Notice of Opposition to Claim of Exemption and a copy of the Notice of Hearing on Claim of Exemption.

5. Once the levying officer receives your papers, she will file with the court the Claim of Exemption sent to her by the debtor. If you don't get these notices to the levying officer by the deadline, she will immediately return any property claimed to be exempt to the debtor or other claimant.

5. Attend Hearing

If you attend the hearing, review your argument the day before. On the day of the hearing, try to get to the courtroom a little early. At the entrance, there may be a bulletin board with a list of the cases to be heard that day. If your case isn't listed, check with the clerk.

Step forward when your case is called. Be prepared to answer the judge's questions. Call the judge "Your Honor" and don't interrupt the debtor, even if you disagree with what they say. The judge will give you a chance to state your disagreement. Be prepared for the judge to try to get you and the debtor to compromise. While you are entitled to remain adamant and go for it all, that attitude may lead the judge to decide for the debtor.

6. Wait for the Ruling

Until the court issues its decision, the levying officer will hold the property and cannot release, sell or otherwise dispose of it. You will be charged the costs of this storage, which can be very expensive but may be recoverable from the debtor (See Chapter 16).

You will be notified of the judge's decision at the hearing or by mail. If the court decides in your favor, the property can be sold and the proceeds applied toward satisfaction of your judgment. If the debtor wins, the levying officer must release any property, found to be exempt.

A judge may order a variation on these two themes. For instance, the judge might determine property to be partially exempt but require it to be sold and replaced with a less costly item, with part of the proceeds of the sale going to the judgment creditor.

Either you or the debtor can appeal the judge's decision on the Claim of Exemption. In the meantime, the judge's order is in effect. If you lose and appeal, the exemption is allowed while your appeal is pending. If the debtor loses, appeals, and wins on appeal, any property you have seized will have to be returned to the debtor. Appealing is time consuming, and few appeals are granted. We recommend against appealing. It is much easier to simply wait a while and try again.

Blank Page

Chapter 16

Recovering Post-Judgment Costs and Interest

A. Post-Judgment Costs	16/2
1. Costs You Can Recover by Statute	16/2
2. Costs You Can Recover with Court Approval	16/3
3. Costs You Cannot Recover	16/3
4. Keeping Track of Costs	16/3
B. Post-Judgment Interest	16/4
1. Interest Rate	16/4
2. Types of Interest	16/5
3. Keeping Track of Statutory Interest	16/5
C. Memorandum of Costs	16/6
1. Complete the Memorandum of Costs	16/8
2. Have Debtor Served	16/8
3. File the Memorandum of Costs	16/8
4. Give the Debtor Time to Object	16/9

Some court judgments are paid right away, but others take months, or even years to recover. If your judgment isn't paid soon after it's awarded, you're entitled to receive interest on the unpaid portion of your judgment until the judgment is fully paid. You can also tack on most of the costs you incur in trying to enforce the judgment, such as court fees, registered process server fees and the levying officer's costs.

A. Postjudgment Costs

The law identifies specific enforcement costs for which you are entitled, by statute, to be reimbursed, that is, these costs may be added to your judgment [CCP 685.070]. On the other hand, all costs that are not spelled out in the statute are not reimbursable unless the court authorizes them [CCP 685.080].

1. Costs You Can Recover by Statute

There are certain types of costs incurred, from enforcing a judgment, which the legislature has already decided should be recoverable by the creditor. These are called "statutory costs". The following collection costs and fees are permitted to be added to your judgment (form MC-012):

- clerks' filing fees, such as for obtaining a Writ of Execution, OEX, or Abstract of Judgment

- statutory fees charged and costs incurred by a levying officer attempting a levy under a Writ of Execution

- statutory fees charged by a registered process server for serving the Application and Notice of Order of Examination or Subpoena Duces Tecum

- fees charged to issue and serve a bench warrant if the judgment debtor does not appear at a judgment debtor's examination

- fees for issuing and levying an earnings withholding order (Chapter 9)

- fees for recording an Abstract of Judgment to place a lien on the judgment debtor's real estate (Chapter 4)

- fees for filing a Notice of Judgment Lien on Business Personal Property (Chapter 4)

- attorney fees spent on enforcement efforts, if the judgment called for attorney fees on the basis of a contract or statute [CCP 685.040].

Use Form MC-012, (see Section C, below) to add such recoverable costs to your judgment. But what about costs incurred by the levying officer at the moment of seizure? You can instruct the levying officer to recover the amount remaining on the judgment (as listed in the Writ of Execution) as well as their fee and costs.

If the levying officer doesn't recover enough to pay the judgment, or even to cover your levying officer fees (a common occurrence where the judgment debtor has little or no funds in their bank account), then you will need to do another levy on your judgment debtor's monetary assets in the future, once you find such additional funds on which to levy. Until then, you will be temporarily out the money you paid for the unsuccessful levy. Of course, you may recover such fees and costs in the future using a subsequent levy, but only if you list such unrecovered costs on another Memorandum of Costs (will call "Memo of Costs") and file it with the court before you ask the levying officer to perform another levy.

What if you decide to use a Registered Process Server to serve your bank levy or wage garnishment? These additional costs are fully recoverable when serving a Writ of Execution [CCP 685.095] and a Notice of Levy [CCP 699.080(f)] and will be added to the judgment balance. These costs should be written in under the "other" (item "h") on the Memo of Costs.

2. Costs You Can Recover With Court Approval

Any costs that are reasonable and necessary, for the enforcement, may be claimed and added to the balance owed on the judgment. If there is no statute or law that has already decided that those costs should be recovered, then the creditor must;

1) prepare a motion asking for the recovery of those non-statutory costs,

2) schedule the motion with the court

3) serve the motion on the debtor,

4) file the motion/proof of service with the court

5) attend the hearing on that motion [CCP 685.080]. Creditor will need to convince the court that the costs you are claiming were "reasonable and necessary".

Example: You examined the debtor in court. The debtor testified that he did not own any cars and did not have a job. You believed that this was a lie so you hired a private investigator to find out where the debtor works and what cars they own. You wanted the information so that you could do a wage garnishment and levy on the cars. It turned out that the debtor did lie at the examination. The private investigator expenses are not automatically recoverable. You will need the court's approval in order to recover those costs. Having evidence that the debtor was less than forthcoming with the information may help sway the judge that the expense was necessary under the circumstance.

We don't cover filing a motion for costs in this book. But in Chapter 19 we explain how to bring a motion for an assignment order. The process is similar.

3. Costs You Cannot Recover

Costs other than those detailed in Section 1 generally may not be added to the judgment. For, example, the following costs will most likely be disallowed by the court if the judgment debtor objects:

- fees for the time you spend enforcing the judgment

- fees for parking (including fines for parking tickets) while visiting the levying officer or court

- lunch expenses while interviewing investigators or collection professionals

- long distance telephone charges

- fax and copying charges

- postage charges

- mileage.

Despite this list, you are entitled to recover the "reasonable and necessary costs of enforcing a judgment" [CCP 685.040], as long as you can convince the judge of the necessity of the costs.

4. Keeping Track of Costs

A form entitled "Keeping Track of Costs" is included in the Appendix. If you fill it out as you incur various expenses, you'll have all the information you need at your fingertips when you prepare your Memo of Costs.

Be sure to keep all your receipts and/or invoices for costs you incur, especially if you pay cash. If the judgment debtor raises any questions about the cost, you'll have proof that it's a legitimate claim. The costs are recoverable when you incur them, whether or not you have paid for them yet [CCP 1033.5(c) (1)]

When the Judgment Debtor Bounces a Check

If the judgment debtor writes you a check to pay your judgment and it bounces, you will need court approval to add the bank and other fees to your cost of enforcement. But the court should easily approve the cost.

Alternatively, you can send a certified letter demanding payment, within 30 days, on the bounced check. Keep photocopies of the bounced checks, your demand letter to the judgment debtor and the original signed certified mail receipt. If the judgment debtor does not make the check good, you can sue in small claims court for the original amount of the bounced check plus three times the amount of the check, up to a total of $1,500 [Civil Code 1719].

If you'd rather not get involved in a second lawsuit with your judgment debtor, see if your county's District Attorney's office has a check diversion program. To avoid criminal prosecution, the person who wrote a bad check must make the check good and comply with other rules. You cannot seek triple ("treble") damages, but you'll be spared the hassle of another lawsuit.

If you get paid on the bounced check, don't forget to credit the debtor with that payment on the original judgment (not including penalties and costs).

Here's how to fill in the form:

Date Expended: Specify the date on which you incurred each cost.

Cost Amount: Specify the amount of each cost.

Type of Cost: Specify the kind of cost. For example, it might be a filing fee for a Writ of Execution, a sheriff's deposit for a bank levy or a recording fee for an Abstract of Judgment.

Expense Record: Specify how you paid the cost. If you paid by check, insert the check number.

Date Costs Claimed: Leave this blank until you actually claim this cost on a Memo of Costs or by a motion to the court. At that time, fill in the date you file it with the court.

If you've already been reimbursed, you cannot also claim the cost on a Memo of Costs. For example, if the sheriff repaid your Writ of Execution filing fees and deposit from the proceeds of a bank levy, you aren't entitled to recover them again. Make a note of any reimbursed costs.

B. Postjudgment Interest

You can recover statutory interest on the unpaid portion of your judgment, including on unpaid costs that have been claimed in a Memo of Costs or approved by the court on a motion [CCP 685.010(a) & CCP 685.090]. Interest accrues from the date the judgment was first entered, even if the judgment debtor appealed the judgment and lost (except interest on the costs accrues from the date the cost is incurred). If the judgment is an installment judgment, then interest accrues on each installment from the date it becomes due until it is paid by the judgment debtor.

1. Interest Rate

Statutory interest accrues at the rate of 10% simple interest per year on state court civil money judgments [CCP 685.010]. There is one exception: Interest on a judgment against the State of California or any of its agencies accrues at the statutory rate of only 7% simple interest per year, as set forth in Article XV, § 1, of the California Constitution

[California Fed. Sav. & Loan Assn. v. City of Los Angeles, 11 Cal.4th 342 (1995)].

2. Types of Interest

For enforcement purposes, there are two types of statutory interest after a judgment is entered:

- interest that accrues between the time the judgment is entered and the time the Writ of Execution is issued by the clerk (we will call this interest "pre-writ"); and

- interest that accrues between the date on which the Writ of Execution is issued and the date that an actual levy occurs (we will call this interest "post-writ").

The first type of interest must be documented before the levying officer can collect it. You do this by completing the Memo of Costs and listing the amount of such interest on the Writ of Execution.

The levying officer can recover the second type of interest without your documenting it because the Writ of Execution directs the levying officer to collect added interest each day after the Writ of Execution is issued. A Writ of Execution is valid for 180 days, so several months of added interest may accrue by the time a levy is completed. If the levying officer recovers enough funds from the judgment debtor's assets to cover such interest, he will send it to you.

3. Keeping Track of Statutory Interest

How much interest accrues on a judgment depends, not only on the amount of the judgment, but also on how long it remains unpaid. For example, at 10% simple interest, a $3,000.00 judgment accrues about $75.00 interest over 3 months. However, the exact amount depends on which 3 months, since some months are longer (or shorter) than others.

Of course, if a judgment is paid in a lump sum, then computing accrued interest is relatively easy. But it's more common for payments to dribble in over time, either voluntarily or through levies and wage garnishments. If you receive partial payments, you must apply the payments;

1) first toward statutory and court approved costs and pre-writ interest [CCP 695.220(a)]

2) post-writ interest [CCP 695.220(c)]

3) toward reduction of the principal balance owed on the judgment [CCP 695.220(d)].

You must recalculate the interest every time a payment reduces the principal balance of the judgment. A computer spreadsheet can be a real timesaver.

Before getting started, make several copies of the Keeping Track of Payments form found in the Appendix.

Shortcut Alert !!!!!

Figuring out interest and balances can be complicated and frustrating. If you have access to the internet, go to

ijcalc.sdcourt.ca.gov (no www.)

You can use this software and print out your reports. Input one cost, or payment, at a time (you can add more) to make sure the calculations are correct.

You can skip this next section on how to use our form.

Here is how to use the form to calculate interest and when should you complete a line?

You should complete a line when one of the following happens:

1) When you are completing a Memo of Costs

2) The day you receive a payment

A–Starting Date: Fill in the date your judgment was entered (if you have already filed a Memo of Costs, with the court, calculating everything since day one will allow you to verify that you are doing it correctly). After your first line entry, all further entries should be the day after your last "ending date.

B–Ending Date: Fill in the date you are completing that form line. You should complete a line 1) the day prior to receiving a payment, 2) the day your costs were allowed by the court, 3) you receive a payment, or on the judgment, whether you will be filing a Memo of Costs or not.

C–Number of Days: Enter the number of days between the Starting Date (Column A) and Ending Date (Column B). If you do not have a computer spreadsheet, it's best to have an actual calendar in front of you and then you can count the number of days manually. Do not guess or estimate.

D–Balance: Enter the original amount of your judgment on the first line entry. For all subsequent lines, Column D should be calculated as the previous Column D minus the previous Column G.

E–Interest Due: To calculate the interest due, multiply the Balance amount (Column D) by 10% (or 7% if your judgment is against the State of California or one of its agencies). Then, multiply the result by the Number of Days (Column C) and divide by 365. Now do the same for the amount of costs that were accrued by the court. Then add them both.

F-Payment: Enter the amount of the payment you received on the Ending Date (Column B).

G-Payment Applicable to Principal: Subtract the Interest Due amount (Column E) from the Payment amount (Column F). You will apply any payments to accrued interest first. Now subtract the approved costs from the remainder. If you had any unpaid interest from previous pay periods (Column H), subtract that amount, as well. That way, you will have applied the payment to all accrued interest before you use any part of the payment to reduce the judgment principal.

Subtract the remainder of the payment, what's left after you subtract all accrued interest, from your original balance to get the balance for the next pay period. Enter this amount in Column D on the next line. If the payment was less than the interest due, you'll have to fill in Column H, below.

H-Unpaid Interest: If the payment was less than the interest due, then no remainder will be available to pay down the judgment principal, so the Balance amount will stay the same, and you are still entitled to any interest that wasn't paid. Subtract the Payment amount (Column F) from the Interest Due amount (Column E), and enter the result in Column H.

When you receive another payment, repeat the process described above for the next pay period.

C. Memorandum of Costs

You must file the Memo of Costs form (form MC-012) with the court in order to recover post judgment costs and statutory interest. Post judgment statutory interest can be claimed at any time using this form, but you can only claim your costs if you file the Memo of Costs within two years of the date that such costs were incurred [CCP 685.070(b)]. When you do so, such costs are added to the judgment amount, which also means that you can recover statutory interest on them. Therefore, it makes sense to file an additional Memo of Costs each time your recoverable costs exceed $100.00.

We suggest you file a Memo of Costs at least once a year, unless, of course, you don't want the judgment debtor to know that you're actively pursuing collection of the judgment. If you claim such costs, then you must have the judgment debtor served with a copy of each Memo of Costs, so filing a Memo of Costs will definitely cost you the "element of surprise".

However, if you only claim statutory interest, then you only have to file the Memo of Costs with the court, but you do not have to serve the judgment debtor with a copy of the Memo of Costs. In practical terms, this means that, if you discover a potentially successful recovery in the form of a bank account with a large balance, and you want to preserve the element of surprise and have the levying officer to levy on the account before the judgment debtor has an opportunity to move, or, worse, to spend such funds, then you can choose to simply not claim the recoverable costs, but only claim the statutory interest on your Memo of Costs. This strategy can be particularly appealing when the judgment is large, the accrued statutory interest has also become large, but the recoverable costs have been quite low.

Don't "double dip". Once you have filed a Memo of Costs, make sure you don't claim "interest on interest" i.e. compound interest. The second time you prepare a Memo of Costs, subtract the interest previously claimed on a Memo of Costs from the total due before you start calculating. If you want to earn interest on the interest you've claimed, you must renew your judgment, an option that's available only once every five years (See Chapter 20).

If Service of Process is Not Performed by the Levying Officer

It used to be that only the sheriff or constable served levying papers and collected funds for the judgment creditor. But, although the sheriff or constable is still called the 'levying officer', there are some counties where such services have been severely curtailed, and in other counties, discontinued altogether due to budget cuts or staffing reductions.

If you intend to have a bank levy or wage garnishment and must, or wish to, hire a registered process server to do so, as mentioned in Section A, a registered process server cannot automatically add their fee to the levy.

There is a way around this. Prepay for the process servers' assistance (tell them that the paperwork will follow). Now complete the Memo of Costs and Writ of Execution and file them with the court. Include the fee you just paid the process server. The debtor may contest the fee, but you will have the opportunity to explain it to the judge.

Simultaneous Writ of Execution and Memo of Costs

If you ask the clerk of the court to issue a Writ of Execution at the same time as you file a Memo of Costs, you can claim up to $100.00 in statutory costs on the Writ of Execution, if they are listed in the Memo of Costs, without having to wait the mandatory time to give the debtor a chance to oppose the costs. In order to do this you must add the following statement to the Memo of Costs – "The fees sought under this Memorandum may be disallowed by a court upon a Motion to Tax filed by the debtor notwithstanding the fees having been included in the Writ of Execution".

If you don't include this statement then the court will wait the mandatory time, giving the debtor a chance to oppose your charges. If the debtor does nothing then the court will issue your Writ and file the Memo of Costs. **Do not take advantage of this and request fees that are not allowed. If the debtor can show that you did something unethical, you could wind up having to pay for their attorney fees.**

1. Complete the Memorandum of Costs

A blank form can be found in the Appendix. A completed sample follows.

Caption: Fill in your name, address and telephone number, the name and address of the court, the case name and case number.

Line 1a through h: List the costs you have incurred in each category, and the dates on which you incurred each cost. Use line 1h to list any additional statutory costs (review the lists in Section A to make sure you haven't forgotten any).

Line 1i: Add up lines 1a through 1h, and write the total here.

Line 2: If you have previously filed one or more Memo of Costs, enter the total amount claimed on all previous Memoranda. If this is the first time you're claiming costs, write '$0'.

Line 3: Add lines 1 and 2 together, and write the total here.

Line 4: Enter the total amount you have received as payments on the judgment to date. This is the total of all amounts listed in the Payment column of the Keeping Track of Payments form. If you haven't received any payments, write '$0'.

Line 5: Write down the total amount of statutory interest that has accrued on the judgment since the date of entry. If you have not received any partial payments from the judgment debtor, calculate interest by multiplying the judgment amount times 10%, and divide by 365 to obtain the daily interest amount, and then multiply that amount by the total number of days since the judgment was awarded.

For example, if you had a judgment for $2,000.00 that was entered 180 days ago, you would claim total statutory interest, as follows: $2,000.00 x 10% = $200.00 divided by 365 days = $0.5479 per day. Truncate this number to two decimal places = $0.54 (54 cents) per day. Do not round up. Then, multiply $0.54 x 180 days, which equal $97.20. That is the total interest to claim. In reality, the amount you claim using this method is about $1.42 less than you are entitled to claim. However, if you do not truncate to two decimal places before you multiply the daily interest amount by the number of days since the judgment was entered, you risk claiming too much interest. If this happens, the levying officer will have to release all levied funds because you claimed too much interest. Even claiming a penny too much is a serious violation.

If you have received partial payments, add up all of the interest you entered in Column E of your Keeping Track of Payments worksheet. Then add any interest that has accrued since you received your last payment, using the formula in Section B, above. Write the total on Line 5.

Line 6: Check the box next to "judgment creditor."
Type or print your name, date and sign the bottom of the form in blue or black ink.

2. Have Debtor Served

You must have a copy of the Memo of Costs served on the judgment debtor. Service can be by U.S. first-class mail to their last known address or in person. Have the person who serves the judgment debtor complete the Proof of Service. (One is printed on the reverse side of the Memo of Costs form). Anyone not involved in the case and over the age of 18 can serve this document.

3. File the Memorandum of Costs

After the judgment debtor is served, make two copies of the Memo of Costs and signed proof of service. Send the court the original and one copy of the Memo of Costs and signed proof of service, along with a self-addressed, stamped envelope. There is no filing fee. (Generic cover letter can be found in the Appendix.)

4. Give the Debtor Time to Object

If you have the judgment debtor served personally, the debtor has 10 days (but 15 days if you have them served by U.S. first-class mail) to contest the costs that are listed in your Memo of Costs. If the judgment debtor contests, which rarely happens, you should seriously consider opposing their "motion to tax costs" by filing an opposition and then going to court, since losing such a motion may require you to pay their attorneys' costs in bringing such a motion, if the court believes that you added unreasonable costs deliberately or negligently. (See Chapter 19 for more information on making and opposing motions.) If it is necessary to oppose a motion to tax costs, you should consider using the services of a licensed California attorney to represent you. The specific techniques for drafting a written opposition and representing yourself at such a motion hearing are beyond the scope of this book.

If the judgment debtor does not file a motion to tax costs, then the Memo of Costs is considered final after 10 days (or 15 days, if you served the judgment debtor by U.S. first-class mail), and you are then entitled to recover whatever costs you claimed. If you are in the midst of a levy and want to recover the costs claimed, get a "certification" from the court clerk stating the costs have been added to the judgment [CCP 685.090(c) (2)] and send it to the levying officer. The levying officer can then add the amount of your claimed costs to the amount shown on your Writ of Execution and recover the total amount indicated.

MC-012

ATTORNEY OR PARTY WITHOUT ATTORNEY (Name, State Bar number, and address):

Amy Right
1000 My st
Mytown, Ca 90000

TELEPHONE NO.: 310-555-5555   FAX NO.:
ATTORNEY FOR (Name): In Pro Per

NAME OF COURT: Superior Court of California
STREET ADDRESS: 111 Hill st
MAILING ADDRESS:
CITY AND ZIP CODE: Los Angeles, Ca 90012
BRANCH NAME: Stanley Mosk Courthouse

PLAINTIFF: Amy Right

DEFENDANT: Jeff Isbad

MEMORANDUM OF COSTS AFTER JUDGMENT, ACKNOWLEDGMENT OF CREDIT, AND DECLARATION OF ACCRUED INTEREST

CASE NUMBER: 14K5000

1. I claim the following costs after judgment incurred within the last two years (indicate if there are multiple items in any category):

		Dates Incurred	Amount
a	Preparing and issuing abstract of judgment	02/01/2014	$ 25.00
b	Recording and indexing abstract of judgment	02/01/2014	$ 35.00
c	Filing notice of judgment lien on personal property	02/01/2014	$ 10.00
d	Issuing writ of execution, to extent not satisfied by Code Civ. Proc., § 685.050 (specify county): Los Angeles	02/01/2014	$ 25.00
e	Levying officers fees, to extent not satisfied by Code Civ. Proc., § 685.050 or wage garnishment	02/01/2014	$ 35.00
f	Approved fee on application for order for appearance of judgment debtor, or other approved costs under Code Civ. Proc., § 708.110 et seq.		$
g	Attorney fees, if allowed by Code Civ. Proc., § 685.040		$
h	Other: (Statute authorizing cost):		$
i	Total of claimed costs for current memorandum of costs (add items a-h)		$ 130.00

2. All previously allowed postjudgment costs: .... $ 0.00

3. **Total** of all postjudgment costs (add items 1 and 2): .... **TOTAL** $ 130.00

4. **Acknowledgment of Credit.** I acknowledge total credit to date (including returns on levy process and direct payments) in the amount of: $ 0.00

5. **Declaration of Accrued Interest.** Interest on the judgment accruing at the legal rate from the date of entry on balances due after partial satisfactions and other credits in the amount of: $ 49.20

6. I am the [✔] judgment creditor   [ ] agent for the judgment creditor   [ ] attorney for the judgment creditor.
I have knowledge of the facts concerning the costs claimed above. To the best of my knowledge and belief, the costs claimed are correct, reasonable, and necessary, and have not been satisfied.

I declare under penalty of perjury under the laws of the State of California that the foregoing is true and correct.

Date: 02/01/2014

Amy Right
(TYPE OR PRINT NAME)   ▶   (SIGNATURE OF DECLARANT)

NOTICE TO THE JUDGMENT DEBTOR
If this memorandum of costs is filed at the same time as an application for a writ of execution, any statutory costs, *not exceeding $100 in aggregate* and not already allowed by the court, may be included in the writ of execution. *The fees sought under this memorandum may be disallowed by the court upon a motion to tax filed by the debtor, notwithstanding the fees having been included in the writ of execution.* (Code Civ. Proc., § 685.070(e).) A motion to tax costs claimed in this memorandum must be filed within 10 days after service of the memorandum. (Code Civ. Proc., § 685.070(c).)

(Proof of service on reverse)

Form Adopted for Mandatory Use
Judicial Council of California
MC-012 [Rev. January 1, 2011]

MEMORANDUM OF COSTS AFTER JUDGMENT, ACKNOWLEDGMENT OF CREDIT, AND DECLARATION OF ACCRUED INTEREST

Code of Civil Procedure
§ 685.070
www.courts.ca.gov

SHORT TITLE: Right v Isbad	CASE NUMBER: 14K5000

MC-012

PROOF OF SERVICE
☐ Mail ☐ Personal Service

1. At the time of service I was at least 18 years of age and not a party to this legal action.

2. My residence or business address is *(specify)*:

3. I mailed or personally delivered a copy of the *Memorandum of Costs After Judgment, Acknowledgment of Credit, and Declaration of Accrued Interest* as follows *(complete either a or b)*:

   a. ☐ **Mail.** I am a resident of or employed in the county where the mailing occurred.
      (1) I enclosed a copy in an envelope AND
         (a) ☐ **deposited** the sealed envelope with the United States Postal Service with the postage fully prepaid.
         (b) ☐ **placed** the envelope for collection and mailing on the date and at the place shown in items below following our ordinary business practices. I am readily familiar with this business's practice for collecting and processing correspondence for mailing. On the same day that correspondence is placed for collection and mailing, it is deposited in the ordinary course of business with the United States Postal Service in a sealed envelope with postage fully prepaid.
      (2) The envelope was addressed and mailed as follows:
         (a) Name of person served:
         (b) Address on envelope:

         (c) Date of mailing:
         (d) Place of mailing *(city and state)*:

   b. ☐ **Personal delivery.** I personally delivered a copy as follows:
      (1) Name of person served:
      (2) Address where delivered:

      (3) Date delivered:
      (4) Time delivered:

I declare under penalty of perjury under the laws of the State of California that the foregoing is true and correct.

Date:

.... ▶ _____
(TYPE OR PRINT NAME)   (SIGNATURE OF DECLARANT)

MC-012 [Rev. January 1, 2011] **MEMORANDUM OF COSTS AFTER JUDGMENT, ACKNOWLEDGMENT OF CREDIT, AND DECLARATION OF ACCRUED INTEREST**

Blank Page

Chapter 17

If the Debtor Files for Bankruptcy

A. Types of Bankruptcy	17/3
B. Bankruptcy and Enforcement.	17/3
1. If You Have Started Levying	17/4
2. Enforcing Against Codebtors	17/4
3. Getting Your Money in Bankruptcy	17/4
C. Examine the Bankruptcy Papers You Receive	17/5
1. Notice of Case, Meeting of Creditors and Deadlines.	17/5
2. Chapter 13 Repayment Plan.	17/6
D. File Proof of Claim	17/6
1. Completing the Proof of Claim	17/7
2. Filing Proof of Claim	17/8
3. If Debtor or Trustee Objects	17/8
E. After Filing the Proof of Claim	17/8
1. Chapter 7 Bankruptcy.	17/8
2. Chapter 13 Bankruptcy	17/8
3. When the Case is Over	17/9
F. What Else Can You Do?	17/9
1. Ask Debtor to Reaffirm the Debt	17/9
2. Challenge the Dischargeability of Certain Debts.	17/10
3. Object to Exemptions	17/10
4. Make Other Objections	17/11
5. Enforce Liens That Survive Bankruptcy	17/11
6. Enforcing Nondischargeable Debts.	17/12

Collection Factor	High	Moderate	Low
Potential cost to you	✓		✓
Potential for producing $$$			✓
Potential for settlement			✓
Potential time and trouble	✓		✓
Potential for bankruptcy	✓		

If the judgment debtor files for bankruptcy, you may be at the end of the line. As soon as the debtor files for bankruptcy, all enforcement activity must stop. Furthermore, funds received from enforcement, shortly before the filing, usually have to be turned over to the bankruptcy court. And through the bankruptcy case, a debtor may be able to wipe out your judgment, and may even be able to remove any lien you recorded against their house and/or personal property.

But creditors also have rights in bankruptcy. The debtor may have to surrender property to be sold to pay some of their debts. Certain debts survive bankruptcy fully intact. Also, if the debtor's bankruptcy papers and any papers they gave you as a creditor contain serious inconsistencies, the court may throw out the bankruptcy case or refuse to let the debtor discharge (cancel) your judgment. Finally, if the debtor lied in their bankruptcy papers, the bankruptcy court might dismiss the case outright.

Debts That Survive Chapter 7 Bankruptcy

Several types of debts survive bankruptcy intact. Others may survive if you successfully challenge the debtor's request to have them discharged. So if you have any of the following types of debts, take heart, your debt probably won't be wiped out by the debtor's bankruptcy case (Note that this list applies to Chapter 7 bankruptcy, commonly filed by individuals and small businesses. If your debtor files for Chapter 13 bankruptcy, some of these debts might be wiped out).

Debts that survive bankruptcy (see Section F5):

- Debts that the debtor does not list on their bankruptcy papers, as long as the creditor doesn't otherwise learn of the bankruptcy case.
- Student loans, unless repayment would cause the debtor undue hardship.
- Most federal, state and local taxes and any money borrowed to pay those taxes.
- Child and spousal support, and debts in the nature of support.
- Court-ordered fines or restitution owed to the victim of a crime.
- Court Fees
- Debts for the death of, or personal injury to, someone due to the debtor's intoxicated driving.

Debts that may be declared nondischargeable if you successfully object in court (see Section F2):

- Debts incurred on the basis of fraud.
- Debts from willful and malicious acts.
- Debts from embezzlement, larceny or breach of fiduciary duty.
- Debts arising from a marital settlement or divorce decree, unless discharging the debt would result in a benefit to the debtor that outweighs the detriment to the debtor's former spouse or child.

Bankruptcy Laws Change

The Bankruptcy Abuse Prevention and Consumer Protection Act of 2005 (BAPCPA), was one of the more significant legislative changes to personal finance passed by the United States and applies to cases filed on or after October 17, 2005. It made sweeping changes to American bankruptcy laws, affecting both consumer and business bankruptcies. Many of the Bill's provisions were explicitly designed by the Bill's Congressional sponsors to make it "more difficult for people to file for bankruptcy". The BAPCPA was intended to make it more difficult for debtors to file a Chapter 7 and instead required them to file a Chapter 13 Bankruptcy, under which the debts they incurred are discharged only after the debtor has repaid some portion of these debts.

Prior to the BAPCPA Amendments, debtors of all incomes could file for bankruptcy under Chapter 7. BAPCPA restricted the number of debtors that could declare Chapter 7 bankruptcy. The act sets out a method to calculate a debtor's income, and compares this amount to the median income of the debtor's state. IF the debtor's income is above the median income amount of the debtor's state, the debtor is subject to a "means test".

The most noteworthy change brought by the 2005 BAPCPA amendments occurred within 11 U.S.C. §707(b). Congress amended this section of the Bankruptcy Code to provide for the dismissal or conversion of a Chapter 7 case upon a finding of "abuse" by an individual debtor (or married couple) with "primarily consumer debt".

A. Types of Bankruptcy

The different kinds of bankruptcy are named after specific chapters of the federal Bankruptcy Code.

- **Chapter 7 bankruptcy:** This is the most common form of bankruptcy filed by individuals and small businesses. A debtor asks the court to discharge (cancel) their debts. In exchange, the debtor hands over to the court any property that isn't considered exempt. The property is sold and the proceeds are distributed to creditors. If the debtor doesn't have any non-exempt assets (called "no-asset"), their creditors won't get paid anything.

- **Chapter 13 bankruptcy:** Also known as the "wage earners' plan". A debtor creates a plan under which they pay a portion of their debts over a three to five year period. The amount that the debtor must pay depends on several factors, and can vary from a few cents on the dollar to 100%. In general, the debtor holds on to all of their property and uses their income to fund the plan. If the debtor successfully completes the plan, any balances still owing on most debts are wiped out. Debtors must owe less than $ 336,900 in unsecured debt, and less than $ 1,010,650 in secured debt, in order to qualify for this plan.

- **Other types of bankruptcy:**

    Chapter 11 bankruptcy is primarily designed to let a business restructure its debt while it continues to operate. Although individuals are permitted to file Chapter 11 bankruptcy, few do.

    Chapter 12 bankruptcy is designed especially for family farmers. Chapter 11 and Chapter 12 bankruptcies are beyond the scope of this book.

B. Bankruptcy and Enforcement

The moment a debtor files a bankruptcy petition, the court automatically issues an order called the "automatic stay". This order requires creditors and debt collectors to end all collection and enforcement efforts against the debtor and their property [11 U.S.C. § 362]. It remains in effect until the case is closed or the court lifts the stay for a particular creditor.

If you know of the bankruptcy filing, whether through court papers served on you or through rumors on the street, and try to enforce your judgment anyway, you can be held in contempt of court and fined. So if you get even a whiff that the judgment debtor has gone bankrupt, immediately stop your enforcement efforts until you learn otherwise or until the court says you may proceed with enforcing your judgment.

1. If You Have Started Levying

If you started levying on the debtor's wages or property before they filed for bankruptcy, immediately let the levying officer know about the bankruptcy. Give him the case name and number, and 1) tell him to release to the bankruptcy court any funds already received as a result of your levy 2) if the levying officer is expecting to receive any property, ask him to return the property or instruct the sending party to cancel the levy (unless you plan on asking the court for an immediate relief from stay, which is beyond the scope of this book). Later, you may be required to turn over funds collected during the 90 days preceding the bankruptcy filing. If you're related to the debtor or were in business with him, you may be required to turn over funds received during the entire year directly preceding the bankruptcy filing.

2. Enforcing against Codebtors

A codebtor is another person legally responsible for paying your judgment. In your situation, a codebtor is a codefendant, that is, someone else who was named in your judgment and specifically found liable to pay you. If you have a judgment against just one person, you might still have a codebtor, such as:

- a cosignor or guarantor of your original debt, or

- the debtor's spouse, if the underlying debt was incurred during marriage.

After the automatic stay goes into effect, your right to enforce your judgment from codebtors depends on which type of bankruptcy the debtor filed.

- **Chapter 7 bankruptcy.** You may enforce from any codebtor before, during or after the bankruptcy proceeding.

- **Chapter 13 bankruptcy.** The automatic stay prevents enforcement activity against a codebtor while the bankruptcy case is pending [11 U.S.C.1301]. If the court approves a repayment plan in which you will receive less than 100% of your judgment, you can petition the court for relief from the stay to collect the unpaid portion from the codebtor or wait until the case is over and collect the remaining balance from the codebtor. These procedures are beyond the scope of this book.

3. Getting your Money in Bankruptcy

As explained below, you will be notified by the court of the type of bankruptcy the debtor has filed. If there's a chance you will be paid something through the bankruptcy case, you will be invited to file what's called a "Proof of Claim" with the bankruptcy court. We suggest always filing a claim.

Don't give up yet. If your debtor files for bankruptcy, you may worry that you'll never collect your judgment. But not every debtor who seeks bankruptcy protection actually goes through with the procedure. Some file solely to get the protection of the automatic stay (see above), or simply to convince their creditors to quit trying to collect. If the debtor backs out before receiving a discharge, your judgment is still good and you are entitled to enforce it. So remember to keep tabs on the debtor's bankruptcy case, from start to finish.

C. Examine the Bankruptcy Papers You Receive

When a debtor files for bankruptcy, they are supposed to list all of their debts and creditors. They cannot pick and choose which ones to list, even if they hope to repay a specific creditor after their bankruptcy ends. This means that you are likely to be listed in the debtor's bankruptcy petition, unless they forgot about your debt or submits incomplete papers to the bankruptcy court.

1. Notice of Case, Meeting of Creditors and Deadlines

Assuming you are listed and notified of the bankruptcy, you will receive one of the following types of notices.

- **Chapter 7 "no asset" case.** A Chapter 7 debtor claims that all of their assets are exempt, that is, unavailable to pay their creditors. We suggest you file a Proof of Claim even if the court does not require you to. But keep reading this chapter, as you may have other remedies.

- **Chapter 7 "asset" case.** A Chapter 7 debtor has nonexempt assets that may be used to pay their creditors. You may get paid a portion of your judgment, depending on the value of the assets and the rights of other creditors. You must file a Proof of Claim to be paid.

- **Chapter 13 case.** The debtor intends to repay a portion of their debts through a repayment plan. A copy of the plan will be enclosed with the notice or sent separately. You must file a Proof of Claim to be paid.

If you receive a bankruptcy notice but don't recognize the name of the debtor, contact the trustee. The debtor may be using a different name. For example, your judgment may be in the name of the business while the bankruptcy filing may be in the name of an individual.

> **If You Don't Receive Notice**
>
> If you believe the debtor has filed for bankruptcy but you don't receive any notice from the bankruptcy court, you probably weren't listed in the papers or the notice was sent to an old address. Still, act like you received the notice. Cease all enforcement activities. Then call the bankruptcy court for the area in which the debtor lives (www.uscourts.gov/court_locator) and ask if the debtor has filed bankruptcy. If so, get the name and phone number of the trustee handling the case. Call the trustee, state that you are a judgment creditor who did not get notice of the case and ask for notice so you can file a claim.
>
> If you are completely unaware of a bankruptcy filing and not listed in the bankruptcy papers, your judgment might legally survive the bankruptcy. While it may be tempting to pretend you don't know about the bankruptcy if you receive no notice, debtors often can amend their papers after their cases are over to add omitted creditors and have the debts wiped out. You are better off pursuing your rights as soon as you hear that the debtor has filed.

We have included copies of notices commencing a Chapter 7 "no asset" bankruptcy, a Chapter 7 "asset" bankruptcy and a Chapter 13 bankruptcy. The fine print at the top left of each form tells you the type of case. Each notice states the name of the court and the date the debtor filed the case.

Next are boxes identifying the debtor and any attorney, the case number, and the name, address and telephone number of the trustee. As mentioned earlier, the trustee is a court-appointed official who represents the unsecured creditors in a bankruptcy case. Their role is to make sure the debtor coughs up as much property (Chapter 7) or cash (Chapter 13) as possible. In most consumer bankruptcy cases, the proceedings are controlled by the trustee. Generally, the debtor can't dispose of any property without

Meeting of Creditors

This section gives you the date, time and location of the meeting of the creditors. It is usually held one to two months after the debtor files the bankruptcy papers. The debtor must appear to answer a few routine questions or to clarify any ambiguities in the papers. Despite its name, few creditors attend. You can go, and you should, if you are curious about the process or have some questions about information in the debtor's bankruptcy papers that you would like to ask the debtor. Most meetings last under five minutes, although you might be sitting in the room for an hour or longer waiting for the trustee to get to your debtor's case.

If you want to formally object to something in the debtor's papers, the meeting of creditors is not the place to do it. Formal objections must be brought before a bankruptcy judge. But creditors do raise objections at the meeting of creditors with the hope that the debtor will voluntarily address the creditors' concerns, rather than litigate the objection before the bankruptcy judge. (See Section F, below, for objections you can raise.)

Deadlines. In a Chapter 7 asset or Chapter 13 case, you must file a Proof of Claim with the court by the date specified in this box. If you plan to object to the discharge of a debt, a claimed exemption or the debtor's Chapter 13 plan, you must meet the deadlines specified. (See Section F about these and other objections.)

Creditors May Not Take Certain Actions. This is a notice that the automatic stay is in effect. (The automatic stay is discussed above in Section B.)

At the very bottom left is the court's address. The clerk's signature or stamp and date are at the bottom right.

The back page of each form provides explanations of the information on the front page.

2. Chapter 13 Repayment Plan

Enclosed with the Chapter 13 notice, or sent separately, will be the debtor's Chapter 13 plan. Read it carefully. You want to figure out which category of creditor includes you. Generally, creditors fall into three categories: priority, secured and general unsecured. Priority and secured creditors usually receive 100% of what they are owed. General unsecured creditors usually receive less. Somewhere on the plan should be a number, written as a percentage, such as 33%, 54%, 72% or 100%. This indicates how much the debtor intends to repay each general unsecured creditor. So if you are a general unsecured creditor owed $8,000 and the debtor files a "54%" plan, you can hope to receive $4,320 through the debtor's bankruptcy.

The percentage is determined through a complex formula based on the debtor's disposable income each month (the amount left after basic living expenses are paid), how much the debtor owes to priority and secured creditors and the value of the debtor's nonexempt assets. (The debtor must pay their unsecured creditors at least the value of their nonexempt property).

You are not bound by how the debtor classifies you if you feel it is wrong. For example, if the debtor lists you as a general unsecured creditor but you recorded an Abstract of Judgment in the county in which the debtor owns real estate (and there is equity in the property), be sure to identify yourself as a secured creditor on the Proof of Claim (See Section D).

D. File Proof of Claim

If the debtor filed a Chapter 7 asset case, you must file a Proof of Claim to claim a share of the proceeds generated from the sale of the debtor's nonexempt assets. If the debtor filed a Chapter 13 bankruptcy, you must file a Proof of Claim to receive payments under the plan. The bankruptcy notice (see Section C) gives the deadline for filing the Proof of Claim. If you miss the deadline, you will probably be out of luck. There is one exception: if your debt is automatically not dischargeable, you don't have to file a Proof of Claim. Even then, however, it can never hurt.

Even if you file a Proof of Claim, don't get too excited. In a Chapter 7 case, the assets may produce only a few cents on the dollar. Even if they generate a decent amount of money, the proceeds are distributed to creditors in a specific order, and you may get very little. Similarly, in a Chapter 13 case, priority and secured creditors must be paid in full under the plan. Many Chapter 13 plans propose paying no more than 25% to general unsecured creditors.

Still, you should complete your Proof of Claim. Getting paid something is better than getting paid nothing at all.

1. Completing the Proof of Claim

In a Chapter 7 asset case or a Chapter 13 case, the court should have sent a Proof of Claim with the bankruptcy notice. If it didn't, use the blank in the Appendix or get a copy from the bankruptcy court. A completed sample is attached.

READ THE FORM AND COMPLETE

Name of Debtor and Case Number: Get the information off of the debtor's bankruptcy papers.

Name of Creditor: Enter your name spelled correctly, even if it was misspelled on the notice.

Name and address where notices should be sent: Enter your name, mailing address and telephone number. Check any of the boxes at the right that apply.

Item 1: Enter the total amount of your judgment, including costs and interest that accrued prior to the bankruptcy filing date, less any payments that have been made on the judgment, even if this amount differs from what the debtor listed in the bankruptcy papers. Check the bottom box if your claim includes post-judgment interest or costs (See Chapter 16).

Item 2: Enter the name of the court from which your judgment comes and the case number, such as "Superior Court of California – Stanley Mosk Courthouse, Case # 14K5000"

Item 3: Enter the last 4 digits of the debtor's social security number.

Item 4: Check this box if you have created liens that still exist against the debtor's property (See Chapter 4). Then indicate whether your liens are against the debtor's real estate, motor vehicle or other property, and specify that other property. Where you are asked to enter the value of the collateral, enter the estimated value of the property to which the liens attach. If you don't know, write "don't know." In the space asking for the amount of arrearage and other charges, enter the amount you entered in Item 4.

Item 5: Priority creditors are entitled to be paid first in bankruptcy. Check the first box if your judgment is based on a priority debt. Then enter the amount of your debt entitled to priority (certain priority debts have a ceiling), and check the box describing the kind of debt you have.

Item 7: Attach to the Proof of Claim copies of all documents that substantiate your claim, including:
- the judgment
- the latest filed Memorandum of Costs
- your written computation of interest accrued and costs incurred after the last Memorandum of Costs was filed
- Abstract of Judgment
- Notice of Judgment Lien on Personal

Property, and
- Proof of Service of Application and Order for Appearance and Examination.

Item 8: Follow the instructions. You are usually the "creditor". Enter the date, and sign and print your name.

2. Filing Proof of Claim

Make a copy of the Proof of Claim for your records. You should file the Proof of Claim with the clerk, at the office of the United States Bankruptcy Court, and receive a conformed copy (dated and stamped "filed"), indicating that you filed the Proof timely. There is no need to serve the Proof of Claim on the debtor or their attorney.

3. If Debtor or Trustee Objects

The amount you list on your Proof of Claim will be deemed correct unless the debtor or the trustee objects. The most likely objections are:

- you failed to attach proper documentation in support of your claim
- the amount you claim is incorrect, or
- you improperly stated that your claim was a priority claim.

See a bankruptcy attorney if your claim is rejected for a reason you can't correct and the amount you are seeking warrants the expense.

E. After Filing the Proof of Claim

What happens after you file the Proof of Claim depends on the type of case.

1. Chapter 7 Bankruptcy

After all Proofs of Claim are filed and the meeting of the creditors takes place, the trustee sells any nonexempt property and distributes the funds to creditors. You just sit back and hope to get a check. The entire process usually takes no more than six months.

2. Chapter 13 Bankruptcy

A bankruptcy judge will accept or reject the debtor's plan at a confirmation hearing. The judge will generally accept a plan that was submitted in good faith and is feasible. The judge relies heavily on the recommendation of the trustee.

You can object to the confirmation of a debtor's plan on a number of grounds, including that the debtor's living expenses are unreasonable, that the debtor's total payments will not reach the value of their nonexempt property, that a creditor has been improperly classified as a priority or,
secured creditor and therefore is being paid off in full when they shouldn't be, or that the plan unfairly discriminates, meaning that the debtor is treating similarly situated creditors differently. For example, if your judgment isn't secured and the debtor proposes paying one unsecured creditor 100%, his brother, for example, while you and the other unsecured creditors receive less, the plan discriminates.

You can raise your objections informally at the meeting of the creditors. If the debtor or trustee does not adequately address your problem, you will have to file a formal motion with the court to be determined at the confirmation hearing.

Once the plan is approved, the trustee's job is to receive payments and distribute them to the creditors. It may take some time before you get paid. As mentioned, priority debts are paid first, then secured creditors. Only after those debts are paid are funds distributed to general unsecured creditors. Before you see a cent, the debtor may miss payments, modify the plan, dismiss the case or convert to a Chapter 7 bankruptcy.

If the debtor has problems making

payments, it's up to the bankruptcy trustee, not you, to decide how to proceed. The trustee may give the debtor a grace period of a month or two or may allow minor adjustments in the plan. As long as the debtor appears to be acting in good faith, the trustee will try to be accommodating. If the debtor cannot complete the plan, the debtor may do any of the following:

- Ask to amend the plan to reduce the percentage paid general unsecured creditors or extend the repayment period to as much as five years. This may reduce the total amount you receive under the plan.

- Convert to a Chapter 7 case; you will receive a notice of conversion if this happens.

- Request a discharge of debts, without converting to Chapter 7, on the basis of hardship, if the debtor's inability to pay is due to circumstances beyond their control, such as a serious illness that prevents the debtor from working.

- Dismiss the Chapter 13 case. This means that you can pick up your enforcement activities where you left off when the bankruptcy was filed. (But note our caution in Section E3, below, in the event the debtor refiles.)

3. When the Case Is Over

In a Chapter 7 case, when the trustee has mostly completed their work, you will receive a final notice of discharge from the court. If you have been paid nothing, it means that few assets were available to be distributed to general unsecured creditors. If the debtor successfully completes a Chapter 13 case, you will receive a final notice of discharge.

After the debtor receives a discharge, the automatic stay ends. Any balance owed on your judgment will be wiped out unless you have liens on the debtor's property that survived the bankruptcy, your judgment automatically escapes discharge or the bankruptcy court declared your judgment nondischargeable (See Section F, below).

If the court notifies you that the bankruptcy case has been dismissed rather than discharged, you may resume enforcing your judgment, unless and until the debtor files another bankruptcy case. If that happens, a new automatic stay will take effect. Be especially wary of this in a Chapter 13 bankruptcy. One strategy used by debtors who file for Chapter 13 bankruptcy is to wait until Proofs of Claims are filed, dismiss their case and then refile, hoping the creditor won't notice it's a new case and won't refile the necessary Proof of Claim, thinking they've already done so.

F. What Else Can You Do?

In addition to filing a Proof of Claim, a number of possible avenues are open to judgment creditors in bankruptcy. Before you invest time and money pursuing your rights, keep in mind that the paramount purpose of bankruptcy is to give the debtor a fresh start. The debtor, almost always, get the benefit of the doubt and a court is generally inclined to discharge every allowable debt. Still, if you do your homework, you may be able to snatch victory from the jaws of defeat.

1. Ask Debtor to Reaffirm the Debt

Under the Bankruptcy Code, a debtor who wants to keep property that secures a debt, such as a car or house, can do so by "reaffirming" the judgment, that is, agreeing to keep making payments under the original, or adjusted, agreement. Some unsecured creditors use this section of the Bankruptcy Code to convince debtors who might have engaged in fraud or other questionable behavior to pay their debt rather than have the debt challenged in the bankruptcy court. You may be able to convince the debtor to reaffirm the debt, especially if you notice that the bankruptcy papers are inconsistent with papers the debtor gave you.

You can call the debtor and ask for reaffirmation or raise it at the creditors' meeting. If the debtor agrees, you will have to draft a reaffirmation agreement. If the debtor does not have a lawyer, you will have to schedule a hearing to obtain the judge's approval on the agreement. And whether or not the debtor has an attorney, the reaffirmation agreement must be filed with the bankruptcy court to be valid. You can get a Reaffirmation Agreement at www.cacb.uscourts.gov, search for "reaffirmation agreement". Please read page 5, section "your right to rescind". The debtor can cancel the agreement at any time prior to their discharge, by then all of your other options may no longer be available to you. Enter into a reaffirmation agreement cautiously. An application for approval of the agreement and order are included.

2. Challenge the Dischargeability of Certain Debts

Certain debts can survive a Chapter 7 bankruptcy, but only if the creditor formally contests the discharge of the debt in court by filing a Complaint to Determine Dischargeability of Debt within 60 days of the date set for the first meeting of creditors. Debts that creditors can successfully preserve through the bankruptcy process are:

- Debts incurred on the basis of fraud, such as loans made in reliance on false or misleading written statements, debts based on intentional misrepresentation or debts of more than $1,075 incurred for luxuries or non-necessary items incurred within 60 days of filing for bankruptcy [11 U.S.C. 523(a)(2)].

- Debts from willful and malicious acts, including civil judgments for damages resulting from assault and battery, theft, intentional infliction of emotional distress and other intentional torts [11 U.S.C. 523(a)(6)].

- Debts from embezzlement, larceny or breach of fiduciary duty [11 U.S.C. 523(a)(4)].

- Debts arising from a marital settlement or divorce decree, other than support, if the debtor has the ability to pay the debt from income or property not reasonably necessary for their support or if discharging the debt would result in a benefit to the debtor that outweighs the detriment to the debtor's former spouse or child [11 U.S.C. 523(a)(15)].

Does it make sense for you to challenge the discharge of a debt? That depends on the amount at stake and how much it will cost you to do so. Although it is theoretically possible to handle a non-dischargeability proceeding yourself, you'll probably have to hire an attorney.

3. Object to Exemptions

In a Chapter 13 bankruptcy, general unsecured creditors must receive, at least, the value of the debtor's nonexempt property. Otherwise, exemptions have no role in a Chapter 13 case. In a Chapter 7 bankruptcy, however, exemptions are a key component. All nonexempt property may be taken by the trustee and sold to pay off the general unsecured creditors.

When the debtor files for bankruptcy, they must complete several forms. On Schedules A and B, the debtor lists all of their property. On Schedule C, they list the property they claim as exempt. Most debtors in California find a way to include all of their valuable property on Schedule C. You can visit the court and examine the schedules your debtor files or you can set up an account at www.pacer.gov.

In California, a debtor can choose between two sets of exemptions, those authorized by various provisions of section 704 of the Code of Civil Procedure (called the "System 1" exemptions) and those authorized by various provisions of section 703 of the Code of Civil Procedure (called the "System 2" exemptions). For the most updated lists see Chapter A.

If you examine the debtor's schedules and discover bogus exemptions or property that has been greatly undervalued to bring it within the limit of an exemption, you can object. Written objections must be made within 30 days after the Meeting of the Creditors. The court will accept any exemption claimed by a debtor if no one objects, even if the exemption has no basis in reality. Formally objecting to a claimed exemption is beyond the scope of this book. You can report your findings to the trustee, however, and hope that he'll do the job for you.

4. Make Other Objections

In every Chapter 7 bankruptcy case, a debtor must list all their property, debts, income and expenses and describe all property transactions that occurred during the year before filing. On the basis of the debtor's papers, the trustee decides whether the debtor has nonexempt assets that should be sold to repay the creditors.

That's not the only thing the trustee looks for. The trustee, and creditors, can examine the papers to see if the debtor made payments to any creditors during the 90 days preceding the bankruptcy, and during the last year to creditors who are relatives or business associates. If so, these payments are considered illegal preferences and the trustee may demand that the creditor turn the money over to the trustee to be apportioned among all of the creditors.

It might also be that the debtor has obviously unloaded (sold cheaply or given away) assets in order to hide them from creditors. This may be a basis for denying the bankruptcy altogether. Bankruptcy laws impose severe penalties on debtors who try to cheat their creditors or lie about their assets or income. Several bankruptcy courts, including the one in Los Angeles, aggressively go after debtors who try to commit fraud.

If you discover this type of questionable behavior, bring it to the attention of the trustee at once. The trustee can file a motion asking the bankruptcy court to dismiss the case. A dismissal would free you up to continue your enforcement efforts just as if the bankruptcy were never filed.

If you discover the questionable behavior only after the bankruptcy has ended and the debtor has received a discharge, you have up to one year after the date of the discharge to file a complaint with the bankruptcy court. You'll need a lawyer's help. If you win, the bankruptcy discharge will be nullified and you can enforce your judgment [11 U.S.C. 727(d), 727(e), 1328(d)].

5. Enforce Liens That Survive Bankruptcy

A judgment lien that attaches to exempt property such as a house or car can usually be wiped out in bankruptcy through a process called lien avoidance. There are a few exceptions. First, if the lien existed before the debtor obtained the property, then the lien cannot be wiped out. So if you got your judgment, recorded an Abstract of Judgment, with the county recorder, and then the debtor bought a house in that county, the debtor did not own the property before the lien was affixed and the lien cannot be eliminated.

In addition, the lien can be wiped out only if it "impairs" the exemption. If there's enough equity in the property to allow the debtor to get the full exemption and to pay off the lien, it won't be eliminated. For example, say an unmarried debtor owns a house worth $150,000; the debtor owes $125,000 to the lender, leaving $25,000 of equity. You've recorded a $10,000 judgment. If the homestead exemption, in this example, is $50,000. The equity doesn't cover that much.

Your lien can be wiped out. If the house was worth $200,000, and the debtor owed the lender $125,000, the debtor would have $75,000 of equity, enough to cover the exemption and your judgment. In that case, the lien would stay.

If your lien is wiped out, your debt is treated like any other unsecured debt. If your lien survives bankruptcy, the lien is your only method of collecting the judgment after your bankruptcy case ends, unless the court determines that the debt isn't dischargeable. Oddly, you have to think of your debt as having two parts: 1) the debtor's personal liability to pay you, and 2) your lien. The personal liability gets wiped out in bankruptcy, even if the lien remains. As we said in Chapter 4, this means you'll most likely be paid if the debtor sells or refinances the property before your lien expires. Since the judgment will not be allowed to be renewed, the abstract of judgment will also not be allowed to be renewed.

6. Enforcing Nondischargeable Debts

Certain debts automatically survive the bankruptcy intact, which means you can still enforce them after the bankruptcy case is over. They include:

- **Omitted debts.** Debts not listed in the bankruptcy papers are not discharged, unless the creditor had notice or actual knowledge of the bankruptcy case in time to file a Proof of Claim [11 U.S.C. 523(a)(3)] .

- **Alimony and child support.** Child and spousal support obligations, and debts that are in the nature of support, are not dischargeable [11 U.S.C. 523(a)(5) and 523(a)(18)].

- **Court-ordered restitution.** A court may have ordered a convicted criminal to make restitution to you. If you convert that restitution order into a civil judgment under Penal Code 1214(b), the debt cannot be discharged in bankruptcy [11 U.S.C. 523(a)(19)(B)(iii) & (a)(13)] (Chapter 1, Section D covers converting a restitution order into a civil judgment).

- **Debts from intoxicated driving.**

Debts based on a death or personal injury resulting from the debtor's driving under the influence of alcohol or drugs are nondischargeable in bankruptcy [11 U.S.C. 523(a) (9)].

UNITED STATES BANKRUPTCY COURT

SOUTHERN DISTRICT OF CALIFORNIA

In re:)
Jeff Isbad) Case No.0000-0007
)
) Chapter 7
)
)
)
Debtor(s))

APPLICATION FOR APPROVAL OF REAFFIRMATION

AGREEMENT PURSUANT TO 11 U.S.C. § 524(C)

TO THE HONORABLE, JOHN D. FAIR, JUDGE:

The debtor(s) in this case, Jeff Isbad, hereby apply for approval of their reaffirmation agreement with Amy Right. In support of this application we hereby aver that:

1. Jeff Isbad wishes to reaffirm his debt with Amy Right, to the extent it is secured by debtor's home.

2. The debtor's home is presently worth $195,000.

3. The reaffirmation agreement, signed by the parties and providing for the payment of $ 645.92 at 10% interest, in 33 monthly installments, is attached to this application.

4. The agreement does not impose a hardship on Jeff Isbad, because the debtor(s)' current income is $4,700 per month, and expenses are $4,000 per month.

WHEREFORE, the debtors pray that the reaffirmation of the aforesaid debt be approved.

Dated: 3/17/XX   signed by Jeff Isbad
                   Jeff Isbad

ORDER APPROVING REAFFIRMATION AGREEMENT

AND NOW, this 10th day of May, 2015, the court having found that the reaffirmation agreement proposed by the debtor is in the best interest of the debtor and does not pose a hardship on the debtor or the debtor's dependents, it is hereby ordered that the reaffirmation with Amy Right is approved.

Dated: _____
U.S. Bankruptcy Judge

B9A (Official Form 9A) (Chapter 7 Individual or Joint Debtor No Asset Case) (12/12)

UNITED STATES BANKRUPTCY COURT_____ District of_____

Notice of
Chapter 7 Bankruptcy Case, Meeting of Creditors, & Deadlines

[A chapter 7 bankruptcy case concerning the debtor(s) listed below was filed on _____(date).]
or [A bankruptcy case concerning the debtor(s) listed below was originally filed under chapter_____ on _____(date) and was converted to a case under chapter 7 on_____(date).]

You may be a creditor of the debtor. **This notice lists important deadlines.** You may want to consult an attorney to protect your rights. All documents filed in the case may be inspected at the bankruptcy clerk's office at the address listed below. NOTE: The staff of the bankruptcy clerk's office cannot give legal advice.

**Creditors -- Do not file this notice in connection with any proof of claim you submit to the court.
See Reverse Side for Important Explanations.**

Debtor(s) (name(s) and address):	Case Number:
	Last four digits of Social-Security or Individual Taxpayer-ID (ITIN) No(s)./Complete EIN:
All other names used by the Debtor(s) in the last 8 years (include married, maiden, and trade names):	Bankruptcy Trustee (name and address):
Attorney for Debtor(s) (name and address):	
Telephone number:	Telephone number:

Meeting of Creditors
Date: / /   Time: ( ) A. M.   Location:
                            ( ) P. M.

Presumption of Abuse under 11 U.S.C. § 707(b)
See "Presumption of Abuse" on the reverse side.

Depending on the documents filed with the petition, one of the following statements will appear.

   The presumption of abuse does not arise.
        Or
   The presumption of abuse arises.
        Or
   Insufficient information has been filed to date to permit the clerk to make any determination concerning the presumption of abuse. If more complete information, when filed, shows that the presumption has arisen, creditors will be notified.

Deadlines:
Papers must be *received* by the bankruptcy clerk's office by the following deadlines:
Deadline to Object to Debtor's Discharge or to Challenge Dischargeability of Certain Debts:

Deadline to Object to Exemptions:
Thirty (30) days after the *conclusion* of the meeting of creditors.

Creditors May Not Take Certain Actions:
In most instances, the filing of the bankruptcy case automatically stays certain collection and other actions against the debtor and the debtor's property. Under certain circumstances, the stay may be limited to 30 days or not exist at all, although the debtor can request the court to extend or impose a stay. If you attempt to collect a debt or take other action in violation of the Bankruptcy Code, you may be penalized. Consult a lawyer to determine your rights in this case.

Please Do Not File a Proof of Claim Unless You Receive a Notice To Do So.

Creditor with a Foreign Address:
A creditor to whom this notice is sent at a foreign address should read the information under "Do Not File a Proof of Claim at This Time" on the reverse side.

Address of the Bankruptcy Clerk's Office:	For the Court:
	Clerk of the Bankruptcy Court:
Telephone number:	
Hours Open:	Date:

B9I (Official Form 9I) (Chapter 13 Case) (12/12)

UNITED STATES BANKRUPTCY COURT _____ District of _____

Notice of
Chapter 13 Bankruptcy Case, Meeting of Creditors, & Deadlines

[The debtor(s) listed below filed a chapter 13 bankruptcy case on _____ (date).]
or [A bankruptcy case concerning the debtor(s) listed below was originally filed under chapter _____
on _____ (date) and was converted to a case under chapter 13 on _____ (date).]

You may be a creditor of the debtor. **This notice lists important deadlines.** You may want to consult an attorney to protect your rights. All documents filed in the case may be inspected at the bankruptcy clerk's office at the address listed below.
NOTE: The staff of the bankruptcy clerk's office cannot give legal advice.

Creditors -- Do not file this notice in connection with any proof of claim you submit to the court.
See Reverse Side for Important Explanations.

Debtor(s) (name(s) and address):	Case Number:
	Last four digits of Social-Security or Individual Taxpayer-ID (ITIN) No(s)./Complete EIN:
All other names used by the Debtor(s) in the last 8 years (include married, maiden, and trade names):	Bankruptcy Trustee (name and address):
Attorney for Debtor(s) (name and address):	
Telephone number:	Telephone number:

Meeting of Creditors
Date: / /   Time: ( ) A. M.   Location:
                          ( ) P. M.

Deadlines:
Papers must be *received* by the bankruptcy clerk's office by the following deadlines:
Deadline to File a Proof of Claim:
For all creditors (except a governmental unit):   For a governmental unit (except as otherwise provided in Fed. R. Bankr. P. 3002(c)(1)):

Creditor with a Foreign Address:
A creditor to whom this notice is sent at a foreign address should read the information under "Claims" on the reverse side.

Deadline to Object to Debtor's Discharge or to Challenge Dischargeability of Certain Debts:

Deadline to Object to Exemptions:
Thirty (30) days after the *conclusion* of the meeting of creditors.

Filing of Plan, Hearing on Confirmation of Plan
[The debtor has filed a plan. The plan or a summary of the plan is enclosed. The hearing on confirmation will be held:
Date:_____ Time:_____ Location:_____]
or [The debtor has filed a plan. The plan or a summary of the plan and notice of confirmation hearing will be sent separately.]
or [The debtor has not filed a plan as of this date. You will be sent separate notice of the hearing on confirmation of the plan.]

Creditors May Not Take Certain Actions:
In most instances, the filing of the bankruptcy case automatically stays certain collection and other actions against the debtor, the debtor's property, and certain codebtors. Under certain circumstances, the stay may be limited to 30 days or not exist at all, although the debtor can request the court to extend or impose a stay. If you attempt to collect a debt or take other action in violation of the Bankruptcy Code, you may be penalized. Consult a lawyer to determine your rights in this case.

Address of the Bankruptcy Clerk's Office:	For the Court:
	Clerk of the Bankruptcy Court:
Telephone number:	
Hours Open:	Date:

Information to identify the case:

Debtor 1 _____
          First Name   Middle Name   Last Name

Debtor 2 _____
(Spouse, if filing) First Name Middle Name Last Name

United States Bankruptcy Court for the: _____ District of _____
                                                                (State)

Case number: _____

Last 4 digits of Social Security number or ITIN ___ ___ ___ ___
EIN ___ ___ - ___ ___ ___ ___ ___ ___ ___

Last 4 digits of Social Security number or ITIN ___ ___ ___ ___
EIN ___ ___ - ___ ___ ___ ___ ___ ___ ___

[Date case filed for chapter 11 _____ MM / DD / YYYY] OR

[Date case filed in chapter ____ _____ MM / DD / YYYY

Date case converted to chapter 11 _____ MM / DD / YYYY

Official Form 309E (For Individuals or Joint Debtors)

Notice of Chapter 11 Bankruptcy Case

12/15

For the debtors listed above, a case has been filed under chapter 11 of the Bankruptcy Code. An order for relief has been entered.

This notice has important information about the case for creditors and debtors, including information about the meeting of creditors and deadlines. Read both pages carefully.

The filing of the case imposed an automatic stay against most collection activities. This means that creditors generally may not take action to collect debts from the debtors or the debtors' property. For example, while the stay is in effect, creditors cannot sue, garnish wages, assert a deficiency, repossess property, or otherwise try to collect from the debtors. Creditors cannot demand repayment from debtors by mail, phone, or otherwise. Creditors who violate the stay can be required to pay actual and punitive damages and attorney's fees. Under certain circumstances, the stay may be limited to 30 days or not exist at all, although debtors can ask the court to extend or impose a stay.

Confirmation of a chapter 11 plan may result in a discharge of debt. Creditors who assert that the debtors are not entitled to a discharge of any debts or who want to have a particular debt excepted from discharge may be required to file a complaint in the bankruptcy clerk's office within the deadlines specified in this notice. (See line 10 below for more information.)

To protect your rights, consult an attorney. All documents filed in the case may be inspected at the bankruptcy clerk's office at the address listed below or through PACER (Public Access to Court Electronic Records at www.pacer.gov).

The staff of the bankruptcy clerk's office cannot give legal advice.

To help creditors correctly identify debtors, debtors submit full Social Security or Individual Taxpayer Identification Numbers, which may appear on a version of this notice. However, the full numbers must not appear on any document filed with the court.

Do not file this notice with any proof of claim or other filing in the case. Do not include more than the last four digits of a Social Security or Individual Taxpayer Identification Number in any document, including attachments, that you file with the court.

	About Debtor 1:	About Debtor 2:
1. Debtor's full name		
2. All other names used in the last 8 years		
3. Address		If Debtor 2 lives at a different address:
4. Debtor's attorney Name and address		Contact phone _____ Email _____
5. Bankruptcy clerk's office Documents in this case may be filed at this address. You may inspect all records filed in this case at this office or online at www.pacer.gov.		Hours open _____ Contact phone _____

For more information, see page 2 ▶

B10 (Official Form 10) (04/13)

UNITED STATES BANKRUPTCY COURT Central District of California		PROOF OF CLAIM
Name of Debtor: Jeff Isbad	Case Number: 00000-0007	

NOTE: *Do not use this form to make a claim for an administrative expense that arises after the bankruptcy filing. You may file a request for payment of an administrative expense according to 11 U.S.C. § 503.*

Name of Creditor (the person or other entity to whom the debtor owes money or property):
Amy Right

COURT USE ONLY

Name and address where notices should be sent:
Amy Right
1000 My st
Mytown, Ca 90000

Telephone number: (310) 555-5555   email:

☐ Check this box if this claim amends a previously filed claim.

Court Claim Number: _____
(If known)

Filed on: _____

Name and address where payment should be sent (if different from above):
same as above

Telephone number: email:

☐ Check this box if you are aware that anyone else has filed a proof of claim relating to this claim. Attach copy of statement giving particulars.

1. Amount of Claim as of Date Case Filed: $_____ 3,000.00

If all or part of the claim is secured, complete item 4.

If all or part of the claim is entitled to priority, complete item 5.

☑ Check this box if the claim includes interest or other charges in addition to the principal amount of the claim. Attach a statement that itemizes interest or charges.

2. Basis for Claim: Superior Court of Ca- Stanley Mosk court case # 14K5000
(See instruction #2)

3. Last four digits of any number by which creditor identifies debtor: 6 7 8 9	3a. Debtor may have scheduled account as: _____ (See instruction #3a)	3b. Uniform Claim Identifier (optional): _ (See instruction #3b)

4. Secured Claim (See instruction #4)
Check the appropriate box if the claim is secured by a lien on property or a right of setoff, attach required redacted documents, and provide the requested information.

Nature of property or right of setoff: ☑ Real Estate ☐ Motor Vehicle ☐ Other
Describe: 666 e Cra P st, Helltown, Ca 90666

Value of Property: $ 1,000,000.00

Annual Interest Rate 10.000 % ☑ Fixed or ☐ Variable
(when case was filed)

Amount of arrearage and other charges, as of the time case was filed, included in secured claim, if any:
$_____ 3,000.00

Basis for perfection: abstract filed in
Los Angeles county on 01/01/2014 #14200000015

Amount of Secured Claim: $_____ 3,000.00

Amount Unsecured: $_____ 0.00

5. Amount of Claim Entitled to Priority under 11 U.S.C. § 507 (a). If any part of the claim falls into one of the following categories, check the box specifying the priority and state the amount.

☐ Domestic support obligations under 11 U.S.C. § 507 (a)(1)(A) or (a)(1)(B).

☐ Wages, salaries, or commissions (up to $12,475*) earned within 180 days before the case was filed or the debtor's business ceased, whichever is earlier – 11 U.S.C. § 507 (a)(4).

☐ Contributions to an employee benefit plan – 11 U.S.C. § 507 (a)(5).

Amount entitled to priority:

☐ Up to $2,775* of deposits toward purchase, lease, or rental of property or services for personal, family, or household use – 11 U.S.C. § 507 (a)(7).

☐ Taxes or penalties owed to governmental units – 11 U.S.C. § 507 (a)(8).

☐ Other – Specify applicable paragraph of 11 U.S.C. § 507 (a)(__).

$_____

Amounts are subject to adjustment on 4/01/16 and every 3 years thereafter with respect to cases commenced on or after the date of adjustment.

6. Credits. The amount of all payments on this claim has been credited for the purpose of making this proof of claim. (See instruction #6)

B10 (Official Form 10) (04/13)

7. Documents: Attached are **redacted** copies of any documents that support the claim, such as promissory notes, purchase orders, invoices, itemized statements of running accounts, contracts, judgments, mortgages, security agreements, or, in the case of a claim based on an open-end or revolving consumer credit agreement, a statement providing the information required by FRBP 3001(c)(3)(A). If the claim is secured, box 4 has been completed, and **redacted** copies of documents providing evidence of perfection of a security interest are attached. If the claim is secured by the debtor's principal residence, the Mortgage Proof of Claim Attachment is being filed with this claim. *(See instruction #7, and the definition of "redacted".)*

DO NOT SEND ORIGINAL DOCUMENTS. ATTACHED DOCUMENTS MAY BE DESTROYED AFTER SCANNING.

If the documents are not available, please explain:

---

8. Signature: (See instruction #8)

Check the appropriate box.

☑ I am the creditor. ☐ I am the creditor's authorized agent. ☐ I am the trustee, or the debtor, or their authorized agent. (See Bankruptcy Rule 3004.) ☐ I am a guarantor, surety, indorser, or other codebtor. (See Bankruptcy Rule 3005.)

I declare under penalty of perjury that the information provided in this claim is true and correct to the best of my knowledge, information, and reasonable belief.

Print Name: __Amy Right__
Title:
Company: 05/01/2015
Address and telephone number (if different from notice address above):   (Signature)   (Date)

Telephone number: email:

Penalty for presenting fraudulent claim: Fine of up to $500,000 or imprisonment for up to 5 years, or both. 18 U.S.C. §§ 152 and 3571.

INSTRUCTIONS FOR PROOF OF CLAIM FORM

The instructions and definitions below are general explanations of the law. In certain circumstances, such as bankruptcy cases not filed voluntarily by the debtor, exceptions to these general rules may apply.

Items to be completed in Proof of Claim form

Court, Name of Debtor, and Case Number:
Fill in the federal judicial district in which the bankruptcy case was filed (for example, Central District of California), the debtor's full name, and the case number. If the creditor received a notice of the case from the bankruptcy court, all of this information is at the top of the notice.

Creditor's Name and Address:
Fill in the name of the person or entity asserting a claim and the name and address of the person who should receive notices issued during the bankruptcy case. A separate space is provided for the payment address if it differs from the notice address. The creditor has a continuing obligation to keep the court informed of its current address. See Federal Rule of Bankruptcy Procedure (FRBP) 2002(g).

1. Amount of Claim as of Date Case Filed:
State the total amount owed to the creditor on the date of the bankruptcy filing. Follow the instructions concerning whether to complete items 4 and 5. Check the box if interest or other charges are included in the claim.

2. Basis for Claim:
State the type of debt or how it was incurred. Examples include goods sold, money loaned, services performed, personal injury/wrongful death, car loan, mortgage note, and credit card. If the claim is based on delivering health care goods or services, limit the disclosure of the goods or services so as to avoid embarrassment or the disclosure of confidential health care information. You may be required to provide additional disclosure if an interested party objects to the claim.

3. Last Four Digits of Any Number by Which Creditor Identifies Debtor:
State only the last four digits of the debtor's account or other number used by the creditor to identify the debtor.

3a. Debtor May Have Scheduled Account As:
Report a change in the creditor's name, a transferred claim, or any other information that clarifies a difference between this proof of claim and the claim as scheduled by the debtor.

3b. Uniform Claim Identifier:
If you use a uniform claim identifier, you may report it here. A uniform claim identifier is an optional 24-character identifier that certain large creditors use to facilitate electronic payment in chapter 13 cases.

4. Secured Claim:
Check whether the claim is fully or partially secured. Skip this section if the claim is entirely unsecured. (See Definitions.) If the claim is secured, check the box for the nature and value of property that secures the claim, attach copies of lien documentation, and state, as of the date of the bankruptcy filing, the annual interest rate (and whether it is fixed or variable), and the amount past due on the claim.

5. Amount of Claim Entitled to Priority Under 11 U.S.C. § 507 (a).
If any portion of the claim falls into any category shown, check the appropriate box(es) and state the amount entitled to priority. (See Definitions.) A claim may be partly priority and partly non-priority. For example, in some of the categories, the law limits the amount entitled to priority.

6. Credits:
An authorized signature on this proof of claim serves as an acknowledgment that when calculating the amount of the claim, the creditor gave the debtor credit for any payments received toward the debt.

7. Documents:
Attach redacted copies of any documents that show the debt exists and a lien secures the debt. You must also attach copies of documents that evidence perfection of any security interest and documents required by FRBP 3001(c) for claims based on an open-end or revolving consumer credit agreement or secured by a security interest in the debtor's principal residence. You may also attach a summary in addition to the documents themselves. FRBP 3001(c) and (d). If the claim is based on delivering health care goods or services, limit disclosing confidential health care information. Do not send original documents, as attachments may be destroyed after scanning.

8. Date and Signature:
The individual completing this proof of claim must sign and date it. FRBP 9011. If the claim is filed electronically, FRBP 5005(a)(2) authorizes courts to establish local rules specifying what constitutes a signature. If you sign this form, you declare under penalty of perjury that the information provided is true and correct to the best of your knowledge, information, and reasonable belief. Your signature is also a certification that the claim meets the requirements of FRBP 9011(b). Whether the claim is filed electronically or in person, if your name is on the signature line, you are responsible for the declaration. Print the name and title, if any, of the creditor or other person authorized to file this claim. State the filer's address and telephone number if it differs from the address given on the top of the form for purposes of receiving notices. If the claim is filed by an authorized agent, provide both the name of the individual filing the claim and the name of the agent. If the authorized agent is a servicer, identify the corporate servicer as the company. Criminal penalties apply for making a false statement on a proof of claim.

Blank Page

Chapter 18

If the Debtor Passes Away

A. Recovering Your Judgment Through Probate	18/2
1. When to File a Creditor's Claim	18/4
2. Complete the Creditor's Claim	18/4
3. Send and File the Claim	18/5
4. After You Submit the Claim	18/5
B. Recovering Outside of Probate	18/6

Learning of a judgment debtor's death can be deeply sobering. No matter how zealously you have pursued your judgment, the final reality of the debtor's death will certainly make you pause. Perhaps you'll be grateful that the same fate did not befall you and simply drop the matter. Perhaps you'll think of the debtor's survivors, want to leave them in peace and abandon your claim. Or perhaps you are hoping that the deceased left assets from which you can enforce your judgment.

If either of the first two scenarios describe how you feel, put down the book, hug your loved ones and celebrate what you have. If the third one is closer to how you feel, keep reading this chapter, if the debtor lived in California. If the debtor lived elsewhere, you will probably need a lawyer's help to follow the procedures of that state.

Whether you can enforce your judgment against the property the debtor owned at their death depends on the value of the property and how it passes to the debtor's heirs. If the assets pass through a formal court process known as probate, you may be in luck. Probate provides an orderly procedure for you to present your claim and be paid. On the other hand, if the assets pass directly to the debtor's heirs outside of probate, there is no special enforcement procedure for creditors. You must track down the assets one by one, much the same as when the debtor was alive.

Note that the debtor's surviving relatives, parents, adult children and others, are not personally responsible for your judgment. Your only course is to seek payment from the debtor's estate. The one possible exception is if the judgment was a community debt, in which case the debtor's spouse is personally responsible for paying it.

There is a misconception that when a person dies, the heirs just automatically get what the decedent's Will says they get. Not so. First, the Executor of the Will must go to court to prove the decedent's Will is valid and that the decedent owned each item or asset prior to distributing those assets. Once it is proved that the decedent owned each item, then and only then, can the Executor look to the Will to see who gets each item. Probate Court is the process of validating the Will and proving ownership in court after death.

In order to avoid the expense and delay of Probate Court, anyone may, while they are alive, create a revocable living trust. After creating the trust, the person must transfer all of their assets into the trust by changing title or ownership of each asset into the name of the trust. Basically, the person is proving ownership during their lifetime instead of ownership being proven after their death.

A. Recovering Your Judgment Through Probate

You cannot enforce a judgment against a Debtor who has died using regular creditor remedies in Title 9 of the Code of Civil Procedure. You must use the Probate Code statutes to claim against the assets of the decedent [CCP 686.020]. Assets pass to heirs through probate when they are left in a will or when the deceased made no provision for how they should be passed. But not all assets pass through probate. If the debtor's assets are worth less than $150,000 [Probate Code 13151 & 13100], they can pass to heirs without probate. Or if the debtor arranged to transfer assets through a living trust, joint tenancy property or a pay-on-death account, the assets don't go through probate. The deceased's share of community property automatically passes to a surviving spouse absent a will or other estate planning document. Section B, below, explains how to pursue assets if there's no probate proceeding.

Important Terms Used in This Chapter

Intestate succession: The rules under which property is passed to a person's heirs when he dies without a will, trust or other estate planning document, or when an estate planning document fails to pass the property for one reason or another.

Joint tenancy: A way of holding title to property that avoids probate. When one joint tenant dies, her share automatically passes to the surviving joint tenants.

Living trust: A probate-avoidance device by which a person transfers property to a trust with instructions that the trust property be transferred to a named beneficiary at the owner's death.

Non-probate property: Property that does not go through probate because the deceased, while alive, set up a mechanism to avoid probate. Examples are life insurance proceeds payable to named beneficiaries, property held in joint tenancy, property held in a living trust and pay-on-death bank account trusts.

Personal representative: A person authorized to act on behalf of a deceased's estate. If named in the will, this person is called an executor; otherwise, he is called an administrator.

Probate: The court-supervised process by which a deceased's assets are distributed and debts are paid.

Probate estate: The assets of the deceased that are distributed through probate.

There are several different ways in which you may learn of the debtor's death.

• If you are looking for the debtor or actively involved in enforcing the judgment, you may learn of the death from relatives, an employer or other creditors.

• If you live in the same community as the debtor, you may read of his death in an obituary in a newspaper.

• If the debtor had a will or other estate planning document and sufficient assets to pass through probate, and the personal representative knows of your judgment, he must send you a document called a Notice of Administration to Creditors

The notice informs you of your right to file a Creditor's Claim against the estate. The notice must be mailed within four months of when the personal representative is named.

• If the debtor had a will or other estate planning document and sufficient assets to pass through probate, the personal representative for the estate must file a document called Notice of Petition to Administer Estate in the probate court. The court will set a date and time for a hearing. The personal representative then must publish a legal death notice in a general circulation newspaper in the city in which the debtor died, giving the date of the hearing. Collection agencies read these notices, but few others do, as a practical matter, you are unlikely to learn of the debtor's death this way.

If you learn of the debtor's death through a notice from the personal representative or you see the legal death notice in a newspaper, there will be a probate proceeding. If you learn of the death from some other source, you will need to ask around to find out if there will be a probate proceeding. First, contact the Probate Division of the Superior Court for the county in which the debtor died and ask if a probate petition has been filed in the debtor's name or look on the Court's website in the County where the debtor lived if Probate cases are shown on that website. If one hasn't, you can monitor the newspaper that carries legal notices for that area or Google the debtor's name to see if an obituary was published to find out who are the survivors. You might also contact any other creditors to whom the debtor owed money and ask if they know. After a respectable amount of time (a few weeks), you can call relatives, offer your condolences and then ask politely whether there will be a probate proceeding.

Once you know that a probate proceeding has been opened, you must file a Creditor's Claim in order to request payment.

In a Creditor's Claim, you assert your right to be paid out of the debtor's assets, if enough assets remain after higher priority creditors are paid. If you don't file a Creditor's Claim, you give up all right to enforce your judgment.

1. When to File a Creditor's Claim

Your deadline for filing a Creditor's Claim depends on how you learned about the probate proceeding.

- If you receive a Notice of Administration to Creditors from the personal representative, you must file your claim within four months after the date the personal representative was appointed by the court or 60 days after the notice was sent to you, whichever is later [Probate Code 9100].

- If you saw the Notice of Petition to Administer Estate in a newspaper, the deadline is four months from the hearing date stated on the Petition.

- If you learn from the court or another source, contact the probate court and find out when the personal representative was appointed. File your Creditor's Claim within four months of that date.

If you don't find out about the probate proceedings until after the deadline for filing a Creditor's Claim, see a probate attorney. If you did not receive notice of the probate proceeding, you can petition the court to file a late claim, but only if the probate court has not yet made a final order for distribution of the estate [Probate Code 9103].

2. Complete the Creditor's Claim

The Creditor's Claim is Judicial Council form DE-172 and can be found at http://www.courts.ca.gov/forms.htm

To complete the Creditor's Claim, you will need the following information:

- title and address of the probate court
- probate case number, and
- name and address of the personal representative.

A sample completed form is attached.

Caption: Enter your name, address and phone number and indicate that you are appearing in pro per. Enter the name and address of the court handling the probate, the debtor's name and the probate case number.

Item 1: Fill in the total amount of the judgment still due. Deduct any payments you have received and add post-judgment interest and court costs (See Chapter 16). If you haven't filed a Memorandum of Costs within the past few months, do so and serve it on the personal representative before filing this claim.

Item 2: Enter your name and check the box that best describes your status as the creditor. If you check 2b, be sure to enter your business' fictitious name. 2e might apply if you are the creditor's conservator or attorney-in-fact under a power of attorney.

Item 3: Enter your address.

Item 4: Check the first box if you are the creditor. Check the second box if you are acting on behalf of a creditor and state your authority.

Item 5: Leave this blank.

Item 6: Check both boxes (if the computer will not allow it, manually check the second after you print the form).

Fill in the date, print or type your name and sign the form.

Page Two

Caption: Fill in the name of the debtor and the probate case number.

Facts Supporting the Creditor's Claim: Check the "See attachment" box because you'll be attaching a copy of your judgment and possibly the most recent Memorandum of Costs.

Date of Item: Fill in the date your judgment was entered.

Item and Supporting Facts: Provide a brief description of your judgment. For example: "Judgment against Jeff Isbad for failure to pay back a loan." State whether costs were claimed in Memoranda of Costs and the amount of these costs. Also describe any judicial liens that you created on the debtor's personal property or real estate. Provide copies of all recorded or filed liens.

Amount Claimed: Enter the total from Item 1 on the front of the form.

Total: Enter the same amount.

Proof of Mailing/Personal Delivery: Unlike most court documents, you can serve the Creditor's Claim yourself. Depending on whether you plan to mail or hand deliver the document; check the appropriate box before "Mailing" or "Personal delivery." Complete the rest of the Proof of Service following the guidelines in Chapter 21.

3. Send and File the Claim

Make four copies of the Creditor's Claim, including your attachments. Mail or hand deliver a copy to the personal representative. If you mail the Creditor's Claim, it is best to mail using a USPS Certificate of Mailing, which is a little white form showing how the envelope was addressed. It is not Certified Mail and the recipient does not sign anything when the envelope is received. The Post Office will stamp the Certificate of Mailing form showing the date you mailed the envelope. This is confirmation that you mailed the form. Staple it to your copy of the Creditor's Claim form in case there is a question of the date you mailed your form. Send the original and one copy to the court to be file-stamped and returned to you in a self-addressed, stamped envelope.

File your Creditor's Claim, and Proof of Service, at the Court.

4. After You Submit a Claim

After receiving your claim, the personal representative should send you an Allowance or Rejection of Claim form. If payment of your judgment is approved, you may be paid immediately or the personal representative may wait until the court issues a final order stating how estate property is to be distributed.

What if the personal representative ignores or rejects your claim? You can dispute the decision formally by filing a lawsuit against the estate within 90 days [Probate Code 9353] of the date you receive a notice of rejection. You should receive some kind of notice, from the personal representative within 30 days. If you do not, contact them to find out why. If they don't respond then assume that the claim is rejected. You can file a lawsuit within 90 days of the "presumed" date of rejection.

If the personal representative disputes your claim, the court may require the estate to deposit the entire amount of the claim with the court, where it will remain until the matter is settled [Probate Code 11463].

Before you run to court, contact the personal representative by phone or letter. The personal representative might explain the reason for the rejection or dispute. For example, if they claim the judgment has been paid, you should ask them for evidence of the payment, it is impossible for you to prove that it has not been paid. Or you might be able to reach a compromise that settles the judgment.

> **How the Representative Pays Claims**
>
> The personal representative must pay off debts in the order set out below, except that debts owed the federal or state government have priority. The first five categories must be paid before the others [Probate Code 11420 & 11421].
>
> 1. Expenses of administering the estate.
>
> 2. Funeral expenses.
>
> 3. Expenses of last illness.
>
> 4. Family allowance to support the deceased's family during probate. Note also that if the debtor had filed a homestead declaration, her family members will be allowed to claim the homestead exemption if they inherit all or part of the house and are living in it at the time of the debtor's death [CCP 704.995].
>
> 5. Wages due the deceased's employees.
>
> 6. Mortgages, judgment liens and other liens. These are paid from the proceeds of the property subject to the lien; if the proceeds aren't enough, the remaining amount is classed with general debts.
>
> 7. General debts, including judgments not secured by liens.

If your claim is ignored or rejected because the estate has no money, you can check the court file to learn how funds are being disbursed. There may truly be no assets to pay you with, in which case you are out of luck.

If there appear to be funds or assets from which your claim can be paid, consider suing the personal representative for payment from the estate. If the amount in question is a relatively small sum, say up to $10,000 [CCP 116.221], you can probably handle it yourself in Small Claims court. There are special notice requirements for suing an estate, so check with the Small Claims advisor, your Court's Self-Help Center, a probate lawyer or your local Bar Association. If the amount is large enough for a regular court action, see a lawyer.

> **If Probate Is Opened But Assets Pass Outside of Probate**
>
> Many people pass some of their assets through probate avoidance devices such as a living trust or pay-on-death bank account, but leave enough property in their will to require a probate proceedings. Property that passes through a trust is liable for the payment of the deceased's creditors, if the property passing through probate is insufficient for that purpose [Probate Code 19001]. If the probate proceeding won't produce enough in assets to pay off your judgment, try collecting from assets passed outside of probate. See Section B, just below, for some suggestions on how to approach this task.

B. Recovering Outside of Probate

If the debtor left insufficient assets to require probate, or left insufficient funds to pay your judgment through probate but did leave property in a trust, the only way to get paid is to find assets that formerly belonged to the debtor but are now in the hands of heirs. You can attempt to levy on that property as if the debtor was alive. One possible source is a surviving spouse. Because California is a community property state, you can go after the surviving spouse's share of any community property owned prior to the debtor's death as well as property inherited by the spouse.

It may be possible for you to open a probate proceeding on behalf of a deceased debtor. Whether or not this makes sense will depend on your case. A consultation with a probate lawyer can help you decide.

It can be difficult to trace the debtor's assets once they are passed on; there is seldom a public record of what happened to the debtor's property. Real estate and business assets are the exception. So where do you turn? If the debtor was single but had children, you can reasonably expect that the children inherited most of the property. If the debtor was unmarried but had a companion, look to that person. To locate assets owned by heirs, you will have to use the procedures outlined in Chapter 6 or hire an asset-tracing firm.

If you created liens on the debtor's property, you will have an easier time collecting. Liens remain on property that passes to heirs. If the heir wants to sell the property, the liens will have to be paid off in order for the property to sell with clear title. Inherited property is often sold soon after it is received, so you may be paid.

There is one important exception to this rule: liens on property held in joint tenancy property are extinguished when the joint tenant-debtor dies. This is based on the legal principle that joint tenancy property isn't technically inherited; a joint tenant's interest (including the lien) simply ends when he dies.

DE-172

ATTORNEY OR PARTY WITHOUT ATTORNEY (Name, state bar number, and address):	TELEPHONE AND FAX NOS.: 310-555-5555	FOR COURT USE ONLY
Amy Right 1000 My st Mytown, Ca 90000 ATTORNEY FOR (Name): In Pro Per		

SUPERIOR COURT OF CALIFORNIA, COUNTY OF Los Angeles
STREET ADDRESS: 111 Hill st
MAILING ADDRESS:
CITY AND ZIP CODE: Los Angeles, Ca 90012
BRANCH NAME: Stanley Mosk Courthouse

ESTATE OF (Name):
Jeff Isbad
                                                    DECEDENT

CREDITOR'S CLAIM	CASE NUMBER: PB10666

You must file this claim with the court clerk at the court address above before the LATER of (a) four months after the date letters (authority to act for the estate) were first issued to the personal representative, or (b) sixty days after the date the *Notice of Administration* was given to the creditor, if notice was given as provided in Probate Code section 9051. You must also mail or deliver a copy of this claim to the personal representative and his or her attorney. A proof of service is on the reverse.
WARNING: Your claim will in most instances be invalid if you do not properly complete this form, file it on time with the court, and mail or deliver a copy to the personal representative and his or her attorney.

1. Total amount of the claim: $ 3,000.00
2. Claimant (name): Amy Right
   a. [✓] an individual
   b. [ ] an individual or entity doing business under the fictitious name of (specify):
   c. [ ] a partnership. The person signing has authority to sign on behalf of the partnership.
   d. [ ] a corporation. The person signing has authority to sign on behalf of the corporation.
   e. [ ] other (specify):
3. Address of claimant (specify): 1000 My st
                                   Mytown, Ca 90000
4. Claimant is [✓] the creditor [ ] a person acting on behalf of creditor (state reason):

5. [ ] Claimant is [ ] the personal representative [ ] the attorney for the personal representative.
6. I am authorized to make this claim which is just and due or may become due. All payments on or offsets to the claim have been credited. Facts supporting the claim are [ ] on reverse [✓] attached.

I declare under penalty of perjury under the laws of the State of California that the foregoing is true and correct.
Date: 12/01/2015

Amy Right   ▶
(TYPE OR PRINT NAME AND TITLE)   (SIGNATURE OF CLAIMANT)

INSTRUCTIONS TO CLAIMANT

A. On the reverse, itemize the claim and show the date the service was rendered or the debt incurred. Describe the item or service in detail, and indicate the amount claimed for each item. Do not include debts incurred after the date of death, except funeral claims.
B. If the claim is not due or contingent, or the amount is not yet ascertainable, state the facts supporting the claim.
C. If the claim is secured by a note or other written instrument, the original or a copy must be attached (state why original is unavailable.) If secured by mortgage, deed of trust, or other lien on property that is of record, it is sufficient to describe the security and refer to the date or volume and page, and county where recorded. (See Prob. Code, § 9152.)
D. Mail or take this original claim to the court clerk's office for filing. If mailed, use certified mail, with return receipt requested.
E. Mail or deliver a copy to the personal representative and his or her attorney. Complete the *Proof of Mailing or Personal Delivery* on the reverse.
F. The personal representative or his or her attorney will notify you when your claim is allowed or rejected.
G. Claims against the estate by the personal representative and the attorney for the personal representative must be filed within the claim period allowed in Probate Code section 9100. See the notice box above.

(Continued on reverse)

Form Approved by the
Judicial Council of California
DE-172 [Rev. January 1, 1998]

CREDITOR'S CLAIM
(Probate)

Probate Code, §§ 9000 et seq., 9153

ESTATE OF (Name): Jeff Isbad	DECEDENT	CASE NUMBER: PB10666

FACTS SUPPORTING THE CREDITOR'S CLAIM
☐ See attachment (if space is insufficient)

Date of item	Item and supporting facts	Amount claimed
01/01/2014	Judgment entered in Right v Isbad in Los Angeles County, California Superior Court, case no. 14K5000 Case was heard by the court and Jeff Isbad was present at the hearing. Debt was for some work Jeff Isbad was to complete on my car and never did. An Abstract of Judgment was recorded in the County of Los Angeles Recorder's Office as recorder number 1420000015 on May 1, 2014 A copy of the judgment and Abstract is attached.	3,000.00
	TOTAL:	$

PROOF OF ☐ MAILING ☐ PERSONAL DELIVERY TO PERSONAL REPRESENTATIVE
(Be sure to mail or take the original to the court clerk's office for filing)

1. I am the creditor or a person acting on behalf of the creditor. At the time of mailing or delivery I was at least 18 years of age.
2. My residence or business address is *(specify)*:

3. I mailed or personally delivered a copy of this *Creditor's Claim* to the personal representative as follows *(check either a or b below)*:
   a. ☐ **Mail.** I am a resident of or employed in the county where the mailing occurred.
      (1) I enclosed a copy in an envelope AND
         (a) ☐ **deposited** the sealed envelope with the United States Postal Service with the postage fully prepaid.
         (b) ☐ **placed** the envelope for collection and mailing on the date and at the place shown in items below following our ordinary business practices. I am readily familiar with this business' practice for collecting and processing correspondence for mailing. On the same day that correspondence is placed for collection and mailing, it is deposited in the ordinary course of business with the United States Postal Service in a sealed envelope with postage fully prepaid.
      (2) The envelope was addressed and mailed first-class as follows:
         (a) Name of personal representative served:
         (b) Address on envelope:

         (c) Date of mailing:
         (d) Place of mailing *(city and state)*:
   b. ☐ **Personal delivery.** I personally delivered a copy of the claim to the personal representative as follows:
      (1) Name of personal representative served:
      (2) Address where delivered:

      (3) Date delivered:
      (4) Time delivered:

I declare under penalty of perjury under the laws of the State of California that the foregoing is true and correct.
Date:

▶

_____   _____
(TYPE OR PRINT NAME OF CLAIMANT)   (SIGNATURE OF CLAIMANT)

DE-172 [Rev. January 1,1998]

CREDITOR'S CLAIM
(Probate)

Blank Page

Chapter 19

Help from a Judge: Filing Motions to Enforce Your Judgment

A. Seizure and Turnover Orders	19/2
1. Motion for Seizure Order	19/2
2. Motion for Turnover Order	19/3
3. Preparing a Motion for a Seizure Order or Turnover Order	19/3
B. Assignment and Restraining Orders	19/5
1. Payments Not Subject to an Assignment Order	19/5
2. Grounds for Granting an Assignment Order	19/5
3. Preparing a Motion for Assignment Order	19/6
4. Preparing a Restraining Order	19/6
C. After You Prepare the Papers	19/7
1. Serve (If Applicable) and File Papers with Court	19/7
2. Provide Informal Notice (If Applicable)	19/7
3. Review Objections or Claim of Exemption	19/7
4. Attend the Hearing	19/8
5. Serve Order	19/8
6. Change of Circumstances	19/9

Collection Factor	High	Moderate	Low
Potential cost to you		✓	
Potential for producing $$$		✓	
Potential for settlement		✓	
Potential time & trouble	✓		
Potential for bankruptcy			✓

There are situations in which the enforcement methods outlined in this book won't get you any money for your judgment. For example, the debtor may own valuable property that you can't levy on it because it's in the debtor's private residence or the debtor is concealing it. Or, the debtor may receive periodic payments from a nonexempt source, which makes a levy impractical because a levy only seizes what is due at the time the levy is made.

In these situations, you may be able to reach the elusive assets if you obtain a court order from a judge. You can file a motion requesting one of the following kinds of orders.

- **Seizure order:** Allows a levying officer to levy on personal property which is located in a private place, of the debtor.

- **Turnover order:** Requires the debtor to turn over specified property to the levying officer.

- **Assignment order:** Requires the debtor to assign the right to receive certain payments to you.

You have two choices in filing your motion, you can give the debtor several weeks advance notice or not. When you give the debtor no, or very little, advance notice, your motion is called an ex parte motion. You simply prepare the paperwork and argue your motion before the judge at an informal hearing. If you do give the debtor notice, your motion is called a noticed motion. You prepare the necessary paperwork, schedule a formal hearing for a date and give the debtor 16 court days' notice.

Ex parte motions can be either <u>with</u> notice to the debtor or <u>without</u> notice to the debtor. Ex parte motions <u>without</u> notice to the debtor are allowed if you convince the court that giving notice to the debtor would defeat the purpose for the order [California Rules of Court, Rules 3.1200-3.1207]. For instance, if you seek an order permitting a levy on property in the debtor's home, the debtor is likely to remove the property if you give advance notice. In cases where you will use a No Notice Ex Parte motion, you should consider also using a Restraining Order (section B). When the property in question can be simply moved, to avoid a levy, then the motion should be No Notice Ex Parte. If the property would require a non-interested third party to cooperate with the moving or transferring of the asset, then the No Notice can be used only for the Restraining Order motion.

On ex parte motions in which you give the debtor notice, a court will require advance notice before the hearing, without requiring a fully noticed hearing. Typically, you'll have to phone the debtor by 10:00 a.m. the day before the hearing. In extreme cases, the judge will dispense with even this type of notice. Be sure to also check the Local Rules for Ex Parte Hearings in whatever courthouse the hearing will be held.

A. Seizure and Turnover Orders

A motion for a Seizure Order or Turnover Order is typically brought ex parte, unless the judge or a local court rule requires a noticed motion. If the local rules don't address this issue, ask the court clerk if your motion can be brought ex parte. If the answer isn't clear, proceed ex parte. If the court requires a noticed motion, you'll have to start over.

1. Motion for Seizure Order

Also known as a Break In Order, technically a "Levy on Personal Property in Private Place" order. A levying officer cannot forcibly enter a debtor's private residence, or other private place, to seize assets unless the officer has a Writ of Execution and Seizure Order from the court [CCP 699.030]. A judge will not grant a Seizure Order unless you convince them that all of the following are true:

- the debtor has property that you need to seize and sell to apply toward all or part of your judgment

- you have "probable cause" for believing that the assets are on the premises in question, and

- you have no reasonable alternative method to enforce your judgment.

2. Motion for Turnover Order

A Turnover Order requires the debtor to give the levying officer tangible personal property or certificates of title to personal property, such as a motor vehicle or stock certificates [CCP 699.040]. You must first obtain a Writ of Execution (See Chapter 7). A Turnover Order may be useful in these situations:

- you know the judgment debtor has specific items of property, but you are having trouble locating them for a levy

- property belonging to the judgment debtor can't be reached by an ordinary levy and you don't want to, or can't, obtain a Seizure Order, or

- you need specific evidence, which the debtor possesses, of debts owed to the debtor by third parties, and you'd rather proceed this way than through a subpoena and debtor's examination (see Chapter 6).

Difference Between Seizure Order and Turnover Order

A Seizure Order authorizes the levying officer to enter a private place to levy on assets. A Turnover Order requires the debtor to deliver specifically named property to the levying officer.

You use a Seizure Order if you want to levy on an item that can't easily be concealed, a piano, for instance.

You use a Turnover Order for items that are easy to hide, such as jewelry or documents.

3. Preparing a Motion for a Seizure Order or Turnover Order

If your judgment is from small claims court, check with the small claims court advisor or clerk for the specific forms you need and procedures to follow to file your motion. Most likely, filing a motion in small claims court means simplified paperwork. On the other hand, if your judgment is from regular civil court, you'll have to prepare several documents.

a. Consult Court Rules

California's Rules of Court establish the general procedures for filing and serving motions in every court [California Rules of Court, Rules 3.1110-3.1116]. In addition, your court may have adopted local rules of procedure. You must read, and follow, both. To find out if your court has adopted local rules, contact the court clerk where you obtained your judgment. Ask if the court has adopted local rules for filing motions. If yes, ask the court clerk for a copy of the local rules. If the court doesn't have the local rules, visit your county law library or look on the homepage of the county court's website.

The specific rules you need to know, whether contained in Rules of Court or your local rules, cover the following topics:

- the days and times your motion may be heard by the court

- the location of the hearing

- how to schedule a noticed hearing or request an ex parte hearing, and

- whether you must file the documents electronically

b. Prepare Documents

If you think you can't deal with one more piece of paperwork, filing a motion is going to tax your patience. Even the simplest motion papers, called pleadings, must be typed on 8.5" x 11" numbered paper, called pleading paper. All documents prepared for the court should be one-sided only. The Judge will not be turning the pages over in order to read them.

To prepare your papers, find the blank sheet of pleading paper in the Appendix. Make several copies. If you have Microsoft Word, or similar, go to "file", then "new", then search "pleading" for the prepared format.

On one sheet, type your name, address and phone number, followed by the words "Appearing in Pro Per," single-spaced in the upper left corner. Then go down to line 8. In the center of the page, type the name of the court in capital letters. Type the caption; your name vs. the debtor's name, the case number (your judgment case number), the documents included, and the date, time and location of the hearing. We have a sample included here for you.

The documents included are the same no matter which motion you file; the content however, is different.

- **Notice of Motion (if applicable) and Motion:** This gives the court and debtor (if applicable) written notice of your request and the date, time and location of the hearing. The notice is required for noticed motions only.

- **Declaration:** Your declaration is a statement of the facts that gives the court a basis to grant your motion. In most situations, only your statement will be necessary. If you are relying on somebody else's observations, you must submit that person's statement as well, for example, if you are seeking a Seizure Order and the debtor's ex-roommate has information about property in the debtor's home, ask the ex-roommate to state what they know in a signed declaration.

- **Memorandum of Points and Authorities:** This is a short statement of citations to the legal authority entitling you to your requested order.

- **Proposed Court Order:** This gives the judge a place to sign if he grants your motion.

We have included sample documents. You must prepare three separate documents. The first contains a Notice of Motion and a Memorandum of Points and Authorities. The second document is the Declaration, and the third is the Proposed Order. If you submit additional declarations (from witnesses other than yourself), those should be separate documents as well.

Be sure to modify these samples to fit your situation. Do not copy instructions word-for-word into your document. As you type, be sure to number the pages of each document at the bottom. You also have to include a "footer" at the bottom of each page, which identifies the document (for example, "Notice of Motion and Motion for Seizure Order" or "Declaration of Amy Right in Support of Motion for Seizure Order"). The sample notices contain language asking the court to dispense with the advance notice requirement. If the judge rejects this no-notice option, you'll have to reschedule your hearing with the judge and provide notice to the debtor. If you'd rather not risk the delay, leave the language out and provide the debtor with notice of the hearing.

When you're done preparing your documents, make at least three copies. Staple each set in the upper left-hand corner. You will also have to two-hole punch the top of the set you file with the court.

B. Assignment and Restraining Orders

If the debtor receives regular payments that you can't readily garnish or levy, it may be possible to have all or a portion of them paid directly to you. You do this through an Assignment Order, an order from the court requiring the judgment debtor to assign to you their right to receive some or all of the payments [CCP 708.510]. The assignment puts you in the shoes of the debtor for the purposes of receiving the payments until your judgment is satisfied. Then the right to receive the payments reverts to the debtor.

Typical sources of income subject to assignment include:

- rents from tenants
- sales commissions
- royalties from a patent, copyright or other type of license
- payments due on account (called accounts receivable), and
- installment payments on promissory notes.

EXAMPLE: Jeff is an author who receives royalties of approximately $3,000 from one of his publishers each quarter. Amy obtains a judgment against Jeff for $15,000. Amy requests a court order requiring Jeff to assign her the right to receive these royalties until the judgment is satisfied. If the royalties were Jeff's sole or primary source of income, the judge would probably order considerably less than 100% assigned.

1. Payments Not Subject to an Assignment Order

Several types of income are legally nonassignable or exempt from enforcement, meaning that you cannot use an Assignment Order to have the payments directed to you [CCP 703.140(b) (10)]. These income sources include:

- Social Security
- Supplemental Security Income (SSI)
- Medicare and Medicaid payments (if the debtor is a medical provider)
- public assistance benefits (welfare)
- worker's compensation
- unemployment insurance
- IRAs or Keogh plans
- most payments from pension or retirement plans, and
- payments from an irrevocable trust.

2. Grounds for Granting an Assignment Order

The court will consider several issues when deciding whether or not to grant an Assignment Order:

- **The reasonable needs of the debtor and his family.** The court will not order an assignment that will strip the debtor of income necessary to meet a basic standard of living.

- **How long the payments are likely to continue.** If the payments to the debtor won't last much more than a few months, the court is not likely to order the payments assigned to you.

- **The balance remaining compared to the payments sought to be assigned.** If little is left on the judgment, only one or two assigned payments will cover the balance, the court may not order the assignment, especially if a levy could do the job. But if your entire judgment is outstanding and many payments will be needed to pay it off, the court is more likely to order the assignment.

- Whether the debtor already has any other payments or wage assignments going towards other judgments.

3. Preparing a Motion for Assignment Order

Follow the material in Section A3, above, on finding out the applicable rules. In addition, follow the general information in the same section on preparing court papers.

We have provided you with a sample motion and order. Please make changes based on your particular facts. Normally, the debtor must sign the Assignment Order before it can take effect. You may be able to get around this by changing the language of the Order slightly. You want to avoid having to have the debtor sign the Order because the debtor may not do so, and your only recourse then is to hire a lawyer to bring a motion for contempt against the debtor.

The statute doesn't authorize this change, but many judges accept it anyway. If you want to chance it, do the following:

- Eliminate the following, as shown in the sample Order:

"I hereby make the assignments required by this Court Order.

_____

Judgment Debtor"

- Replace it with the following:

"The judgment debtor Jeff Isbad's right to receive the following payments shall be and hereby is assigned to the judgment creditor Amy Right until the judgment is satisfied or this order is amended.

_____

Signed by Judge"

4. Preparing a Restraining Order

We recommend always getting a Restraining Order issued by the court **before** serving the Motion for Assignment Order on the debtor.

A Restraining Order is a temporary order that requires the debtor not to alienate themselves from the income stream, you are asking the court to assign to you, until the court has a chance to rule on the Motion for Assignment. When using a Motion for Restraining Order, the Restraining motion is heard ex parte, the Assignment motion is heard on a regularly scheduled hearing (unless there is an urgent need otherwise).

Example 1: Jeff receives royalty checks, for a book he authored, from XYZ Publishing. Amy filed a motion to assign these payments to pay the judgment she has against Jeff. Once Jeff got served with a copy of the Motion for Assignment Order, Jeff signed over all of his rights, to payments from XYZ Publishing, to his brother Bob. Once they got to court, the judge could not assign the payments to Amy because they no longer belong to Jeff.

Example 2: Jeff receives royalty checks, for a book he authored, from XYZ Publishing. Amy planned to file a motion to assign these payments to her, in order to satisfy the judgment she has against Jeff. Amy worried that Jeff may try to pull a fast one, so Amy went into court with a no-notice ex parte Motion for a Restraining Order, asking the judge to restrict Jeff's ability to transfer his rights to those payments until the Motion for Assignment could be heard. The judge gave Amy the Restraining Order, which Amy had personally served on XYZ Publishing and on Jeff, at the same time she had the Motion for Assignment Order served on him. Now, if Jeff tries to transfer his rights to someone else XYZ Publishing has been notified that there is a court order that states that he is not allowed to do it. Most third parties do not want to chance getting in trouble with a judge, and will probably not allow Jeff to do anything with this payment stream until the court reaches a final decision.

We provide you with a sample Motion for a Restraining Order. The Restraining Order should be done on a no-notice ex parte manner. This means that you find out from the court:

- in what division ex parte's are heard

- what days and time they are heard

- schedule the Motion for Assignment

Then you would:

- you file both motions and pay the fees, within an hour before the Motion will be heard, you take your original motion for a Restraining Order and a copy of the motion for Assignment Order to the ex parte judge.

- you give no notice to the debtor about the motions.

If the judge agrees to give you the Restraining Order then you would:

- personally serve the third party with a copy of the Restraining Order and Motion for Assignment Order

- file and serve the debtor with the Restraining Order and the Motion for Assignment, by personal service, at the same time and as quickly as possible. You don't want to chance that the third party may notify your debtor that they were served. It will only make serving your debtor that much harder. Use of Professional Process Servers is recommended.

If the judge does not agree to give you the Restraining Order then you move on to serving the Motion for Assignment.

C. After You Prepare the Papers

Once you have completed your papers, you must file them with the court.

1. Serve (If Applicable) and File Papers With Court

After scheduling a noticed motion, you must have one set of your papers served on the debtor before you file them with the court. Most judgment creditors have the debtor served by mail at his last known address. Service by mail must take place at least 16 court days before the hearing date (plus 5 additional calendar days if by mail) [CCP 1005(b)].

After the papers are served, have the person who did the serving complete and sign a Proof of Service (Instructions for serving documents and preparing Proofs of Service are in Chapter 21). Attach the signed Proof of Service to your motion papers.

At least a week before the hearing date, visit the court or send in your documents. Take the original and the remaining copies of the papers and your checkbook. If you mail the papers, find out the fee in advance, enclose a self-addressed, stamped envelope and ask that a file-stamped copy of your documents be returned to you. The current fee to file a motion is $60 [Government Code 70617(a)].

2. Provide Informal Notice (If Applicable)

The judgment debtor is entitled to short advance notice of an ex parte hearing unless you convince the judge that even 24-hours' notice would defeat the purpose of your motion. You would try to convince the judge when you go to court to request the order. If the judge disagrees then you will have to do everything all over again, but this time with notice given. To give notice, call the debtor, inform them of your motion, its date, time and location, and find out if the debtor plans on attending or opposing your motion (You don't need to do this if you've filed a noticed motion).

3. Review Objections or Claim of Exemption

If the debtor objects to your motion, they must file and serve a Claim of Exemption at least three days before the hearing [CCP 708.550(a)]. The debtor may claim that the property you seek to seize or the payments you want assigned are exempt, or that a portion of the payments are needed to support the debtor and their family. Review the documents carefully. To win your motion, you will have to counter the debtor's arguments at the hearing.

If the motion is being heard without notice, then the debtor will not be present and therefore any objection will come after the hearing. If the debtor received 24 hour notice then the objection will be heard at the hearing, for the first time. You will have to think on your feet, so be ready.

4. Attend the Hearing

The day before the hearing, review your motion papers. On the day of the hearing, go a little early. Go right to the designated room or courtroom. Before you go in, check outside for a bulletin board listing the cases to be heard. If your case isn't listed, check with the courtroom clerk.

Bring copies of all your documents, including the unsigned Order and any unfiled Proofs of Service. Let the clerk or bailiff know you are present.

When your case is called, step forward. Always address the judge as "Your Honor." Some judges prefer to ask questions, but others will ask you to begin. Explain your request in your own words.

EXAMPLE: Good morning, Your Honor. I am the judgment creditor in this case and I am seeking an order assigning to me certain payments due the judgment debtor from third parties. Specifically, the judgment debtor receives monthly payments from Katherine Piper on a promissory note, monthly rent from Paul Simonson and quarterly royalty payments from Lilac Press. The judgment debtor owes $17,000 on the judgment, plus costs and interest. If the assignments are ordered as I request, the judgment will be satisfied in approximately 15 months. Otherwise, I will have to repeatedly levy on these payments.

If the debtor has filed a Claim of Exemption, or otherwise responded to your motion, he has an opportunity to speak after you. You then have a chance to reply. Your reply to a Claim of Exemption must be either that the payments or property are not exempt, or that the payments are not needed to support the judgment debtor or their family (Chapter 15 covers how to oppose a Claim of Exemption).

Once the court hears your motion, the judge must make a ruling. The judge may grant your request in full or part, deny it, or take the matter under submission, which means they will mail out their decision in a few days. If you lose, nothing happens and you may proceed with other enforcement efforts. While it is possible to appeal the judge's decision, it's almost never worth the time and expense. Regardless of the outcome, you can claim costs incurred, such as filing fees and service of process fees (See Chapter 16).

If the judge grants your motion, they will sign your proposed Order, possibly with changes. Once the Order is signed, the Judicial Assistant will usually stamp it filed and give you a copy or they may give you the Order to file. You must give all parties notice of entry of the order as well.

5. Serve Order

Once you receive the filed, and signed, order from the court, you must have a copy personally served on the judgment debtor for it to be valid, unless the judge orders otherwise. In addition, you must have any affected third parties served with a notice of the order. For example, you should have one copy of your Assignment Order mailed to each source of payments being assigned (See Chapter 21 for instructions on personal service and service by mail).

After you prepare your notices, have the orders served on the affected parties and have the original Proofs of Service filed with the court (See Chapter 21). Any third party must comply with the order. If the third party does not, send a letter reminding them of their obligation under the order. If they still don't comply, and there is enough at stake to justify pursuing the matter, consult an attorney for assistance pursuing contempt against the third party.

6. Change of Circumstances
If circumstances change after an Assignment Order is made, either party can bring a noticed motion to amend or set aside the order [CCP 708.560]. For example, the debtor might argue that they now need the assigned payments to support a new child or you might argue that the debtor can afford to assign a greater portion of the payments because they received a raise in pay. This rule doesn't apply to Seizure Orders or Turnover Orders because they are not ongoing.

Seizure Order

Amy Right

1000 My st

Mytown, Ca 90000

In Pro Per

SUPERIOR COURT OF THE STATE OF CALIFORNIA

COUNTY OF LOS ANGELES - CENTRAL DISTRICT

AMY RIGHT, Plaintiff, vs. JEFF ISBAD, Defendant.	Case No. 14K5000 CREDITOR'S EX PARTE NO NOTICE APPLICATION FOR A LEVY ORDER ON PROPERTY IN A PRIVATE PLACE; MEMORANDUM OF POINTS AND AUTHORITIES; DECLARATIONS OF AMY RIGHT, PRO SERVE1, AND PRO SERVE2 IN SUPPORT FILED CONCURRENTLY HEREWITH; [PROPOSED] ORDER SUBMITTED CONCURRENTLY **No Notice Required:** [CCP 699.030; CRC 3.1204(b)(3)] Date: April 28, 2015 Time: 9:00 a.m. Dept.: 5D

Amy Right (Creditor) applies ex parte without notice to the debtor or his attorney, for a Levy Order on Property in a Private Place against the personal property of judgment debtor, JEFF ISBAD ("Debtor"). Said property consists of a safe located in a front room of Debtors' residence, 666 e. Cra P st, Helltown, Ca 90666 ("Residence"). This safe is visible from the front porch of the Residence.

This application is supported by photographs showing a safe clearly visible from the front porch of the Debtors' Residence, the declaration of the registered process server who captured the images while standing on the front porch of the Debtor's Residence, a second registered process server who observed the safe from the front porch of the Residence, and the declaration of Creditor who reviewed all the photographs. This application is made ex-parte and without notice pursuant to California Rules of Court 3.1202(c), 3.1203(a), and 3.1204(b)(3), and for the reasons shown in this application.

This application is based upon the following:

1. CCP§ 699.030(b) plainly states a motion for levy on personal property located in a private place is sought, that motion may be sought ex parte, and as such this ex parte application is proper.

2. Under CRC 3.1204(b)(3) there is valid justification that Creditor should not be required to inform the Debtor of the instant motion. Personal property, by its very nature, is moveable and concealable on very short notice. Creditor believeS that Debtor will likely empty the safe of all valuables if he or HIS attorney were put on notice of this instant motion. Debtor have shown zero cooperation to voluntarily pay this judgement. Despite an Earnings Withholding Order, an Assignment Order, and a Levy, Judgment Creditor has yet to receive any property, money or any other consideration of any value.

3. CCP§ 3.1202(c) requires an ex parte application make an affirmative and factual showing of irreparable harm or immediate danger. Here the irreparable harm is that personal property by its very nature is easily moveable and concealable. If the Debtor or their attorney were to be put on notice, there is the real threat that the personal property sought to be levied upon on with this order would be moved, concealed or otherwise placed out of the reach of creditors.

4. One year has passed since this $3,000.00 judgment was entered against the Debtor. He has

failed and refused to pay a single cent toward the debt. With interest accruing at the legal rate of 10% per annum, as of April 24, 2015, the judgment now stands at approximately $3,927.50 dollars.[1]

2. Creditor believes Debtor has and will continue to make all attempts possible to conceal and/or transfer their personal property in order to avoid execution and to avoid paying this court-ordered obligation.

3. Creditor believes Debtor maintains cash, jewelry and other items of value within this safe located at 666 e. Cra P st, Helltown, Ca 90666, and these items of value can begin to satisfy their approximately $3,927.50 dollar judgment.

Since it is unlikely that this execution will satisfy Debtors' entire obligation, other relief has been or is being sought, concurrently herewith.

4. This Order is necessary so that Creditor can, in some part, satisfy its judgment for the Debtors' long overdue obligation. Should this order not be granted, Creditor's likelihood of satisfying its judgment will be greatly diminished.

6. Based on the still photographs and the eyewitness testimony of two registered process servers, one of whom obtained these images, probable cause exists to believe that the property sought is still in the possession of the debtor and is housed within Debtors' Residence.[2]

7. In light of Debtors' refusal to pay the judgment entered against him, and the difficulty of finding and levying upon other assets to satisfy this obligation, Creditor requests that the attached order be granted, empowering the levying officer to:

> a. At the time delivery of the property by the levying officer is demanded, pursuant to the order, that he or she announce his or her identity, purpose and authority, and if the property is not delivered voluntarily, cause the building or enclosure where the property is believed to be located to be broken open in such manner as the levying officer reasonably believes will cause the least damage, in order to effectuate this levy of the items described herein.

---

[1] See Exhibit B attached to the Declaration of Amy Right filed concurrently with the instant ex parte application, a true and correct copy of the current Writ of Execution
[2] See Declaration of RPS Pro Serve1 filed herewith; See Declaration of RPS Pro Serve2 filed herewith

9. There is no concern of prejudice to Debtor based on this court's granting of the requested relief, as Debtor will have ample opportunity to defend against Creditor's actions.

In addition, because the Sheriff of Los Angeles County requires Creditor to arrange for a "spotter", described on the LACS website as *"an agent of the creditor who can identify the property"*, any possibility of misidentifying the property in question would be alleviated. Conversely, should this court deny the requested relief, Debtors will most certainly attempt to further conceal or transfer their remaining mobile personal property, thereby diminishing Creditor's likelihood of satisfying the substantial debt owed by Debtor.

Without the relief requested, this judgment is likely to remain unsatisfied.

Executed at Pasadena, California on April 24, 2015.

Respectfully submitted,

_____

Amy Right, Plaintiff/Creditor

CREDITOR'S EXPARTE APPLICATION FOR A LEVY ORDER ON PROPERTY IN PRIVATE PLACE

MEMORANDUM OF POINTS & AUTHORITIES

I. ALL OF THE DEBTORS' PROPERTY IS SUBJECT TO ENFORCEMENT

This motion will ask the court to order the Sheriff to enter the Debtors' home and take the Debtors' personal property. Under CCP § 695.070, **ALL PROPERTY** of the Debtors is subject to enforcement of a money judgment.[3] While Debtors may file exemptions as allowed, that does not prevent enforcement remedies requested in this instant motion. The Creditor in this case seeks compromise and cooperation from the Debtor and Debtors' counsel. Having received no cooperation whatsoever from Debtor or their counsel, Creditor seeks the assistance of this court to use lawful remedies that do not require the cooperation of the Debtors to enforce the judgment of this court.

II. BACKGROUND

A. The Judgment

On January 1, 2014, this court entered judgment in the amount of $3,000.00 against Judgment Debtor, JEFF ISBAD ("Debtor").

B. Attempts at Informal Resolution:

RIGHT has made substantial and repeated efforts to informally resolve this matter with the judgment debtor prior to bringing the underlying action; however, Debtor ISBAD has failed and refused to pay the amount due under the judgment.

C. Balance Due Under the Judgment

The balance due after being amended, including statutory interest, is approximately $3,927.50 dollars.

D. Unwillingness of Debtors to Pay the Judgment

Debtor have not voluntarily paid the Judgment they owe, and the remedies at law used by the Creditors to date have not yielded any assets of value. Creditor believes Debtor have and will continue to make all attempts possible to conceal and/or transfer their property in order to avoid execution and to avoid paying this court-ordered obligation. Therefore, by way of this ex-parte application, Creditor seeks this

---

[3] CCP§ 695.070

court's assistance in executing on property in Debtors' possession which, without a Private Place Order, will likely be concealed and/or transferred, making execution nearly impossible.

As described with particularity herein, Creditor seeks to levy on a safe and all its contents, that belongs to the Debtor, which sits in a front room in the home of Debtor, 666 e Cra P. st, Helltown, Ca 90666.

III. PRIVATE PLACE ORDER

Creditor is entitled to an order in aid of execution allowing the levying officer to demand entry and execute on the Debtors' personal property to satisfy the judgment. Section 699.030(b) of the California Code of Civil Procedure provides as follows: "If personal property sought to be levied upon is located in a private place of the Judgment Debtor:

The judgment creditor may apply to the court ex parte, or on noticed motion if the

court so directs or a court rule so requires, for an order directing the levying

officer to seize the property in the private place. The application may be made

whether or not a writ has been issued and whether or not demand has been made

pursuant to subdivision (a). The application for the order shall describe with

particularity both the property sought to be levied upon, and the place where it is to be found, according to the best knowledge, information, and belief of the judgment creditor. Therefore, this court has the authority to issue a Levy Order on Personal Property located in a Private Place pursuant to CCP 699.030.

IV. PROPRIETY OF EX-PARTE AND NO NOTICE

As specifically provided in CCP §699.030, the Creditor may apply for a Private Place Order on an ex parte basis. And, pursuant to California Rules of Court, Rules 3.1202(c), 3.1203(a) and 3.1204(b) (3), issuance of ex parte orders without notice may be proper when appropriate justification exists and said basis is presented to the court. If any situation is appropriate for relief without notice, it is the relief requested herein. As the California legislators correctly anticipated, when levying on moveable items of personal property, ex parte relief is the only way to ensure that the property sought to be levied upon will actually be available, instead of being subject to the efforts of a motivated debtor to hide, conceal, transfer, encumber, or otherwise frustrate execution.

Here, Debtor have not paid a single dime toward the satisfaction of this judgment, despite driving luxury vehicles, living in the exclusive and affluent gated community of Helltown and running a successful business for years.[4]

V. **BASED ON CREDITOR'S BEST KNOWLEDGE, INFORMATION AND BELIEF, CREDITOR CAN DESCRIBE WITH PARTICULARITY THE LOCATION OF THE PERSONAL PROPERTY TO BE LEVIED UPON**

A. **Creditor has Personally Viewed Images of a Safe within a Room of Debtors' Residence**

Creditor has attempted to personally serve Debtor at their residence, 666 e Cra P st, Helltown, Ca 90666. During several attempts, while standing on the front porch of the Debtors' residence, two registered process servers ("RPS") have noticed a safe clearly visible through a glass door without curtains or window coverings.[5] One RPS recorded images of a safe, as instructed by the Creditor. In the Creditor's possession are images depicting a safe in a front room of the Debtors' residence, clearly visible and in plain view through a glass door without curtains or other coverings.[6]

Creditor's counsel has reviewed the images and has printed a color photograph, which is attached to the Declaration of RPS Pro Serve1 filed concurrently with this application.[7]

Therefore, Creditor can state with great certainty the location of the safe within the Residence of Debtors and the nature of the property to be levied (the safe and all its contents.)

Therefore, Creditor can describe with particularity the exact items to be levied.

---

[4] See Exhibit C to Declaration of Amy Right, filed concurrently with the instant ex parte application, a true and correct certified copy of Debtors' BK Petition at pg 17-25 of 33 in "Statement of Financial Affairs". BK petition shows address of debtors and business generating over 1 million dollars a year.
[5] See Exhibit A to the Declaration of RPS Pro Serve1, filed concurrently with the instant ex parte application, a true and correct copy of the photograph of the subject safe

[7] See Exhibit A to the Declaration of Pro Serve1 filed concurrently herewith

B. Creditor has Established that there is Probable Cause to Believe that Property Sought to be Levied upon is Located at Debtors' Residence

Probable cause is defined as "a reasonable ground to suspect" or a "reasonable belief."[8] Creditor has established probable cause by virtue of two eyewitnesses that the property is located at Debtors' Residence.

VI. THE GRANTING OF THIS ORDER WILL NOT DEPRIVE THE JUDGMENT DEBTOR OF DUE PROCESS.

If the court grants the requested Levy Order on Property in a Private Place, the judgment debtors will not be deprived of their right to claim exemptions or to other procedural due process. Once the property is within the levying officer's custody, the levying officer is required to serve the judgment debtor with a copy of the writ, a notice of levy, and if the judgment debtor is a natural person [as here], a copy of the form listing exemptions.[9] Once a notice of levy is served, the exemption and third party claim statutes become operable. Specifically, pursuant to CCP §703.520(a): "The claimant may make a claim of exemption by filing with the levying officer a claim of exemption."[10]

Therefore, Debtors' rights to claim of exemption or other procedural due process will be protected in the event the court orders the turnover of the specified property.

VII. CONCLUSION

Creditor has shown with particularity the property to be levied and the location of the property, and has further shown probable cause that these items are located at Debtors' residence. This property is:

1) A safe, clearly visible from the front porch, identified by two separate RPS eye witnesses.

For these reasons, an Order is necessary, authorizing the Levying Officer to seize the safe described from the Residence of Debtors before it can be transferred out of the reach of lawful enforcement efforts.

Respectfully Submitted,

_____

Amy Right, Plaintiff/Creditor

---

[8] Black's Law Abridged 8th Edition
[9] CCP §700.010
[10] *Imperial Bank*, 33 Cal.App 4th at 554

Amy Right

1000 My st

Mytown, Ca 90000

(310)555-5555

In Pro Per

SUPERIOR COURT OF THE STATE OF CALIFORNIA

COUNTY OF LOS ANGELES

AMY RIGHT,	Case No. 14K5000
Plaintiff,	DECLARATION OF AMY RIGHT IN SUPPORT OF NO NOTICE EX PARTE APPLICATION
vs.	§699.030
JEFF ISBAD,	[NO HEARING REQUIRED]
Defendant.	
	Date: April 28, 2015
	Time: 9:00 a.m.
	Dept.: 5D

I, AMY RIGHT, declare as follows:

1. I am the Plaintiff/Creditor in the above-entitled case, and I am over the age of 18 years old. This declaration is specifically filed in support of CREDITOR'S EX PARTE NO NOTICE APPLICATION FOR A LEVY ORDER ON PROPERTY IN A PRIVATE PLACE.

2. If called upon to testify, I could and would competently testify to the matters contained herein based upon my personal knowledge, except as to those matters stated upon information and belief, and as to those matters I am informed and believe and thereon allege that they are true and correct.

3. In the above-entitled action, Judgment was entered on January 1, 2014.

4. Defendant/Judgment Debtor have completely failed and refused to pay a single cent toward the aforementioned judgment. With interest accruing at the legal rate of 10% per annum, as of April 24, 2015, the judgment stands at approximately $3,927.50 dollars owed to Judgment Creditor, AMY RIGHT.

5. Creditor believes Debtor has and will continue to make all attempts possible to conceal and/or transfer their personal property in order to avoid execution and to avoid paying this court-ordered obligation.

6. Creditor believes Debtor maintains cash, jewelry and other items of value within this safe located at 666 e. Cra P st, Helltown, Ca 90666, and these items of value can begin to satisfy their approximately $3,927.50 dollar judgment. Since it is unlikely that this execution will satisfy Debtors' entire obligation, other relief has been or is being sought, concurrently herewith.

7. Creditor believes Debtor truthfully disclosed the existence and particular nature of personal property in their recent application for bankruptcy which was voluntarily dismissed on September 22, 2014, and this personal property is located at their residence, 666 e Cap P st, Helltown, Ca 90666.

8. This Order is necessary so that Creditor can, in some part, satisfy its judgment for the Debtors' long overdue obligation. Should this order not be granted, Creditor's likelihood of satisfying its judgment will be greatly diminished.

DECLARATION OF AMY RIGHT IN SUPPORT OF EXPARTE APPLICATION FOR A NO NOTICE LEVY ORDER

9. Based on the still photographs and the eyewitness testimony of the registered process server who obtained these images, probable cause exists to believe that the property sought is still in the possession of the debtor and is housed within Debtors' Residence.

10. Personal property or evidence of Title sought to be levied upon is described as follows:

    a. The safe.

11. On July 16, 2014, Debtors filed for bankruptcy. Attached hereto as Exhibit "A" is a true and correct certified copy of Judgment Debtors' Voluntary Petition.

12. In February 2015, I prepared a Writ of Execution in this matter. The court issued the Writ on February 17, 2015. Attached hereto as Exhibit "C" is a true and correct copy of the current, operative Writ for this action.

I declare under penalty of perjury under the laws of the State of California that the foregoing is true and correct. Executed in Mytown, California on April 24, 2015.

By: _____

Amy Right, Plaintiff/Creditor

DECLARATION OF AMY RIGHT IN SUPPORT OF EXPARTE APPLICATION FOR A NO NOTICE LEVY ORDER

Amy Right

1000 My st

Mytown, Ca 90000

(310)555-5555

In Pro Per

SUPERIOR COURT OF THE STATE OF CALIFORNIA

COUNTY OF LOS ANGELES

AMY RIGHT, Plaintiff, vs. JEFF ISBAD, Defendant.	Case No. 14K5000 [PROPOSED] ORDER FOR LEVY ON PERSONAL PROPERTY IN A PRIVATE PLACE §699.030 [NO HEARING REQUIRED] Date: April 28, 2015 Time: 9:00 a.m. Dept.: 5D Judge: Honorable Matt Bander

IT IS ORDERED AS FOLLOWS:

The Ex Parte No Notice Motion of Judgment Creditor AMY RIGHT ("Creditor") for a Levy Order on Property in a Private Place of the Judgment Debtor JEFF ISBAD ("Debtor"), came for hearing before this Court on the above date, the Honorable _____, Presiding. The Court, having considered the pleadings filed in connection with this motion, records on file in this matter, oral argument at the hearing, and good cause found:

1. The Creditor has described with particularity the property to be levied upon: a safe located in a front room, visible from the front porch.

2. The Creditor has described with particularity the location of the property to be levied; in a front room of the debtors' residence, visible from the front porch.

3. The Creditor has established there is probable cause to believe that the property sought to be levied upon is located in the place described.

THEREFORE, IT IS HEREBY ORDERED:

1. Any levying officer acting under an Order from this court issued in the above-referenced case, in satisfaction of the responsibilities for levying on that Order, is ordered to go to the residence at 666 e. Cra P st, Helltown, Ca 90666 for the purpose of levying and taking possession of:

    a. The Safe, located in a front room and visible from the front porch, and all its contents.

2. The levying officer is directed to seize said property from the private place listed above.

3. The levying offer shall announce his or her identity, purpose, and authority. If the property is not voluntarily delivered, the levying officer is authorized and directed to cause the building or enclosure to be broken open in such manner as the levying officer reasonably believes will cause the least damage and enter the premises and seize the above property.

ORDER PURSUANT TO CCP 699.030

4. Nothing contained herein shall require the levying officer to act in a manner which the levying officer reasonably believes will involve a substantial risk of death or serious bodily harm to any person.

5. Once the property is within the custody of the levying officer, the levying officer is required to provide notice to the Debtor of the levy and notify the Debtors of CCP 703.520 (making of Claim of Exemption) per the levying officer's internal policy.

Dated:

_____
Judicial Officer, Department 5D

Turnover Order

Amy Right

1000 My st

Mytown, Ca 90000

(310)555-5555

In Pro Per

SUPERIOR COURT OF CALIFORNIA

COUNTY OF LOS ANGELES-CENTRAL JUSTICE CENTER

AMY RIGHT		Case No. 14K5000
	Plaintiff,	NOTICE OF MOTION AND MOTION FOR TURNOVER ORDER PURSUANT TO CCP §699.040; MEMORANDUM OF POINTS AND AUTHORITIES; DECLARATION OF AMY RIGHT FILED CONCURRENTLY HEREWITH
vs.		[CCP §699.040(a)]
JEFF ISBAD,		
	Defendant.	
		Date: April 23, 2015 Time: 1:30 p.m. Crtrm: 5D Judge: Honorable Matt Bander

// TO ALL PARTIES AND TO THEIR ATTORNEYS OF RECORD:

PLEASE TAKE NOTICE THAT on April 23, 2015, at 1:30 p.m. in Department D5 of the above-entitled court located at 111 Hill st, Los Angeles, California 90012, Judgment Creditor/Assignee of Record will and hereby does move the court pursuant to CCP §699.040(a), for a turnover order.

NOTICE OF MOTION AND MOTION FOR TURNOVER ORDER

This motion is made pursuant to California Code of Civil Procedure §699.040 and is based upon this Notice of Motion, the attached Memorandum of Points and Authorities, the Declaration of Amy Right, along with the attached exhibits, the court's own record and such further evidence and oral argument as may be presented at the hearing of this motion.

Executed at Mytown, California on March 24, 2015.

_____
Amy Right, Plaintiff/Creditor

MEMORANDUM OF POINTS AND AUTHORITIES

I. FACTUAL BACKGROUND

A. The Judgment:

On January 1, 2014 this court entered judgment in the amount of $3,000.00 against Judgment Debtors, JEFF ISBAD.

Attempts at Informal Resolution:

RIGHT has made substantial and repeated efforts to informally resolve this matter with the judgment debtor prior to bringing the underlying action; however Debtor ISBAD has failed and refused to pay the amount due under the judgment, or enter into a payment plan agreement for payment of the same.

B. Balance Due Under the Judgment:

The balance, including statutory interest, is $3,927.50.

C. Debtor Falsely Claims No Value For his Two Corporations

Debtor lists the current value of his three companies, Southern Termite, EJ Investments Inc., as $0.00.[11] In fact, Southern Termite itself has generated 120,000 in gross profits during the time period of 2012 through 2014.[12]

D. Requested Relief:

Based upon the foregoing, the judgment creditor requests this court issue a Turnover Order pursuant to Code of Civil Procedure §699.040, requiring the judgment debtor to deliver the following personal property to the levying officer: *1)* All stock share certificates for Southern Termite; *2)* All stock share certificates for EJ Investments; *3)* One (1) Camera and photographic equipment; *4)* One (1) Shotgun. Debtor Jeff Isbad has testified he own all the property listed above.[13]

II. LEGAL ARGUMENT: TURNOVER

---

[11] See *Exhibit "K"* at Schedule B, p.6 of 33

[12] See *Exhibit "K"* at SOFA p.17 of 33

[13] See *Exhibit "E"* at p.12:13-25, p.13:1-18, p 20:9-25 to 21:1-6; p.30:13-25, p.31:1-2; See *Exhibit "B"* at p 59:25 to 60:1-5; p.65:16-25, p.70:8-13

A. **The Creditor Meets All Requirements for the Court to Issue the Requested Turnover Order Pursuant to CCP §699.040**:

California Code of Civil Procedure §699.040 states:

(a) **If a writ of execution is issued**, the judgment creditor may apply to the court ex parte, or on a noticed motion if the court so directs or a court rule so requires, for an order directing the judgment debtor to transfer to the levying officer either or both of the following: 1) **Possession of the property sought to be levied upon if the property is sought to be levied upon by taking it into custody.** 2) Possession of documentary evidence of title to property of or a debt owed to the judgment debtor that is sought to be levied upon. An order pursuant to this paragraph may be served when the property or debt is levied upon or thereafter. **a) The court may issue an order pursuant to this section upon a showing of need for the order.** b) The order shall be personally served on the judgment debtor and shall contain a notice to the judgment debtor that failure to comply with the order may subject the judgment debtor to arrest and punishment for contempt. [Bold emphasis added to show key factors]

As argued and supported *infra*, the judgment creditor meets every requirement for the court to issue the requested Turnover Order:

B. **This Court has Jurisdiction to Issue a Turnover Order:**
California courts have inherent power to enforce their judgments, and statutory power to compel obedience to their judgments, orders and process.[14] Jurisdiction over the subject matter and the parties continues post-judgment throughout subsequent proceedings in the action. Thus, a court of competent jurisdiction that rendered the original judgment has continuing jurisdiction to enforce the judgment.[15]

C. **A Writ of Execution has been Issued**:
On February 17, 2015, this court issued a Writ of Execution which remains valid and unexpired.[16]

Therefore, a Writ of Execution has been issued per the requirement of CCP §699.040(a).

D. **CCP §699.040(a)(1) Expressly Authorizes Issuance of a Turnover Order for the Type of Property Sought Herein**

---

[14] See Code of Civil Procedure §§128(a)(4), 177; *Security Trust & Sav. Bank v. Southern Pac. R.R. Co.*, 6 Cal.App.2d 585, 588, 45 P.2d 268, 270 (1935); *Brown v. Brown*, 22 Cal.App.3d 82, 84; 99 Cal.Rptr. 311, 312 (1971).

[15] CCP §410.50(b) and comment thereto; See *Goldman v. Simpson*, 160 Cal.App.4th 255, 263–264, 72 Cal.Rptr.3d 729, 734–735 (2008) (Court that entered original judgment had continuing jurisdiction to enforce the judgment even though the debtor had moved out of state)

[16] See *Exhibit "M"*-True and correct copy of Writ of Execution issued 2/17/15

By this application, Judgment Creditor seeks the turnover of the following property:

1) All stock share certificates of Southern Termite;
2) All stock share certificates of EJ Investments;
3) One (1) Camera plus photographic equipment(as described by Debtor Jeff Isbad during February 5, 2015, examination)
4) One (1) Shotgun (as described by debtor during the February 5, 2015, examination)

Except as otherwise provided by law, all property of the judgment debtors is subject to enforcement of a money judgment[17], and Code of Civil Procedure §699.710 further provides:

> Except as otherwise provided by law, all property that is subject to enforcement of a money judgment pursuant to Article 1 (commencing with §695.010) of Chapter 1 is subject to levy under a writ of execution to satisfy a money judgment.

Notably, Code of Civil Procedure §699.720(a) lists the types of property *not* subject to execution; however, none of the exclusions are applicable to the property sought here.

In addition, the court put a freeze order on all property listed above until this turnover order is heard.[18]

Therefore, because all of the property sought by the turnover order requested herein is subject to execution, Code of Civil Procedure §699.040(a)(1) provides the court with authority to order the turnover of the above-listed property to the levying officer.

E. Creditor has an Absolute Need for the Requested Turnover Order:

The judgment debtors have not paid any amount towards satisfaction of this judgment, and the total judgment amount, including accrued interest, now stands at $3,927.50. Moving beyond a mere refusal to pay, the debtors claimed that their termite business *"makes enough money to stay in business"*[19]; however, his bankruptcy petition filed only three months later contradicted this claim, demonstrating the debtors had received over 120,000 dollars in gross income from the operation of the business during the previous three years.[20]

---

[17] CCP §695.010(a)

[18] **See** Court's own record at ROA 711.

[19] **See** *Exhibit "N"*-True and authentic copy of May 14, 2014, correspondence from Debtors' attorney, Tom Bad (California Evidence Code 1152 does not prevent the use of this evidence as the judgment creditor is not using the evidence to establish the judgment debtors' liability, but instead their bad faith.) **See also** *Young v. Keele (1987), 188 Cal.App.3d 1090* (limiting CEC §1152 in the post judgment setting)

[20] **See** *Exhibit "K"*-Page 17

These actions, coupled with the debtors' dubious bankruptcy filing,[21] demonstrate a level of recalcitrance rarely seen, providing Creditor with just cause to believe the judgment will remain unsatisfied without the assistance of this court.

The court should also take note that the Creditor has a long-established lien pursuant to CCP §708.110(d)[22] on all of the personal property sought by this order.

From a practical standpoint, a turnover order is more likely to succeed when compared to the standard levy procedure: To levy on the personal property sought by this order, the levying officer would need to take the property into custody.[23] The judgment debtors are in actual and/or constructive possession of the specific property, and only they would have knowledge of its current location, thus placing the levying officer at a severe disadvantage in trying to gain physical custody of the property. The least intrusive and damaging remedy Creditor can use is to request the court order Debtors to deliver the property described herein to the levying officer in accordance with CCP §699.040.

Therefore, the creditor has a demonstrated need for the requested order.

F. The Granting of this Order Ex Parte will not Deprive the Judgment Debtors of Due Process:

If the court grants the requested turnover order, the judgment debtors will not be deprived of their right to claim exemptions or to other procedural due process: Once the property is within the levying officer's custody the levying officer is required to serve the judgment debtor with a copy of the writ, a notice of levy, and if the judgment debtor is a natural person [as here], a copy of the form listing exemptions.[24] Once a notice of levy is served, the exemption and third party claim statutes become operable. Specifically, pursuant to CCP §703.520(a): "The claimant may make a claim of exemption by filing with the levying officer a claim of exemption."[25]

Therefore, the judgment debtors' rights to claim of exemption or other procedural due process will be protected in the event the court orders the turnover of the specified property.

G. Upon Issuance of the Requested Turnover Order, the Court Should also Issue an Order to Show Cause-Re: Turnover:

---

[21] See *Exhibit "D"*

[22] CCP §708.110(d): "……Service of the order [Order for Appearance] creates a lien on the personal property of the judgment debtor for a period of one year from the date of the order unless extended or sooner terminated by the court." See *Exhibit "O"*-True and correct copy of Order for Examination with Proof of Service upon Judgment Debtor Jeff Isbad

[23] CCP §700.030

[24] CCP §700.010

[25] *Imperial Bank, 33 Cal.App 4th at 554*

Upon issuance of the requested turnover order pursuant to §699.040, Creditor requests this court immediately issue an *Order to Show Cause-Re: Turnover* ("OSC"), requiring Debtors to appear before this court on a date shortly after the date for compliance with the order. Such an order might work to preempt the debtors' prospective non-compliance with the Turnover Order, thus preventing the creditor from having to bring contempt motions and/or other time-consuming motions before the court. Moreover, if the debtors attempt to avoid service [of the orders], as they have done in the past[26], the OSC would provide the court with an additional means to ensure compliance with the order.

California courts are empowered to exercise their supervisory power in such a manner to provide for the orderly conduct of the court's business and guard against inept procedures and unnecessary indulgences which would tend to hinder, hamper or delay the conduct and dispatch of its proceedings.[27] In addition, CCP §128(a)(4) provides the court with statutory authority to compel obedience to its orders. It is worth repeating that issuance of an OSC to provide a control date for the debtors' compliance with the turnover order could go far in achieving both turnover of the specified property, but also result in significant judicial economies.

Therefore, the court should issue an *OSC-Re: Turnover* concurrent with its approval of the turnover order requested herein.

H. Summary:

As demonstrated, *infra,* the judgment creditor meets all of the requirements for the court to issue a Turnover Order pursuant to CCP §699.040: The judgment creditor has been issued a valid and active Writ of Execution; has demonstrated the property requested by the turnover order is the type of property subject to levy as required by §699.040(a)(1), and that the judgment creditor has shown need for the turnover order. Finally, the court can be assured that the issuance of the requested order will not act to deprive the judgment debtors of their applicable due process rights.

Therefore, the court has just cause to issue the requested Turnover Order.

III. CONCLUSION:

As argued and supported herein, the judgment creditor has met all of the requirements, including a demonstrated need for the requested order.

Therefore, the court is authorized and justified in ordering the judgment debtors to deliver the above-specified personal property to the levying officer

---

[27] *Ellis v. Roshei Corp. (1983) 143 Cal.App.3d. 642, 648-649*

DATED: March 24, 2015   Respectfully submitted,

                                         _____
                                         Amy Right Plaintiff/Creditor

Amy Right

1000 My st

Mytown, Ca 90000

(310)555-5555

In Pro Per

SUPERIOR COURT OF CALIFORNIA

COUNTY OF LOS ANGELES-CENTRAL JUSTICE CENTER

AMY RIGHT, Plaintiff, vs. JEFF ISBAD, Defendant.	Case No. 14K5000 DECLARATION OF AMY RIGHT IN SUPPORT OF MOTION FOR TURNOVER ORDER Date: April 23, 2015 Time: 1:30 p.m. Crtrm: 5D Judge: Honorable Matt Bander

//

//

I, AMY RIGHT, declare:

1. I am the Plaintiff in the above-entitled case, and I am over the age of 18 years old.

2. The statements herein are based on my personal knowledge and are true and correct. If called upon to testify to their accuracy, I could and would do so.

3. On January 1, 2014, this court entered judgment in the amount of $3,000.00 against Judgment Debtor, Jeff Isbad ("DEBTOR").

4. To date, the balance due on the judgment, including statutory interest, is approximately $3,972.50 dollars.

5. On February, 2015, I prepared a Writ of Execution in this matter. (See *Exhibit "M"* - A true and correct copy of Writ of Execution issued on February 17, 2015.)

6. On February 18, 2014, the court issued an Application and Order for Appearance and Examination, which was served on Jeff Isbad on March 31, 2014, for an April 17, 2014 judgment debtor exam. (See *Exhibit "O"* - A true and correct copy of Jeff Isbad's Order for Examination, with Proof of Service.)

7.
I declare under penalty of perjury under the laws of the State of California that the foregoing is true and correct.

DATED: March 24, 2015   Respectfully submitted,

_____

Amy Right, Plaintiff/Creditor

DECLARATION OF AMY RIGHT IN SUPPORT OF MOTION FOR TURNOVER ORDER

Amy Right

1000 My st

Mytown, Ca 90000

(310)555-5555

In Pro Per

SUPERIOR COURT OF THE STATE OF CALIFORNIA

COUNTY OF LOS ANGELES – CENTRAL JUSTICE CENTER

AMY RIGHT,
 	
       Plaintiff,
 	
vs.
 	
JEFF ISBAD,
 	
       Defendant.
	Case No. 14K5000
	
	[PROPOSED] ORDER FOR TURNOVER IN AID OF EXECUTION
	
	Date: April 23, 2015
	Time: 1:30 p.m.
	Dept.: 5D

[PROPOSED] ORDER FOR TURN OVER

The motion of AMY RIGHT ("Creditor") for a turnover order in aid of execution against Judgment Debtor JEFF ISBAD ("Debtor") came before this court on the above date, the Honorable _____, Presiding. The Court, having considered the pleadings filed in connection with the application, records on file in this matter, oral argument at the hearing, and good cause appearing has found:

1) A Writ of Execution in Los Angeles County has been issued and is currently valid;
2) There is a need for this order, as the debtor has failed to recognize valid ORAP liens, have taken deliberate actions to evade enforcement and have not voluntarily paid the outstanding amount owed on this judgment.

THEREFORE IT IS HEREBY ORDERED that Jeff Isbad, shall within 10 or_____ days of the date of the entry of this order, deliver the Levying Officer of the Los Angeles County Sheriff Department, located at 111 Hill st, Los Angeles, California 90012, or _____ all of the property described in Exhibit "A", previously described by Debtor in their bankruptcy case 8:14-bk-00000-ES, and/or in the February 5, 2015, debtor examination of Jeff Isbad, which shall be applied toward the satisfaction of the judgment entered herein on April 20, 2005, in which the total sum of $3,000.00 was entered against Judgment Debtor, JEFF ISBAD. The total amount due under the most recent Writ of Execution is $3,927.50.

In addition, an Order to Show Cause re: Turnover, has been set for May 4, 2015, at 9:00 a.m. in Department 5D of this court, or on _____, to insure that Debtors have turned over the enumerated property.

The property listed in Attachment "A" turned over to the Los Angeles County Sheriff will be held by the Sheriff until Debtors have had the opportunity to claim any and all reasons why the said property should not be turned over to the Creditor to be applied to the satisfaction of said judgment.

NOTICE IS HEREBY GIVEN THAT FAILURE TO COMPLY WITH THIS ORDER MAY SUBJECT _____ **TO ARREST AND PUNISHMENT FOR CONTEMPT OF COURT. JUDGMENT CREDITOR SHALL PROVIDE NOTICE OF THIS ORDER TO JUDGMENT DEBTOR, JEFF ISBAD AND/OR THIRD PARTY** _____.

DATED:

By: _____
Honorable Judge of the Superior Court

[PROPOSED] ORDER FOR TURN OVER

ATTACHMENT "A"

1) All Stock Shares for Southern Termite
2) All Stock Shares for EJ Investments
3) One shotgun
4) One Camera and all corresponding Photographic Equipment

Assignment Order

Amy Right

1000 My st

Mytown, Ca 90000

(310) 555-5555

In Pro Per

SUPERIOR COURT OF CALIFORNIA, COUNTY OF LOS ANGELES

STANLEY MOSK COURTHOUSE, CENTRAL DISTRICT

AMY RIGHT

                      Plaintiff,

vs.

JEFF ISBAD,

                      Defendant.

Case Number: **14K5000**

NOTICE OF MOTION AND MOTION FOR ASSIGNMENT ORDER; MEMORANDUM OF POINTS AND AUTHORITIES; DECLARATIONS OF AMY RIGHT IN SUPPORT OF MOTION FOR ASSIGNMENT ORDER ATTACHED HEREWITH

[CCP §**708.510** et seq.]

Date:	December 3, 2015
Time:	1:30 p.m.
Crtrm:	Department 95
Judge:	Honorable John Smitherines

TO THE ABOVE-ENTITLED COURT, AND TO THE DEFENDANT/JUDGMENT DEBTOR AND HIS COUNSEL OF RECORD:

PLEASE TAKE NOTICE that on the date, time and place indicated above, Plaintiff/Judgment Creditor, AMY RIGHT ("RIGHT" or "PLAINTIFF") shall move the court to issue an Assignment Order pursuant to Cal. Code of Civil Procedure §708.510[28] et seq. against Defendant/Judgment Debtor, JEFF ISBAD ("DEFENDANT", "ISBAD" or "DEBTOR").

PLEASE TAKE FURTHER NOTICE that this motion is made pursuant to a judgment entered by this court; Defendant's failure and/or refusal to pay any monies pursuant to this judgment; Code of Civil Procedure §708.510 et seq.; and on the grounds that enforcement of the judgment against JEFF ISBAD is not stayed and the amount due on the judgment remains wholly unsatisfied.

PLEASE TAKE FURTHER NOTICE that this motion is supported by this notice, and is based on the accompanying Memorandum of Points and Authorities; Exhibits; the Declaration of Amy Right; the documents and pleadings on file in this case, and by other such evidence and oral argument that may be presented at the hearing on this motion.

Executed at Mytown, California on October 22, 2015.

By: _____

Amy Right, Judgment Creditor

---

[28] CITATIONS ARE TO THE CALIFORNIA CODE OF CIVIL PROCEDURE UNLESS OTHERWISE NOTED.

MEMORANDUM OF POINTS AND AUTHORITIES

SUMMARY OF MOTION

Plaintiff/Creditor AMY RIGHT ("RIGHT", "PLAINTIFF" or "CREDITOR") hereby submits the following Memorandum of Points and Authorities in support of her Motion for an Assignment Order. Creditor's application is based upon this Court's Judgment against DEFENDANT/Debtor JEFF ISBAD ("ISBAD", "DEFENDANT" or "DEBTOR") in the amount of Three thousand dollars ($3,000) entered in this court on January 1, 2014; ISBAD's right to receive payments, distributions, loans, commissions or other revenue/payments from XYZ Publishing, LLC ("XYZ"); and the fact that no monies have been paid towards satisfaction of this judgment.

FACTUAL BACKGROUND

The Judgment: On January 1, 2014, this court entered judgment requiring DEFENDANT/Debtor ISBAD to pay PLAINTIFF/Creditor RIGHT the principal amount of Three thousand dollars ($3,000). This judgment resulted from unpaid amounts due from ISBAD to RIGHT pursuant to some work that ISBAD did not complete.

Attempts at Informal Resolution: RIGHT has made substantial and repeated efforts to informally resolve this matter with the judgment debtor prior to bringing this motion, including attempting to reach a payment plan agreement with the debtor for the amount due; however, DEFENDANT/Debtor ISBAD has failed and refused to pay the amount due under the judgment, or enter into a payment plan agreement for payment of the same.

Payments Received By DEFENDANT/Debtor: ISBAD is known to be receiving monthly interest (only) payments of five hundred dollars ($500.00) per month pursuant to a promissory note (loan) made to XYZ Publishing, LLC.

Balance Due Under the Judgment. The principal balance due under the judgment is three thousand ($3,000), plus nine hundred seventy-two dollars, eighty-seven cents ($972.87) in accrued statutory interest for a total judgment amount of three thousand nine hundred seventy-two dollars, eighty-seven cents ($3,972.87).

Requested Relief. Based upon the foregoing, PLAINTIFF/Creditor requests the Court grant this Motion for Assignment Order assigning ISBAD's rights to monthly interest payments, received pursuant to the note received from XYZ Publishing, LLC, to PLAINTIFF/Creditor RIGHT.

LEGAL ARGUMENT

This Court has Jurisdiction over this Matter.

California courts have inherent power to enforce their judgments and statutory power to compel obedience to their judgments, orders and process.[29] Jurisdiction over the subject matter and the parties continues post-judgment throughout subsequent proceedings in the action. Thus, a court of competent jurisdiction that rendered the original judgment has continuing jurisdiction to enforce the judgment.[30]

Therefore, this court has jurisdiction to order DEFENDANT to assign his rights to the XYZ Publishing monthly interest payment to PLAINTIFF, until such time as the judgment is satisfied.

The Court May Issue an Assignment Order.

The Motion for an Assignment Order. A judgment creditor may bring a motion for an Assignment Order to assign rights to payments owed a judgment debtor (from a third party) directly to the judgment creditor. All or part of a right to payment due, or to become due, may be ordered

---

[29] See Code of Civil Procedure §§128(a)(4), 177; *Security Trust & Sav. Bank v. Southern Pac. R.R. Co.*, 6 CA2d 585, 588, 45 P2d 268, 270 (1935); *Brown v. Brown*, 22 CA3d 82, 84, 99 CR 311, 312 (1971).

[30] See §410.50(b) and Comment thereto; *See Goldman v. Simpson*, 160 CA4th 255, 263–264, 72 CR3d 729, 734–735 (2008)(Court that entered original judgment had continuing jurisdiction to enforce the judgment even though the debtor had moved out of state)

assigned, whether or not such right is conditioned upon future developments.[31] The right to payment may include, but is not limited to, deferred compensation, accounts receivables, general intangibles or instruments, and/or insurance payments.[32]

PLAINTIFF has an unsatisfied judgment against the DEFENDANT, and can demonstrate that DEFENDANT/Debtor ISBAD has an interest in monies due for principal and interest payments on a promissory note (pursuant to a loan transaction) received from XYZ Publishing, LLC.[33], and that the interest payments on the note alone are approximately five hundred dollars ($500.00).[34],[35]

In determining whether to order an assignment order or the amount of any ordered assignment, the court may take into consideration all relevant factors, including the following:[36]

1. <u>The reasonable requirements of the judgment debtor who is a natural person and of persons supported by the judgment debtor</u>:

The judgment debtor is a single man with recurring business income from other sources, and is not wholly reliant on the XYZ Publishing monthly interest payments for his own support.[37] Of course, the debtor will be free to list his reasonable living expenses, and support any claimed expenses with evidence in any opposition to this motion; however, the court should weigh in contrast that PLAINTIFF RIGHT is a single mother with sole custody of her 12 year old son, and needs the judgment amount to pay for the basic living expenses of both herself and her minor child. The court should further consider that DEFENDANT, during the past year, DEFENDANT has chosen to keep all proceeds from the XYZ Publishing promissory notes for his own use, while paying nothing towards satisfaction of the judgment.

2. <u>Payments the judgment debtor is required to make or that are deducted in satisfaction of</u>

---

[31] See Code of Civil Procedure §708.510(a)
[32] See Code of Civil Procedure§ 708.510(a)(1); Comment to C.C.P. §708.510 & <u>Ahart Cal. Prac. Guide: Enforcing Judgments and Debts,</u> §§ 6:1422, 6:1423, 6:1432 (The Rutter Group 2009)
[33] See Exhibit "B"-True and authentic copy of XYZ Publishing, LLC promissory note
[34] See Exhibit "C"-True and authentic copy of XYZ Publishing, LLC "Statement of Account"
[35] See Right Decl.¶5; ¶6
[36] CCP 708.510(c)
[37] See Right Decl. ¶8

other judgments and wage assignments, including earnings assignment orders for support:

Plaintiff is not aware of any deductions or payments being deducted in satisfaction of other judgments or wage assignments, including assignments related to support orders.

    3. The amount remaining due on the money judgment:

The amount due on the judgment is three thousand ($3,000), plus nine hundred seventy-two dollars, eighty-seven cents ($3,972.87) in accrued statutory

interest, for a total judgment amount of three thousand nine hundred seventy-two dollars, eighty-seven cents ($3,972.87).[38] The payment of this judgment amount is long overdue[39] and the judgment debtor has failed and refused to pay any amount towards satisfaction of the judgment despite clearly having the means to do so.

    4. The amount being or to be received in satisfaction or the right to payment that may be assigned:

Even with the requested assignment of the entire five hundred dollars, ($500.00) monthly (interest-only) payment, the judgment owed to PLAINTIFF would not be satisfied for eight months. The court should also consider that instead of paying the judgment amount 15 months ago when due, ISBAD instead stonewalled the debtor, pocketing 100% of the XYZ Publishing monthly payments for his own unknown uses.

In summary, all of the above factors articulated in §708.510(c)(1),(2),(3), and (4) justify this court ordering DEFENDANT to assign the entire monthly interest-only payment to PLAINTIFF until such time as the judgment amount is paid in full. In the alternative, PLAINTIFF requests that no less than three hundred dollars ($300) of each monthly payment be ordered assigned.

The Court Has Authority To Require The DEFENDANT/Debtor To Provide Regular Accountings of Payments Or Other Funds Received From XYZ Publishing, LLC:

---

[38] See Right Decl.¶4
[39] See Exhibit "A"-Certified copy of judgment

This court has authority pursuant to Code of Civil Procedure §128(a)(4) and (8)[40] to require the debtor to provide creditor with a regular accounting of all principal and interest payments received from XYZ Publishing, LLC, while the requested assignment order is in effect. Such an order will make it less likely that the debtor will take action to circumvent the assignment order, and alleviate the need for additional motions and/or frequent judgment debtor examinations to police the effectiveness of any granted order. This will have the added benefit of reducing burdens on the court's busy calendar, and on the court's already over-worked staff.

CONCLUSION

Based upon the foregoing, PLAINTIFF/Creditor RIGHT requests this Court grant the Assignment Order against DEFENDANT/Debtor JEFF ISBAD for the entire monthly payment amount received from XYZ Publishing, LLC; or that in the alternative the court order a partial assignment of this payment stream. A proposed order is filed concurrently with this motion.

DATED: October 22, 2015

Respectfully submitted,

By:_____

Amy Right, PLAINTIFF/Judgment Creditor

---

[40] Code of Civil Procedure 128(a): *"Every court shall have the power to do all of the following: (4) To compel obedience to its judgments, orders and process, and to the orders of a judge out of court, in an action or proceeding therein" (8): "To amend and control its process and orders to make them conform to law and justice...."*

Amy Right

1000 My St.

Mytown, Ca 90000

In Pro Per

SUPERIOR COURT OF CALIFORNIA, COUNTY OF LOS ANGELES

STANLEY MOSK COURTHOUSE, CENTRAL DISTRICT

AMY RIGHT
 	
                Plaintiff,
 	
vs.
 	
JEFF ISBAD,
 	
                Defendant.
	Case Number: **14K5000**
	
	DECLARATION OF AMY RIGHT IN SUPPORT OF EXPARTE NO NOTICE APPICATION FOR A RESTRAINING ORDE PENDING ASSIGNMENT
	
	ORDER
	
	Date: December 3, 2013
	Time: 1:30 PM
	Crtrm: Department 95
	Judge: Honorable John Shimmering

I, Amy Right, declare as follows:

8. I am the Plaintiff in the above-entitled case, and I am over the age of 18 years old.

9. If called upon to testify, I could and would competently testify to the matters contained herein based upon my personal knowledge, except as to those matters stated upon information and belief, and as to those matters I am informed and believe and thereon allege that they are true and correct based upon my reasonable investigation.

10. The judgment in this case resulted from uncompleted work by Defendant, JEFF ISBAD.

11. I have made substantial and repeated efforts to informally resolve this matter with Defendant JEFF ISBAD. These efforts include numerous verbal and written demands for payments, and also include demand letters written by my former attorney. In addition, I have attempted to negotiate a payment plan agreement with Defendant without success. To date, Defendant ISBAD has failed and refused to pay any amount towards satisfaction of the judgment.

12. Exhibit "B" is a true and authentic copy of Promissory Note between XYZ Publishing, LLC and Defendant JEFF ISBAD. This document was provided to me by the Defendant.

13. Exhibit "C" is a true and authentic copy of the Statement of Account for the account of Defendant JEFF ISBAD. This document was provided to me by the Defendant.

14. I am unaware of any deductions or payments being deducted in satisfaction of other judgments, or wage assignments, including assignments related to support orders.

15. To my knowledge, Defendant JEFF ISBAD is a single man with recurring business income from other sources, and is not wholly reliant on the XYZ Publishing, LLC monthly interest payments for his own support. I need to collect the judgment amount so that I will be able to pay basic living expenses for both myself and my 12 year old son.

16. I have personal first-hand knowledge that Defendant JEFF ISBAD has transferred his personal assets to a family member in the past in order to hinder and frustrate the collection efforts of his creditors.

Executed at Mytown, California on June 9, 2016.

By: _____

Amy Right, Judgment Creditor

DECLARATION OF AMY RIGHT IN SUPPORT OF MOTION FOR ASSIGNMENT ORDER

Amy Right

1000 My St.

Mytown, Ca 90000

(310) 555-5555

In Pro Per

SUPERIOR COURT OF CALIFORNIA, COUNTY OF LOS ANGELES

STANLEY MOSK COURTHOUSE, CENTRAL DISTRICT

AMY RIGHT,	Case Number: **14K5000**
Plaintiff,	
vs.	
	[PROPOSED] ASSIGNMENT ORDER
JEFF ISBAD,	
Defendant.	Date: December 3, 2013
	Time: 1:30 P.M.
	Crtrm: Department 95
	Judge: Honorable John Shimmering

The Motion of Plaintiff/Judgment Creditor AMY RIGHT ("CREDITOR") to be assigned the rights of Defendant/Judgment Debtor JEFF ISBAD ("DEBTOR") to payments from specified payment sources, was heard before this Court on the above date, the Honorable John Shimmering, Presiding. The Court, having considered the pleadings filed in connection with this motion, the pleadings and records on file in this matter, oral argument at the hearing, and good cause appearing therefore:

IT IS HEREBY ORDERED that the following rights to payment of Debtor, JEFF ISBAD, be and hereby are assigned to the Judgment Creditor AMY RIGHT, until such time as the judgment herein is fully satisfied or this order is amended per California Code of Civil Procedure §708.560. This assignment covers:

1. One Hundred Percent (100%) or _____ of any and all rights to any interest or principal payments, distributions, loans, commissions or any other payments types from XYZ Publishing, LLC ("XYZ"), until such time as the judgment amount stated in Paragraph 3 below is satisfied (paid) in full;

2. Debtor, JEFF ISBAD, shall provide Creditor, AMY RIGHT, an accounting of all payments, including, but not limited to, interest or principal payments, distributions, loans, commissions, or any other payment types received from XYZ Publishing, LLC every SIXTY (60) days starting from the date of this order.

3. The current amount of the judgment remaining unsatisfied is three thousand nine hundred seventy-two dollars, eighty-seven cents ($3,972.87).

IT IS HEREBY FURTHER ORDERED that Debtor, JEFF ISBAD, along with any third parties who are served with notice, shall pay any and all monies due and owing under this Order to "AMY RIGHT" 1000 My St, Mytown, Ca 90000, to be applied to the judgment herein until such judgment is fully satisfied, or this Order is amended.

NOTICE IS HEREBY GIVEN THAT FAILURE BY JUDGMENT DEBTOR, JEFF ISBAD, OR OTHER THIRD PARTIES, TO OBEY THIS ORDER MAY SUBJECT HIM/THEM TO BEING SANCTIONED AND/OR HELD IN CONTEMPT OF COURT.

IT IS SO ORDERED.

Dated:_____   _____

                                                                                                   The Honorable Judge of the Superior Court

Restraining Order

Amy Right

1000 My st

Mytown, Ca 90000

In Pro Per

SUPERIOR COURT OF CALIFORNIA, COUNTY OF LOS ANGELES

STANLEY MOSK COURTHOUSE ON HILL STREET-CENTRAL DISTRICT

AMY RIGHT, 　　　　　　　　　　Plaintiff, vs. JEFF ISBAD, 　　　　　　　　　　Defendant.	Case Number: **14K5000** **CREDITORS EX PARTE NO NOTICE APPLICATION AND MEMORANDUM OF POINTS AND AUTHORITIES FOR A RESTRAINING ORDER PENDING ASSIGNMENT ORDER** [CCP §708.520; CCP §708.510 *et seq.*] Date:　　October 22, 2015 Time:　　8:30am Crtrm:　　Department 5D Judge:　　Matt Bander Motion for Assignment Order: 11/21/13 Time:　　8:30 a.m. Crtrm:　　5D Judge:　　Honorable Matt Bander

PLEASE TAKE NOTICE that on the date, time and place indicated above, Plaintiff/Judgment Creditor, AMY RIGHT ("RIGHT", "PLAINTIFF" or "CREDITOR") hereby submits the following *Ex Parte* Application for Restraining Order Pending Assignment Order pursuant to Cal. Code of Civ. Proc. §708.520[41] *et seq.* against DEFENDANT/Judgment Debtor JEFF ISBAD ("ISBAD or "DEBTOR").

PLEASE TAKE FURTHER NOTICE that this motion is made pursuant to a Judgment entered by this court, Defendant's failure and/or refusal to pay any monies on the Judgment, Codes of Civil Procedure §§708.520 et seq.,708.510 et seq., and on the grounds that enforcement of the Judgment against JEFF ISBAD is not stayed and the Judgment remains wholly unsatisfied.

PLEASE TAKE FURTHER NOTICE that this application is based on this *Ex Parte* Application, all of the records and files in this action, the accompanying Memorandum of Points and Authorities, Exhibits, Declaration of Amy Right, and on such evidence that may be presented at the hearing on this Application.

Ex Parte Notice: This application is made ex-parte and without notice pursuant to California Rules of Court 3.1202(c), 3.1203(a), and 3.1204(b)(3), and for the reasons shown in this application.

This application is based upon the following:

1. CCP 708.520(a) plainly states an application for Order Restraining Disposition of Right to Payment may be sought ex parte, and as such this ex parte application is proper.

2. Under CRC 3.1204(b)(3) there is justification that Creditor should not be required to inform the Debtor of the instant motion. A right to payment can easily be transferred. Creditor believes that Debtor will likely transfer his right to payment if they, or their attorney, were put on notice of this instant motion. Debtor has shown zero cooperation to voluntarily pay this judgment.

---

[41] CITATIONS ARE TO THE CALIFORNIA CODE OF CIVIL PROCEDURE UNLESS OTHERWISE NOTED.

Despite a bank levy, wage garnishment, and an Order for Appearance and Examination, Creditor has yet to receive any property, money, or any other consideration of any value.

3. CRC 3.1202(c) requires an ex parte application make an affirmative and factual showing of irreparable harm or immediate danger. Here the irreparable harm is that a right to payment can be transferred by writing one letter of authorization. If the Debtor, or their attorney, were to be put on notice, there is the real threat that the right to payment sought to be assigned would be transferred away from the Debtor, and thereby out of the reach of creditors.

4. This Order is necessary so that Debtor will not alienate his right to payment until the Motion for Assignment Order can be heard by the Court.

5. In light of Debtor's refusal to pay the judgment entered against him, and the difficulty of finding and levying upon other assets to satisfy this obligation, Creditor requests that the attach order be granted, requiring the Debtor to hold off on transferring and/or encumbering the right to payment being sought in the Motion for Assignment Order.

6. There is no concern of prejudice to Debtor, based on this court's granting of the requested relief, as Debtor will continue to receive his payments until the court decides on the Motion for Assignment Order, scheduled reasonably soon.

//

Executed at Mytown, California, on October 21, 2015.

By: _____

Amy Right, Plaintiff/ Judgment Creditor

MEMORANDUM OF POINTS AND AUTHORITIES

SUMMARY OF MOTION

Plaintiff/Creditor AMY RIGHT ("RIGHT", "PLAINTIFF" or "Creditor") hereby submits the following Memorandum of Points and Authorities in support of her *Ex Parte Application for a Restraining Order Pending Assignment Order*. Creditor's application is based upon this Court's Judgment against Defendant/Judgment Debtor JEFF ISBAD ("ISBAD or "DEBTOR") in the amount of $3,000.00 entered by this court on January 1, 2014; ISBAD's right to receive payments, distributions, loans, commissions or other payments types from XYZ PUBLISHING, LLC ("XYZ") and/or other entities or persons sufficiently identified as making or owing payments to ISBAD; and the fact that no monies have been paid towards this judgment amount. A need exists to hear this matter on the *Ex Parte* calendar because the Plaintiff/Creditor has great concerns that the Defendant/Debtor will take steps to dissipate his rights to these identified payment streams, and/or other personal assets during the pendency of the *Motion for Assignment Order*, thus making the motion moot. This restraining order is expressly authorized by Code of Civil Procedure §708.520, which was instituted in recognition of, and to prevent the potential harms alleged herein.[42]

FACTUAL BACKGROUND

The Judgment: On January 1, 2014, this court entered judgment against Defendant/Debtor ISBAD requiring him to pay Plaintiff/Creditor RIGHT the principal amount of $3,000.00. This judgment resulted from unpaid amounts due from ISBAD to RIGHT.

Attempts at Informal Resolution: RIGHT has made substantial and repeated efforts to informally resolve this matter with the judgment debtors prior to bringing the underlying action, including reaching a payment plan agreement for the amount due; however, Defendant/Debtor ISBAD has failed and refused to pay the amount due under the judgment, or enter into a payment plan agreement for payment of the same.[43]

Creditor's Investigation Into Defendant: Defendant/Debtor ISBAD is known to be receiving monthly interest (only) payments of approximately $5,00.00[44] per month from a promissory note (loan) made to XYZ PUBLISHING, LLC.[45]

---

[42] California Code of Civil Procedure §708.520(a): *"When an application is made pursuant to Section 708.510 or thereafter, the judgment creditor may apply to the court for an order restraining the judgment debtor from assigning or otherwise disposing of the right to payment that is sought to be assigned....."*

[43] See RIGHT Decl.¶4

[44] See Exhibit "C"-True and authentic copy of XYZ PUBLISHING, LLC "Statement of Account"

[45] See Exhibit "B"-True and authentic copy of promissory note between Defendant/Debtor and XYZ PUBLISHING, LLC

Balance Due Under the Judgment. The present balance due under the judgment is $3,000.00, plus $972.87 in accrued statutory interest for a total judgment amount of $3,972.87.[46]

Requested Relief. Based upon the foregoing, Plaintiff/Creditor requests the Court issue the attached, proposed restraining order pending the hearing on the *Motion for an Assignment Order* that was concurrently filed with this court as this instant motion for an ex-parte restraining order. Creditor's proposed order is concurrently submitted with this application.

LEGAL ARGUMENT

A. This Court has Jurisdiction over this Matter

California courts have inherent power to enforce their judgments and statutory power to compel obedience to their judgments, orders and process.[47] Jurisdiction over the subject matter and the parties continues post-judgment throughout subsequent proceedings in the action. Thus, a court of competent jurisdiction that rendered the original judgment has continuing jurisdiction to enforce the judgment.[48]

Therefore, this court has jurisdiction to order Defendant to assign his rights to the XYZ PUBLISHING monthly interest payment to Plaintiff, until such time as the judgment is satisfied.

B. The Court May Issue a Restraining Order Pending an Assignment Motion.

The Motion for an Assignment Order. A creditor may bring a motion for an *Assignment Order* to assign rights to payments owed a judgment debtor (from a third party) directly to the judgment creditor. All or part of a right to payment due, or to become due, may be ordered assigned, whether or not such right is conditioned upon future developments.[49]. The right to payment may include, but is not limited to, deferred compensation, accounts receivables, general

---

[46] See Right Decl. ¶4

[47] See Code of Civil Procedure §§ 128(a)(4), 177; *Security Trust & Sav. Bank v. Southern Pac. R.R. Co.*, 6 CA2d 585, 588, 45 P2d 268, 270 (1935); *Brown v. Brown*, 22 CA3d 82, 84, 99 CR 311, 312 (1971).

[48] See § 410.50(b) and Comment thereto; *See Goldman v. Simpson*, 160 CA4th 255, 263–264, 72 CR3d 729, 734–735(2008)(Court that entered original judgment had continuing jurisdiction to enforce judgment even though debtor had moved out of state)

[49] CCP 708.510(a)

intangibles or instruments, and/or insurance payments.[50]

Plaintiff/Creditor RIGHT can show that Debtor ISBAD has an interest in a promissory note received from XYZ PUBLISHING, LLC and that ISBAD is currently realizing monthly interest income in the amount of $500.00 from this note.

Restraining Order When a motion for an assignment order is pending, or anytime thereafter, a creditor may apply for an order restraining the transfer, assignment, disposal or encumbrance of payments sought to be assigned. The application further may be made by *Ex Parte* application.[51] Thus, for the *emergency* reasons set forth below, Creditor requests this Court immediately issue the proposed Restraining Order until such time as the Court rules on Creditor's pending *Motion for an Assignment Order*.

C. Creditor's Emergency Basis for the Restraining Order.

The Judgment Debtor presently owes Creditor $3,972.87, and have refused to voluntarily pay any portion of this judgment. Furthermore, Creditor has knowledge that the Defendant/Debtor has transferred his personal assets to a family member in the past to hinder and frustrate the collection efforts of his creditors.[52] Therefore, there is a real risk that if the debtor is not restrained from assigning or transferring his rights to payments to others during pendency of the concurrently filed *Motion for Assignment Order* that he would in fact alienate his rights to payments sought to be assigned, thus making the *Motion for Assignment Order* fruitless and moot. The restraining order authorized in §708.520, and sought by Plaintiff here, was instituted for this very purpose-the protection of creditors during the short interim period between the filing of, and ultimate ruling on the motion.

---

[50] See §708.510(a)(1); Comment to C.C.P. §708.510 & Ahart Cal. Prac. Guide: Enforcing Judgments and Debts, §§ 6:1422, 6:1423, 6:1432 (The Rutter Group 2009).
[51] CCP 708.520(a)

[52] See RIGHT Decl ¶10

Therefore, Plaintiff respectfully requests that this Court grant its *Ex Parte* Application for a Restraining Order until such time as the Court can rule on Creditor's noticed *Motion for an Assignment Order*.

D. An Undertaking Is Not Required For The Restraining Order Requested Herein:

Although a court has authority to require an undertaking from a creditor seeking a restraining order under §708.520(a)[53]; it is not mandatory and given the limited nature of the relief provided for under §708.520(a), is not normally required. The restraining order requested herein will *not* limit in any way the PLAINTIFF's right or ability to spend or use the payment stream sought to be assigned (via Plaintiff/Creditor's concurrently filed *Motion For Assignment Order)*, but would *only* limit the PLAINTIFF's right to assign, encumber or alienate the right to payment during the time period before the court has the opportunity to rule on the motion. For this reason, there is little or no risk of harm or damage to the PLAINTIFF's property rights in the payment stream or otherwise.

Therefore, the court should not require any undertaking from the creditor.

E. Creditor Should Not be Required to give *Ex Parte* Notice to Debtor.

Under CRC 3.1204(b)(3), a Court may allow a No Notice Ex Parte if the Creditor has shown valid justification for there not to be notice. We ask this Court to accept the justifications shown here, and in the Declaration, as valid.

CONCLUSION

---

[53] CCP 708.520(b): *"The court may issue an order pursuant to this section upon a showing of need for the order. The court in its discretion **may** require the judgment creditor to provide an undertaking."* [Bold Emphasis Added]

Creditor meets all of the *Ex Parte* application requirements for a *Temporary Restraining Order* pending the outcome of the *Assignment Order* motion. Creditor has a statutory as well as emergency basis as shown above for the issuance of a *Temporary Restraining Order*.

Dated: October 21, 2015   Respectfully submitted,

_____
Amy Right, Plaintiff/Judgment Creditor

Amy Right

1000 My St.

Mytown, Ca 90000

In Pro Per

SUPERIOR COURT OF CALIFORNIA, COUNTY OF LOS ANGELES

STANLEY MOSK COURTHOUSE, CENTRAL DISTRICT

AMY RIGHT

                    Plaintiff,

vs.

JEFF ISBAD,

                    Defendant.

Case Number: **14K5000**

DECLARATION OF AMY RIGHT IN SUPPORT OF EXPARTE NO NOTICE APPICATION FOR A RESTRAINING ORDER PENDING ASSIGNMENT ORDER

Date: December 3, 2013

Time: 1:30 PM

Crtrm: Department 95

Judge: Honorable John Shimmering

I, Amy Right, declare as follows:

1. I am the Plaintiff in the above-entitled case, and I am over the age of 18 years

old.

18. If called upon to testify, I could and would competently testify to the matters contained herein based upon my personal knowledge, except as to those matters stated upon information and belief, and as to those matters I am informed and believe and thereon allege that they are true and correct based upon my reasonable investigation.

19. The judgment in this case resulted from uncompleted work by Defendant, JEFF ISBAD.

20. I have made substantial and repeated efforts to informally resolve this matter with Defendant JEFF ISBAD. These efforts include numerous verbal and written demands for payments, and also include demand letters written by my former attorney. In addition, I have attempted to negotiate a payment plan agreement with Defendant without success. To date, Defendant ISBAD has failed and refused to pay any amount towards satisfaction of the judgment.

21. Exhibit "B" is a true and authentic copy of Promissory Note between XYZ Publishing, LLC and Defendant JEFF ISBAD. This document was provided to me by the Defendant.

22. Exhibit "C" is a true and authentic copy of the Statement of Account for the account of Defendant JEFF ISBAD. This document was provided to me by the Defendant.

23. I am unaware of any deductions or payments being deducted in satisfaction of other judgments, or wage assignments, including assignments related to support orders.

24. To my knowledge, Defendant JEFF ISBAD is a single man with recurring business income from other sources, and is not wholly reliant on the XYZ Publishing, LLC monthly interest payments for his own support. I need to collect the judgment amount so that I will be able to pay basic living expenses for both myself and my 12 year old son.

25. I have personal first-hand knowledge that Defendant JEFF ISBAD has

transferred his personal assets to a family member in the past in order to hinder and frustrate the collection efforts of his creditors.

Executed at Mytown, California on June 9, 2016.

By: _____

Amy Right, Judgment Creditor

Amy Right

1000 My st.

Mytown, Ca 90000

In Pro Per

SUPERIOR COURT OF CALIFORNIA, COUNTY OF LOS ANGELES
STANLEY MOSK COURTHOUSE ON HILL STREET-CENTRAL DISTRICT

AMY RIGHT, 　　　　　　　　　　　Plaintiff, vs. JEFF ISBAD, 　　　　　　　　　　　Defendant.	Case Number: **14K5000** *[PROPOSED]TEMPORARY RESTRAINING ORDER AUTHORITIES FOR A RESTRAINING ORDER PENDING ASSIGNMENT ORDER* [CCP §708.520; CCP §708.510 *et seq.*] Date:　October 22, 2015 Time:　8:30am Crtrm:　Department 5D Judge:　Matt Bander

The Ex Parte Application of Plaintiff/Creditor AMY RIGHT for a Temporary Restraining Order (pending *Motion for Assignment Order* filed with this court) against Defendant/Judgment Debtor JEFF ISBAD came before this court on the above date, the Honorable Matt Bander presiding. The Court, having considered the pleadings filed in connection with the application, the pleadings and records on file in this matter, oral argument at the hearing, and good cause appearing; *therefore,*

IT IS HEREBY ORDERED that Petitioner/Judgment Debtor JEFF ISBAD is hereby restrained from transferring, assigning, disposing, encumbering, or interfering with any right to payment from:

1) Any and all rights to any interest or payment now due or to become due in the future to Petitioner/Judgment Debtor JEFF ISBAD, in any money or property due from XYZ Publishing, LLC, or their affiliates, and assigns, including but not limited to payments for principal, interest, share distributions, profit distributions, dividends, bonus payments, loan payments, or other payments of every kind.

NOTICE IS HEREBY GIVEN THAT FAILURE BY DEFENDANT/JUDGMENT DEBTOR JEFF ISBAD TO COMPLY WITH THIS ORDER MAY SUBJECT THE DEFENDANT/JUDGMENT DEBTOR TO BEING SANCTIONED AND/OR HELD IN CONTEMPT OF COURT.

IT IS SO ORDERED

DATED: _____

_____

Honorable Matt Bander, Judge

Chapter 20

Renewing Your Judgment and Liens

A. Renewing a Judgment	20/2
1. Get Current Renewal Forms	20/2
2. Prepare the Application	20/2
3. Send Notice of Renewal	20/3
4. File Papers with Court	20/4
5. Have Debtor Served	20/4
B. Renewing Liens	20/4
1. Real Estate Lien	20/4
2. Business Asset Lien	20/5
3. Personal Property Lien	20/5

A judgment (and any real estate liens associated with that judgment) issued by a California state or federal court lasts for ten years. With any luck, you will be able to fully enforce your judgment within that ten-year period.

If you don't, however, you can renew your judgment along with any judgment liens you created on the debtor's real estate. The judgment and liens can be renewed for successive ten-year periods.

There are exceptions: Judgments for child or spousal support do not need to be renewed [CCP 683.310] nor do criminal restitution orders. They are enforceable until paid in full.

A. Renewing a Judgment

If your judgment isn't fully satisfied and it's been close to ten years since your judgment was entered, you need to act quickly. That is because you must renew a judgment **before** it expires. If you try to renew a judgment even one day after it expires, you are out of luck. You may be able to file another lawsuit to obtain a judgment on your judgment, but there are limitations to doing this and you will need a lawyer's help [CCP 683.050].

When you renew a judgment, all interest and costs you've claimed in A Memorandum of Costs form previously (see Chapter 16) become part of the new judgment. In effect, this entitles you to receive compound interest on your judgment, because you'll now be allowed to earn interest on accrued interest. The interest for the years prior to renewal now become part of the principal of the judgment moving forward and are no longer considered 'interest' after renewal.

1. Get Current Renewal Forms

The first step is to make sure that you have the most current version of the forms. Go into the Self Help Center at your local courthouse or get the forms from the internet at http://www.courts.ca.gov/forms.htm. The forms needed are the Application for and Renewal of Judgment (EJ-190) and the Notice of Renewal of Judgment (EJ-195).

2. Prepare the Application

First you have to calculate and declare all accrued interest up to the date you will be renewing your judgment. The easiest way to figure the interest is to use the Judgment Calculator found here:

http://ijcalc.sdcourt.ca.gov./default.aspx

Enter the total amount of your judgment, as it was entered by the court, in the first box.

Then, enter the date the judgment was entered by the court in the "Judgment Date" box.

Then, enter the date you are preparing the forms for in the *'End Date'* box.

If you have received any payments or have claimed any costs, enter each one separately and then hit the "add" button. After you finish entering all Payments and all Costs, click the *'Calculate'* button. You will then see 'Total Interest' in the box along the bottom. Put that number into Item 5 on the Memorandum of Costs form MC-012, which can be found at:

http://www.courts.ca.gov/forms.htm (see Chapter 16, part B and C).

Date and sign the form and make a copy.

This is not when you want to claim any new costs, that should be done at least 30 days before filing the Renewal of Judgment.

The "Application for and Renewal of Judgment" (form EJ-190) is the form you use to request an extension of your judgment. A sample completed form and instructions follow.

Caption: Follow the format of your other court papers.

Check the box that says "judgment creditor." Leave the "case number" box empty. Some courts may give you a new case number.

Item 1: Enter your name exactly as it appears on the original judgment and your current address.

Item 2: Enter the judgment debtor's name exactly as it appears on the original judgment and last known address.

Item 3a: Enter the case number of the original judgment.

Item 3b: Enter the date the original judgment was entered.

Item 3c: If you've created real estate liens by recording an Abstract of Judgment, or by recording a certified copy of the judgment, in any county, indicate here the date and county in which you recorded the Abstract, as well as the recorded document's instrument number. If you haven't recorded an Abstract or certified judgment, leave this section blank. If you have recorded an abstract in more than one county, type in "see Attachment 3" and add a separate page with the information for all of the recorded Abstracts.

Item 4: Check this box and enter the dates if you've previously renewed your judgment.

Item 5: Check this box.

Item 5a: Enter the total amount of the original judgment.
Item 5b: Enter the total post-judgment costs you have claimed in previously filed Memorandum of Costs forms (MC-012) (See Chapter 16).

Item 5c: Enter the total of Items 5a and 5b.

Item 5d: Enter the total credits made on the judgment, voluntary payments and money recovered through levies.

Item 5e: Subtract Item 5d from Item 5c and enter the difference.

Item 5f: Enter the total post-judgment interest you have claimed in previously filed Memorandum of Costs forms along with the current up-to-date interest you are declaring along with this Application, see above interest calculation website (See Chapter 16)

Item 5g: Enter the fee for filing the renewal application. The fee is currently $30 [Government Code 70626(b) (4) & CCP 683.150(b)]. You can verify the fee with the court clerk.

Item 5h: Enter the total of Items 5e, 5f and 5g. This is the amount of your renewed judgment.

Item 5i: Leave this box blank unless your judgment is against different debtors, and each owes you different amounts. In this case, include a separate page, labeled Attachment 5, listing each debtor and the amount owed.

Page two

Short Title: Enter the name of the plaintiff and defendant. Leave the case number blank.

Item 6: Skip this entire item. This book covers only money judgments.

At the bottom, date the form, enter your name and sign.

3. Prepare Notice of Renewal of Judgment

The Notice of Renewal of Judgment is used to notify the debtor that you are renewing the judgment. A sample completed form and instructions follow.

To judgment debtor (name): Enter the name of the judgment debtor exactly as it appears on the original judgment.

Leave the rest of the form blank.

4. File Papers with Court

Give or send the clerk of the court the original and two copies of the Application for and Renewal of Judgment and the original and two copies of the Notice of Renewal of Judgment along with the original and one copy of the Memorandum of Costs declaring the accrued interest. If you mail the documents to the court clerk, be sure to include a self-addressed stamped envelope so the clerk can return the file-stamped copies to you. After filing the original, the clerk will stamp all your copies and return them to you in the self-addressed stamped envelope you provide. Make sure to put sufficient postage on the envelope to cover all the documents being returned to you. Make sure you keep a copy of each item for yourself before mailing anything to the court.

The filing fee for an Application for and Renewal of Judgment is currently $30 to renew a court judgment, whether in Small Claims or Superior Court [Government Code 70626(b) (4) and CCP 683.150(b)].

Don't miss the deadline! If you're facing the ten-year renewal deadline, take your papers to the court for filing. Don't rely on the mail, if you made any errors filling in the forms and the court doesn't accept them, you may be out of luck.

5. Have Debtor Served

After you renew your judgment, you must have a copy of the "Application for and Renewal of Judgment" and the "Notice of Renewal of Judgment" served personally or by first-class mail on the debtor before you can initiate enforcement activities [CCP 683.160(a)] (Chapter 21 covers service). You do not have to serve the debtor prior to filing your documents at the court. You just have to serve the debtor prior to attempting any enforcement of the renewed judgment [CCP 683.160(b)].

Once the judgment debtor has been served with the renewal papers, prepare a Proof of Service (See Chapter 21). You can use form POS-020 if the debtor is served personally or form POS-030 if the debtor is served by mail. The forms can be found at http://www.courts.ca.gov/forms.htm. Have the person who served the documents sign the Proof of Service, make an extra copy and then file the original with the court. Be sure to get the extra copy file-stamped by the court for your records.

The judgment is actually renewed once the clerk files the Application for and Renewal of Judgment [CCP 683.150(a)].

You don't need to serve the debtor to renew the judgment, but you must serve him before you can resume enforcing your judgment.

After the debtor is served, they have 30 days to file a motion asking the court to vacate or modify the renewal. If the debtor makes such a motion, they must serve you personally or by mail, and schedule a court hearing on the motion [CCP 683.170(b)]. It is very unlikely that a debtor will object to renewal, he has few grounds to do so. If he does, however, see Chapter 19 on noticed motion procedures.

B. Renewing Liens

In Chapter 4, we explained how to record real estate, business asset and personal property liens against the debtor. As with judgments, liens expire after a certain period of time. Some liens may be renewed; others may be re-recorded.

1. Real Estate Lien

Liens on a debtor's real estate expire when the underlying judgment expires. This means that you must renew your liens before the judgment expires. Logically, before the ten years are up, you can renew your judgment and then renew your liens. To be safe, renew your judgment several months before the expiration of the ten-year period, so you have time to renew the liens.

EXAMPLE: Amy obtains a $3,000 judgment against Jeff, which is entered on July 1, 1991. Amy records an Abstract of Judgment to establish a lien against Jeff's cabin in Tahoe. On April 1, 2001, Amy renews the judgment for another ten years. Amy also renews the lien. If Jeff continues to avoid payment, Amy can renew the judgment and lien again. If, however, Amy forgets about or gives up on the judgment and lien and fails to renew them by April 1, 2011, they both will be unenforceable.

As soon as you renew your judgment, you can renew your real estate liens following these steps:

1. Obtain a certified copy of your Application for and Renewal of Judgment from the court [CCP 683.180(a)]. You must pay a small fee, which is currently $25 [Government Code 70626(a) (4)]. You will need one certified copy of your Application for each county in which you recorded a lien.

2. Record the certified Application with each county where you have recorded an Abstract of Judgment or certified copy of the judgment (See Chapter 4, Section A2, for information on recording documents).

2. Business Asset Lien

If you have not fully recovered your judgment within five years of creating a business asset lien, your lien will expire. You can renew your lien prior to the five year expiration date by completing a Judgment Lien Change Form (JL3), which can be found at http://www.sos.ca.gov/business-programs/ucc/judgment-lien-amendment/ (See Chapter 4, Section B).

3. Personal Property Lien

As explained in Chapters 4 and 6, it is possible to create a short-term lien against a judgment debtor's personal property when you schedule a debtor's examination. It remains in effect for a year. You can renew the lien by serving the debtor with a new Application and Order for Appearance and Examination.

EJ-190

ATTORNEY OR PARTY WITHOUT ATTORNEY *(Name, address, and State Bar number):*
After recording, return to:
Amy Right
1000 My st
Mytown, Ca 90000

TEL NO.: 310-555-5555   FAX NO. (optional):
E-MAIL ADDRESS *(Optional):*
☐ ATTORNEY FOR   ☒ JUDGMENT CREDITOR   ☐ ASSIGNEE OF RECORD

SUPERIOR COURT OF CALIFORNIA, COUNTY OF Los Angeles
STREET ADDRESS: 111 Hill st
MAILING ADDRESS:
CITY AND ZIP CODE: Los Angeles, Ca 90012
BRANCH NAME: Stanley Mosk Courthouse

PLAINTIFF: Amy Right
DEFENDANT: Jeff Isbad

APPLICATION FOR AND RENEWAL OF JUDGMENT

FOR RECORDER'S USE ONLY

CASE NUMBER:

FOR COURT USE ONLY

☒ Judgment creditor
☐ Assignee of record
applies for renewal of the judgment as follows:

1. Applicant *(name and address):*
   Amy Right
   1000 My st, Mytown, Ca 90000

2. Judgment debtor *(name and last known address):*
   Jeff Isbad
   666 e Cra P st, Helltown, Ca 90666

3. Original judgment
   a. Case number *(specify):* 14K5000
   b. Entered on *(date):* 01/01/2014
   c. Recorded: Abstract
      (1) Date: 02/01/2014
      (2) County: Los Angeles
      (3) Instrument No.: 142000000005

4. ☐ Judgment previously renewed *(specify each case number and date):*

5. ☒ Renewal of money judgment
   a. Total judgment . . . . $ 3,000.00
   b. Costs after judgment . . . . $ 0.00
   c. Subtotal *(add a and b)* . . . . $ 3,000.00
   d. Credits after judgment . . . . $ 0.00
   e. Subtotal *(subtract d from c)* . . . . $ 3,000.00
   f. Interest after judgment . . . . $ 2,999.16
   g. Fee for filing renewal application . . . . $ 30.00
   h. **Total renewed judgment** *(add e, f, and g)* $ **6,029.16**

   i. ☐ The amounts called for in items a–h are different for each debtor.
      These amounts are stated for each debtor on Attachment 5.

Form Approved for Optional Use
Judicial Council of California
EJ-190 [Rev. July 1, 2014]

APPLICATION FOR AND RENEWAL OF JUDGMENT

Code of Civil Procedure, § 683.140

SHORT TITLE: Right v Isbad	CASE NUMBER:

6. ☐ Renewal of judgment for ☐ possession.
   ☐ sale.

   a. ☐ If judgment was not previously renewed, terms of judgment as entered:

   b. ☐ If judgment was previously renewed, terms of judgment as last renewed:

   c. ☐ Terms of judgment remaining unsatisfied:

I declare under penalty of perjury under the laws of the State of California that the foregoing is true and correct.

Date: 12/10/2023

Amy Right
_____
(TYPE OR PRINT NAME)

▶ _____
(SIGNATURE OF DECLARANT)

APPLICATION FOR AND RENEWAL OF JUDGMENT

EJ-195

ATTORNEY OR PARTY WITHOUT ATTORNEY *(Name and Address)*	TELEPHONE NO.: 310-555-5555	FOR COURT USE ONLY
Amy Right 1000 My st Mytown, Ca 90000 ATTORNEY FOR *(Name):* In Pro Per		

NAME OF COURT: Superior Court of California
STREET ADDRESS: 111 Hill st
MAILING ADDRESS:
CITY AND ZIP CODE: Los Angeles, Ca 90012
BRANCH NAME: Stanley Mosk Courthouse

PLAINTIFF: Amy Right

DEFENDANT: Jeff Isbad

NOTICE OF RENEWAL OF JUDGMENT	CASE NUMBER: 14K5000

TO JUDGMENT DEBTOR *(name):* Jeff Isbad

1. **This renewal extends** the period of enforceability of the judgment until 10 years from the date the application for renewal was filed.
2. **If you object** to this renewal, you may make a motion to vacate or modify the renewal with this court.
3. You must make this motion within **30 days** after service of this notice on you.
4. A copy of the *Application for and Renewal of Judgment* is attached (Cal. Rules of Court, rule 3.1900).

Date: Clerk, by _____, Deputy

[SEAL]

See CCP 683.160 for information on method of service

Form Adopted for Mandatory Use
Judicial Council of California
EJ-195 [Rev. January 1, 2007]

NOTICE OF RENEWAL OF JUDGMENT

Code of Civil Procedure, § 683.160
www.courtinfo.ca.gov

of your intentions, it will become much harder from that point on.

2. Personal Service on a Corporation

If the debtor or third party is a domestic or foreign corporation, personal service must be made either on an officer of the corporation such as a president, vice-president, secretary, treasurer, or on the person who has been designated as agent for service of process [CCP 416.10]. Call the corporation and ask who the officers are and in which office they are located.

If you can't get the information this way, either because the business won't give you the information or the business is a large corporation doing business in California, go to the website of the Secretary of State, at http://kepler.sos.ca.gov/. You can look up the agent for service of process on this website. Follow the instructions on the left side of their Business Search webpage to learn who the corporation's officers are.

Once you have the name and location of an officer or the agent for service of process, have your process server simply hand deliver the papers. They shouldn't meet with any resistance.

3. Personal Service on a Partnership

To serve a partnership, your process server must personally serve one of the partners or it's agent for service (See Section B1, above) [Corporations Code 15901.16(b)]. If you cannot serve one of the partners, you may be able to serve a limited partnership or foreign general partnership by serving the Secretary of State. That procedure is beyond the scope of this book.

4. Personal Service on a Limited Liability Company (LLC)

To serve an LLC, your process server must personally serve it's agent for service. (See Section B1, above) [Corporations Code 17701.16(b)]. If you cannot serve the agent, you may be able to serve an LLC or foreign LLC by serving the Secretary of State. That procedure is beyond the scope of this book.

C. Service by Mail

Often, depending on the type of document being served, the debtor or third party can be served by mail. Someone other than yourself who is over 18 and not a party to the case must do the mailing. It may cost you no more than the first-class postage.

Here's how to serve papers through the mail:

1. Gather together the papers to be served.

2. Complete a Proof of Service by mail form (see Section E, below), except for the signature.

3. Make copies of the papers to be served and copies of the unsigned Proof of Service, keeping one set for yourself.

4. Put one copy of the papers, including one copy of the unsigned Proof of Service, in an envelope addressed to the person to be served. Use the person's residence address or office address stated on any document the person filed in your court case. If the person has an attorney, you can send it to the attorney if the debtor has provided you with a signed statement that all service shall be upon his attorney. Otherwise, all documents must be served on the judgment debtor [CCP 684.020(a)].

5. Affix sufficient postage on the envelope for first-class mail.

6. Have the process server put the envelope into a mailbox. If the process server mails the papers from a business, they may deposit them in the business's outgoing mail, as long as it will be taken for collection that day.

7. Have the server complete their address, phone information, and sign the Proof

of Service, then give it to you so you can copy it and file it with the court (See Section E, below).

When service is done by mail, the person being served is usually entitled to an extra five to ten days to respond, assuming they have been served with papers requiring a response. For example, if you are required to give the judgment debtor 16 court days' notice of a hearing, and you serve the judgment debtor with notice through the mail, the hearing must be scheduled at least 28 days in the future, 33 days if the debtor does not live in California [CCP 1013(a)].

Certified mail is not necessary unless a statute specifically requires certified mail. Otherwise, certified mail may be to a disadvantage. When you mail something first class, the party to whom it is addressed is presumed to receive it. But when you send something certified mail, the party is not presumed to have received it unless they sign for it. Certified mail is often signed for by other people in the house or isn't picked up at the post office.

D. Proof of Service Form

After papers are served, the process server must fill out a document called a Proof of Service, which states when and how service was made and then the completed and signed Proof of Service must be filed with the court. Subpoenas, and their corresponding Proofs of Service, are not filed with the court [California Rules of Court, Rule 3.250(a) (1) & (2)].

Throughout the book we tell you when a Proof of Service must be filed. If you are notifying the debtor, of a court hearing (except on an ex parte motion; see Chapter 19), the Proof of Service must be filed before the hearing. How long in advance varies by court and procedure, but five business days is common.

Some documents have an official Proof of Service form on the back or as the last page of the document; if so, use that form. If not, you can use a generic form, which covers personal service and service by mail, see the Judicial Council form POS-040. For service by First Class Mail, you can use form POS-030 or for personal service, you can use form POS-020. The content of these various Proof of Service forms is pretty much the same. The Judicial Council forms can be found at any Law Library or online at http://www.courts.ca.gov/forms.htm

POS-020

ATTORNEY OR PARTY WITHOUT ATTORNEY *(Name, State Bar number, and address):*
Amy Right
1000 My st
Mytown, Ca 90000

TELEPHONE NO.: 310-555-5555   FAX NO. *(Optional):*
E-MAIL ADDRESS *(Optional):*
ATTORNEY FOR *(Name):* In Pro Per

SUPERIOR COURT OF CALIFORNIA, COUNTY OF Los Angeles
STREET ADDRESS: 111 Hill st
MAILING ADDRESS:
CITY AND ZIP CODE: Los Angeles, Ca 90012
BRANCH NAME: Stanley Mosk Courthouse

PETITIONER/PLAINTIFF: Amy Right

RESPONDENT/DEFENDANT: Jeff Isbad

FOR COURT USE ONLY

PROOF OF PERSONAL SERVICE—CIVIL

CASE NUMBER: 14K5000

(Do not use this Proof of Service to show service of a Summons and Complaint.)

1. I am over 18 years of age and **not a party to this action**.
2. I served the following **documents** *(specify):*

   1) Application and Order for Appearance and Examination
   2) Subpoena Duces Tecum

   ☐ The documents are listed in the *Attachment to Proof of Personal Service—Civil (Documents Served)* (form POS-020(D)).

3. I personally served the following **persons** at the address, date, and time stated:
   a. Name: Jeff Isbad
   b. Address: 666 e Cra P st, Helltown, Ca 90666
   c. Date: 02/30/2015
   d. Time: 6:25 pm

   ☐ The persons are listed in the *Attachment to Proof of Personal Service—Civil (Persons Served)* (form POS-020(P)).

4. I am
   a. ☑ not a registered California process server.
   b. ☐ a registered California process server.
   c. ☐ an employee or independent contractor of a registered California process server.
   d. ☐ exempt from registration under Business & Professions Code section 22350(b).

5. My name, address, telephone number, and, if applicable, county of registration and number are *(specify):*

   Betty Bestfriend
   160 Helpful st
   Los Angeles, Ca 90016

6. ☑ I declare under penalty of perjury under the laws of the State of California that the foregoing is true and correct.
7. ☐ I am a California sheriff or marshal and certify that the foregoing is true and correct.

Date: 02/30/2015

Betty Bestfriend
(TYPE OR PRINT NAME OF PERSON WHO SERVED THE PAPERS)   ▶   (SIGNATURE OF PERSON WHO SERVED THE PAPERS)

Form Approved for Optional Use
Judicial Council of California
POS-020 [New January 1, 2005]

PROOF OF PERSONAL SERVICE—CIVIL

Code of Civil Procedure, § 1011
www.courtinfo.ca.gov

POS-030

ATTORNEY OR PARTY WITHOUT ATTORNEY (Name, State Bar number, and address):	FOR COURT USE ONLY
Amy Right 1000 My st Mytown, Ca 90000 TELEPHONE NO.: 310-555-5555 FAX NO. (Optional): E-MAIL ADDRESS (Optional): ATTORNEY FOR (Name): In Pro Per	

SUPERIOR COURT OF CALIFORNIA, COUNTY OF Los Angeles
STREET ADDRESS: 111 Hill st
MAILING ADDRESS:
CITY AND ZIP CODE: Los Angeles, Ca 90012
BRANCH NAME: Stanley Mosk Courthouse

PETITIONER/PLAINTIFF: Amy Right

RESPONDENT/DEFENDANT: Jeff Isbad

PROOF OF SERVICE BY FIRST-CLASS MAIL—CIVIL	CASE NUMBER: 14K5000

(Do not use this Proof of Service to show service of a Summons and Complaint.)

1. I am over 18 years of age and **not a party to this action.** I am a resident of or employed in the county where the mailing took place.

2. My residence or business address is:
   160 Helpful st
   Los Angeles, Ca 90016

3. On *(date)*: 02/30/2015   I mailed from *(city and state):* Los Angeles, Ca
   the following **documents** *(specify)*:
   name of forms mailed and how many pages. Make sure that it is allowed to serve them by mail
   Read chapter that covers the document you are mailing

   ☐ The documents are listed in the *Attachment to Proof of Service by First-Class Mail—Civil (Documents Served)* (form POS-030(D)).

4. I served the documents by enclosing them in an envelope and *(check one)*:
   a. ☑ **depositing** the sealed envelope with the United States Postal Service with the postage fully prepaid.
   b. ☐ **placing** the envelope for collection and mailing following our ordinary business practices. I am readily familiar with this business's practice for collecting and processing correspondence for mailing. On the same day that correspondence is placed for collection and mailing, it is deposited in the ordinary course of business with the United States Postal Service in a sealed envelope with postage fully prepaid.

5. The envelope was addressed and mailed as follows:
   a. **Name** of person served: Jeff Isbad
   b. **Address** of person served:
      666 e Cra P st
      Helltown, Ca 90666

   ☐ The name and address of each person to whom I mailed the documents is listed in the *Attachment to Proof of Service by First-Class Mail—Civil (Persons Served)* (POS-030(P)).

I declare under penalty of perjury under the laws of the State of California that the foregoing is true and correct.

Date: 02/30/2015

Betty Bestfriend   ▶
(TYPE OR PRINT NAME OF PERSON COMPLETING THIS FORM)   (SIGNATURE OF PERSON COMPLETING THIS FORM)

Form Approved for Optional Use
Judicial Council of California
POS-030 [New January 1, 2005]

PROOF OF SERVICE BY FIRST-CLASS MAIL—CIVIL
(Proof of Service)

Code of Civil Procedure, §§ 1013, 1013a
www.courtinfo.ca.gov

Chapter 22

After the Judgment is Paid

A. Why File an Acknowledgment	21/2
1. Complete Acknowledgement Form	21/3
2. Have your Signature Notarized	21/4
3. Serve and File Acknowledgment	21/4
B. Release Any Liens	21/4
1. Real Estate Liens	21/4
2. Business Personal Property Liens	21/4

Congratulations. Let's hope you are reading this chapter because your enforcement efforts have reached a happy end. Either you've recovered your judgment in full or you've accepted less as payment in full [CCP 724.010(a)].

Before you get carried away celebrating, you must complete a bit more paperwork. The task is simple, but essential; if you don't do this promptly, you could end up owing the debtor money.

Here are the steps you need to take when your judgment is **paid**.

1. Complete an Acknowledgment of Satisfaction of Judgment form, form EJ-100, which can be found at http://www.courts.ca.gov/forms.htm. Your signature will need to be notarized.

2. File the form with the court to show that the judgment has been paid, (technically, "satisfied") [CCP 116.850(a) and 724.030].

3. Release any liens you created on the debtor's real estate or personal business property.

4. Serve the debtor with a copy of all filed and/or recorded forms, by either personal or mail service.

5. File the original Proof of Service with the court.

If your judgment was from small claims court and the debtor paid the small claims court directly, the court clerk is responsible for filing a Satisfaction of Judgment [CCP 116.860(b)]. You must release any liens you've created [CCP 724.040].

A. Why File an Acknowledgment?

The debtor has the right to demand that you file an Acknowledgment of Satisfaction of Judgment within 15 days after your judgment is satisfied, if your case is Limited Civil or Unlimited Civil [CCP 724.050(c)], 14 days for small claims judgments [CCP 116.850(b)]. In addition, the debtor can serve you with a written demand to file an Acknowledgment for partial satisfaction of the judgment if you have collected some payments on the judgment. Again, you must comply with the 15-day deadline or the 14-day deadline, depending on which type of case you have. A debtor might want a partial Acknowledgment filed, for example, if they are selling or refinancing real estate and need proof of how much they have paid on the judgment [CCP 724.110 & 724.120].

If you don't file the Acknowledgment, the debtor can take you to court. You may be liable for any damages the debtor sustains because you failed to file the Acknowledgment, plus reasonable attorneys' fees and court costs [CCP 724.080]. On top of all that, you may be ordered to pay the debtor $100 in damages [CCP 724.050(e)]. Although this scenario is unlikely to happen, why chance it?

What harm can a debtor suffer if you don't promptly file an Acknowledgment? If the judgment shows up on the debtor's credit report, the debtor might be denied credit or prevented from buying real estate or renting an apartment. If you have recorded a lien, they might not be able to sell their property.

EXAMPLE: Amy and Jeff had a business dispute. Amy got a judgment against Jeff for $3,000, which Jeff paid over a ten-month period. Amy never filed a Satisfaction of Judgment, although Jeff asked Amy to do it, twice. Jeff filed a small claims action of $2,500 against Amy, claiming his bad credit report lost him two profitable jobs. Amy ended up owing Jeff $1,400.

The deadline begins when you

1) received the full (final) payment from the levying officer [CCP 724.010(b)].

2) when the payment made by the debtor is honored by your bank. If you deposit a check (money order, cashier's check, etc.) into your bank account. Do not wait until you receive your bank statement to confirm that the funds are good. Be proactive and call your bank within days (unless you have a statement showing that the bank will place the check on hold) [CCP 724.010(c)].

In either case, don't wait for trouble; file the documents as early as possible.

1. Complete Acknowledgment Form

You have to complete the Acknowledgment of Satisfaction of Judgment form after your judgment is paid. A completed sample copy follows and instructions are below; a blank fillable form EJ-100 can be found at http://www.courts.ca.gov/forms.htm.

Caption: Follow the format of your previous court papers for the first three sections and the case number.

Acknowledgment of Satisfaction of Judgment:

- Check the first box if the judgment is fully satisfied. This means you are willing to end the matter with regard to the debtors you name. It doesn't necessarily mean that you received full payment.

- Check the second box if the judgment is partially satisfied. This means that only part of the judgment has been paid and you intend to try and recover the rest of the money due you.

- Check the third box if the debtor has been paying you on an installment judgment and all installments have been paid.

Item 1a: Check this box if the judgment is fully satisfied, as defined above.

Item 1a (1): Check this box if the judgment, costs and interest were paid in full.

Item 1a(2): Check this box if you have settled for less than the total amount but consider the judgment fully satisfied.

Item 1b: Check this box if the judgment is only partially satisfied, as defined above. Then enter the amount you have received to date.

Item 1c: Check this box if all matured installments have been paid on an installment judgment. In other words, all payments that have become due have been paid. Enter the date the last installment was paid [CCP 724.210 thru 724.260].

Item 2: Enter your full name, as it appears on the judgment and your current address.

Item 3: Leave this blank unless you were assigned the right to enforce this judgment.

Item 4: Enter the full name of the judgment debtor exactly as it appears on the judgment, and enter the debtor's address. If more than one judgment debtor is liable for your judgment, name only the debtors being released.

Item 5a: Enter the date the judgment was entered by the court.

Item 5b: Check this box if you renewed the judgment, then enter the date the court filed the renewal.

Item 6: Check this box if you have recorded any Abstracts of Judgment or certified copies of the judgment with any County Recorder's Offices, that is, if you recorded any liens on the debtor's property. Then specify what you recorded by checking the appropriate box. Enter the county(ies) where you recorded the forms, the dates of recording and the instrument number(s), which is the unique number in the upper right hand corner of the Abstract you recorded}.

You can find this information on the documents you recorded or at the recorder's office.

Item 7: Check this box if you created a judgment lien against the debtor's business personal property by filing a Notice of Judgment Lien with the Secretary of State; then enter the file number you were given.

Do not sign or date the Acknowledgment of Satisfaction of Judgment yet; you must do so in front of a notary public [CCP 724.060(b)].

2. Have Your Signature Notarized

Find a notary public. Real estate offices and title companies are good places to call, your bank, the Automobile Club, or you can look in the yellow pages or search the internet.

Take your original Acknowledgment of Satisfaction of Judgment form and ask that your signature be notarized. The notary will ask you to provide some identification, such as your driver's license. After you sign, the notary will fill out a short form for you to attach to the Acknowledgment of Satisfaction of Judgment [Government Code 8211].

3. File and Serve Acknowledgment

You must file the original Acknowledgement of Satisfaction of Judgment, along with the Notary Acknowledgement attachment, with the court. Take two extra copies of the Acknowledgement of Satisfaction of Judgment form with the Attachment and have the court stamp the extra copies. One copy is for you and one is for the debtor.

Have one of the stamped copies served on the debtor. The debtor may be served either personally or by mail with a copy of the Acknowledgment of Satisfaction of Judgment (See Chapter 21 for information on serving papers). Have the person who served the debtor fill out a Proof of Service. They can use either the POS-020 form or the POS-030 form, depending on whether the debtor was served personally or by mail (see Chapter 21). Those forms can be found at http://www.courts.ca.gov/forms.htm.

Finally file the Proof of Service at the court. Be sure to take an extra copy so the court can stamp it and keep a file-stamped copy of the form for your records.

B. Release Any Liens

Once you have officially informed the court that the judgment has been satisfied, you should take steps to release any liens you have created against the debtor's property. The procedures and costs are about the same as recording the lien (See Chapter 4). If you have recorded several liens, this can add up, and it's not money you can recover. But you must still remove the liens or give the debtor the paperwork they need in order to remove the liens themselves. There is no statute that requires you, the creditor, to record the Acknowledgment of Satisfaction of Judgment. As long as you provided the debtor with a file-stamped copy of the Acknowledgement of Satisfaction of Judgment, then the debtor can record it [CCP 724.040]. You had the right to collect and the debtor has the right to have liens removed.

1. Real Estate Liens

If you recorded an Abstract of Judgment with any county recorder, you have two choices. You must either record a certified copy of the Acknowledgment with that county recorder or send a certified copy of the Acknowledgment to the debtor (one for each county where you recorded an Abstract), along with a letter telling them that they will have to record the document in order to release the lien (see sample letter, below). Once the Acknowledgment is filed with the county recorder, the judgment lien is released.

2. Business Personal Property Liens

If you created a judgment lien on any business personal property belonging to the debtor by filing a Notice of Judgment Lien with the California Secretary of State, you'll need to file a form called Judgment Lien

Change Form (Form JL3) in order to release the lien [CCP 697.650]. This form can be found at http://www.sos.ca.gov/business-programs/ucc/judgment-lien-amendment/. A sample completed form is below. Instructions are printed on the back of the form, but three items require further explanation.

Item 2: Be sure NOT to check this box}

Item 5: Be sure to check this box

Item 7: In this space, write "All property subject to judgment lien #" In the blank, insert the number the Secretary of State assigned to your judgment lien.

Once you have completed the form, send the original and one copy to the Secretary of State's office at P.O. Box 942835, Sacramento, CA 94235-0001, along with a $10 filing fee. Once the State mails you confirmation that the form has been filed, serve a copy of the Release on the debtor.

Sample Letter to Debtor to Release Lien

September 26, 2015

Jeff Isbad
666 e Cra P st
Helltown, Ca 90666

Dear Jeff,

I have enclosed a certified, notarized copy of the Acknowledgment of Satisfaction of Judgment. I filed this document with the Los Angeles County Superior Court on September 24, 2015. The document informs the court that you have paid the judgment in full.

As you know, I recorded a real estate lien against your property in Los Angeles County. In order to release this lien, you need to record the enclosed Acknowledgment with the recorder's office in Los Angeles County. Unless and until you record this acknowledgment, the county's property records will continue to show that you have a lien against your property.

Sincerely,

Amy Right

EJ-100

ATTORNEY OR PARTY WITHOUT ATTORNEY (Name, address, and State Bar number):
After recording, return to:

Amy Right
1000 My st
Mytown, Ca 90000

TEL NO.: 310-555-5555   FAX NO. (optional):
E-MAIL ADDRESS (Optional):

[ ] ATTORNEY FOR   [X] JUDGMENT CREDITOR   [ ] ASSIGNEE OF RECORD

SUPERIOR COURT OF CALIFORNIA, COUNTY OF Los Angeles
STREET ADDRESS: 111 Hill st
MAILING ADDRESS:
CITY AND ZIP CODE: Los Angeles, Ca 90012
BRANCH NAME: Stanley Mosk Courthouse

PLAINTIFF: Amy Right
DEFENDANT: Jeff Isbad

CASE NUMBER: 14K5000

ACKNOWLEDGMENT OF SATISFACTION OF JUDGMENT
[X] FULL   [ ] PARTIAL   [ ] MATURED INSTALLMENT

1. Satisfaction of the judgment is acknowledged as follows:
   a. [X] Full satisfaction
      (1) [X] Judgment is satisfied in full.
      (2) [ ] The judgment creditor has accepted payment or performance other than that specified in the judgment in full satisfaction of the judgment.
   b. [ ] Partial satisfaction
      The amount received in partial satisfaction of the judgment is $
   c. [ ] Matured installment
      All matured installments under the installment judgment have been satisfied as of (date):

2. Full name and address of judgment creditor:*
   Amy Right
   1000 My st, Mytown, Ca 90000

3. Full name and address of assignee of record, if any:

4. Full name and address of judgment debtor being fully or partially released:*
   Jeff Isbad
   666 e Cra P st, Helltown, Ca 90666

5. a. Judgment entered on (date): 01/01/2014
   b. [ ] Renewal entered on (date):

6. [X] An [X] abstract of judgment [ ] certified copy of the judgment has been recorded as follows (complete all information for each county where recorded):

COUNTY	DATE OF RECORDING	INSTRUMENT NUMBER
Los Angeles	02/01/2014	1420000005

7. [ ] A notice of judgment lien has been filed in the office of the Secretary of State as file number (specify):

NOTICE TO JUDGMENT DEBTOR: If this is an acknowledgment of full satisfaction of judgment, it will have to be recorded in each county shown in item 6 above, if any, in order to release the judgment lien, and will have to be filed in the office of the Secretary of State to terminate any judgment lien on personal property.

Date: 12/31/2016

▶

(SIGNATURE OF JUDGMENT CREDITOR OR ASSIGNEE OF CREDITOR OR ATTORNEY**)

*The names of the judgment creditor and judgment debtor must be stated as shown in any Abstract of Judgment which was recorded and is being released by this satisfaction. ** A separate notary acknowledgment must be attached for each signature.

Form Approved for Optional Use
Judicial Council of California
EJ-100 [Rev. July 1, 2014]

ACKNOWLEDGMENT OF SATISFACTION OF JUDGMENT

Code of Civil Procedure, §§ 724.060, 724.120, 724.250

JUDGMENT LIEN CHANGE FORM

FOLLOW INSTRUCTIONS CAREFULLY (front and back of form)

A. NAME & PHONE NUMBER OF FILER'S CONTACT (optional)

B. SEND ACKNOWLEDGMENT TO: (Name and Address)

THE ABOVE SPACE IS FOR FILING OFFICE USE ONLY

1a. SECRETARY OF STATE FILE NO. (Original Notice of Judgment Lien)

1b. DATE OF FILING ORIGINAL NOTICE OF JUDGMENT LIEN

2. NOTICE OF CONTINUATION OF JUDGMENT LIEN ON PERSONAL PROPERTY

☐ THIS NOTICE IS FILED TO CONTINUE THE EFFECTIVENESS OF THE NOTICE OF JUDGMENT LIEN IDENTIFIED IN ITEMS 1a & 1b. (California Code of Civil Procedure section 697.510.)

3. JUDGMENT DEBTOR'S EXACT LEGAL NAME – Insert a name in 3a or 3b only. Do not abbreviate or combine names.

3a. ORGANIZATION'S NAME

3b. INDIVIDUAL'S LAST NAME	FIRST NAME	MIDDLE NAME		SUFFIX
3c. MAILING ADDRESS	CITY	STATE	POSTAL CODE	COUNTRY

4. JUDGMENT CREDITOR'S EXACT NAME – Insert a name in 4a or 4b only. Do not abbreviate or combine names.

4a. ORGANIZATION'S NAME

4b. INDIVIDUAL'S LAST NAME	FIRST NAME	MIDDLE NAME		SUFFIX
4c. MAILING ADDRESS	CITY	STATE	POSTAL CODE	COUNTRY

5. RELEASE OF JUDGMENT LIEN ON PERSONAL PROPERTY

☐ THE JUDGMENT LIEN ON THE PERSONAL PROPERTY SUBJECT TO LIEN IS HEREBY RELEASED AS DESCRIBED IN ITEM 7 BELOW. (California Code of Civil Procedure section 697.650.)

6. SUBORDINATION OF JUDGMENT LIEN ON PERSONAL PROPERTY

☐ THE JUDGMENT LIEN ON THE PERSONAL PROPERTY SUBJECT TO LIEN IS HEREBY SUBORDINATED AS DESCRIBED IN ITEM 7 BELOW. (California Code of Civil Procedure section 697.650.)

7. DESCRIPTION OF RELEASE OR SUBORDINATION OF PERSONAL PROPERTY

8.

SIGNATURE OF JUDGMENT CREDITOR (See instructions for Item 8.)   DATE

FOR _____

FILING OFFICE COPY   JUDGMENT LIEN (FORM JL3) - (REV. 04/2010)   APPROVED BY SECRETARY OF STATE

Blank Page

Appendix

Sample Forms

This Appendix contains a blank copy of most of the forms you will need to complete the procedures covered in this book. A completed sample is available in the Chapter named.

Form	Chapter
Cover Letter to Clerk /Instructions to Levying Officer	Throughout
Numbered Pleading Paper	Throughout
Change of Address	1
Substitution of Attorney	1
Abstract of Judgment /Abstract of Support Judgment	4
Notice of Judgment Lien on Personal Property	4
Financial Statement (Income and Expense Statement)	5
Declaration of Default in Payment of Judgment/Order	5B
Declaration Re: Default in Installment Payments and Order	5B
Declaration of Default Re: Stipulated Agreement and Judgment	5B
Application and Order for Appearance and Examination	6
Subpoena	6
Questions for Debtor's Examination	6
Writ of Execution	7
Application for Federal Employee Commercial Garnishment	9
Application for Earnings Withholding Order	9
Notice of Opposition to Claim of Exemption (Wage Garnishment)	15
Notice of Opposition to Claim of Exemption (Levy)	15
Notice of hearing on Claim of Exemption (Wage & Levy)	15
Memorandum of Costs After Judgment	16
Attachment (can be used with any Judicial Council form)	16
Keeping Track of Costs	16
Keeping Track of Payments	16
Proof of Claim	17
Creditor's Claim	18
Application for and Renewal of Judgment	20
Notice of Renewal of Judgment	20
Proof of Service	21
Acknowledgment of Satisfaction of Judgment	22
Notice of Judgment Lien Release or Subordination	22

Tips on Using Forms

- Never fill out forms without making photocopies first. You may make a mistake, or you may need another copy of the original form later on.
- If a form has printing on both sides, make sure you copy both sides. You can make a two-sided copy or you can copy them on two single-sided pages and staple them together.
- When preparing documents on Pleading Paper, always type on one side only. Use Times Roman font, size 12.
- Carefully follow the instructions in this book for completing the forms. Use the completed samples as guides.
- If possible, type the forms. If that is not possible, print clearly and neatly.
- Whenever you send forms to the court or levying officer, keep copies for yourself. Forms can get lost in the mail, get misplaced by a clerk or end up in the twilight zone.
- If you type up your forms on Pleading paper, remember to include the name of the form in the footing (bottom of page).

Judicial Council Forms

Many of the forms you will be using are published by the California Judicial Council for use in all California Courts. At the bottom of each Judicial Council Form is its title, the form number and the revision date.

The forms were current when this book was published. Judicial Council forms are subject to change, however. We suggest that you fill out these forms at the Court's website. These forms can be filled out online and printed out as a completely typed forms. This way you will always be using the most up-to-date forms available.

The website is:

http://www.courts.ca.gov/forms.htm

Cover Letter to Clerk

Date:_____

To: _____
    _____
    _____
    _____

Re: _____ v. _____

Court: _____

Case No. _____

Dear Clerk:

Enclosed please find:

1) Original and _____ copy/copies of the following document(s):

_____
_____
_____
_____

2) Check in the amount of $ _____ (if required);

3) Self-addressed stamped envelope; and

4) Other:

_____
_____
_____
_____

Please file, issue or file these documents and return conformed copies to me.

Sincerely,

_____

Address:

_____
_____
_____

Phone: (____) _____-_____

Instructions to Levying Officer

Date:_____

Instructions to Levying Officer, County of _____

Please take the action described below to enforce this court judgment. Please hole the Writ for its entire 180-day duration, or until the judgment has been satisfied, unless I contact and instruct you differently.

1. Case Information:

   Case: _____ v. _____

   Court: _____

   Case No. _____

2. Enclosures:

   ☐ Original Writ of Execution and _____ copy/copies.

   ☐ Check or money order in the amount of $ _____

   ☐ Separate written levy instructions (Check only if applicable)

3. Levy Instructions:

   ☐ Type of Levy: _____

   ☐ Please proceed as follows: _____

   _____
   _____
   _____
   _____
   _____
   _____
   _____
   _____

Sincerely,   Address:

_____   _____
                                                  _____
                                                  _____

Printed name: Phone No.

_____   (_____) _____-_____

Numbered Pleading Paper

Change of Address

	MC-040
ATTORNEY OR PARTY WITHOUT ATTORNEY *(Name, State Bar number, and address):*	FOR COURT USE ONLY
TELEPHONE NO.: FAX NO. *(Optional):*	
E-MAIL ADDRESS *(Optional):*	
ATTORNEY FOR *(Name):*	

SUPERIOR COURT OF CALIFORNIA, COUNTY OF
STREET ADDRESS:
MAILING ADDRESS:
CITY AND ZIP CODE:
BRANCH NAME:

PLAINTIFF/PETITIONER:

DEFENDANT/RESPONDENT:

NOTICE OF CHANGE OF ADDRESS OR OTHER CONTACT INFORMATION	CASE NUMBER:
	JUDICIAL OFFICER:
	DEPT.:

1. **Please take notice** that, as of *(date):*
   ☐ the following self-represented party or
   ☐ the attorney for:
      a. ☐ plaintiff *(name):*
      b. ☐ defendant *(name):*
      c. ☐ petitioner *(name):*
      d. ☐ respondent *(name):*
      e. ☐ other *(describe):*

   has **changed his or her address** for service of notices and documents or other contact information in the above-captioned action.
   ☐ A list of additional parties represented is provided in Attachment 1.

2. The **new address** or other contact information for *(name):*
   is as follows:
   a. Street:
   b. City:
   c. Mailing address *(if different from above):*
   d. State and zip code:
   e. Telephone number:
   f. Fax number (if available):
   g. E-mail address (if available):

3. **All notices and documents** regarding the action should be sent to the above address.
   Date:

   ▸ _____
   (TYPE OR PRINT NAME)   (SIGNATURE OF PARTY OR ATTORNEY)

Form Approved for Optional Use
Judicial Council of California
MC-040 [Rev. January 1, 2013]

NOTICE OF CHANGE OF ADDRESS OR OTHER CONTACT INFORMATION

Cal. Rules of Court, rules 2.200 and 8.816
www.courts.ca.gov

		MC-040
PLAINTIFF/PETITIONER: DEFENDANT/RESPONDENT:	CASE NUMBER:	

PROOF OF SERVICE BY FIRST-CLASS MAIL
NOTICE OF CHANGE OF ADDRESS OR OTHER CONTACT INFORMATION

(NOTE: This page may be used for proof of service by first-class mail of the **Notice of Change of Address or Other Contact Information**. *Please use a different proof of service, such as* **Proof of Service—Civil** *(form POS-040), if you serve this notice by a method other than first class-mail, such as by fax or electronic service. You cannot serve the* **Notice of Change of Address or Other Contact Information** *if you are a party in the action. The person who served the notice must complete this proof of service.)*

1. At the time of service, I was at least 18 years old and **not a party to this action.**

2. I am a resident of or employed in the county where the mailing took place. My residence or business address is *(specify):*

3. I served a copy of the *Notice of Change of Address or Other Contact Information* by enclosing it in a sealed envelope addressed to the persons at the addresses listed in item 5 and *(check one):*
   a. ☐ deposited the sealed envelope with the United States Postal Service with postage fully prepaid.
   b. ☐ placed the sealed envelope for collection and for mailing, following our ordinary business practices. I am readily familiar with this business's practice for collecting and processing correspondence for mailing. On the same day correspondence is placed for collection and mailing, it is deposited in the ordinary course of business with the United States Postal Service in a sealed envelope with postage fully prepaid.

4. The *Notice of Change of Address or Other Contact Information* was placed in the mail:
   a. on *(date):*
   b. at *(city and state):*

5. The envelope was addressed and mailed as follows:

   a. Name of person served:

   Street address:
   City:
   State and zip code:

   b. Name of person served:

   Street address:
   City:
   State and zip code:

   c. Name of person served:

   Street address:
   City:
   State and zip code:

   d. Name of person served:

   Street address:
   City:
   State and zip code:

☐ Names and addresses of additional persons served are attached. *(You may use form POS-030(P).)*

I declare under penalty of perjury under the laws of the State of California that the foregoing is true and correct.

Date:

▶

_____ _____
(TYPE OR PRINT NAME OF DECLARANT)   (SIGNATURE OF DECLARANT)

NOTICE OF CHANGE OF ADDRESS OR OTHER CONTACT INFORMATION

Substitution of Attorney

MC-050

ATTORNEY OR PARTY WITHOUT ATTORNEY *(Name, State Bar number, and address)*:	FOR COURT USE ONLY
TELEPHONE NO.: FAX NO. *(Optional)*:	
E-MAIL ADDRESS *(Optional)*:	
ATTORNEY FOR *(Name)*:	

SUPERIOR COURT OF CALIFORNIA, COUNTY OF
STREET ADDRESS:
MAILING ADDRESS:
CITY AND ZIP CODE:
BRANCH NAME:
CASE NAME:

SUBSTITUTION OF ATTORNEY—CIVIL (Without Court Order)	CASE NUMBER:

THE COURT AND ALL PARTIES ARE NOTIFIED THAT *(name)*:   makes the following substitution:

1. **Former legal representative** ☐ Party represented self   ☐ Attorney *(name)*:
2. **New legal representative** ☐ Party is representing self*   ☐ Attorney
   a. Name: b. State Bar No. *(if applicable)*:
   c. Address *(number, street, city, ZIP, and law firm name, if applicable)*:

   d. Telephone No. *(include area code)*:
3. The party making this substitution is a   ☐ plaintiff   ☐ defendant   ☐ petitioner   ☐ respondent   ☐ other *(specify)*:

---

*NOTICE TO PARTIES APPLYING TO REPRESENT THEMSELVES

- Guardian
- Conservator
- Trustee
- Personal Representative
- Probate fiduciary
- Corporation
- Guardian ad litem
- Unincorporated association

If you are applying as one of the parties on this list, you may NOT act as your own attorney in most cases. Use this form to substitute one attorney for another attorney. SEEK LEGAL ADVICE BEFORE APPLYING TO REPRESENT YOURSELF.

NOTICE TO PARTIES WITHOUT ATTORNEYS
A party representing himself or herself may wish to seek legal assistance. Failure to take timely and appropriate action in this case may result in serious legal consequences.

---

4. I consent to this substitution.
   Date:

   _____   ▶ _____
   (TYPE OR PRINT NAME)   (SIGNATURE OF PARTY)

5. ☐ I consent to this substitution.
   Date:

   _____   ▶ _____
   (TYPE OR PRINT NAME)   (SIGNATURE OF FORMER ATTORNEY)

6. ☐ I consent to this substitution.
   Date:

   _____   ▶ _____
   (TYPE OR PRINT NAME)   (SIGNATURE OF NEW ATTORNEY)

(See reverse for proof of service by mail)

Form Adopted For Mandatory Use
Judicial Council of California
MC-050 [Rev. January 1, 2009]

SUBSTITUTION OF ATTORNEY—CIVIL
(Without Court Order)

Code of Civil Procedure, §§ 284(1), 285;
Cal. Rules of Court, rule 3.1362
www.courtinfo.ca.gov

CASE NAME:	CASE NUMBER:

MC-050

PROOF OF SERVICE BY MAIL
Substitution of Attorney—Civil

Instructions: After having all parties served by mail with the Substitution of Attorney—Civil, have the person who mailed the document complete this Proof of Service by Mail. An <u>unsigned</u> copy of the Proof of Service by Mail should be completed and served with the document. Give the Substitution of Attorney—Civil and the completed Proof of Service by Mail to the clerk for filing. If you are representing yourself, someone else must mail these papers and sign the Proof of Service by Mail.

1. I am over the age of 18 and **not a party to this cause.** I am a resident of or employed in the county where the mailing occurred. My residence or business address is *(specify):*

2. I served the Substitution of Attorney—Civil by enclosing a true copy in a sealed envelope addressed to each person whose name and address is shown below and depositing the envelope in the United States mail with the postage fully prepaid.

    (1) Date of mailing: (2) Place of mailing *(city and state):*

3. I declare under penalty of perjury under the laws of the State of California that the foregoing is true and correct.

Date:

_____   _____
(TYPE OR PRINT NAME)   (SIGNATURE)

NAME AND ADDRESS OF EACH PERSON TO WHOM NOTICE WAS MAILED

4. a. Name of person served:
   b. Address *(number, street, city, and ZIP):*

   c. Name of person served:
   d. Address *(number, street, city, and ZIP):*

   e. Name of person served:
   f. Address *(number, street, city, and ZIP):*

   g. Name of person served:
   h. Address *(number, street, city, and ZIP):*

   i. Name of person served:
   j. Address *(number, street, city, and ZIP):*

   ☐ List of names and addresses continued in attachment.

MC-050 [Rev. January 1, 2009]

SUBSTITUTION OF ATTORNEY—CIVIL
(Without Court Order)

Abstract of Judgment

EJ-001

ATTORNEY OR PARTY WITHOUT ATTORNEY *(Name, address, and State Bar number):*
After recording, return to:

TEL NO.: FAX NO. *(optional):*
E-MAIL ADDRESS *(Optional):*
☐ ATTORNEY FOR ☐ JUDGMENT CREDITOR ☐ ASSIGNEE OF RECORD

SUPERIOR COURT OF CALIFORNIA, COUNTY OF
STREET ADDRESS:
MAILING ADDRESS:
CITY AND ZIP CODE:
BRANCH NAME:

FOR RECORDER'S USE ONLY

PLAINTIFF:
DEFENDANT:

CASE NUMBER:

ABSTRACT OF JUDGMENT—CIVIL AND SMALL CLAIMS ☐ Amended

FOR COURT USE ONLY

1. The ☐ judgment creditor ☐ assignee of record applies for an abstract of judgment and represents the following:
   a. Judgment debtor's
      Name and last known address

   b. Driver's license no. [last 4 digits] and state: ☐ Unknown
   c. Social security no. [last 4 digits]: ☐ Unknown
   d. Summons or notice of entry of sister-state judgment was personally served or mailed to *(name and address):*

2. ☐ Information on additional judgment debtors is shown on page 2.
3. Judgment creditor *(name and address):*

4. ☐ Information on additional judgment creditors is shown on page 2.
5. ☐ Original abstract recorded in this county:
   a. Date:
   b. Instrument No.:

Date:

_____
(TYPE OR PRINT NAME)

_____
(SIGNATURE OF APPLICANT OR ATTORNEY)

6. Total amount of judgment as entered or last renewed:
   $
7. All judgment creditors and debtors are listed on this abstract.
8. a. Judgment entered on *(date):*
   b. Renewal entered on *(date):*
9. ☐ This judgment is an installment judgment.

[SEAL]

10. ☐ An ☐ execution lien ☐ attachment lien is endorsed on the judgment as follows:
    a. Amount: $
    b. In favor of *(name and address):*

11. A stay of enforcement has
    a. ☐ not been ordered by the court.
    b. ☐ been ordered by the court effective until *(date):*
12. a. ☐ I certify that this is a true and correct abstract of the judgment entered in this action.
    b. ☐ A certified copy of the judgment is attached.

This abstract issued on *(date):*

Clerk, by _____, Deputy

Form Adopted for Mandatory Use
Judicial Council of California
EJ-001 [Rev. July 1, 2014]

ABSTRACT OF JUDGMENT—CIVIL AND SMALL CLAIMS

Page 1 of 2
Code of Civil Procedure, §§ 488.480, 674, 700.190

Abstract of Support Judgment

FL-480

ATTORNEY OR PARTY WITHOUT ATTORNEY *(name, address, and State Bar number):*
After recording, return to:

TEL NO.: FAX NO. *(optional):*
E-MAIL ADDRESS *(optional):*
[ ] ATTORNEY FOR [ ] JUDGMENT CREDITOR [ ] ASSIGNEE OF RECORD

SUPERIOR COURT OF CALIFORNIA, COUNTY OF
STREET ADDRESS:
MAILING ADDRESS:
CITY AND ZIP CODE:
BRANCH NAME:

PETITIONER/PLAINTIFF:
RESPONDENT/DEFENDANT:

ABSTRACT OF SUPPORT JUDGMENT

FOR RECORDER'S USE ONLY

CASE NUMBER:

FOR COURT USE ONLY

1. The [ ] original judgment creditor [ ] assignee of record applies for an abstract of a support judgment and represents the following:
   a. Judgment debtor's
       name and last known address

   b. Driver's license no. and state: [ ] Unknown
   c. Social security number [last four digits]:   [ ] Unknown
   d. Birth date: [ ] Unknown
   Date:

   _____   ▶ _____
   (TYPE OR PRINT NAME)   (SIGNATURE OF APPLICANT OR ATTORNEY)

2. I CERTIFY that the judgment entered in this action contains an order for payment of spousal, family, or child support.

3. Judgment creditor *(name):*
   whose address appears on this form above the court's name.

4. [ ] The support is ordered to be paid to the following county officer *(name and address):*

5. Judgment debtor *(full name as it appears in judgment):*

6. a. A judgment was entered on *(date):*
   b. Renewal was entered on *(date):*
   c. Renewal was entered on *(date):*

7. [ ] An execution lien is endorsed on the judgment as follows:
   a. Amount: $
   b. In favor of *(name and address):*

[SEAL]

8. A stay of enforcement has
   a. [ ] not been ordered by the court.
   b. [ ] been ordered by the court effective until *(date):*

9. [ ] This is an installment judgment.

This abstract issued on *(date):*

Clerk, by _____, Deputy

Page 1 of 1

Form Adopted for Mandatory Use
Judicial Council of California
FL-480 [Rev. January 1, 2015]

ABSTRACT OF SUPPORT JUDGMENT

Code of Civil Procedure, §§ 488.480, 674, 697.320, 700.190
www.courts.ca.gov

Notice of Judgment Lien on Personal Property

NOTICE OF JUDGMENT LIEN
FOLLOW INSTRUCTIONS CAREFULLY (front and back of form)

A. NAME & PHONE OF FILER'S CONTACT (optional)

B. SEND ACKNOWLEDGMENT TO: (NAME AND ADDRESS)

THIS SPACE FOR FILING OFFICE USE ONLY

1. JUDGMENT DEBTOR'S EXACT LEGAL NAME – Insert only one name, either 1a or 1b. Do not abbreviate or combine names.

1a. ORGANIZATION'S NAME

1b. INDIVIDUAL'S LAST NAME	FIRST NAME	MIDDLE NAME	SUFFIX
1c. MAILING ADDRESS	CITY	STATE	POSTAL CODE	COUNTRY

2. JUDGMENT CREDITOR'S NAME – Do not abbreviate or combine names.

2a. ORGANIZATION'S NAME

2b. INDIVIDUAL'S LAST NAME	FIRST NAME	MIDDLE	SUFFIX
2c. MAILING ADDRESS	CITY	STATE	POSTAL CODE	COUNTRY

3. ALL PROPERTY SUBJECT TO ENFORCEMENT OF A MONEY JUDGMENT AGAINST THE JUDGMENT DEBTOR TO WHICH A JUDGMENT LIEN ON PERSONAL PROPERTY MAY ATTACH UNDER SECTION 697.530 OF THE CODE OF CIVIL PROCEDURE IS SUBJECT TO THIS JUDGMENT LIEN.

    A. Title of court where judgment was entered: _____

    B. Title of the action: _____

    C. Number of this action: _____

    D. Date judgment was entered: _____

    E. Date of subsequent renewals of judgment (if any): _____

    F. Amount required to satisfy judgment at date of this notice: $ _____

    G. Date of this notice: _____

4. I declare under penalty of perjury under the laws of the State of California that the foregoing is true and correct:

_____ Dated: _____
SIGNATURE – SEE INSTRUCTION NO. 4   (If not indicated, use same as date in item 3G.)

FOR: _____

FILING OFFICE COPY

NOTICE OF JUDGMENT LIEN (FORM JL1) (Rev. 6/01)
Approved by the Secretary of State

JUDGMENT LIEN ADDENDUM
FOLLOW INSTRUCTIONS CAREFULLY (FRONT AND BACK OF FORM)

5. NAME OF JUDGMENT DEBTOR: (NAME OF FIRST DEBTOR ON RELATED JUDGMENT LIEN)

5a. ORGANIZATION'S NAME			
5b. INDIVIDUAL'S LAST NAME	FIRST NAME	MIDDLE NAME	SUFFIX

6. ADDITIONAL JUDGMENT DEBTOR – insert only one name (6a or 6b):

6a. ORGANIZATION'S NAME				
6b. INDIVIDUAL'S LAST NAME	FIRST NAME	MIDDLE NAME		SUFFIX
6c. MAILING ADDRESS	CITY	STATE	POSTAL CODE	COUNTRY

7. ADDITIONAL JUDGMENT DEBTOR – insert only one name (7a or 7b):

7a. ORGANIZATION'S NAME				
7b. INDIVIDUAL'S LAST NAME	FIRST NAME	MIDDLE NAME		SUFFIX
7c. MAILING ADDRESS	CITY	STATE	POSTAL CODE	COUNTRY

8. ADDITIONAL JUDGMENT DEBTOR – insert only one name (8a or 8b):

8a. ORGANIZATION'S NAME				
8b. INDIVIDUAL'S LAST NAME	FIRST NAME	MIDDLE NAME		SUFFIX
8c. MAILING ADDRESS	CITY	STATE	POSTAL CODE	COUNTRY

9. ADDITIONAL JUDGMENT CREDITOR – insert only one name (9a or 9b):

9a. ORGANIZATION'S NAME				
9b. INDIVIDUAL'S LAST NAME	FIRST NAME	MIDDLE NAME		SUFFIX
9c. MAILING ADDRESS	CITY	STATE	POSTAL CODE	COUNTRY

10. ADDITIONAL JUDGMENT CREDITOR – insert only one name (10a or 10b):

10a. ORGANIZATION'S NAME				
10b. INDIVIDUAL'S LAST NAME	FIRST NAME	MIDDLE NAME		SUFFIX
10c. MAILING ADDRESS	CITY	STATE	POSTAL CODE	COUNTRY

(1) FILING OFFICER COPY – JUDGMENT LIEN ADDENDUM FORM (REV. 6/01)

CA Secretary of State

Financial Statement (Income & Expense Statement)

SHORT TITLE:	LEVYING OFFICER FILE NO.	COURT CASE NO.

WG-007/EJ-165

FINANCIAL STATEMENT
(Wage Garnishment—Enforcement of Judgment)

NOTE: If you are married, this form must be signed by your spouse unless you and your spouse are living separate and apart. If this form is not signed by your spouse, check the applicable box on the reverse in item 9.

1. The following persons other than myself depend, in whole or in part, on me or my spouse for support:

	NAME	AGE	RELATIONSHIP TO ME	MONTHLY TAKE-HOME INCOME & SOURCE
a.			Spouse	
b.				
c.				
d.				
e.				

2. My monthly income
   a. My gross monthly pay is: .... 2a. $ _____
   b. My payroll deductions are (specify *purpose* and amount):
      (1) Federal and state withholding, FICA, and SDI. . . . . $ _____
      (2) _____ $ _____
      (3) _____ $ _____
      (4) _____ $ _____
      My TOTAL payroll deduction amount is (add (1) through (4)): .... b. $ _____
   c. My monthly take-home pay is (a minus b): .... c. $ _____
   d. Other money I get each month from (specify source):
      _____ is .... d. $ _____

   e. **TOTAL MONTHLY INCOME** (c plus d) .... e. $ _____

3. I, my spouse, and my other dependents own the following property:
   a. Cash .... 3a. $ _____
   b. Checking, savings, and credit union accounts (list banks):
      (1) _____ $ _____
      (2) _____ $ _____
      (3) _____ $ _____   b. $ _____
   c. Cars, other vehicles, and boat equity (list make, year of each):
      (1) _____ $ _____
      (2) _____ $ _____
      (3) _____ $ _____   c. $ _____
   d. Real estate equity .... d. $ _____
   e. Other personal property (jewelry, furniture, furs, stocks, bonds, etc.) (list separately):

   e. $ _____

Form Adopted by the Judicial Council of California
WG-007/EJ-165 [Rev. January 1, 2007]

FINANCIAL STATEMENT
(Wage Garnishment—Enforcement of Judgment)

Code of Civil Procedure, §§ 706.124, 703.530
www.courtinfo.ca.gov

SHORT TITLE:	LEVYING OFFICER FILE NO.	COURT CASE NO.

WG-007/EJ-165

4. **The monthly expenses for me, my spouse, and my other dependents**
   a. Rent or house payment and maintenance .... 4 a. $ _____
   b. Food and household supplies .... b. $ _____
   c. Utilities and telephone .... c. $ _____
   d. Clothing .... d. $ _____
   e. Medical and dental payments .... e. $ _____
   f. Insurance (life, health, accident, etc.) .... f. $ _____
   g. School, child care .... g. $ _____
   h. Child, spousal support (prior marriage) .... h. $ _____
   I. Transportation & auto expenses (insurance, gas, repair) *(list car payments in item 5)* .... i. $ _____
   j. Installment payments *(insert total and itemize below in item 5)* .... j. $ _____
   k. Laundry and cleaning .... k. $ _____
   l. Entertainment .... l. $ _____
   m. Other *(specify):*

   m. $ _____

   n. **TOTAL MONTHLY EXPENSES** *(add a through m):* .... n. $ _____

5. **I, my spouse, and my other dependents owe the following debts:**

CREDITOR'S NAME	FOR	MO. PAYMENTS	BALANCE OWED	OWED BY *(State person's name)*

6. Other facts which support this Claim of Exemption (i.e., unusual medical needs, school tuition, expenses for recent family emergencies, or other unusual expenses to help your creditor and the judge understand your budget) *(describe):* *(If more space is needed, attach page labeled Attachment 6.)*

7. ☐ An earnings withholding order is now in effect with respect to my earnings or those of my spouse or dependents named in item 1 (specify *each person's name and monthly amount*):

8. ☐ A wage assignment for support is now in effect with respect to my earnings or those of my spouse or dependents named in item 1 (specify *each person's name and monthly amount*):

9. ☐ My spouse has signed below.
   ☐ I have no spouse.
   ☐ My spouse and I are living separate and apart.

I declare under penalty of perjury under the laws of the State of California that the foregoing is true and correct.

Date:

_____   ▶ _____
(TYPE OR PRINT NAME)   *(SIGNATURE)*

_____   ▶ _____
(TYPE OR PRINT NAME OF SPOUSE)   *(SIGNATURE OF SPOUSE)*

WG-007/EJ-165 [Rev. January 1, 2007]

FINANCIAL STATEMENT
(Wage Garnishment—Enforcement of Judgment)

Declaration of Default in Payment of Judgment

| SC-223 | **Declaration of Default in Payment of Judgment** | *Clerk stamps here when form is filed.* |

Important: Read the other side before you fill out this form or if it was mailed to you. If you are the judgment debtor named in ② and you disagree with this *Declaration of Default in Payment of Judgment*, you may file *Response to Declaration of Default in Payment of Judgment* (Form SC-224) within 10 days after the declaration was mailed to you.

① I am asking the court to order that the remaining balance of a small claims judgment is now due and collectible because payments were not made as the court ordered.

My name is: _____

Mailing address: _____

_____

Phone: _____ E-mail *(optional)*: _____

Fill in the court name and street address:

Superior Court of California, County of

② The judgment debtor who has not made payments as the court ordered is *(complete a separate form for each judgment debtor who has not paid as ordered)*:

Name: _____

Mailing address: _____

_____

Phone: _____ E-mail *(optional)*: _____

Fill in your case number and case name:

Case Number:

Case Name:

③ On *(date)*: _____ the court ordered that the judgment debtor named in ② must pay me, or someone who assigned the judgment to me, principal, prejudgment interest, and costs in the total amount of $_____.

④ On *(date)*: _____ the court ordered that the judgment debtor named in ② may pay the judgment described in ③ as follows:

  a. ☐ Payments of $_____ on the _____ day of each *(month, week, other)*: _____
     starting *(date)*: _____, until *(date of final payment)*: _____; amount of final payment: $_____

  b. ☐ Other payment schedule *(specify)*: _____

⑤ The payments listed below, and no others, have been made on the judgment described in ③.

  ☐ *Check here if there is not enough space below. List the date and amount of each payment on a separate page and write "SC-223, Item 5" at the top.*

Date	Amount	Date	Amount	Date	Amount	Date	Amount

⑥ The total amount of the payments that have been made on the judgment described in ③ is $_____, and the balance due, without adding any interest after the judgment, is $_____.

⑦ I request interest on the judgment, in the amount of $_____, calculated as follows:

  ☐ *Check here if there is not enough space below. Explain how you calculated interest on a separate page and write "SC-223, Item 7" at the top.*

_____

_____

I declare under penalty of perjury under the laws of the State of California that the information above is true and correct.

Date: _____

▶

Type or print your name   *Sign here*

Judicial Council of California, www.courts.ca.gov
New July 1, 2013, Optional Form
Code of Civil Procedure, § 116.620;
Cal. Rules of Court, rule 3.2107

Declaration of Default in Payment of Judgment
(Small Claims)

Default in Payments on Small Claims Judgment
General Information

If the court ordered that another plaintiff or defendant (judgment debtor) may pay a small claims judgment in payments, and that judgment debtor has not made the payments as ordered, you can ask the court to order that the full balance of the judgment is due and collectible. Here's how:

- Read this form.
- Fill out page 1 of Form SC-223, *Declaration of Default in Payment of Judgment*. Fill out a separate form for each judgment debtor who did not make payments as ordered.
- File your completed form(s) with the small claims court clerk.

The court will mail all other plaintiffs and defendants in the case copies of the *Declaration* and a blank Form SC-224, *Response to Declaration of Default in Payment of Judgment*.

The judgment debtor will have 10 days to file a Response. Then the court will mail all plaintiffs and defendants in the case:

- A decision, or
- A notice to go to a hearing.

If the court ordered that you may make payments on a judgment, and another plaintiff, defendant, or person to whom the judgment has been assigned (judgment creditor) has filed Form SC-223, *Declaration of Default in Payment of Judgment*, asking the court to order that the full balance is now due and collectible because you did not make the payments:

- Read this form and the *Declaration*.
- If you agree with the court ordering that the amounts claimed in the *Declaration* are now due in full, you do not need to do anything.
- **If you do not agree with the *Declaration* or with the court ordering that the amounts it claims are now due in full, file a *Response* within 10 calendar days after the court clerk mailed the *Declaration* to you.** (This date is on the *Clerk's Certificate of Mailing*.)

To file your *Response*:

- Fill out Form SC-224, *Response to Declaration of Default in Payment of Judgment*.
- Have your *Response* served on the judgment creditor and all other plaintiffs and defendants in your case. (See Form SC-112A, *Proof of Service by Mail*.)
- File your *Response* and *Proof of Service* with the small claims court clerk.

Answers to Common Questions

When is the judgment due?
Unless the court orders otherwise, small claims judgments are due immediately. If the judgment is not paid in full within 30 days, the judgment creditor (person to whom the money is owed) can take legal steps to collect any unpaid amount. (Collection may be postponed if an appeal or a request to vacate (cancel) or correct the judgment is filed.)

When can the judgment debtor make payments?
A plaintiff or defendant who was ordered to pay a small claims judgment (judgment debtor) can ask the court for permission to make payments. If the court agrees, the plaintiff or defendant who is owed money (the judgment creditor) cannot take any other steps to collect the money as long as the payments are made on time. If payments are not made on time, the judgment creditor can ask the court to order that the remaining balance of the judgment is due and collectible.

Is interest added after the judgment?
Interest (10 percent per year) is usually added to the unpaid amount of the judgment from the date the judgment is entered until it is paid in full. Interest can only be charged on the unpaid amount of the judgment (the principal); interest cannot be charged on any unpaid interest. If a partial payment is received, the money is applied first to unpaid interest and then to unpaid principal.

When the court allows payments, the court often does not order any interest, as long as all payments are made in full and on time. Unless the judgment creditor asks for interest to be included in the order allowing payments, the judgment creditor may lose any claims for interest. But if the judgment debtor does not make full payments on time, interest on the missed payment or the entire unpaid balance might become due and collectible.

How do I calculate interest?
If you are asking for interest or disagreeing with a request for interest, you need to explain your interest calculation. Interest, at the rate of 10 percent per year (.0274 percent per day), may be added to the full unpaid balance of the judgment or only to payments that were not made on time. To calculate interest, show the unpaid principal balance, the dates and number of days you want the court to allow interest on that amount, and the total interest for that period. If payments were made, you will need to make separate calculations for the reduced principal balance after each payment.

 Need help?
For free help, contact your county's small claims advisor:

Or go to *www.courts.ca.gov/smallclaims/advisor*

Declaration of Default in Payment of Judgment
(Small Claims)

Order on Declaration of Default in Payments

SC-225 Order on Declaration of Default in Payments

Clerk stamps here when form is filed.

① A judgment was entered in this case on *(date):* _____
against *(name of judgment debtor):* _____

② On *(date):* _____, the court ordered that the judgment debtor named in ① may pay the judgment as follows:

  a. ☐ Payments of $_____, on the _____ day of each *(month, week, other):* _____
  starting *(date):* _____
  until *(date of final payment):* _____,
  amount of final payment: $_____

  b. ☐ The payment schedule is stated on Form SC-225A, item ①.

③ On *(date):* _____ the judgment creditor *(name):*
_____
informed the court that the judgment debtor had not made one or more payments as provided in ② and asked the court to order that the remaining balance of the judgment is due and collectible.

④ ☐ On *(date):* _____ the judgment debtor filed a response to the judgment creditor's request.

Fill in the court name and street address:
Superior Court of California, County of

Fill in your case number and case name:
Case Number:

Case Name:

The court orders:

⑤ ☐ **The payment order referred to in** ② *(check one):*
  a. ☐ is terminated and the balance of the judgment is collectible.
  b. ☐ remains in effect, without modification.
  c. ☐ is modified as stated on Form SC-225A, item ②.

⑥ ☐ **The following amounts are owing on the judgment as of** *(date):* _____
  a. ☐ Principal balance of judgment and costs included in judgment *(amount):* $_____
  b. ☐ Interest *(amount):* $_____

⑦ ☐ **Other orders are stated on Form SC-225A, item ③.**

⑧ ☐ **The court will make orders on the matter after a hearing,** which will take place on:

Hearing Date → _____ Time: _____ Dept. _____
Name and address of court if different than address above:
_____
_____

Request for Accommodations Assistive listening systems, computer-assisted real-time captioning, or sign language interpreter services are available if you ask at least five days before the hearing. Contact the clerk's office or go to www.courts.ca.gov/forms for *Request for Accommodations by Persons With Disabilities and Response* (Form MC-410). (Civil Code, § 54.8)

Date: _____

_____
Judicial officer

Need help?
For free help, contact your county's small claims advisor:

Or go to *www.courts.ca.gov/smallclaims/advisor*

Order on Declaration of Default in Payments
(Small Claims)

Declaration Re: Default in Installment Payments and Order Thereon

ATTORNEY OR PARTY WITHOUT ATTORNEY (Name, State Bar number, and address): TELEPHONE NO.: FAX NO.(Optional): EMAIL ADDRESS (Optional): ATTORNEY FOR (Name):	FOR COURT USE ONLY

SUPERIOR COURT OF CALIFORNIA, COUNTY OF

PLAINTIFF(S)

DEFENDANT(S)

DECLARATION RE: DEFAULT IN INSTALLMENT PAYMENTS AND ORDER THEREON	CASE NUMBER

The undersigned judgment creditor in the above-entitled action declares:

Judgment was entered against judgment debtor _____ on

_____ for $_____; the court ordered the judgment paid in installments of

$_____ per month commencing on _____ and on the _____ day of

each month thereafter until paid in full. $_____ has been paid on the judgment.

Debtor has failed to comply with the terms of the judgment by failing to make the payment due and payable on or before

_____.

Therefore, judgment creditor requests that writ of execution be issued for the balance due.

I declare under penalty of perjury under the laws of the State of California that the foregoing is true and correct.

Date: _____   _____

IT IS SO ORDERED.

Date: _____   _____

SDSC CIV-242 (Rev. 12/14)
Optional Form

DECLARATION RE: DEFAULT IN INSTALLMENT PAYMENTS AND ORDER THEREON

Declaration of Default Re: Stipulated Agreement and Judgment Thereon

ATTORNEY OR PARTY WITHOUT ATTORNEY (Name, State Bar number, and address):	FOR COURT USE ONLY
TELEPHONE NO.: FAX NO.(Optional): EMAIL ADDRESS (Optional): ATTORNEY FOR (Name):	

SUPERIOR COURT OF CALIFORNIA, COUNTY OF

PLAINTIFF(S)

DEFENDANT(S)

DECLARATION OF DEFAULT RE: STIPULATED AGREEMENT AND JUDGMENT THEREON	CASE NUMBER

The undersigned states that on _____, a Stipulated Agreement was entered into by _____
_____. The Stipulated Agreement was as follows: _____
_____
_____

1. ☐ Plaintiff ☐ Defendant has failed to comply with the terms of the Stipulated Agreement signed by both parties.
2. ☐ Plaintiff ☐ Defendant hereby requests that the dismissal be set aside and the matter be set for hearing.
3. ☐ Plaintiff ☐ Defendant hereby requests that the dismissal be set aside and judgment be entered in favor of the
   ☐ Plaintiff ☐ Defendant as follows:

   $ _____ Stipulated amount (not including court costs)
   $ _____ Costs of filing and service*
   $ _____ Attorney fees
   $ _____ Interest
   $ (_____) Less payments received
   $ _____ Total

4. ☐ Possession of the premises located at _____.

I declare under penalty of perjury under the laws of the State of California that the foregoing is true and correct.

Date: _____   _____
                                                                                                  Signature of Declarant

NOTE: If this is a Small Claims case, you must attach the original contract, check, or documents to support your claim.

FOR COURT USE ONLY

*REIMBURSEMENT FOR WAIVED COSTS

☐ Plaintiff(s) ☐ Defendant(s) _____
☐ to pay costs of $_____ to the San Diego Superior Court ☐ to pay costs of $_____ to the San Diego County Sheriff.
Pursuant to Gov. Code § 68637(b)(1), the court may refuse to enter satisfaction of judgment until the order requiring payment of waived fees and costs has been satisfied.

IT IS SO ORDERED.

Date: _____   _____
                                                                                  Judge/Commissioner of the Superior Court

DECLARATION OF DEFAULT RE: STIPULATED AGREEMENT AND JUDGMENT THEREON

Application and Order for Appearance and Examination

AT-138/EJ-125

ATTORNEY OR PARTY WITHOUT ATTORNEY:	STATE BAR NO.:	FOR COURT USE ONLY
NAME:		
FIRM NAME:		
STREET ADDRESS:		
CITY:	STATE: ZIP CODE:	
TELEPHONE NO.:	FAX NO.:	
E-MAIL ADDRESS:		
ATTORNEY FOR (name):		

SUPERIOR COURT OF CALIFORNIA, COUNTY OF
STREET ADDRESS:
MAILING ADDRESS:
CITY AND ZIP CODE:
BRANCH NAME:

PLAINTIFF
DEFENDANT

APPLICATION AND ORDER FOR APPEARANCE AND EXAMINATION	CASE NUMBER:
☐ ENFORCEMENT OF JUDGMENT ☐ ATTACHMENT (Third Person) ☐ Judgment Debtor ☐ Third Person	

ORDER TO APPEAR FOR EXAMINATION

1. TO (name):
2. YOU ARE ORDERED TO APPEAR personally before this court, or before a referee appointed by the court, to
   a. ☐ furnish information to aid in enforcement of a money judgment against you.
   b. ☐ answer concerning property of the judgment debtor in your possession or control or concerning a debt you owe the judgment debtor.
   c. ☐ answer concerning property of the defendant in your possession or control or concerning a debt you owe the defendant that is subject to attachment.

Date: Time: Dept. or Div.:   Rm.:
Address of court ☐ is shown above ☐ is:

3. This order may be served by a sheriff, marshal, registered process server, **or** the following specially appointed person (name):

Date: _____
                                          JUDGE

This order must be served not less than 10 days before the date set for the examination.

IMPORTANT NOTICES ON REVERSE

APPLICATION FOR ORDER TO APPEAR FOR EXAMINATION

4. ☐ Original judgment creditor ☐ Assignee of record ☐ Plaintiff who has a right to attach order
   applies for an order requiring (name):
   to appear and furnish information to aid in enforcement of the money judgment or to answer concerning property or debt.
5. The person to be examined is
   a. ☐ the judgment debtor.
   b. ☐ a third person (1) who has possession or control of property belonging to the judgment debtor or the defendant or (2) who owes the judgment debtor or the defendant more than $250. An affidavit supporting this application under Code of Civil Procedure section 491.110 or 708.120 is attached.
6. The person to be examined resides or has a place of business in this county or within 150 miles of the place of examination.
7. ☐ This court is **not** the court in which the money judgment is entered or (attachment only) the court that issued the writ of attachment. An affidavit supporting an application under Code of Civil Procedure section 491.150 or 708.160 is attached.
8. ☐ The judgment debtor has been examined within the past 120 days. An affidavit showing good cause for another examination is attached.

I declare under penalty of perjury under the laws of the State of California that the foregoing is true and correct.

Date:

_____   ▶   _____
(TYPE OR PRINT NAME)   (SIGNATURE OF DECLARANT)

(Continued on reverse)

Page 1 of 2

Form Adopted for Mandatory Use
Judicial Council of California
AT-138/EJ-125 [Rev. January 1, 2017]

APPLICATION AND ORDER FOR APPEARANCE AND EXAMINATION
(Attachment—Enforcement of Judgment)

Code of Civil Procedure,
§§ 491.110, 708.110, 708.120, 708.170
www.courts.ca.gov

AT-138/EJ-125

Information for Judgment Creditor Regarding Service

If you want to be able to ask the court to enforce the order on the judgment debtor or any third party, you must have a copy of the order personally served on the judgment debtor by a sheriff, marshal, registered process server, or the person appointed in item 3 of the order at least 10 calendar days before the date of the hearing, and have a proof of service filed with the court.

IMPORTANT NOTICES ABOUT THE ORDER

APPEARANCE OF JUDGMENT DEBTOR (ENFORCEMENT OF JUDGMENT)

NOTICE TO JUDGMENT DEBTOR If you fail to appear at the time and place specified in this order, you may be subject to arrest and punishment for contempt of court, and the court may make an order requiring you to pay the reasonable attorney fees incurred by the judgment creditor in this proceeding.

APPEARANCE OF A THIRD PERSON (ENFORCEMENT OF JUDGMENT)

(1) **NOTICE TO PERSON SERVED** If you fail to appear at the time and place specified in this order, you may be subject to arrest and punishment for contempt of court, and the court may make an order requiring you to pay the reasonable attorney fees incurred by the judgment creditor in this proceeding.

(2) **NOTICE TO JUDGMENT DEBTOR** The person in whose favor the judgment was entered in this action claims that the person to be examined under this order has possession or control of property that is yours or owes you a debt. This property or debt is as follows *(describe the property or debt)*:

If you claim that all or any portion of this property or debt is exempt from enforcement of the money judgment, you must file your exemption claim in writing with the court and have a copy personally served on the judgment creditor not later than three days before the date set for the examination. You must appear at the time and place set for the examination to establish your claim of exemption or your exemption may be waived.

APPEARANCE OF A THIRD PERSON (ATTACHMENT)

NOTICE TO PERSON SERVED If you fail to appear at the time and place specified in this order, you may be subject to arrest and punishment for contempt of court, and the court may make an order requiring you to pay the reasonable attorney fees incurred by the plaintiff in this proceeding.

APPEARANCE OF A CORPORATION, PARTNERSHIP, ASSOCIATION, TRUST, OR OTHER ORGANIZATION

It is your duty to designate one or more of the following to appear and be examined: officers, directors, managing agents, or other persons who are familiar with your property and debts.

 **Request for Accommodations.** Assistive listening systems, computer-assisted real-time captioning, or sign language interpreter services are available if you ask at least 5 days before your hearing. Contact the clerk's office for *Request for Accommodation* (form MC-410). (Civil Code, § 54.8.)

APPLICATION AND ORDER FOR APPEARANCE AND EXAMINATION
(Attachment—Enforcement of Judgment)

Subpoena

	SUBP-002
ATTORNEY OR PARTY WITHOUT ATTORNEY *(Name, State Bar number, and address):*	*FOR COURT USE ONLY*
TELEPHONE NO.: FAX NO.: E-MAIL ADDRESS: ATTORNEY FOR *(Name):*	
NAME OF COURT: STREET ADDRESS: MAILING ADDRESS: CITY AND ZIP CODE: BRANCH NAME:	
PLAINTIFF/ PETITIONER: DEFENDANT/ RESPONDENT:	
CIVIL SUBPOENA (DUCES TECUM) for Personal Appearance and Production of Documents, Electronically Stored Information, and Things at Trial or Hearing and DECLARATION	CASE NUMBER:

THE PEOPLE OF THE STATE OF CALIFORNIA, TO *(name, address, and telephone number of witness, if known):*

1. **YOU ARE ORDERED TO APPEAR AS A WITNESS** in this action at the date, time, and place shown in the box below UNLESS your appearance is excused as indicated in box 3b below or you make an agreement with the person named in item 4 below.

   a. Date: Time: ☐ Dept.:   ☐ Div.:   ☐ Room:
   b. Address:

2. **IF YOU HAVE BEEN SERVED WITH THIS SUBPOENA AS A CUSTODIAN OF CONSUMER OR EMPLOYEE RECORDS UNDER CODE OF CIVIL PROCEDURE SECTION 1985.3 OR 1985.6 AND A MOTION TO QUASH OR AN OBJECTION HAS BEEN SERVED ON YOU, A COURT ORDER OR AGREEMENT OF THE PARTIES, WITNESSES,** *AND* **CONSUMER OR EMPLOYEE AFFECTED MUST BE OBTAINED BEFORE YOU ARE REQUIRED TO PRODUCE CONSUMER OR EMPLOYEE RECORDS.**

3. **YOU ARE** *(item a or b must be checked):*

   a. ☐ Ordered to appear in person and to produce the records described in the declaration on page two or the attached declaration or affidavit. The personal attendance of the custodian or other qualified witness and the production of the original records are required by this subpoena. The procedure authorized by Evidence Code sections 1560(b), 1561, and 1562 will not be deemed sufficient compliance with this subpoena.

   b. ☐ Not required to appear in person if you produce (i) the records described in the declaration on page two or the attached declaration or affidavit and (ii) a completed declaration of custodian of records in compliance with Evidence Code sections 1560, 1561, 1562, and 1271. (1) Place a copy of the records in an envelope (or other wrapper). Enclose the original declaration of the custodian with the records. Seal the envelope. (2) Attach a copy of this subpoena to the envelope or write on the envelope the case name and number; your name; and the date, time, and place from item 1 in the box above. (3) Place this first envelope in an outer envelope, seal it, and mail it to the clerk of the court at the address in item 1. (4) Mail a copy of your declaration to the attorney or party listed at the top of this form.

4. **IF YOU HAVE ANY QUESTIONS ABOUT THE TIME OR DATE YOU ARE TO APPEAR, OR IF YOU WANT TO BE CERTAIN THAT YOUR PRESENCE IS REQUIRED, CONTACT THE FOLLOWING PERSON BEFORE THE DATE ON WHICH YOU ARE TO APPEAR:**

   a. Name of subpoenaing party or attorney: b. Telephone number:

5. **Witness Fees:** You are entitled to witness fees and mileage actually traveled both ways, as provided by law, if you request them at the time of service. You may request them before your scheduled appearance from the person named in item 4.

DISOBEDIENCE OF THIS SUBPOENA MAY BE PUNISHED AS CONTEMPT BY THIS COURT. YOU WILL ALSO BE LIABLE FOR THE SUM OF FIVE HUNDRED DOLLARS AND ALL DAMAGES RESULTING FROM YOUR FAILURE TO OBEY.

Date issued:

_____ ▶ _____
(TYPE OR PRINT NAME)   (SIGNATURE OF PERSON ISSUING SUBPOENA)

_____
(TITLE)

(Declaration in support of subpoena on reverse)

| Form Adopted for Mandatory Use
 Judicial Council of California
 SUBP-002 [Rev. January 1, 2012] | **CIVIL SUBPOENA (DUCES TECUM) for Personal Appearance and Production of Documents, Electronically Stored Information, and Things at Trial or Hearing and DECLARATION** | Code of Civil Procedure,
 § 1985 et seq.
 www.courts.ca.gov |

PLAINTIFF/PETITIONER:	CASE NUMBER:
DEFENDANT/RESPONDENT:	

The production of the documents, electronically stored information, or other things sought by the subpoena on page one is supported by *(check one)*:

☐ the attached affidavit or   ☐ the following declaration:

DECLARATION IN SUPPORT OF CIVIL SUBPOENA (DUCES TECUM) FOR PERSONAL APPEARANCE AND PRODUCTION OF DOCUMENTS, ELECTRONICALLY STORED INFORMATION, AND THINGS AT TRIAL OR HEARING
(Code Civ. Proc., §§ 1985, 1987.5)

1. I, the undersigned, declare I am the ☐ plaintiff ☐ defendant ☐ petitioner ☐ respondent
   ☐ attorney for *(specify)*:   ☐ other *(specify)*:
   in the above-entitled action.

2. The witness has possession or control of the documents, electronically stored information, or other things listed below, and shall produce them at the time and place specified in the Civil Subpoena for Personal Appearance and Production of Records at Trial or Hearing on page one of this form *(specify the exact documents or other things to be produce; if electronically stored information is demanded, the form or forms in which each type of information is to be produced may be specified)*:

   ☐ Continued on Attachment 2.

3. Good cause exists for the production of the documents, electronically stored information, or other things described in paragraph 2 for the following reasons:

   ☐ Continued on Attachment 3.

4. The documents, electronically stored information, or other things described in paragraph 2 are material to the issues involved in this case for the following reasons:

   ☐ Continued on Attachment 4.

I declare under penalty of perjury under the laws of the State of California that the foregoing is true and correct.

Date:

_____   ▶ _____
(TYPE OR PRINT NAME)   (SIGNATURE OF ☐ SUBPOENAING PARTY ☐ ATTORNEY FOR SUBPOENAING PARTY)

Request for Accommodations

Assistive listening systems, computer-assisted real-time captioning, or sign language interpreter services are available if you ask at least five days before the date on which you are to appear. Contact the clerk's office or go to www.courts.ca.gov/forms for *Request for Accommodations by Persons With Disabilities and Response* (form MC-410). (Civil Code, § 54.8.)

(Proof of service on page 3)

CIVIL SUBPOENA (DUCES TECUM) for Personal Appearance and Production of Documents, Electronically Stored Information, and Things at Trial or Hearing and DECLARATION

PLAINTIFF/PETITIONER:	CASE NUMBER:
DEFENDANT/RESPONDENT:	

PROOF OF SERVICE OF CIVIL SUBPOENA (DUCES TECUM) for Personal Appearance and Production of Documents, Electronically Stored Information, and Things at Trial or Hearing and DECLARATION

1. I served this *Civil Subpoena (Duces Tecum) for Personal Appearance and Production of Documents, Electronically Stored Information, and Things at Trial or Hearing and Declaration* by personally delivering a copy to the person served as follows:

   a. Person served *(name)*:

   b. Address where served:

   c. Date of delivery:

   d. Time of delivery:

   e. Witness fees *(check one)*:
   - (1) ☐ were offered or demanded and paid. Amount: ...... $ _____
   - (2) ☐ were not demanded or paid.

   f. Fee for service: .... $ _____

2. I received this subpoena for service on *(date)*:

3. Person serving:
   - a. ☐ Not a registered California process server.
   - b. ☐ California sheriff or marshal.
   - c. ☐ Registered California process server.
   - d. ☐ Employee or independent contractor of a registered California process server.
   - e. ☐ Exempt from registration under Business and Professions Code section 22350(b).
   - f. ☐ Registered professional photocopier.
   - g. ☐ Exempt from registration under Business and Professions Code section 22451.
   - h. Name, address, telephone number, and, if applicable, county of registration and number:

I declare under penalty of perjury under the laws of the State of California that the foregoing is true and correct.

Date:

▶ _____
(SIGNATURE)

(For California sheriff or marshal use only)
I certify that the foregoing is true and correct.

Date:

▶ _____
(SIGNATURE)

Questions for Debtor's Examination

Questions for Debtor's Examination

Questions for Debtor's Examination

Questions for Debtor's Examination

1. What is your full name and your spouse's full name (if married)?

2. Have you ever used another name or nickname on any documents such as a driver's license, credit application or other important papers? If so:
   a. give name, and
   b. give location and approximate time when name was used.

3. What is your current address and length of time lived there?

4. What is your current phone number?

5. What was your previous address?

6. What was your previous phone number?

7. What is your California driver's license (or California identification card) number?

8. What is your Social Security number?

9. What is your date of birth?

10. If married, what is your spouse's maiden name?

11. Are you employed as an employee, either part-time or full-time? If so:
    a. name, address, and phone number of employer,
    b. frequency of payment (weekly, bi-weekly, monthly, etc.),
    c. gross pay,
    d. take-home pay,
    e. commissions if any,
    f. how much is due you at the pr.esent time, and
    g. how long on this job?

12. Where and with whom was your previous job?

13. Do you perform labor or services for someone else as an independent contractor rather than as an employee? If so:
    a. names, addresses and phone numbers of persons or businesses for whom you perform services,
    b. nature of services performed for each such person or business,
    c. frequency of services, and
    d. method of billing (e.g., flat rate, hourly rate, job rate).

14. Do you own a business (in whole, in part, as a partner or as a corporation), or have you owned a business within the past five years? If so:
    a. describe business,
    b. name who you do business with,
    c. describe major people or businesses who owe you money (names, addresses and telephone numbers),
    d. describe any business assets such as tools, equipment, computers, furniture, fixtures, machinery, etc., wholly owned by business,
    e. identify which of these assets you still owe money on and the approximate amount owed,
    f. describe, generally, method of doing business, and
    g. provide names and addresses of partners (if the business is a partnership), and corporate officers (if the business is a corporation).

15. Do you own stock in any corporation or shares in a mutual fund? If so:
    a. name of corporation or mutual fund,
    b. form of ownership (certificates, computer account, etc.),
    c. location of certificates or account, and
    d. amount of ownership and approximate value.

16. Do you maintain a brokerage account with any stock broker? If so:
    a. name and address of broker,
    b. account number(s), and
    c. approximate amount in brokerage account.

17. Do you or your spouse have any funds in banks, savings and loans, money market accounts, certificates of deposit, escrow accounts, credit

unions, or any other financial institutions, either in your name or jointly with any other individual? If so:
   a. name of each financial institution and address of branch possessing the funds,
   b. the account number of each account,
   c. name(s) the account is under,
   d. the approximate balance in the account,
   e. date the last deposit was made,
   f. source of the funds in the account, and
   g. when you typically make deposits and withdrawals.

18. Do you or your spouse own a safe-deposit box? If so:
    a. name of bank and address of branch,
    b. name(s) of holder of safe-deposit box, and
    c. contents of box.

19. Do you own any securities (that is, any document which grants a share of ownership in exchange for a loan or investment) such as bonds, annuities, etc.? If so:
    a. describe nature of security, bond, annuity, etc.,
    b. institution or person issuing it, and
    c. approximate worth.

20. Do you own any whole life insurance policies? If so:
    a. the name of the insurance company,
    b. the name of your insurance agent,
    c. the face amount of the policy, and
    d. the cash value of the policy, if any.

21. Do you own any of the following items? If so, describe the item, the item's location, approximate value and any joint owner.
    a. office equipment,
    b. gemstones, gems or jewelry,
    c. camera equipment,
    d. computers,
    e. antiques,
    f. precious metals (gold, silver),
    g. musical instruments including pianos and organs,
    h. weapons (guns, swords, other),
    i. furs,
    j. watches,
    k. stamp or coin collections,
    l. china,
    m. original artworks,
    n. crystal,
    o. sports equipment, including exercise machines,
    p. stereo or musical equipment, and
    q. any other items of value not mentioned above.

22. Do you own, in your own name, or jointly with others, an automobile, truck, motorcycle, RV, motor home, mobile home, boat or plane? If so, provide the following information:
    a. brief description (make, model and year),
    b. approximate value,
    c. legal owner,
    d. registered owner,
    e. license number,
    f. vehicle identification number,
    g. amount owed, if any, to a legal owner, and
    h. any other lienholder you are aware of.

23. Does a person, company or institution owe you money? If so:
    a. name, address and telephone number of person or institution,
    b. amount of each debt, and
    c. how each debt arose (e.g., judgment, loan, inheritance).

24. Do you owe money to anyone else besides this current judgment creditor where you have been sued and the other person or business has received a judgment? If so:
    a. to whom (address and telephone no.),
    b. amount owed, and
    c. amount currently paid.

25. Did you ever file for bankruptcy? If so:
    a. when,
    b. where (district and branch),
    c. type of bankruptcy (Chapter 7 or Chapter 13, if you know), and
    d. case number of the bankruptcy.

26. Are you a party (e.g., defendant or plaintiff) in **any current action? This could be an action** brought against you for a money judgment, an action in which you are the plaintiff, or any other action (including divorce, will contest, etc.)? If so:
    a. **Who are the parties in each action?**
    b. Who are the attorneys in each action (names, addresses and phone numbers; include information for parties if they are appearing in pro per)?
    c. Supply a brief description of each lawsuit.
    d. What is your position in the lawsuit, and do you expect to win?

27. Does your wife or husband receive any salary, **commissions or other income, as an employee or independent contractor, from an employer or** business? If so:
    a. Name, address and telephone number of employer, and
    b. income and pay period

28. Any other sources of income? If so:
    a. **amount of income,**
    b. **when income is received, and is it received on a regular basis, and**
    c. brief description of source.

29. Do you own any real estate individually or jointly (single family home, vacation home, co-op/condominium, duplex, rental property, business property, mobile home park, time share, undevelopecj land, agricultural land, boat/ **marina dock space, airplane hangar, stationary** mobile home)? If so:
    a. **address and county,**
    b. **approximate fair market value,**
    c. amount owed (first mortgage, second deed of trust), and
       1. **to whom, and**
       2. amount and frequency of payments,
    d. when the property was obtained,
    e. **what names are on the deed,**
    f. has title to the property been transferred **since its acquisition by you,**
    g. known debts or claims that affect the title **(easements, tax liens, judgment liens, etc.),**
    h. **approximate amount of your actual ownership (equity) in the property,**
    i. if a declaration of homestead been filed,
    j. anyone lives on the property, and
    k. if the property is developed, what kind of building(s)?

30. Are you a landlord? If so:
    a. **name and address of tenants, and**
    b. amount of rent paid and interval of payment.

31. Do you rent where you are now living? If so:
    a. **amount of rent paid,**
    b. landlord's name, and
    c. landlord's address and phone number.

32. Are you the trustee for, or beneficiary of, any property held in trust for yourself or a third person? If so:
    a. briefly describe type of trust (e.g., living, bank account, spousal, Q-TIP),
    b. identify whether you are the trustee or **beneficiary, or both, and**
    c. describe what the nature of the property is that is being held in trust.

33. Do you receive benefits from any government agency (e.g., unemployment insurance, disability **insurance, workers' compensation, Social Security, retirement, pension)? If so:**
    a. **name of agency,**
    b. type of benefit,
    c. **amount of benefit,**
    d. frequency of benefit,
    e. the expected duration of the payments, and
    f. basis for the benefit (e.g., unemployment, industrial injury, etc.).

34. Do you receive benefits from or through a **private business or entity such as an insurance company or financial institution** (e.g., **insurance, annuity, retirement, pension, workers' compen-**sation benefits)? If so:
    a. **name of provider,**
    b. type of benefit,
    c. **amount of benefit,**
    d. frequency of benefit,

e. the expected duration of the payments, and
f. the basis for the benefit.

35. Do you pay alimony/child support? If so:
    a. name, address and telephone number of recipient, and
    b. amount and frequency of support.

36. Do you receive alimony/child support? If so:
    a. name, address and telephone number of provider, and
    b. amount and frequency of support.

37. Do you own any property (cash, tangible personal property items) that is currently in the possession of others? If so:
    a. briefly describe the property,
    b. name, address and telephone number of possessor,
    c. purpose of possession, and
    d. physical location of property.

38. Is there any reason why you can't pay on this judgment now or in the future? If so, briefly describe reason.

39. Do you foresee your financial position changing in the future? If so, how?

40. Identify each item of property (cash, other personal property including motor vehicles, or real estate) you have sold or given away within the past three months, and when the transaction occurred.

41. Identify each service you have received from an individual or business (e.g., medical care, legal consultation, car repair) within the past three months, and when the service was provided. Also indicate whether you have paid for that service, and in what manner (cash, check, credit card, etc.).

42. Do you hold an occupational license of any type? If so:
    a. name of license,
    b. agency granting the license,
    c. expiration date of license, and
    d. license number.

43. Do you own any mortgages or deeds of trust on any real estate? If so:
    a. property involved (address, county),
    b. approximate value of mortgage,
    c. date of mortgage or deed of trust, and
    d. persons or institutions involved.

44. Do you own, solely or jointly, any copyrights, patents, trademarks, trade names or trade secrets? If so:
    a. item protected by the copyright, patent, etc.,
    b. where registered (if registered) and registration number,
    c. co-owners, if any,
    d. royalties or other payments received under the copyright patent, etc.

45. Do you or your spouse have any personal property in pawn? If so:
    a. name and address of pawnbroker, and
    b. brief description of property and approximate value.

46. Have you made a will? If so:
    a. describe bequests, and
    b. physical location of will.

47. How much money in cash or traveller's checks do you have with you at this time? Identify specifically.

48. Any checks or money orders payable to you? If so, describe.

49. Do you or your spouse have an IRA or Keogh account? If so:
    a. institution and branch where account is maintained, and
    b. amount in account.

Writ of Execution

EJ-130

ATTORNEY OR PARTY WITHOUT ATTORNEY *(Name, State Bar number and address)*:	FOR COURT USE ONLY
TELEPHONE NO.: FAX NO.: E-MAIL ADDRESS: ATTORNEY FOR *(Name)*: ☐ ATTORNEY FOR ☐ JUDGMENT CREDITOR ☐ ASSIGNEE OF RECORD	

SUPERIOR COURT OF CALIFORNIA, COUNTY OF
STREET ADDRESS:
MAILING ADDRESS:
CITY AND ZIP CODE:
BRANCH NAME:

PLAINTIFF:

DEFENDANT:

WRIT OF	☐ EXECUTION (Money Judgment) ☐ POSSESSION OF ☐ Personal Property ☐ Real Property ☐ SALE	☐ Limited Civil Case ☐ Small Claims Case ☐ Unlimited Civil Case ☐ Other_____

CASE NUMBER:

1. **To the Sheriff or Marshal of the County of:**
   You are directed to enforce the judgment described below with daily interest and your costs as provided by law.
2. **To any registered process server:** You are authorized to serve this writ only in accord with CCP 699.080 or CCP 715.040.
3. *(Name):*
   is the ☐ judgment creditor ☐ assignee of record   whose address is shown on this form above the court's name.
4. **Judgment debtor** *(name, type of legal entity stated in judgment if not a natural person, and last known address):*

   ┌─────────────────────────┐
   │   │
   │   │
   │   │
   │   │
   └─────────────────────────┘
   ☐ Additional judgment debtors on next page
5. **Judgment entered** on *(date):*
6. ☐ **Judgment renewed** on *(dates):*
7. **Notice of sale** under this writ
   a. ☐ has not been requested.
   b. ☐ has been requested *(see next page).*
8. ☐ Joint debtor information on next page.

   [SEAL]

9. ☐ See next page for information on real or personal property to be delivered under a writ of possession or sold under a writ of sale.
10. ☐ This writ is issued on a sister-state judgment.
11. Total judgment .... $
12. Costs after judgment (per filed order or memo CCP 685.090) .... $
13. Subtotal *(add 11 and 12)* .... $ _____
14. Credits .... $
15. Subtotal *(subtract 14 from 13)* ..... $ _____
16. Interest after judgment (per filed affidavit CCP 685.050) (not on GC 6103.5 fees)... $
17. Fee for issuance of writ .... $
18. **Total** *(add 15, 16, and 17)* .... $ _____
19. Levying officer:
    (a) Add daily interest from date of writ *(at the legal rate on 15)* (not on GC 6103.5 fees) of .... $
    (b) Pay directly to court costs included in 11 and 17 (GC 6103.5, 68637; CCP 699.520(i)) .... $
20. ☐ The amounts called for in items 11–19 are different for each debtor. These amounts are stated for each debtor on Attachment 20.

Issued on *(date):* _____ Clerk, by _____, Deputy

NOTICE TO PERSON SERVED: SEE NEXT PAGE FOR IMPORTANT INFORMATION.

Page 1 of 2

Form Approved for Optional Use
Judicial Council of California
EJ-130 [Rev. January 1, 2012]

WRIT OF EXECUTION

Code of Civil Procedure, §§ 699.520, 712.010, 715.010
Government Code, § 6103.5
www.courts.ca.gov

		EJ-130
PLAINTIFF:	CASE NUMBER:	
DEFENDANT:		

— Items continued from page 1—

21. ☐ **Additional judgment debtor** *(name, type of legal entity stated in judgment if not a natural person, and last known address):*

22. ☐ **Notice of sale** has been requested by *(name and address):*

23. ☐ **Joint debtor** was declared bound by the judgment (CCP 989–994)
    a. on *(date):*   a. on *(date):*
    b. name, type of legal entity stated in judgment if not a   b. name, type of legal entity stated in judgment if not
        natural person, and last known address of joint debtor: a natural person, and last known address of joint debtor:

    c. ☐ additional costs against certain joint debtors *(itemize):*

24. ☐ *(Writ of Possession or Writ of Sale)* **Judgment** was entered for the following:
    a. ☐ Possession of real property: The complaint was filed on *(date):*
        (Check (1) or (2)):
        (1) ☐ The Prejudgment Claim of Right to Possession was served in compliance with CCP 415.46.
               The judgment includes all tenants, subtenants, named claimants, and other occupants of the premises.
        (2) ☐ The Prejudgment Claim of Right to Possession was NOT served in compliance with CCP 415.46.
            (a) $ was the daily rental value on the date the complaint was filed.
            (b) The court will hear objections to enforcement of the judgment under CCP 1174.3 on the following
                dates *(specify):*
    b. ☐ Possession of personal property.
          ☐ If delivery cannot be had, then for the value *(itemize in 24e)* specified in the judgment or supplemental order.
    c. ☐ Sale of personal property.
    d. ☐ Sale of real property.
    e. Description of property:

NOTICE TO PERSON SERVED

WRIT OF EXECUTION OR SALE. Your rights and duties are indicated on the accompanying *Notice of Levy* (Form EJ-150).
WRIT OF POSSESSION OF PERSONAL PROPERTY. If the levying officer is not able to take custody of the property, the levying officer will make a demand upon you for the property. If custody is not obtained following demand, the judgment may be enforced as a money judgment for the value of the property specified in the judgment or in a supplemental order.
WRIT OF POSSESSION OF REAL PROPERTY. If the premises are not vacated within five days after the date of service on the occupant or, if service is by posting, within five days after service on you, the levying officer will remove the occupants from the real property and place the judgment creditor in possession of the property. Except for a mobile home, personal property remaining on the premises will be sold or otherwise disposed of in accordance with CCP 1174 unless you or the owner of the property pays the judgment creditor the reasonable cost of storage and takes possession of the personal property not later than 15 days after the time the judgment creditor takes possession of the premises.
► A *Claim of Right to Possession* form accompanies this writ (unless the Summons was served in compliance with CCP 415.46).

WRIT OF EXECUTION

Application for Federal Employee Commercial Garnishment

APPLICATION FOR FEDERAL EMPLOYEE COMMERCIAL GARNISHMENT

Approved by OMB 3206-0229

Date Received in Office of Designated Agent

INSTRUCTIONS

1. Federal law, 5 U.S.C. § 5520a, provides for the commercial garnishment of the pay of Federal employees.
2. Each garnishment order or similar legal process in the nature of garnishment must be delivered to the agency's Designated Agent. (See 5 CFR Part 582 Appendix A and 5 CFR Part 581 Appendix A for the lists of Designated Agents to receive legal process.)
3. Employing agencies will generally begin to disburse amounts withheld from employee-obligor's pay within 30 days of receipt by Designated Agent.
4. Employing agencies will **not** modify compensation schedules or pay disbursement cycles in responding to legal process.
5. 31 CFR Part 210 governs funds remitted by Electronic Funds Transfer.
6. See reverse side for Public Burden Statement.

Title and Address of Employing Agency's Designated Agent

Note: Service of legal process **may** be accomplished by certified or registered mail, return receipt requested, or by personal service only upon the agent to receive process as explained in 5 CFR 582.201, or if no agent has been designated, then upon the head of the employee-obligor's employing agency.

A. EMPLOYEE IDENTIFICATION - 5 U.S.C. § 5520a requires sufficient information to enable the employing agency to identify the employee-obligor. Please provide as much of the information in items 1 through 5 as possible.

1. Full Name of Employee-Obligor
2. Date of Birth
3. Employee/Social Security Number
4. Employing Agency, Component, and Employee's Official Duty Station/Worksite Address and ZIP Code
5. Home Address or Current Mailing Address and ZIP Code
6. For Agency Use

B. CASE INFORMATION

1. Name of Court and Case Number in Garnishment Order
2. Garnishment Amount $
3. Legal process expiration date (if time limited)
4. Is there a dollar amount or percentage limitation under the applicable law of the jurisdiction where the order has been issued that will result in a lower amount to be garnished than would otherwise be applicable under the Consumer Credit Protection Act, 15 U.S.C. § 1673? ☐ Yes ☐ No If Yes, provide a citation and a copy of the applicable provision:_____
5. Does the law of the jurisdiction where this legal process is issued have a "one order at a time" rule that precludes employers from garnishing more than one order at a time? ☐ Yes ☐ No
6. Does the law of the jurisdiction where this legal process is issued provide for the garnishment of interest amounts that are not reflected on the order or in item number B2? ☐ Yes ☐ No

C. AUTHORIZED PAYEE IDENTIFICATION

1. Full Name of Person Authorized to Receive Payment, as it appears on Court Order
2. Address of Authorized Payee, including ZIP Code
3. Daytime Telephone - Area Code and Number
4. Signature of Authorized Payee, Creditor, or Creditor's Representative, and Date Signed

D. ELECTRONIC FUNDS TRANSFER (if available)

If you wish to request that the funds be remitted by electronic funds transfer rather than by paper check, please complete items D1 through D5.

1. Name and Address of Authorized Payee's Financial Institution
2. Depositor (Payee) Account No. and Title

Type of Account: ☐ Checking ☐ Savings

3. 9-Digit Routing Transit No. of Authorized Payee's Financial Institution (Verify with Financial Institution)
4. Name and Title of Authorized Payee's Representative
5. Signature of Authorized Payee's Representative and Date Signed

U. S. Office of Personnel Management

Optional Form 311 (March 1997)

Application for Earnings Withholding Order

WG-001

ATTORNEY OR PARTY WITHOUT ATTORNEY *(Name, State Bar number, and address)*:	LEVYING OFFICER *(Name and Address)*:
TELEPHONE NO.: FAX NO.:	
E-MAIL ADDRESS:	
ATTORNEY FOR *(Name)*:	

SUPERIOR COURT OF CALIFORNIA, COUNTY OF
STREET ADDRESS:
MAILING ADDRESS:
CITY AND ZIP CODE:
BRANCH NAME:

PLAINTIFF/PETITIONER:	COURT CASE NUMBER:
DEFENDANT/RESPONDENT:	
APPLICATION FOR EARNINGS WITHHOLDING ORDER (Wage Garnishment)	LEVYING OFFICER FILE NUMBER:

TO THE SHERIFF OR ANY MARSHAL OR CONSTABLE OF THE COUNTY OF:
OR ANY REGISTERED PROCESS SERVER

1. The judgment creditor *(name)*: requests issuance of an Earnings Withholding Order directing the employer to withhold the earnings of the judgment debtor (employee).

   Name and address of employer   Name and address of employee

2. The amounts withheld are to be paid to   Social Security no. ☐ on form WG-035 ☐ unknown
   a. ☐ The attorney (or party without an attorney)   b. ☐ Other *(name, address, and telephone)*:
      named at the top of this page.

3. a. Judgment was entered on *(date)*: _____
   b. Collect the amount directed by the Writ of Execution unless a lesser amount is specified here: $ _____

4. *Check any that apply:*
   a. ☐ The Writ of Execution was issued to collect delinquent amounts payable for the **support** of a child, former spouse, or spouse of the employee.
   b. ☐ The Writ of Execution was issued to collect a judgment based entirely on a claim for elder or dependent adult financial abuse.
   c. ☐ The Writ of Execution was issued to collect a judgment based in part on a claim for elder or dependent adult financial abuse. The amount that arises from the claim for elder or dependent adult financial abuse is *(state amount)*: $ _____

5. ☐ Special instructions *(specify)*:

6. *Check a or b:*
   a. ☐ I have not previously obtained an order directing this employer to withhold the earnings of this employee.
      —OR—
   b. ☐ I have previously obtained such an order, but that order *(check one)*:
      ☐ was terminated by a court order, but I am entitled to apply for another Earnings Withholding Order under the provisions of Code of Civil Procedure section 706.105(h).
      ☐ was ineffective.

▶

_____   ▶ _____
(TYPE OR PRINT NAME)   (SIGNATURE OF ATTORNEY OR PARTY WITHOUT ATTORNEY)

I declare under penalty of perjury under the laws of the State of California that the foregoing is true and correct.
Date:

▶

_____   ▶ _____
(TYPE OR PRINT NAME)   (SIGNATURE OF DECLARANT)

Form Adopted for Mandatory Use
Judicial Council of California
WG-001 [Rev. January 1, 2012]

APPLICATION FOR EARNINGS WITHHOLDING ORDER
(Wage Garnishment)

Code Civ. Procedure, § 706.121
www.courts.ca.gov

Notice of Opposition to Claim of Exemption

(Wage Garnishment)

WG-009

ATTORNEY OR PARTY WITHOUT ATTORNEY *(Name, State Bar number, and address):*	LEVYING OFFICER *(Name and Address):*
TELEPHONE NO.: FAX NO.:	
E-MAIL ADDRESS:	
ATTORNEY FOR *(Name):*	

SUPERIOR COURT OF CALIFORNIA, COUNTY OF
STREET ADDRESS:
MAILING ADDRESS:
CITY AND ZIP CODE:
BRANCH NAME:

PLAINTIFF/PETITIONER:
DEFENDANT/RESPONDENT:

COURT CASE NUMBER:

NOTICE OF OPPOSITION TO CLAIM OF EXEMPTION
(Wage Garnishment)

LEVYING OFFICER FILE NUMBER.:

TO THE LEVYING OFFICER:

1. Name and address of judgment creditor

2. Name and address of employee

   Social Security No. ☐ on form WG-035   ☐ unknown

3. The Notice of Filing Claim of Exemption states it was mailed on *(date):*

4. The earnings claimed as exempt are
   a. ☐ not exempt.
   b. ☐ partially exempt. The amount not exempt per month is: $

5. The judgment creditor opposes the claim of exemption because
   a. ☐ the following expenses of the debtor are not necessary for the support of the debtor or the debtor's family *(specify):*

   b. ☐ the debt was for attorney's fees based on a court order under Family Code section 2030, 3121, or 3557.

   c. ☐ other *(specify):*

6. ☐ The judgment creditor will accept: $ _____ per pay period for payment on account of this debt.

I declare under penalty of perjury under the laws of the State of California that the foregoing is true and correct.

Date:

_____   ▶   _____
(TYPE OR PRINT NAME)   (SIGNATURE OF DECLARANT)

Form Adopted for Mandatory Use
Judicial Council of California
WG-009 [Rev. January 2, 2012]

NOTICE OF OPPOSITION TO CLAIM OF EXEMPTION
(Wage Garnishment)

Code of Civil Procedure, § 706.128
www.courts.ca.gov

Notice of Opposition to Claim of Exemption

(Levy of Personal Property)

ATTORNEY OR PARTY WITHOUT ATTORNEY *(Name and Address)*:	TELEPHONE NO.:	FOR COURT USE ONLY
ATTORNEY FOR *(Name)*:		

NAME OF COURT:
STREET ADDRESS:
MAILING ADDRESS:
CITY AND ZIP CODE:
BRANCH NAME:

PLAINTIFF:

DEFENDANT:

NOTICE OF OPPOSITION TO CLAIM OF EXEMPTION (Enforcement of Judgment)	LEVYING OFFICER FILE NO.:	COURT CASE NO.:

— *DO NOT USE THIS FORM FOR WAGE GARNISHMENTS* —

The original of this form and a Notice of Hearing on Claim of Exemption must be filed with the court.
A copy of this Notice of Opposition and the Notice of Hearing *must* be filed with the levying officer.
A copy of this Notice of Opposition and the Notice of Hearing must be served on the judgment debtor and other claimant at least 10 days *before* the hearing.

TO THE LEVYING OFFICER:

1. Name and address of judgment creditor

2. Name and address of judgment debtor

   Social Security Number *(if known)*:

3. ☐ Name and address of claimant *(if other than judgment debtor)*

4. The notice of filing claim of exemption states it was mailed on *(date)*:

5. The item or items claimed as exempt are
   a. ☐ not exempt under the statutes relied upon in the Claim of Exemption.
   b. ☐ not exempt because the judgment debtor's equity is greater than the amount provided in the exemption.
   c. ☐ other *(specify)*:

6. The facts necessary to support item 5 are
   ☐ continued on the attachment labeled Attachment 6.
   ☐ as follows:

I declare under penalty of perjury under the laws of the State of California that the foregoing is true and correct.

Date:

_____
(TYPE OR PRINT NAME)

▶ _____
(SIGNATURE OF DECLARANT)

Form Approved by the
Judicial Council of California
EJ-170 [New July 1, 1983]

NOTICE OF OPPOSITION TO CLAIM OF EXEMPTION
(Enforcement of Judgment)

CCP 703.550

Notice of Hearing on Claim of Exemption

(Wage & Levy)

WG-010/EJ-175

ATTORNEY OR PARTY WITHOUT ATTORNEY *(Name, State Bar number, and address):*

TELEPHONE NO.:

FOR COURT USE ONLY

ATTORNEY FOR *(Name):*

NAME OF COURT, JUDICIAL DISTRICT OR BRANCH COURT, IF ANY

PLAINTIFF:

DEFENDANT:

NOTICE OF HEARING ON CLAIM OF EXEMPTION
(Wage Garnishment—Enforcement of Judgment)

LEVYING OFFICER FILE NO.:

COURT CASE NO.:

1. TO:

   Name and address of levying officer

   Name and address of judgment debtor

   ☐ Claimant, if other than judgment debtor *(name and address):*

   ☐ Judgment debtor's attorney *(name and address):*

2. **A hearing to determine the claim of exemption of**
   ☐ judgment debtor
   ☐ other claimant
   will be held as follows:

   a. date: time: ☐ dept.:   ☐ div.:   ☐ rm.:

   b. address of court:

3. ☐ **The judgment creditor will not appear at the hearing and submits the issue on the papers filed with the court.**

Date:

....
(TYPE OR PRINT NAME)

▶

....
(SIGNATURE OF JUDGMENT CREDITOR OR ATTORNEY)

If you do not attend the hearing, the court may determine your claim based on the Claim of Exemption, Financial Statement (when one is required), Notice of Opposition to Claim of Exemption, and other evidence that may be presented.

Form Approved by the Judicial Council of California
WG-010/EJ-175 [Rev. January 1, 2007]

NOTICE OF HEARING ON CLAIM OF EXEMPTION
(Wage Garnishment—Enforcement of Judgment)

Code of Civil Procedure, § 703.550, 706.107
www.courtinfo.ca.gov

SHORT TITLE:	LEVYING OFFICER FILE NO.	COURT CASE NO.

WG-010/EJ-175

PROOF OF SERVICE BY MAIL

I am over the age of 18 and not a party to this cause. I am a resident of or employed in the county where the mailing occurred. My residence or business address is *(specify)*:

I served the attached Notice of Hearing on Claim of Exemption and the attached Notice of Opposition to Claim of Exemption by enclosing true copies in a sealed envelope addressed to each person whose name and address is given below and depositing the envelope in the United States mail with the postage fully prepaid.

(1) Date of deposit: (2) Place of deposit *(city and state)*:

NAME AND ADDRESS OF EACH PERSON TO WHOM NOTICE WAS MAILED

I declare under penalty of perjury under the laws of the State of California that the foregoing is true and correct.

Date:

_____
(TYPE OR PRINT NAME)

▶ _____
(SIGNATURE OF DECLARANT)

PROOF OF SERVICE—PERSONAL DELIVERY

I am over the age of 18 and not a party to this cause. My residence or business address is *(specify)*:

I served the attached Notice of Hearing on Claim of Exemption and the attached Notice of Opposition to Claim of Exemption by personally delivering copies to the person served as shown below.

PERSONS SERVED

Name   **Delivery At**
               Date: Time: Address:

I declare under penalty of perjury under the laws of the State of California that the foregoing is true and correct.

Date:

_____
(TYPE OR PRINT NAME)

▶ _____
(SIGNATURE OF DECLARANT)

WG-010/WJ-175 [Rev. January 1, 2007]

NOTICE OF HEARING ON CLAIM OF EXEMPTION
(Wage Garnishment—Enforcement of Judgment)

Memorandum of Costs After Judgment

MC-012

ATTORNEY OR PARTY WITHOUT ATTORNEY (Name, State Bar number, and address):	FOR COURT USE ONLY
TELEPHONE NO.: FAX NO.:	
ATTORNEY FOR (Name):	

NAME OF COURT:
STREET ADDRESS:
MAILING ADDRESS:
CITY AND ZIP CODE:
BRANCH NAME:

PLAINTIFF:

DEFENDANT:

MEMORANDUM OF COSTS AFTER JUDGMENT, ACKNOWLEDGMENT OF CREDIT, AND DECLARATION OF ACCRUED INTEREST	CASE NUMBER:

1. I claim the following costs after judgment incurred within the last two years (indicate if there are multiple items in any category):

		Dates Incurred	Amount
a	Preparing and issuing abstract of judgment		$
b	Recording and indexing abstract of judgment		$
c	Filing notice of judgment lien on personal property		$
d	Issuing writ of execution, to extent not satisfied by Code Civ. Proc., § 685.050 (specify county):		$
e	Levying officers fees, to extent not satisfied by Code Civ. Proc., § 685.050 or wage garnishment		$
f	Approved fee on application for order for appearance of judgment debtor, or other approved costs under Code Civ. Proc., § 708.110 et seq.		$
g	Attorney fees, if allowed by Code Civ. Proc., § 685.040		$
h	Other: (Statute authorizing cost):		$
i	Total of claimed costs for current memorandum of costs (add items a-h)		$

2. All previously allowed postjudgment costs: .... $

3. **Total** of all postjudgment costs (add items 1 and 2): .... **TOTAL** $

4. **Acknowledgment of Credit.** I acknowledge total credit to date (including returns on levy process and direct payments) in the amount of: $

5. **Declaration of Accrued Interest.** Interest on the judgment accruing at the legal rate from the date of entry on balances due after partial satisfactions and other credits in the amount of: $

6. I am the ☐ judgment creditor ☐ agent for the judgment creditor ☐ attorney for the judgment creditor.
I have knowledge of the facts concerning the costs claimed above. To the best of my knowledge and belief, the costs claimed are correct, reasonable, and necessary, and have not been satisfied.

I declare under penalty of perjury under the laws of the State of California that the foregoing is true and correct.

Date:

▶

_____   _____
(TYPE OR PRINT NAME)   (SIGNATURE OF DECLARANT)

NOTICE TO THE JUDGMENT DEBTOR
If this memorandum of costs is filed at the same time as an application for a writ of execution, any statutory costs, *not exceeding $100 in aggregate* and not already allowed by the court, may be included in the writ of execution. *The fees sought under this memorandum may be disallowed by the court upon a motion to tax filed by the debtor, notwithstanding the fees having been included in the writ of execution.* (Code Civ. Proc., § 685.070(e).) A motion to tax costs claimed in this memorandum must be filed within 10 days after service of the memorandum. (Code Civ. Proc., § 685.070(c).)

(Proof of service on reverse)

| Form Adopted for Mandatory Use
Judicial Council of California
MC-012 [Rev. January 1, 2011] | **MEMORANDUM OF COSTS AFTER JUDGMENT, ACKNOWLEDGMENT OF CREDIT, AND DECLARATION OF ACCRUED INTEREST** | Code of Civil Procedure
§ 685.070
www.courts.ca.gov |

SHORT TITLE:	CASE NUMBER:

MC-012

PROOF OF SERVICE
☐ Mail ☐ Personal Service

1. At the time of service I was at least 18 years of age and not a party to this legal action.

2. My residence or business address is *(specify):*

3. I mailed or personally delivered a copy of the *Memorandum of Costs After Judgment, Acknowledgment of Credit, and Declaration of Accrued Interest* as follows *(complete either a or b):*
   a. ☐ **Mail.** I am a resident of or employed in the county where the mailing occurred.
      (1) I enclosed a copy in an envelope AND
         (a) ☐ **deposited** the sealed envelope with the United States Postal Service with the postage fully prepaid.
         (b) ☐ **placed** the envelope for collection and mailing on the date and at the place shown in items below following our ordinary business practices. I am readily familiar with this business's practice for collecting and processing correspondence for mailing. On the same day that correspondence is placed for collection and mailing, it is deposited in the ordinary course of business with the United States Postal Service in a sealed envelope with postage fully prepaid.
      (2) The envelope was addressed and mailed as follows:
         (a) Name of person served:
         (b) Address on envelope:

         (c) Date of mailing:
         (d) Place of mailing *(city and state):*

   b. ☐ **Personal delivery.** I personally delivered a copy as follows:
      (1) Name of person served:
      (2) Address where delivered:

      (3) Date delivered:
      (4) Time delivered:

I declare under penalty of perjury under the laws of the State of California that the foregoing is true and correct.

Date:

_____ ▶ _____
(TYPE OR PRINT NAME)   (SIGNATURE OF DECLARANT)

Attachment

(can be used with any Judicial Council form)

SHORT TITLE:	CASE NUMBER:

ATTACHMENT *(Number):* _____

(This Attachment may be used with any Judicial Council form.)

(If the item that this Attachment concerns is made under penalty of perjury, all statements in this Attachment are made under penalty of perjury.)

Page _____ of _____

(Add pages as required)

Form Approved for Optional Use
Judicial Council of California
MC-025 [Rev. July 1, 2009]

ATTACHMENT
to Judicial Council Form

www.courtinfo.ca.gov

MC-025

Keeping Track of Costs

Keeping Track of Costs

Date Expended	Cost Amount	Type of Cost	Expense Record	Date Costs Claimed

Keeping Track of Payments

Keeping Track of Payments

A Starting Date	B Ending Date	C No. of Days	D Balance	E Interest Due (D x ☐% x C/365)	F Payment	G Balance Reduction (F-E)	H Unpaid Interest

Proof of Claim

B10 (Official Form 10) (04/13)

UNITED STATES BANKRUPTCY COURT		**PROOF OF CLAIM**
Name of Debtor:	Case Number:	

NOTE: *Do not use this form to make a claim for an administrative expense that arises after the bankruptcy filing. You may file a request for payment of an administrative expense according to 11 U.S.C. § 503.*

Name of Creditor (the person or other entity to whom the debtor owes money or property):

COURT USE ONLY

Name and address where notices should be sent:

❏ Check this box if this claim amends a previously filed claim.

Court Claim Number:_____
(*If known*)

Telephone number: email:

Filed on:_____

Name and address where payment should be sent (if different from above):

❏ Check this box if you are aware that anyone else has filed a proof of claim relating to this claim. Attach copy of statement giving particulars.

Telephone number: email:

1. Amount of Claim as of Date Case Filed: $_____

If all or part of the claim is secured, complete item 4.

If all or part of the claim is entitled to priority, complete item 5.

❏ Check this box if the claim includes interest or other charges in addition to the principal amount of the claim. Attach a statement that itemizes interest or charges.

2. Basis for Claim: _____
(See instruction #2)

3. Last four digits of any number by which creditor identifies debtor: ___ ___ ___ ___	3a. Debtor may have scheduled account as: _____ (See instruction #3a)	3b. Uniform Claim Identifier (optional): _ (See instruction #3b)

4. Secured Claim (See instruction #4)
Check the appropriate box if the claim is secured by a lien on property or a right of setoff, attach required redacted documents, and provide the requested information.

Amount of arrearage and other charges, as of the time case was filed, included in secured claim, if any:

$_____

Nature of property or right of setoff: ❏ Real Estate ❏ Motor Vehicle ❏ Other
Describe:

Basis for perfection: _____

Value of Property: $_____

Amount of Secured Claim: $_____

Annual Interest Rate_____% ❏ Fixed or ❏ Variable
(when case was filed)

Amount Unsecured: $_____

5. Amount of Claim Entitled to Priority under 11 U.S.C. § 507 (a). If any part of the claim falls into one of the following categories, check the box specifying the priority and state the amount.

❏ Domestic support obligations under 11 U.S.C. § 507 (a)(1)(A) or (a)(1)(B).

❏ Wages, salaries, or commissions (up to $12,475*) earned within 180 days before the case was filed or the debtor's business ceased, whichever is earlier – 11 U.S.C. § 507 (a)(4).

❏ Contributions to an employee benefit plan – 11 U.S.C. § 507 (a)(5).

Amount entitled to priority:

❏ Up to $2,775* of deposits toward purchase, lease, or rental of property or services for personal, family, or household use – 11 U.S.C. § 507 (a)(7).

❏ Taxes or penalties owed to governmental units – 11 U.S.C. § 507 (a)(8).

❏ Other – Specify applicable paragraph of 11 U.S.C. § 507 (a)(__).

$_____

Amounts are subject to adjustment on 4/01/16 and every 3 years thereafter with respect to cases commenced on or after the date of adjustment.

6. Credits. The amount of all payments on this claim has been credited for the purpose of making this proof of claim. (See instruction #6)

B10 (Official Form 10) (04/13) 2

7. Documents: Attached are **redacted** copies of any documents that support the claim, such as promissory notes, purchase orders, invoices, itemized statements of running accounts, contracts, judgments, mortgages, security agreements, or, in the case of a claim based on an open-end or revolving consumer credit agreement, a statement providing the information required by FRBP 3001(c)(3)(A). If the claim is secured, box 4 has been completed, and **redacted** copies of documents providing evidence of perfection of a security interest are attached. If the claim is secured by the debtor's principal residence, the Mortgage Proof of Claim Attachment is being filed with this claim. *(See instruction #7, and the definition of "redacted".)*

DO NOT SEND ORIGINAL DOCUMENTS. ATTACHED DOCUMENTS MAY BE DESTROYED AFTER SCANNING.

If the documents are not available, please explain:

---

8. Signature: (See instruction #8)

Check the appropriate box.

☐ I am the creditor.   ☐ I am the creditor's authorized agent.   ☐ I am the trustee, or the debtor, or their authorized agent. (See Bankruptcy Rule 3004.)   ☐ I am a guarantor, surety, indorser, or other codebtor. (See Bankruptcy Rule 3005.)

I declare under penalty of perjury that the information provided in this claim is true and correct to the best of my knowledge, information, and reasonable belief.

Print Name: _____
Title: _____
Company: _____
Address and telephone number (if different from notice address above):   (Signature)   (Date)
_____
_____
Telephone number: _____ email: _____

Penalty for presenting fraudulent claim: Fine of up to $500,000 or imprisonment for up to 5 years, or both. 18 U.S.C. §§ 152 and 3571.

INSTRUCTIONS FOR PROOF OF CLAIM FORM
The instructions and definitions below are general explanations of the law. In certain circumstances, such as bankruptcy cases not filed voluntarily by the debtor, exceptions to these general rules may apply.
Items to be completed in Proof of Claim form

Court, Name of Debtor, and Case Number:
Fill in the federal judicial district in which the bankruptcy case was filed (for example, Central District of California), the debtor's full name, and the case number. If the creditor received a notice of the case from the bankruptcy court, all of this information is at the top of the notice.

Creditor's Name and Address:
Fill in the name of the person or entity asserting a claim and the name and address of the person who should receive notices issued during the bankruptcy case. A separate space is provided for the payment address if it differs from the notice address. The creditor has a continuing obligation to keep the court informed of its current address. See Federal Rule of Bankruptcy Procedure (FRBP) 2002(g).

1. Amount of Claim as of Date Case Filed:
State the total amount owed to the creditor on the date of the bankruptcy filing. Follow the instructions concerning whether to complete items 4 and 5. Check the box if interest or other charges are included in the claim.

2. Basis for Claim:
State the type of debt or how it was incurred. Examples include goods sold, money loaned, services performed, personal injury/wrongful death, car loan, mortgage note, and credit card. If the claim is based on delivering health care goods or services, limit the disclosure of the goods or services so as to avoid embarrassment or the disclosure of confidential health care information. You may be required to provide additional disclosure if an interested party objects to the claim.

3. Last Four Digits of Any Number by Which Creditor Identifies Debtor:
State only the last four digits of the debtor's account or other number used by the creditor to identify the debtor.

3a. Debtor May Have Scheduled Account As:
Report a change in the creditor's name, a transferred claim, or any other information that clarifies a difference between this proof of claim and the claim as scheduled by the debtor.

3b. Uniform Claim Identifier:
If you use a uniform claim identifier, you may report it here. A uniform claim identifier is an optional 24-character identifier that certain large creditors use to facilitate electronic payment in chapter 13 cases.

4. Secured Claim:
Check whether the claim is fully or partially secured. Skip this section if the claim is entirely unsecured. (See Definitions.) If the claim is secured, check the box for the nature and value of property that secures the claim, attach copies of lien documentation, and state, as of the date of the bankruptcy filing, the annual interest rate (and whether it is fixed or variable), and the amount past due on the claim.

5. Amount of Claim Entitled to Priority Under 11 U.S.C. § 507 (a).
If any portion of the claim falls into any category shown, check the appropriate box(es) and state the amount entitled to priority. (See Definitions.) A claim may be partly priority and partly non-priority. For example, in some of the categories, the law limits the amount entitled to priority.

6. Credits:
An authorized signature on this proof of claim serves as an acknowledgment that when calculating the amount of the claim, the creditor gave the debtor credit for any payments received toward the debt.

7. Documents:
Attach redacted copies of any documents that show the debt exists and a lien secures the debt. You must also attach copies of documents that evidence perfection of any security interest and documents required by FRBP 3001(c) for claims based on an open-end or revolving consumer credit agreement or secured by a security interest in the debtor's principal residence. You may also attach a summary in addition to the documents themselves. FRBP 3001(c) and (d). If the claim is based on delivering health care goods or services, limit disclosing confidential health care information. Do not send original documents, as attachments may be destroyed after scanning.

8. Date and Signature:
The individual completing this proof of claim must sign and date it. FRBP 9011. If the claim is filed electronically, FRBP 5005(a)(2) authorizes courts to establish local rules specifying what constitutes a signature. If you sign this form, you declare under penalty of perjury that the information provided is true and correct to the best of your knowledge, information, and reasonable belief. Your signature is also a certification that the claim meets the requirements of FRBP 9011(b). Whether the claim is filed electronically or in person, if your name is on the signature line, you are responsible for the declaration. Print the name and title, if any, of the creditor or other person authorized to file this claim. State the filer's address and telephone number if it differs from the address given on the top of the form for purposes of receiving notices. If the claim is filed by an authorized agent, provide both the name of the individual filing the claim and the name of the agent. If the authorized agent is a servicer, identify the corporate servicer as the company. Criminal penalties apply for making a false statement on a proof of claim.

B10 (Official Form 10) (04/13)

DEFINITIONS

Debtor
A debtor is the person, corporation, or other entity that has filed a bankruptcy case.

Creditor
A creditor is a person, corporation, or other entity to whom debtor owes a debt that was incurred before the date of the bankruptcy filing. See 11 U.S.C. §101 (10).

Claim
A claim is the creditor's right to receive payment for a debt owed by the debtor on the date of the bankruptcy filing. See 11 U.S.C. §101 (5). A claim may be secured or unsecured.

Proof of Claim
A proof of claim is a form used by the creditor to indicate the amount of the debt owed by the debtor on the date of the bankruptcy filing. The creditor must file the form with the clerk of the same bankruptcy court in which the bankruptcy case was filed.

Secured Claim Under 11 U.S.C. § 506 (a)
A secured claim is one backed by a lien on property of the debtor. The claim is secured so long as the creditor has the right to be paid from the property prior to other creditors. The amount of the secured claim cannot exceed the value of the property. Any amount owed to the creditor in excess of the value of the property is an unsecured claim. Examples of liens on property include a mortgage on real estate or a security interest in a car. A lien may be voluntarily granted by a debtor or may be obtained through a court proceeding. In some states, a court judgment is a lien.

A claim also may be secured if the creditor owes the debtor money (has a right to setoff).

Unsecured Claim
An unsecured claim is one that does not meet the requirements of a secured claim. A claim may be partly unsecured if the amount of the claim exceeds the value of the property on which the creditor has a lien.

Claim Entitled to Priority Under 11 U.S.C. § 507 (a)
Priority claims are certain categories of unsecured claims that are paid from the available money or property in a bankruptcy case before other unsecured claims.

Redacted
A document has been redacted when the person filing it has masked, edited out, or otherwise deleted, certain information. A creditor must show only the last four digits of any social-security, individual's tax-identification, or financial-account number, only the initials of a minor's name, and only the year of any person's date of birth. If the claim is based on the delivery of health care goods or services, limit the disclosure of the goods or services so as to avoid embarrassment or the disclosure of confidential health care information.

Evidence of Perfection
Evidence of perfection may include a mortgage, lien, certificate of title, financing statement, or other document showing that the lien has been filed or recorded.

INFORMATION

Acknowledgment of Filing of Claim
To receive acknowledgment of your filing, you may either enclose a stamped self-addressed envelope and a copy of this proof of claim or you may access the court's PACER system (www.pacer.psc.uscourts.gov) for a small fee to view your filed proof of claim.

Offers to Purchase a Claim
Certain entities are in the business of purchasing claims for an amount less than the face value of the claims. One or more of these entities may contact the creditor and offer to purchase the claim. Some of the written communications from these entities may easily be confused with official court documentation or communications from the debtor. These entities do not represent the bankruptcy court or the debtor. The creditor has no obligation to sell its claim. However, if the creditor decides to sell its claim, any transfer of such claim is subject to FRBP 3001(e), any applicable provisions of the Bankruptcy Code (11 U.S.C. § 101 *et seq.*), and any applicable orders of the bankruptcy court.

Creditor's Claim

DE-172

ATTORNEY OR PARTY WITHOUT ATTORNEY (Name, state bar number, and address):	TELEPHONE AND FAX NOS.:	FOR COURT USE ONLY
ATTORNEY FOR (Name):		

SUPERIOR COURT OF CALIFORNIA, COUNTY OF
    STREET ADDRESS:
    MAILING ADDRESS:
    CITY AND ZIP CODE:
    BRANCH NAME:

ESTATE OF (Name):

DECEDENT

CREDITOR'S CLAIM

CASE NUMBER:

You must file this claim with the court clerk at the court address above before the LATER of (a) four months after the date letters (authority to act for the estate) were first issued to the personal representative, or (b) sixty days after the date the *Notice of Administration* was given to the creditor, if notice was given as provided in Probate Code section 9051. You must also mail or deliver a copy of this claim to the personal representative and his or her attorney. A proof of service is on the reverse.
WARNING: Your claim will in most instances be invalid if you do not properly complete this form, file it on time with the court, and mail or deliver a copy to the personal representative and his or her attorney.

1. Total amount of the claim: $
2. Claimant *(name)*:
   a. ☐ an individual
   b. ☐ an individual or entity doing business under the fictitious name of *(specify)*:

   c. ☐ a partnership. The person signing has authority to sign on behalf of the partnership.
   d. ☐ a corporation. The person signing has authority to sign on behalf of the corporation.
   e. ☐ other *(specify)*:
3. Address of claimant *(specify)*:

4. Claimant is   ☐ the creditor   ☐ a person acting on behalf of creditor *(state reason)*:

5. ☐ Claimant is   ☐ the personal representative   ☐ the attorney for the personal representative.
6. I am authorized to make this claim which is just and due or may become due. All payments on or offsets to the claim have been credited. Facts supporting the claim are   ☐ on reverse   ☐ attached.

I declare under penalty of perjury under the laws of the State of California that the foregoing is true and correct.
Date:

▶

_____   _____
(TYPE OR PRINT NAME AND TITLE)   (SIGNATURE OF CLAIMANT)

INSTRUCTIONS TO CLAIMANT

A. On the reverse, itemize the claim and show the date the service was rendered or the debt incurred. Describe the item or service in detail, and indicate the amount claimed for each item. Do not include debts incurred after the date of death, except funeral claims.
B. If the claim is not due or contingent, or the amount is not yet ascertainable, state the facts supporting the claim.
C. If the claim is secured by a note or other written instrument, the original or a copy must be attached *(state why original is unavailable.)* If secured by mortgage, deed of trust, or other lien on property that is of record, it is sufficient to describe the security and refer to the date or volume and page, and county where recorded. *(See Prob. Code, § 9152.)*
D. Mail or take this original claim to the court clerk's office for filing. If mailed, use certified mail, with return receipt requested.
E. Mail or deliver a copy to the personal representative and his or her attorney. Complete the *Proof of Mailing or Personal Delivery* on the reverse.
F. The personal representative or his or her attorney will notify you when your claim is allowed or rejected.
G. Claims against the estate by the personal representative and the attorney for the personal representative must be filed within the claim period allowed in Probate Code section 9100. See the notice box above.

(Continued on reverse)

Form Approved by the
Judicial Council of California
DE-172 [Rev. January 1, 1998]

CREDITOR'S CLAIM
(Probate)

Probate Code, §§ 9000 et seq., 9153

ESTATE OF (Name):	CASE NUMBER:
DECEDENT	

FACTS SUPPORTING THE CREDITOR'S CLAIM
☐ See attachment *(if space is insufficient)*

Date of item	Item and supporting facts	Amount claimed
	TOTAL:	$

PROOF OF ☐ **MAILING** ☐ **PERSONAL DELIVERY** **TO PERSONAL REPRESENTATIVE**
(Be sure to mail or take the original to the court clerk's office for filing)

1. I am the creditor or a person acting on behalf of the creditor. At the time of mailing or delivery I was at least 18 years of age.
2. My residence or business address is *(specify)*:

3. I mailed or personally delivered a copy of this *Creditor's Claim* to the personal representative as follows *(check either a or b below)*:
   a. ☐ **Mail.** I am a resident of or employed in the county where the mailing occurred.
      (1) I enclosed a copy in an envelope AND
         (a) ☐ **deposited** the sealed envelope with the United States Postal Service with the postage fully prepaid.
         (b) ☐ **placed** the envelope for collection and mailing on the date and at the place shown in items below following our ordinary business practices. I am readily familiar with this business' practice for collecting and processing correspondence for mailing. On the same day that correspondence is placed for collection and mailing, it is deposited in the ordinary course of business with the United States Postal Service in a sealed envelope with postage fully prepaid.
      (2) The envelope was addressed and mailed first-class as follows:
         (a) Name of personal representative served:
         (b) Address on envelope:

         (c) Date of mailing:
         (d) Place of mailing *(city and state)*:
   b. ☐ **Personal delivery.** I personally delivered a copy of the claim to the personal representative as follows:
      (1) Name of personal representative served:
      (2) Address where delivered:

      (3) Date delivered:
      (4) Time delivered:

I declare under penalty of perjury under the laws of the State of California that the foregoing is true and correct.
Date:

▶

_____ _____
(TYPE OR PRINT NAME OF CLAIMANT)   (SIGNATURE OF CLAIMANT)

DE-172 [Rev. January 1, 1998]

CREDITOR'S CLAIM
(Probate)

Application for and Renewal of Judgment

EJ-190

ATTORNEY OR PARTY WITHOUT ATTORNEY *(Name, address, and State Bar number):*
After recording, return to:

TEL NO.:   FAX NO. *(optional):*
E-MAIL ADDRESS *(Optional):*
☐ ATTORNEY FOR   ☐ JUDGMENT CREDITOR   ☐ ASSIGNEE OF RECORD

SUPERIOR COURT OF CALIFORNIA, COUNTY OF
STREET ADDRESS:
MAILING ADDRESS:
CITY AND ZIP CODE:
BRANCH NAME:

FOR RECORDER'S USE ONLY

PLAINTIFF:
DEFENDANT:

CASE NUMBER:

APPLICATION FOR AND RENEWAL OF JUDGMENT

FOR COURT USE ONLY

☐ Judgment creditor
☐ Assignee of record
  applies for renewal of the judgment as follows:

1. Applicant *(name and address):*

2. Judgment debtor *(name and last known address):*

3. Original judgment
   a. Case number *(specify):*
   b. Entered on *(date):*
   c. Recorded:
      (1) Date:
      (2) County:
      (3) Instrument No.:

4. ☐ Judgment previously renewed *(specify each case number and date):*

5. ☐ Renewal of money judgment
   a. Total judgment . . . . $
   b. Costs after judgment . . . . $
   c. Subtotal *(add a and b)* . . . . $_____
   d. Credits after judgment . . . . $
   e. Subtotal *(subtract d from c)* . . . . $_____
   f. Interest after judgment . . . . $
   g. Fee for filing renewal application . . . . $
   h. **Total renewed judgment** *(add e, f, and g)* $_____
   i. ☐ The amounts called for in items a–h are different for each debtor.
      These amounts are stated for each debtor on Attachment 5.

Form Approved for Optional Use
Judicial Council of California
EJ-190 [Rev. July 1, 2014]

APPLICATION FOR AND RENEWAL OF JUDGMENT

Code of Civil Procedure, § 683.140

SHORT TITLE:	CASE NUMBER:

6. ☐ Renewal of judgment for   ☐ possession.
                                                                        ☐ sale.

   a. ☐ If judgment was not previously renewed, terms of judgment as entered:

   b. ☐ If judgment was previously renewed, terms of judgment as last renewed:

   c. ☐ Terms of judgment remaining unsatisfied:

I declare under penalty of perjury under the laws of the State of California that the foregoing is true and correct.

Date:

_____ ▶ _____
(TYPE OR PRINT NAME)   (SIGNATURE OF DECLARANT)

APPLICATION FOR AND RENEWAL OF JUDGMENT

Notice of Renewal of Judgment

EJ-195

ATTORNEY OR PARTY WITHOUT ATTORNEY *(Name and Address)*	TELEPHONE NO.:	FOR COURT USE ONLY
ATTORNEY FOR *(Name)*:		

NAME OF COURT:
STREET ADDRESS:
MAILING ADDRESS:
CITY AND ZIP CODE:
BRANCH NAME:

PLAINTIFF:

DEFENDANT:

NOTICE OF RENEWAL OF JUDGMENT	CASE NUMBER:

TO JUDGMENT DEBTOR *(name)*:

1. **This renewal extends** the period of enforceability of the judgment until 10 years from the date the application for renewal was filed.
2. **If you object** to this renewal, you may make a motion to vacate or modify the renewal with this court.
3. You must make this motion within **30 days** after service of this notice on you.
4. A copy of the *Application for and Renewal of Judgment* is attached *(Cal. Rules of Court, rule 3.1900)*.

Date: _____ Clerk, by _____, Deputy

[SEAL]

See CCP 683.160 for information on method of service

Form Adopted for Mandatory Use
Judicial Council of California
EJ-195 [Rev. January 1, 2007]

NOTICE OF RENEWAL OF JUDGMENT

Code of Civil Procedure, § 683.160
www.courtinfo.ca.gov

Proof of Service

POS-020

ATTORNEY OR PARTY WITHOUT ATTORNEY *(Name, State Bar number, and address):*	FOR COURT USE ONLY
TELEPHONE NO.: FAX NO. *(Optional):*	
E-MAIL ADDRESS *(Optional):*	
ATTORNEY FOR *(Name):*	

SUPERIOR COURT OF CALIFORNIA, COUNTY OF
STREET ADDRESS:
MAILING ADDRESS:
CITY AND ZIP CODE:
BRANCH NAME:

PETITIONER/PLAINTIFF:

RESPONDENT/DEFENDANT:

PROOF OF PERSONAL SERVICE—CIVIL	CASE NUMBER:

(Do not use this Proof of Service to show service of a Summons and Complaint.)

1. I am over 18 years of age and **not a party to this action**.
2. I served the following **documents** *(specify):*

   ☐ The documents are listed in the *Attachment to Proof of Personal Service—Civil (Documents Served)* (form POS-020(D)).
3. I personally served the following **persons** at the address, date, and time stated:
   a. Name:
   b. Address:
   c. Date:
   d. Time:

   ☐ The persons are listed in the *Attachment to Proof of Personal Service—Civil (Persons Served)* (form POS-020(P)).
4. I am
   a. ☐ not a registered California process server.
   b. ☐ a registered California process server.
   c. ☐ an employee or independent contractor of a registered California process server.
   d. ☐ exempt from registration under Business & Professions Code section 22350(b).
5. My name, address, telephone number, and, if applicable, county of registration and number are *(specify):*

6. ☐ I declare under penalty of perjury under the laws of the State of California that the foregoing is true and correct.
7. ☐ I am a California sheriff or marshal and certify that the foregoing is true and correct.

Date:

▶

_____   _____
(TYPE OR PRINT NAME OF PERSON WHO SERVED THE PAPERS)   (SIGNATURE OF PERSON WHO SERVED THE PAPERS)

Form Approved for Optional Use
Judicial Council of California
POS-020 [New January 1, 2005]

PROOF OF PERSONAL SERVICE—CIVIL

Code of Civil Procedure, § 1011
www.courtinfo.ca.gov

INFORMATION SHEET FOR PROOF OF PERSONAL SERVICE—CIVIL
(This information sheet is not a part of the Proof of Service form and does not need to be copied, served, or filed.)

NOTE: This form should **not** be used for proof of service of a summons and complaint. For that purpose, use *Proof of Service of Summons* (form POS-010).

Use these instructions to complete the *Proof of Personal Service* (form POS-020).

A person at least 18 years of age or older must serve the documents. There are two main ways to serve documents: (1) by personal delivery and (2) by mail. Certain documents must be personally served. You must determine whether personal service is required for a document.

The person who personally served the documents must complete a proof of service form for the documents served. **You cannot serve documents if you are a party to the action.**

INSTRUCTIONS FOR THE PERSON WHO SERVED THE DOCUMENTS

The proof of service should be printed or typed. If you have Internet access, fillable versions of the form are available at www.courtinfo.ca.gov/forms.

Complete the top section of the proof of service form as follows:

First box, left side: In this box print the name, address, and phone number of the person *for* whom you served the documents.

Second box, left side: Print the name of the county in which the legal action is filed and the court's address in this box. The address for the court should be the same as on the documents that you served.

Third box, left side: Print the names of the Petitioner/Plaintiff and Respondent/Defendant in this box. Use the same names as are listed on the documents that you served.

First box, top of form, right side: Leave this box blank for the court's use.

Second box, right side: Print the case number in this box. The number should be the same as the case number on the documents that you served.

Complete all applicable items on the form:

1. You are stating that you are over the age of 18 and that you are not a party to this action.
2. List the name of each document that you delivered to the person. If you need more space, check the box in item 2, complete the *Attachment to Proof of Personal Service–Civil (Documents Served)* (form POS-020(D)), and attach it to form POS-020.
3. Provide the name of each person served, the address where you served the documents, and the date and time of service. If you served more than one person, check the box in item 3, complete the *Attachment to Proof of Personal Service–Civil (Persons Served)* (form POS-020(P)), and attach it to form POS-020.
4. Check the box that applies to you. If you are a private person serving the documents for a party, check box "a."
5. Print your name, address, and telephone number. If applicable, include the county in which you are registered as a process server and your registration number.
6. You must check this box if you are not a California sheriff or marshal. You are stating under penalty of perjury that the information you have provided is true and correct.
7. Do not check this box unless you are a California sheriff or marshal.

At the bottom, fill in the date on which you signed the form, print your name, and sign the form at the arrow. By signing, you are stating under penalty of perjury that all the information that you have provided on form POS-020 is true and correct.

PROOF OF PERSONAL SERVICE—CIVIL

POS-030

ATTORNEY OR PARTY WITHOUT ATTORNEY *(Name, State Bar number, and address):*

Amy Right
1000 My st
Mytown, Ca 90000

TELEPHONE NO.: 310-555-5555   FAX NO. *(Optional):*
E-MAIL ADDRESS *(Optional):*
ATTORNEY FOR *(Name):* In Pro Per

FOR COURT USE ONLY

SUPERIOR COURT OF CALIFORNIA, COUNTY OF Los Angeles
STREET ADDRESS: 111 Hill st
MAILING ADDRESS:
CITY AND ZIP CODE: Los Angeles, Ca 90012
BRANCH NAME: Stanley Mosk Courthouse

PETITIONER/PLAINTIFF: Amy Right

RESPONDENT/DEFENDANT: Jeff Isbad

PROOF OF SERVICE BY FIRST-CLASS MAIL—CIVIL

CASE NUMBER:
14K5000

(Do not use this Proof of Service to show service of a Summons and Complaint.)

1. I am over 18 years of age and **not a party to this action.** I am a resident of or employed in the county where the mailing took place.

2. My residence or business address is:
   160 Helpful st
   Los Angeles, Ca 90016

3. On *(date):* 02/30/2015   I mailed from *(city and state):* Los Angeles, Ca
   the following **documents** *(specify):*
   name of forms mailed and how many pages. Make sure that it is allowed to serve them by mail
   Read chapter that covers the document you are mailing

   ☐ The documents are listed in the *Attachment to Proof of Service by First-Class Mail—Civil (Documents Served)* (form POS-030(D)).

4. I served the documents by enclosing them in an envelope and *(check one):*
   a. ☑ **depositing** the sealed envelope with the United States Postal Service with the postage fully prepaid.
   b. ☐ **placing** the envelope for collection and mailing following our ordinary business practices. I am readily familiar with this business's practice for collecting and processing correspondence for mailing. On the same day that correspondence is placed for collection and mailing, it is deposited in the ordinary course of business with the United States Postal Service in a sealed envelope with postage fully prepaid.

5. The envelope was addressed and mailed as follows:
   a. **Name** of person served: Jeff Isbad
   b. **Address** of person served:
      666 e Cra P st
      Helltown, Ca 90666

   ☐ The name and address of each person to whom I mailed the documents is listed in the *Attachment to Proof of Service by First-Class Mail—Civil (Persons Served)* (POS-030(P)).

I declare under penalty of perjury under the laws of the State of California that the foregoing is true and correct.

Date: 02/30/2015

Betty Bestfriend
(TYPE OR PRINT NAME OF PERSON COMPLETING THIS FORM)   ▶   (SIGNATURE OF PERSON COMPLETING THIS FORM)

Form Approved for Optional Use
Judicial Council of California
POS-030 [New January 1, 2005]

PROOF OF SERVICE BY FIRST-CLASS MAIL—CIVIL
(Proof of Service)

Code of Civil Procedure, §§ 1013, 1013a
www.courtinfo.ca.gov

INFORMATION SHEET FOR PROOF OF SERVICE BY FIRST-CLASS MAIL—CIVIL

(This information sheet is not part of the Proof of Service and does not need to be copied, served, or filed.)

NOTE: This form should **not** be used for proof of service of a summons and complaint. For that purpose, use *Proof of Service of Summons* (form POS-010).

Use these instructions to complete the *Proof of Service by First-Class Mail—Civil* (form POS-030).

A person over 18 years of age must serve the documents. There are two main ways to serve documents: (1) by personal delivery and (2) by mail. Certain documents must be personally served. You must determine whether personal service is required for a document. Use the *Proof of Personal Service–Civil* (form POS-020) if the documents were personally served.

The person who served the documents by mail must complete a proof of service form for the documents served. **You cannot serve documents if you are a party to the action.**

INSTRUCTIONS FOR THE PERSON WHO SERVED THE DOCUMENTS

The proof of service should be printed or typed. If you have Internet access, a fillable version of the Proof of Service form is available at www.courtinfo.ca.gov/forms.

Complete the top section of the proof of service form as follows:

<u>First box, left side</u>: In this box print the name, address, and telephone number of the person *for* whom you served the documents.

<u>Second box, left side</u>: Print the name of the county in which the legal action is filed and the court's address in this box. The address for the court should be the same as on the documents that you served.

<u>Third box, left side</u>: Print the names of the Petitioner/Plaintiff and Respondent/Defendant in this box. Use the same names as are on the documents that you served.

<u>First box, top of form, right side</u>: Leave this box blank for the court's use.

<u>Second box, right side</u>: Print the case number in this box. The case number should be the same as the case number on the documents that you served.

Complete items 1–5 as follows:

1. You are stating that you are over the age of 18 and that you are not a party to this action. You are also stating that you either live in or are employed in the county where the mailing took place.

2. Print your home or business address.

3. Provide the date and place of the mailing and list the name of each document that you mailed. If you need more space to list the documents, check the box in item 3, complete the *Attachment to Proof of Service by First-Class Mail—Civil (Documents Served)* (form POS-030(D)), and attach it to form POS-030.

4. For item 4:

    Check box a if you personally put the documents in the regular U.S. mail.
    Check box b if you put the documents in the mail at your place of business.

5. Provide the name and address of each person to whom you mailed the documents. If you mailed the documents to more than one person, check the box in item 5, complete the *Attachment to Proof of Service by First-Class Mail—Civil (Persons Served)* (form POS-030(P)), and attach it to form POS-030.

At the bottom, fill in the date on which you signed the form, print your name, and sign the form. By signing, you are stating under penalty of perjury that all the information you have provided on form POS-030 is true and correct.

PROOF OF SERVICE BY FIRST CLASS MAIL—CIVIL
(Proof of Service)

POS-040

ATTORNEY OR PARTY WITHOUT ATTORNEY:	STATE BAR NO:	FOR COURT USE ONLY
NAME:		
FIRM NAME:		
STREET ADDRESS:		
CITY: STATE: ZIP CODE:		
TELEPHONE NO.: FAX NO.:		
E-MAIL ADDRESS:		
ATTORNEY FOR (name):		

SUPERIOR COURT OF CALIFORNIA, COUNTY OF
STREET ADDRESS:
MAILING ADDRESS:
CITY AND ZIP CODE:
BRANCH NAME:

Plaintiff/Petitioner:
Defendant/Respondent:

PROOF OF SERVICE—CIVIL
Check method of service (only one):
☐ By Personal Service ☐ By Mail ☐ By Overnight Delivery
☐ By Messenger Service ☐ By Fax

CASE NUMBER:
JUDICIAL OFFICER:
DEPARTMENT:

Do not use this form to show service of a summons and complaint or for electronic service.
See USE OF THIS FORM on page 3.

1. At the time of service I was over 18 years of age **and not a party to this action.**
2. My residence or business address is:

3. ☐ The fax number from which I served the documents is *(complete if service was by fax)*:

4. On *(date):*   I served the following **documents** *(specify):*

   ☐ The documents are listed in the *Attachment to Proof of Service–Civil (Documents Served)* (form POS-040(D)).

5. I served the documents on the **person or persons** below, as follows:
   a. Name of person served:
   b. ☐ *(Complete if service was by personal service, mail, overnight delivery, or messenger service.)*
      Business or residential address where person was served:

   c. ☐ *(Complete if service was by fax.)*
      Fax number where person was served:

   ☐ The names, addresses, and other applicable information about persons served is on the *Attachment to Proof of Service—Civil (Persons Served)* (form POS-040(P)).

6. The documents were served by the following means *(specify):*
   a. ☐ **By personal service.** I personally delivered the documents to the persons at the addresses listed in item 5. (1) For a party represented by an attorney, delivery was made (a) to the attorney personally; or (b) by leaving the documents at the attorney's office, in an envelope or package clearly labeled to identify the attorney being served, with a receptionist or an individual in charge of the office; or (c) if there was no person in the office with whom the notice or papers could be left, by leaving them in a conspicuous place in the office between the hours of nine in the morning and five in the evening. (2) For a party, delivery was made to the party or by leaving the documents at the party's residence with some person not younger than 18 years of age between the hours of eight in the morning and six in the evening.

Page 1 of 3

Form Approved for Optional Use
Judicial Council of California
POS-040 [Rev. February 1, 2017]

PROOF OF SERVICE—CIVIL
(Proof of Service)

Code of Civil Procedure, §§ 1011, 1013, 1013a,
2015.5; Cal. Rules of Court, rule 2.306
www.courts.ca.gov

CASE NAME:	CASE NUMBER:

POS-040

6. b. ☐ **By United States mail.** I enclosed the documents in a sealed envelope or package addressed to the persons at the addresses in item 5 and *(specify one)*:

    (1) ☐ deposited the sealed envelope with the United States Postal Service, with the postage fully prepaid.

    (2) ☐ placed the envelope for collection and mailing, following our ordinary business practices. I am readily familiar with this business's practice for collecting and processing correspondence for mailing. On the same day that correspondence is placed for collection and mailing, it is deposited in the ordinary course of business with the United States Postal Service, in a sealed envelope with postage fully prepaid.

I am a resident or employed in the county where the mailing occurred. The envelope or package was placed in the mail at *(city and state)*:

c. ☐ **By overnight delivery.** I enclosed the documents in an envelope or package provided by an overnight delivery carrier and addressed to the persons at the addresses in item 5. I placed the envelope or package for collection and overnight delivery at an office or a regularly utilized drop box of the overnight delivery carrier.

d. ☐ **By messenger service.** I served the documents by placing them in an envelope or package addressed to the persons at the addresses listed in item 5 and providing them to a professional messenger service for service. *(A declaration by the messenger must accompany this Proof of Service or be contained in the Declaration of Messenger below.)*

e. ☐ **By fax transmission.** Based on an agreement of the parties to accept service by fax transmission, I faxed the documents to the persons at the fax numbers listed in item 5. No error was reported by the fax machine that I used. A copy of the record of the fax transmission, which I printed out, is attached.

I declare under penalty of perjury under the laws of the State of California that the foregoing is true and correct.

Date:

_____ ▶ _____
(TYPE OR PRINT NAME OF DECLARANT)   (SIGNATURE OF DECLARANT)

(If item 6d above is checked, the declaration below must be completed or a separate declaration from a messenger must be attached.)

DECLARATION OF MESSENGER

☐ **By personal service.** I personally delivered the envelope or package received from the declarant above to the persons at the addresses listed in item 5. (1) For a party represented by an attorney, delivery was made (a) to the attorney personally; or (b) by leaving the documents at the attorney's office, in an envelope or package clearly labeled to identify the attorney being served, with a receptionist or an individual in charge of the office; or (c) if there was no person in the office with whom the notice or papers could be left, by leaving them in a conspicuous place in the office between the hours of nine in the morning and five in the evening. (2) For a party, delivery was made to the party or by leaving the documents at the party's residence with some person not younger than 18 years of age between the hours of eight in the morning and six in the evening.

At the time of service, I was over 18 years of age. I am not a party to the above-referenced legal proceeding.

I served the envelope or package, as stated above, on *(date)*:

I declare under penalty of perjury under the laws of the State of California that the foregoing is true and correct.

Date:

_____ ▶ _____
(NAME OF DECLARANT)   (SIGNATURE OF DECLARANT)

POS-040 [Rev. February 1, 2017]   **PROOF OF SERVICE—CIVIL**
(Proof of Service)

POS-040

INFORMATION SHEET FOR PROOF OF SERVICE—CIVIL

(This information sheet is not part of the official proof of service form and does not need to be copied, served, or filed.)

USE OF THIS FORM

This form is designed to be used to show proof of service of documents by (1) personal service, (2) mail, (3) overnight delivery, (4) messenger service, or (5) fax.

This proof of service form should **not** be used to show proof of service of a summons and complaint. For that purpose, use *Proof of Service of Summons* (form POS-010).

Also, this proof of service form should **not** be used to show proof of electronic service. For that purpose, use *Proof of Electronic Service* (form POS-050).

Certain documents must be personally served. For example, an order to show cause and temporary restraining order generally must be served by personal delivery. You must determine whether a document must be personally delivered or can be served by mail or another method.

GENERAL INSTRUCTIONS

A person must be over 18 years of age to serve the documents. The person who served the documents must complete the Proof of Service. **A party to the action cannot serve the documents.**

The Proof of Service should be typed or printed. If you have Internet access, a fillable version of this proof of service form is available at *www.courts.ca.gov/forms.htm.*

Complete the top section of the proof of service form as follows:

First box, left side: In this box print the name, address, and telephone number of the person for whom you served the documents.

Second box, left side: Print the name of the county in which the legal action is filed and the court's address in this box. The address for the court should be the same as the address on the documents that you served.

Third box, left side: Print the names of the plaintiff/petitioner and defendant/respondent in this box. Use the same names as are on the documents that you served.

Fourth box, left side: Check the method of service that was used. You should check only one method of service and should show proof of only one method on the form. If you served a party by several methods, use a separate form to show each method of service.

First box, top of form, right side: Leave this box blank for the court's use.

Second box, right side: Print the case number in this box. The case number should be the same as the case number on the documents that you served.

Third box, right side: State the judge and department assigned to the case, if known.

Complete items 1–6:

1. You are stating that you are over the age of 18.
2. Print your home or business address.
3. If service was by fax service, print the fax number from which service was made.
4. List each document that you served. If you need more space, check the box in item 4, complete the *Attachment to Proof of Service—Civil (Documents Served)* (form POS-040(D)), and attach it to form POS-040.
5. Provide the names, addresses, and other applicable information about the persons served. If more than one person was served, check the box on item 5, complete the *Attachment to Proof of Service—Civil (Persons Served)* (form POS-040(P)), and attach it to form POS-040.
6. Check the box before the method of service that was used, and provide any additional information that is required. The law may require that documents be served in a particular manner (such as by personal delivery) for certain purposes. Service by fax generally requires the prior agreement of the parties.

You must sign and date the proof of service form. By signing, you are stating under penalty of perjury that the information that you have provided on form POS-040 is true and correct.

SC-112A	Proof of Service by Mail	Case Number:

See instructions on other side.

☑ This form is attached to the document checked in ② below.

① **Server's information**

Name:_____ Phone:_____

Street or mailing address:_____

City:_____ State:_____ Zip Code:_____

☐ Check here if you are a registered process server, and write:

County where registered:_____ Registration #:_____

② **Form or document served**

a. ☐ Form SC-105, *Request for Court Order and Answer*
b. ☐ Form SC-109, *Authorization to Appear*
c. ☐ Form SC-114, *Request to Amend Claim Before Hearing*
d. ☐ Form SC-133, *Judgment Debtor's Statement of Assets*
e. ☐ Form SC-150, *Request to Postpone Trial*
f. ☐ Form SC-221, *Response to Request to Make Payments*
g. ☐ Other document allowed to be served by mail *(specify)*:

☐ Check here if there is not enough space below to list the document served. List the document on a separate page, and write "SC-112A, Item 2" at the top.

_____
_____

③ **Server's declaration**

a. I am 18 or older. I am not a party to this small claims case. I live or work in the county where I did the mailing described below.

b. I placed copies of the document checked in ② and an unsigned copy of this page in a sealed envelope, addressed as follows:

☐ Check here if there is not enough space below to list all parties served. List their names and addresses on a separate page, and write "SC-112A, Item 3" at the top.

Name of party served	Mailing address on the envelope

c. On *(date of mailing)*:_____, I placed each envelope in the mail, with postage paid, at *(city and state of mailing)*:_____

I declare under penalty of perjury under the laws of the State of California that the information above is true and correct.

Date:_____

▶

_____   _____
Type or print server's name   *Server signs here*

Judicial Council of California, www.courtinfo.ca.gov
New July 1, 2010, Optional Form
Cal. Rules of Court, rule 3.2107

Proof of Service by Mail
(Small Claims)

SC-112A

Instructions for Form SC-112A, *Proof of Service by Mail*

*(This page is **not** part of the Proof of Service and does not need to be copied, served, or filed.)*

Form SC-112A can be used to show the court that these documents were served by mail:
- Form SC-105, *Request for Court Order and Answer*
- Form SC-109, *Authorization to Appear*
- Form SC-114, *Request to Amend Claim Before Hearing*
- Form SC-133, *Judgment Debtor's Statement of Assets*
- Form SC-150, *Request to Postpone Trial*
- Form SC-221, *Response to Request to Make Payments*
- Other documents that are allowed to be served by mail

Form SC-112A cannot be used to prove service of these forms:
- Form SC-100, *Plaintiff's Claim and ORDER to Go to Small Claims Court*
- Form SC-120, *Defendant's Claim and ORDER to Go to Small Claims Court*

For information about serving these forms, see Form SC-104, *Proof of Service*, and Form SC-104B, *What Is "Proof of Service"?*

The server *(the person who will do the mailing):*
- **Must not** be a party (plaintiff or defendant) in the case
- **May** be a friend, relative, co-worker, or other helpful person
- **Must** be 18 or older
- **Must** live or work in the county where the mailing takes place

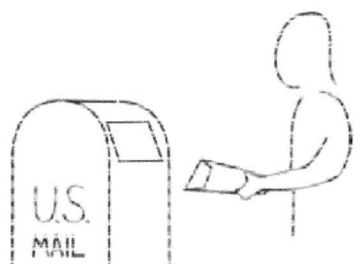

Follow these steps to use Form SC-112A:

1. **Prepare Form SC-112A by filling in:**
   - The case number
   - The document to be served, in item ②*
   - The names and addresses of the parties to be served, in item ③

   *Prepare a separate Form SC-112A for each document to be served.

2. **Give the server:**
   - The partially completed Form SC-112A
   - One copy of the document to be served for each party to be served

3. **Ask the server to:**
   - Fill out the remainder of the Form SC-112A.
   - Mail *each party to be served:*
     - An unsigned copy of the completed Form SC-112A and
     - The document to be served (checked in Item ②).
   - Sign a separate Form SC-112A for each document served, and give it to back you.

4. **File these papers with the small claims court clerk:**
   - The original of each document served, with
   - The signed, original *Proof of Service by Mail* attached

 Need help?
For free help, contact your county's small claims advisor:
[local info here]

Or go to "County-Specific Court Information" at *www.courtinfo.ca.gov/selfhelp/smallclaims*.

SC-104	**Proof of Service**

Clerk stamps date here when form is filed.

Use this form to serve a **person**, a **business**, or a **public entity**. To learn more about proof of service, read *What Is "Proof of Service"?*, Form SC-104B. To learn more about how to serve a business or entity, read *How to Serve a Business or Public Entity,* Form SC-104C.

To serve a **business,** you must serve **one** of the following people:
- Owner (for a sole proprietorship)
- Partner (for a partnership) or general partner (for a limited partnership)
- Any officer or general manager (corporation or association)
- Any person authorized for service by the business (corporation, association, general partnership, limited partnership)
- Any person authorized for service with the Secretary of State (corporation, association, limited liability company [LLC], limited liability partnership [LLP], limited partnership)

To serve a **public entity,** you must first file a claim with that entity, then serve **one** of the following people:
- Clerk (of a city or county)
- Chief officer or director (of a public agency)
- Any person authorized for service by the entity

Fill in court name and street address:

Superior Court of California, County of

Fill in case number, case name, hearing date, day, time, and department below:

Case Number:

Case Name:

Hearing Date:

Time: **Dept.:**

① a. If you are serving a **person,** write the person's name below:

_____

b. If you are serving a **business** or **entity,** write the name of the business or entity, the person authorized for service, and that person's job title:

_____
Business or Agency Name

_____
Person Authorized for Service   Job Title

② **Instructions to Server:**
You must be at least 18 years old and **not be named in this case.** Follow these steps:
- Give a copy of all the documents checked in ③ to the person in ①, *or*
- Give a copy of all the documents checked in ③ to one of the following people:
    a. A competent adult (at least 18) living with, and at the home of the person in ①, *or*
    b. An adult (at least 18) who seems to be in charge at the usual workplace of the person in ①, *or*
    c. An adult (at least 18) who seems to be in charge where the person in ① usually receives mail (but not a U.S. Post Office box), if there is no known physical address for the person in ①.
    and mail a copy of the documents left with one of the adults in a, b, or c above to the person in ①.

THEN
- Complete and sign this form, and
- Give or mail your completed form to the person who asked you to serve these court papers, *in time for the form to be filed with the court at least 5 days before the hearing.*

③ **I served the person in ① a copy of the documents checked below:**
  a. ☐ SC-100, *Plaintiff's Claim and ORDER to Go to Small Claims Court*
  b. ☐ SC-120, *Defendant's Claim and ORDER to Go to Small Claims Court*
  c. ☐ Order for examination *(This form must be personally served. Check the form that was served):*
     Note: *The court can issue a civil arrest warrant if the served party does not come to court **only** if the order for examination was personally served by a registered process server, sheriff, marshal, or someone appointed by the court.*
     (1) ☐ SC-134, *Application and Order to Produce Statement of Assets and to Appear for Examination*
     (2) ☐ AT-138/EJ-125, *Application and Order for Appearance and Examination*
  d. ☐ Other *(specify):* _____

Judicial Council of California, www.courtinfo.ca.gov
Revised January 1, 2009, Optional Form
Code of Civil Procedure, §§ 116.340, 415.10, 415.20

**Proof of Service
(Small Claims)**

Case name: _____

Case Number: _____

④ Fill out "a" or "b" below:

a. ☐ **Personal Service:** I personally gave copies of the documents checked in ③ to the person in ①:

On (date): _____ At (time): _____ ☐ a.m. ☐ p.m.

At this address: _____

City: _____ State: _____ Zip: _____

b. ☐ **Substituted Service:** I personally gave copies of the documents checked in ③ (a, b, or d) to (check one):

☐ A competent adult (at least 18) at the **home** of, and living with the person in ①, or
☐ An adult who seems to be in charge where the person in ① usually **works**, or
☐ An adult who seems to be in charge where the person in ① usually **receives mail**, or has a private post office box (not a U.S. Post Office box), if there is no known physical address for the person in ①.

I told that adult, "Please give these court papers to (name of person in ①)."

I did this on (date): _____ At (time): _____ ☐ a.m. ☐ p.m.

At this address: _____

City: _____ State: _____ Zip: _____

Name or description of the person I gave the papers to: _____

_____

After serving the court papers, I put copies of the documents listed in ③ in an envelope, sealed the envelope, and put first-class prepaid postage on it. I addressed the envelope to the person in ① at the address where I left the copies.

I mailed the envelope on (date): _____ from (city, state): _____

by leaving it (check one):

a. ☐ At a U.S. Postal Service mail drop, or
b. ☐ At an office or business mail drop where I know the mail is picked up every day and deposited with the U.S. Postal Service, or
c. ☐ With someone else I asked to mail the documents to the person in ①, and I have attached that person's completed Form SC-104A.

⑤ Server's Information

Name: _____ Phone: _____

Address: _____

City: _____ State: _____ Zip: _____

Fee for service: $ _____

If you are a registered process server:

County of registration: _____ Registration number: _____

⑥ I declare under penalty of perjury under California state law that I am at least 18 years old and not named in this case and that the information above is true and correct.

Date: _____

▶

_____   _____
Type or print server's name   *Server signs here after serving*

Proof of Service
(Small Claims)

Acknowledgment of Satisfaction of Judgment

EJ-100

ATTORNEY OR PARTY WITHOUT ATTORNEY *(Name, address, and State Bar number)*: After recording, return to:	
TEL NO.: FAX NO. *(optional)*:	
E-MAIL ADDRESS *(Optional)*:	
☐ ATTORNEY FOR ☐ JUDGMENT CREDITOR ☐ ASSIGNEE OF RECORD	

SUPERIOR COURT OF CALIFORNIA, COUNTY OF
STREET ADDRESS:
MAILING ADDRESS:
CITY AND ZIP CODE:
BRANCH NAME:

FOR RECORDER'S OR SECRETARY OF STATE'S USE ONLY

PLAINTIFF:
DEFENDANT:

CASE NUMBER:

ACKNOWLEDGMENT OF SATISFACTION OF JUDGMENT
☐ FULL   ☐ PARTIAL   ☐ MATURED INSTALLMENT

FOR COURT USE ONLY

1. Satisfaction of the judgment is acknowledged as follows:
   a. ☐ Full satisfaction
      (1) ☐ Judgment is satisfied in full.
      (2) ☐ The judgment creditor has accepted payment or performance other than that specified in the judgment in full satisfaction of the judgment.
   b. ☐ Partial satisfaction
      The amount received in partial satisfaction of the judgment is $
   c. ☐ Matured installment
      All matured installments under the installment judgment have been satisfied as of *(date)*:

2. Full name and address of judgment creditor:*

3. Full name and address of assignee of record, if any:

4. Full name and address of judgment debtor being fully or partially released:*

5. a. Judgment entered on *(date)*:
   b. ☐ Renewal entered on *(date)*:

6. ☐ An ☐ abstract of judgment ☐ certified copy of the judgment has been recorded as follows *(complete all information for each county where recorded)*:

COUNTY	DATE OF RECORDING	INSTRUMENT NUMBER

7. ☐ A notice of judgment lien has been filed in the office of the Secretary of State as file number *(specify)*:

NOTICE TO JUDGMENT DEBTOR: If this is an acknowledgment of full satisfaction of judgment, it will have to be recorded in each county shown in item 6 above, if any, in order to release the judgment lien, and will have to be filed in the office of the Secretary of State to terminate any judgment lien on personal property.

Date:

▶ _____
*(SIGNATURE OF JUDGMENT CREDITOR OR ASSIGNEE OF CREDITOR OR ATTORNEY**)*

*The names of the judgment creditor and judgment debtor must be stated as shown in any Abstract of Judgment which was recorded and is being released by this satisfaction. ** A separate notary acknowledgment must be attached for each signature.

Form Approved for Optional Use
Judicial Council of California
EJ-100 [Rev. July 1, 2014]

ACKNOWLEDGMENT OF SATISFACTION OF JUDGMENT

Code of Civil Procedure, §§ 724.060, 724.120, 724.250

Notice of Judgment Lien Release or Subordination

Instructions for Completing the
Judgment Lien Change Form (Form JL3)

Please type or laser-print information on this form. Be sure information provided is legible. Read and follow all instructions completely. Fill out the form very carefully as mistakes may have important legal consequences. Do not insert anything in the open space in the upper right portion of this form as it is reserved for filing office use. Do not staple or otherwise mutilate the barcode in the upper left corner of the document, as this will prevent filing.

Return Acknowledgement: Please do not enclose a duplicate copy. A return acknowledgement automatically will be generated upon filing.

Complete Form JL3 as follows:

Section A. To assist filing office communication with the filer, information in this section should be provided.

Section B. Enter the name and mailing address of filer in this section. This information is required.

Item 1a. Enter the Secretary of State file number assigned to the original Notice of Judgment Lien.

Item 1b. Enter the Secretary of State file date on the original Notice of Judgment Lien.

Item 2. If the Judgment Lien Change Form is being filed as a Continuation Statement, check this box. (California Code of Civil Procedure section 697.510.) Leave Items 3 through 7 blank and complete Item 8.

Item 3a or 3b. Enter the name of the judgment debtor as it appears in the original Notice of Judgment Lien. (Complete Item 3a or 3b, not both.) Use the judgment lien change form addendum to add additional judgment debtor names and addresses.

Item 3c. Enter the current address of the judgment debtor. The address must include a city and state.

Item 4a or 4b. Enter the name of the judgment creditor as it appears in the original Notice of Judgment Lien. (Complete Item 4a or 4b, not both.)

Item 4c. Enter the current address of the judgment creditor. The address must include a city and state.

Item 5. If the lien on personal property covered by the judgment is being released, check the box and describe the personal property being released in Item 7. (California Code of Civil Procedure section 697.650.)

Item 6. If this statement is being filed to subordinate to another security interest, check the box and describe in Item 7 the personal property being subordinated and the security interest to which the judgment lien is being subordinated. (California Code of Civil Procedure section 697.650.)

Item 7. Describe the personal property, or portion thereof, being released or subordinated in this box, and if subordinated, describe the security interest to which the judgment lien is being subordinated.

Item 8: This Judgment Lien Change Form (Form JL3) must be signed by the judgment creditor, or if the judgment creditor has an attorney of record, then the judgment creditor's attorney of record may sign this notice. (California Code of Civil Procedure sections 697.550 and 697.650.)

If the individual signing the notice is signing for a judgment creditor that is an entity, or on behalf of the law firm that is the attorney of record, the name of the entity or law firm, as applicable, should be entered beneath the signature line, not above the signature of the person signing for the judgment creditor entity or law firm of record.

Fee: This Judgment Lien Change Form must be submitted with a filing fee of ten dollars ($10.00) for an original document containing two pages or less, and twenty dollars ($20.00) for an original document containing three pages or more. Please send a check made payable to the **Secretary of State**. Contact the filing office for information concerning the establishment of prepay accounts, use of special handling services, or other payment options. Documents not accompanied by the filing fee will not be processed.

Mailing Address: When properly completed, send the **original form** and **payment of filing fee** to:

Secretary of State
P.O. Box 942835
Sacramento, CA 94235-0001

Instructions for Completing the
Judgment Lien Change Form Addendum (Form JL3AD)

Use this form to list only additional Judgment Debtors to be released or subordinated when filing a Judgment Lien Change Form (Form JL3).

Complete Form JL3AD as follows:

Item 9. Enter file number of the Judgment Lien to which this Additional Party relates, exactly as shown in Item 1a of the Judgment Lien Change Form.

Item 10. Enter the name of the Judgment Creditor exactly as shown in Item 4 of the Judgment Lien Change Form.

Items 11-16. If this change releases or subordinates additional Judgment Debtors pursuant to California Code of Civil Procedure section 697.650, complete Items 11 through 16 in accordance with Instruction 3 of the Judgment Lien Change Form and give complete information for each additional Judgment Debtor. Be sure to complete either the organization's name or individual's name, but not both.

JUDGMENT LIEN CHANGE FORM
FOLLOW INSTRUCTIONS CAREFULLY (front and back of form)

A. NAME & PHONE NUMBER OF FILER'S CONTACT (optional)

B. SEND ACKNOWLEDGMENT TO: (Name and Address)

THE ABOVE SPACE IS FOR FILING OFFICE USE ONLY

1a. SECRETARY OF STATE FILE NO. (Original Notice of Judgment Lien)

1b. DATE OF FILING ORIGINAL NOTICE OF JUDGMENT LIEN

2. NOTICE OF CONTINUATION OF JUDGMENT LIEN ON PERSONAL PROPERTY
☐ THIS NOTICE IS FILED TO CONTINUE THE EFFECTIVENESS OF THE NOTICE OF JUDGMENT LIEN IDENTIFIED IN ITEMS 1a & 1b. (California Code of Civil Procedure section 697.510.)

3. JUDGMENT DEBTOR'S EXACT LEGAL NAME – Insert a name in 3a or 3b only. Do not abbreviate or combine names.

3a. ORGANIZATION'S NAME

3b. INDIVIDUAL'S LAST NAME	FIRST NAME	MIDDLE NAME	SUFFIX
3c. MAILING ADDRESS	CITY	STATE	POSTAL CODE	COUNTRY

4. JUDGMENT CREDITOR'S EXACT NAME – Insert a name in 4a or 4b only. Do not abbreviate or combine names.

4a. ORGANIZATION'S NAME

4b. INDIVIDUAL'S LAST NAME	FIRST NAME	MIDDLE NAME	SUFFIX
4c. MAILING ADDRESS	CITY	STATE	POSTAL CODE	COUNTRY

5. RELEASE OF JUDGMENT LIEN ON PERSONAL PROPERTY
☐ THE JUDGMENT LIEN ON THE PERSONAL PROPERTY SUBJECT TO LIEN IS HEREBY RELEASED AS DESCRIBED IN ITEM 7 BELOW. (California Code of Civil Procedure section 697.650.)

6. SUBORDINATION OF JUDGMENT LIEN ON PERSONAL PROPERTY
☐ THE JUDGMENT LIEN ON THE PERSONAL PROPERTY SUBJECT TO LIEN IS HEREBY SUBORDINATED AS DESCRIBED IN ITEM 7 BELOW. (California Code of Civil Procedure section 697.650.)

7. DESCRIPTION OF RELEASE OR SUBORDINATION OF PERSONAL PROPERTY

8.

SIGNATURE OF JUDGMENT CREDITOR (See instructions for Item 8.)   DATE

FOR _____

FILING OFFICE COPY   JUDGMENT LIEN (FORM JL3) - (REV. 04/2010)   APPROVED BY SECRETARY OF STATE

JUDGMENT LIEN CHANGE FORM ADDENDUM

FOLLOW INSTRUCTIONS CAREFULLY (front and back of form)

9. INITIAL JUDGMENT LIEN FILE # (same as Item 1a on change form)

10. NAME OF JUDGMENT CREDITOR (same as Item 4a or 4b on change form)

10a. ORGANIZATION NAME		
OR		
10b. INDIVIDUAL'S LAST NAME	FIRST NAME	MIDDLE NAME, SUFFIX

THE ABOVE SPACE IS FOR FILING OFFICE USE ONLY

11. ADDITIONAL JUDGMENT DEBTOR'S EXACT FULL LEGAL NAME – insert only <u>one</u> name (11a or 11b) – do not abbreviate or combine names

11a. ORGANIZATION'S NAME				
OR 11b. INDIVIDUAL'S LAST NAME	FIRST NAME	MIDDLE NAME		SUFFIX
11c. MAILING ADDRESS	CITY	STATE	POSTAL CODE	COUNTRY

12. ADDITIONAL JUDGMENT DEBTOR'S EXACT FULL LEGAL NAME – insert only <u>one</u> name (12a or 12b) – do not abbreviate or combine names

12a. ORGANIZATION'S NAME				
OR 12b. INDIVIDUAL'S LAST NAME	FIRST NAME	MIDDLE NAME		SUFFIX
12c. MAILING ADDRESS	CITY	STATE	POSTAL CODE	COUNTRY

13. ADDITIONAL JUDGMENT DEBTOR'S EXACT FULL LEGAL NAME – insert only <u>one</u> name (13a or 13b) – do not abbreviate or combine names

13a. ORGANIZATION'S NAME				
OR 13b. INDIVIDUAL'S LAST NAME	FIRST NAME	MIDDLE NAME		SUFFIX
13c. MAILING ADDRESS	CITY	STATE	POSTAL CODE	COUNTRY

14. ADDITIONAL JUDGMENT DEBTOR'S EXACT FULL LEGAL NAME – insert only <u>one</u> name (14a or 14b) – do not abbreviate or combine names

14a. ORGANIZATION'S NAME				
OR 14b. INDIVIDUAL'S LAST NAME	FIRST NAME	MIDDLE NAME		SUFFIX
14c. MAILING ADDRESS	CITY	STATE	POSTAL CODE	COUNTRY

15. ADDITIONAL JUDGMENT DEBTOR'S EXACT FULL LEGAL NAME – insert only <u>one</u> name (15a or 15b) – do not abbreviate or combine names

15a. ORGANIZATION'S NAME				
OR 15b. INDIVIDUAL'S LAST NAME	FIRST NAME	MIDDLE NAME		SUFFIX
15c. MAILING ADDRESS	CITY	STATE	POSTAL CODE	COUNTRY

16. ADDITIONAL JUDGMENT DEBTOR'S EXACT FULL LEGAL NAME – insert only <u>one</u> name (16a or 16b) – do not abbreviate or combine names

16a. ORGANIZATION'S NAME				
OR 16b. INDIVIDUAL'S LAST NAME	FIRST NAME	MIDDLE NAME		SUFFIX
16c. MAILING ADDRESS	CITY	STATE	POSTAL CODE	COUNTRY

FILING OFFICE COPY   JUDGMENT LIEN CHANGE FORM ADDENDUM (FORM JL3AD) - (REV. 04/2010)   APPROVED BY SECRETARY OF STATE

www.ingramcontent.com/pod-product-compliance
Lightning Source LLC
Chambersburg PA
CBHW080405300426
44113CB00015B/2406